The Purch
Supply Manager's Guide
to the C.P.M. Exam

The Purchasing and Supply Manager's Guide to the C.P.M. Exam

Fred Sollish, C.P.M.

John Semanik, C.P.M.

San Francisco • London

Publisher: Neil Edde
Acquisitions Editor: Heather O'Connor
Developmental Editors: Heather O'Connor, Sally Engelfried
Production Editor: Elizabeth Campbell
Technical Editors: Elizabeth Mortarotti, Mohan Menon
Copyeditor: Sally Engelfried
Compositor: Happenstance Type-O-Rama
Graphic Illustrator: Happenstance Type-O-Rama
CD Coordinator: Dan Mummert
CD Technician: Kevin Ly
Proofreaders: Nancy Riddiough, Jim Brook, Ian Golder, Katherine Perry, Amy Rasmussen, Candace English
Indexer: Ted Laux
Book Designer: Judy Fung
Cover Designer: Richard Miller, Calyx Design
Cover Photograph: Kim Steele, Photodisc Green

Library of Congress Card Number: 2004109309

ISBN: 0-7821-4365-2

To our valued readers,

Harbor Light Press was created as an imprint of Sybex, Inc. to help business professionals acquire the practical skills and knowledge they need to meet today's most pressing business challenges.

Our books serve the people responsible for getting the job done—project managers charged with delivering a product on time and under budget; human resource directors faced with a complex array of resource decisions; support staff determined to exceed the goals set for them; and others who recognize that great business plans are only as good as the people who implement and manage them.

Harbor Light Press is committed to publishing authoritative, reliable, yet engaging business books written by authors who are outstanding instructors and experienced business professionals. The goal for all of our books is to connect with our readers, to understand their needs, and to provide them with solutions that they can put to use immediately.

Neil Edde
Publisher, Harbor Light Press

Software License Agreement: Terms and Conditions

To the dedicated professionals of Supply Management

Illegitimi Non Carborundum!

Acknowledgements

The authors would like to take this opportunity to thank our colleagues, our families and the members of our professional organization—Supply Knowledge (`www.supplyknowledge.com`), The Institute for Supply Management's Silicon Valley affiliate—for the encouragement to write this review. We would especially like to thank one another for the mutual support during the nearly one year it has taken to produce this volume. Without this support, we could have never gone beyond the first paragraph.

We would also like to acknowledge each member of the Board of Directors of Supply Knowledge (past and present) for their continued support of high quality educational programs focused on the advancement of the supply management profession. We also owe our gratitude for the ongoing collaboration of the staff—administrators and instructors—at San Jose State University Continuing Education where our affiliate conducts a professional development program in Purchasing and Supply Chain Management and the Center for Intelligent Supply Networks (C4iSN) at the School of Management, University of Texas, Dallas where we co-produce an online certificate program in Sourcing Management that includes the C.P.M. exam review.

Finally, we are glad to have the opportunity to tell the readers how instrumental the truly dedicated and professional editoral staff at Sybex have been in getting this information out to you in a way that makes sense. The editors—Heather O'Connor, Elizabeth Campbell, and Sally Englefried—added tremendous value to this effort. A special "Thank you" goes to Elizabeth Mortarotti, C.P.M., our Technical Editor and the current President of Supply Knowledge.

Contents at a Glance

Contents

Introduction

Welcome! You are now on your way to becoming a Certified Purchasing Manager (C.P.M.). By taking this path, you are demonstrating your commitment to your profession and will be joining the more than 35,000 people worldwide already certified who lead the field of purchasing and supply chain management. We're certain you understand how complex and challenging this profession can be and that you clearly appreciate the need for rigorous and professional study.

We would like to begin this comprehensive overview by providing some general information about the requirements for certification and what will be included in the following chapters of this book. We will also offer some suggestions for using this book and how you will receive its full educational benefit.

Before beginning, however, we would like to remind you that this book is designed to provide a review of material that you, as a practicing professional, should be cognizant of already. Most likely you have taken some formal training classes or seminars related to the purchasing or supply function and have worked in a related professional supply management capacity for at least three years. The goal of this book, therefore, is to provide enough information about each of the functional areas of purchasing and supply management to enable C.P.M. candidates to prepare themselves to successfully complete and pass the exam. For those of you who have had extensive experience, this book can serve simply to refresh your purchasing and supply management knowledge. Since this book is organized around the C.P.M. exam specifications, it can also help orient candidates to the topics covered by each of the four C.P.M. exam modules.

About Purchasing Manager Certification

Certification is a way of acknowledging individuals who have met predetermined qualifications and standards of competency established by purchasing and supply management academic experts and professional practitioners. It is also a means of informing others of your professional achievement.

Why Become Certified?

Certification provides a way of demonstrating that you have met specific standards of professional competency recognized by others in your chosen field. The C.P.M. designation has become a standard of professional excellence, identifying your achievement to others around the world.

Certification enhances career opportunities and improves your job marketability. It distinguishes you from others competing for the same position and provides a competitive edge in your favor when the final hiring decision is made. It shows that you are serious and dedicated to your professional advancement.

Your certification also demonstrates your commitment to the purchasing and supply management profession and to the practice of continuous professional development. It tells others that you have the ability and drive to achieve significant goals, that you are results oriented and committed to a skill competence. It tells them that you are willing to hold yourself to a higher level of personal, ethical, and professional conduct.

Who Certifies Purchasing Professionals?

The Certified Purchasing Manager (C.P.M) designation is awarded by the Institute for Supply Management, Inc. (ISM). ISM is a not-for-profit association whose mission is to lead the supply management profession through standards of excellence, research, promotional activities, and professional education. ISM's membership includes more than 45,000 supply management professionals in a network of both domestic and international affiliated associations.

ISM offers four C.P.M. certifications: Original Certification, Original Lifetime Certification, Recertification, and Lifetime Certification. To learn the specifics of each requirement, you can visit the ISM website at `www.ism.ws/Certification/Requirements.cfm`.

The American Purchasing Association (APS) also offers certification in purchasing, with two designations: Certified Purchasing Professional (CPP) and Certified Professional Purchasing Manager (CPPM). You can learn more about these certifications on the Web at `www.american-purchasing.com/programs.htm`.

In Canada, the Purchasing Management Association of Canada (PMAC) offers the Certified Professional Purchaser (C.P.P.) designation. C.P.P. is Canada's only "legally" recognized designation for the purchasing profession (`www.pmac.ca/education/cpp_accreditation.asp`).

In the public sector, two professional purchasing organizations offer certification:

- Certified Federal Contracts Manager (CFCM), Certified Commercial Contracts Manager (CCCM) and Certified Professional Contracts Manager (CPCM) are offered by the National Contract Management Association (NCMA) `www.ncmahq.org/`.

- Certified Public Purchasing Officer (CPPO) and Certified Professional Public Buyer (CPPB) are administered by the National Institute for Governmental Purchasing (NIGP) `www.nigp.org`.

How to Achieve Certification

To be eligible for C.P.M. certification, an individual must pass all four modules of the C.P.M. exam and have at least the following minimum experience:

- Three years of professional purchasing or supply management experience and at least a four-year college degree from an accredited educational institution, or

- Five years of professional purchasing or supply management experience.

For the requirements of other organizations, each of their respective websites previously mentioned can provide details on their specifics.

C.P.M. Exam Facts

The C.P.M. exam is constructed of four modules covering the following topics:

- Module 1: Purchasing Process
- Module 2: Supply Environment
- Module 3: Value Enhancement Strategies
- Module 4: Management

Modules 1, 2, and 3 consist of 95 questions (only 90 of which are actually scored). The applicant is allowed 105 minutes to complete the exam. Module 4 consists of 120 questions (110 of which are scored), and the applicant is given 130 minutes to complete it. Those taking the exam will not know which questions are not being scored. The exam specifications can be found on the ISM website at: `www.ism.ws/Certification/CPMExamSpecs.cfm`.

The examination requirement for Module 4 includes a significant number of questions related to "current issues." These issues, reviewed in copyrighted material published by ISM, are not presented in our review or reflected in the chapter or bonus exam questions. You may wish to purchase the latest version directly from ISM by going to its website: `www.ism.ws`.

To learn more about the requirements for each of the other organizations mentioned in the preceding section, please visit their individual websites.

Maintaining Certification

To maintain C.P.M. certification, an individual must recertify every five years until Lifetime Certification has been achieved. To recertify, the candidate is required to complete 12 C.P.M. points, equal to 84 continuing education hours (CEH). Points can be earned from the following categories:

- Seminars and other continuing education courses (taken or taught)
- Formal education (e.g., college courses taken or taught)
- Completion of Modules 3 and/or 4 of the updated exam
- Contributions to the profession

An individual who has achieved 18 years of relevant, verifiable experience in the profession is eligible to recertify (or obtain initial certification) with Lifetime Certification.

How This Book Is Organized

This book covers each of the four modules of the C.P.M. exam.

Chapters 1 through 5 cover **Module 1,** reviewing the elements of the purchasing process:

- Procurement and employing best business practices in the administration of day-to-day activities (Chapter 1).
- Sourcing and locating new suppliers, covering standard practices used in the solicitation process (Chapter 2)
- Selecting suppliers and evaluating supplier performance (Chapter 3)
- Contract formation and purchasing practices (Chapter 4)
- Administering contracts, tracking and expediting delivers, and handling supplier-related deviations from requirements (Chapter 5)

Chapters 6 through 10 cover **Module 2**, reviewing the supply environment:

- Formulating strategies to manage negotiations and conducting negotiations with suppliers (Chapter 6)
- Using computer-based systems and sourcing applications (Chapter 7)
- Managing and measuring quality and ensuring quality performance (Chapter 8)
- Maintaining relationships with internal departments, providing support, and communicating procurement policies (Chapter 9)
- Managing supplier relationships, coordinating supplier activities, and representing your organization in the community (Chapter 10).

Chapters 11 through 14 cover **Module 3**, value enhancement:

- Making sound sourcing decisions, performing make or buy analysis, and formulating financial strategies (Chapter 11)
- Managing material and supply operations including inventory and surplus equipment (Chapter 12)
- Adding value to the organization through material standardization, improved processes, and reduced cost (Chapter 13)
- Strategic procurement planning, developing forecasts, and market analysis (Chapter 14)

Chapters 15 and 16 review **Module 4**, covering the management of the procurement organization:

- Planning procurement strategy and goals, formulating operational policies, and reporting activities to management (Chapter 15)
- Managing the procurement staff (including recruiting, hiring, promoting, training, and terminating employees), handling employee performance issues, and preventing workplace discrimination and harassment (Chapter 16)

In addition, we have provided an Appendix listing some additional resources for your review and assistance in preparing for the examination. We have also included a glossary of the key terms we have used in this book, along with some additional terms you may want to have available as a reference.

The Elements of the Study Guide

As you go through the review, you will encounter a number of repeating elements. They include:

Key Terms   Key terms you should be certain to understand are italicized in the text and defined in the Glossary.

Summary   The "Summary" section is a brief review of the key elements of the chapter as a way of highlighting its important points.

Exam Essentials   The "Exam Essentials" section outlines key topics that you should be certain you are familiar with before taking the exam. While we have no way of knowing the specific questions or the form they will take in the actual exam, we have tried to reinforce important concepts to help you organize and direct your areas of study in advance of taking the C.P.M. exam.

Review Questions   At the conclusion of each chapter, you will find ten questions that help measure how well you know the concepts we have just covered. The answers to these questions appear in an answer section after the question section. If you have difficulty answering the question or answer incorrectly, it might be an indication that you need to do some further review of the material. Remember, the chapter review questions are there to help you measure how much information you have retained from the reading. They are different from the kinds of questions you will see on the actual exam.

What's on the CD?

The CD contains some additional tools to help you further prepare for the exam.

Sybex Test Preparation Software

The test preparation software, made by experts at Sybex, will help you prepare for the C.P.M. exam. This test engine provides all the review and assessment questions from the book, plus four additional bonus exams that you will only find on the CD. You will be able to take the assessment test, take the practice exams, or take a randomly generated exam consisting of all the questions. You can be graded by subject area so you can get a better idea of what you need to review further.

Electronic Flashcards for PC and Palm Devices

Sybex's electronic flashcards include questions designed to challenge you in further preparation for the exam. The review questions, practice exams, and flashcards are there to provide you with a wide variety of preparation materials.

How to Use This Book and CD

There are a number of specific features in this book to help guide your efforts to prepare for the C.P.M. exam. At the beginning of each chapter, you will find a list of topics you should master that are covered in detail in material you are about to read. Be certain you thoroughly understand each of these concepts.

You will also find a number of web links that provide a resource for more detailed information about the subject should you feel you need it. As we've already noted, you also have a Glossary and several exam mechanisms to help you prepare.

Here are some further suggestions you might find helpful:

1. Review the objectives at the beginning of each chapter before you begin reading. You may also want to review the ISM specifications for each module. You'll find them at `www.ism.ws/Certification/CPMExamSpecsGenFormat.cfm`.

   After you have finished each chapter, go back and review the objectives to ensure that you understand and are able to apply them.

2. Answer the questions at the end of each chapter. If you miss any of them, go back to the chapter and review that specific topic or go to one of the additional resources referenced for more information.

3. Download the flashcards to your handheld device and review them whenever you have a few minutes.

4. Take every opportunity to test yourself in the days immediately prior to the exam. Use the bonus exams on the CD.

5. If you can, find a study partner. Taking the exam with someone else provides additional help and motivation for both parties.

6. Consider attending one of the classroom reviews held by local affiliates and the ISM organization. You can generally find information regarding these workshops on the ISM website or the website of your local ISM affiliate.

How to Contact the Authors

Fred Sollish and John Semanik can be reached at `certification@supplyknowledge.com`.

Assessment Test

Module 1

1. What set of data contains a technical description of the material being purchased?

   A. Documentation

   B. Specification

   C. Standard operating procedures

   D. Scope of work

2. What document generated by the user or user department describes the specific quantity and the goods or services to be purchased?

   A. Scope of work

   B. Specification

   C. Requisition

   D. Purchase order

3. What document lists all of the parts that constitute the final product?

   A. Requisition

   B. Catalog

   C. Specification

   D. Bill of Materials

4. What contractual document contains quantity, price, description of the goods or services, required delivery date, and terms and conditions?

   A. Specification

   B. Bill of Materials

   C. Purchase order

   D. Requisition

5. Expenditures that are directly incorporated into a product delivered to the end customer are classified as:

   A. Overhead

   B. Burden

   C. Direct costs

   D. Expenses

6. Sometimes used as a supplemental method of describing specifications.

   A. Benchmarking

   B. Quality control

   C. Standards

   D. Process capability

7. What provides a measurement as a guide for establishing a specific requirement?

   A. Benchmarking

   B. Quality control

   C. Standards

   D. Process capability

8. Document that contains provisions triggering an automatic payment from the buyer's bank to the seller upon proof of shipment:

   A. Bill of lading

   B. Packing slip

   C. Letter of Credit

   D. Requisition

9. Created when only one supplier can produce a particular product due to patents.

   A. Single source

   B. Technical competition

   C. Limited source

   D. Sole source

10. The competitive process that enables the buyer to leverage several potential sources of supply through a single activity to obtain the most favorable business terms.

    A. Sourcing

    B. Negotiation

    C. Benchmarking

    D. Bidding

11. When a supplier has the necessary equipment, tools, and talent to meet your requirements, it is said to have:

    A. Operational capacity

    B. Financial ability

    C. Technical capability

    D. Responsiveness

12. What element is driven by the current supply and demand condition for a particular product?

   A. Service

   B. Technology

   C. Price

   D. Quality

13. Describes the supplier's ability to conform to specifications.

   A. Technology

   B. Quality

   C. Delivery

   D. Service

14. One of the most common tools used to develop an evaluation of a potential supplier's capability.

   A. Site visit

   B. Bidding

   C. Request for Proposal

   D. Request for Information

15. Method of evaluating a supplier where critical areas are ranked by the assessments of the internal team members.

   A. Request for Information

   B. Bidding

   C. Weighted average

   D. Critical path method

16. Article 2 of the Uniform Commercial Code primarily covers:

   A. Goods

   B. Leasing

   C. Services

   D. International

17. Law that requires certain types of contracts to be validated in written form.

   A. Common law

   B. Contract law

   C. Statute of Frauds

   D. Case law

18. Principle that an oral promise can produce substantial or unconscionable injury to the promisee or unjustly enrich the promisor.

    A. Statute of Frauds

    B. Detrimental reliance

    C. Statutory

    D. Estoppel

19. Mutual agreement, legality, consideration, and capacity must be present in order to have a valid:

    A. Purchase order

    B. Specification

    C. Terms and conditions

    D. Contract

20. Defined as an exchange of anything of value except money.

    A. Consideration

    B. Bartering

    C. Exchange

    D. Monetary

21. A seller's guarantee to the buyer that the product or materials being sold performs as specified.

    A. Specification

    B. Terms and conditions

    C. Warranty

    D. Service level agreement

22. This term means that the seller implicitly warrants that the product is fit and suited to be used for the ordinary purposes for which it would be purchased.

    A. Fitness for a particular purpose

    B. Suitability

    C. Functionality

    D. Merchantability

23. The broad process of aligning the goals of your organization and the supplier community, one supplier at a time.

    A. Commodity management

    B. Supplier Relationship Management

    C. Supplier alignment

    D. Strategic planning

24. Method of managing activities on an automated reporting system when there are large amounts of data and the reviewer wishes to limit analysis time.

   A. Standard deviation

   B. Upper control limit

   C. Management by exception

   D. Lower control limit

25. The process of following up with suppliers to determine the current status of a particular purchase order.

   A. Expediting

   B. Root cause analysis

   C. Process improvement

   D. Monitoring

26. Occurs when a supplier is unable or unwilling to perform to the terms and conditions required by the contract.

   A. Anticipatory repudiation

   B. Actual damages

   C. Breach of contract

   D. Consequential damages

27. Provides for a predetermined fixed payment amount in the event of a breach of contract.

   A. Consequential damages

   B. Actual damages

   C. Incidental damages

   D. Liquidated damages

28. Refers to the legal responsibility for the cost of damages in a commercial environment.

   A. Liquidated damages

   B. Liability

   C. Hold harmless

   D. Consequential damages

29. What requires that the buying organization provide the seller with timely notice of its intention to reject nonconforming goods?

   A. Uniform Commercial Code

   B. Contract law

   C. Case law

   D. Terms and conditions

30. What is the most commonly used method outside of the court system for reaching settlement in a dispute with a supplier?

   A. Negotiation

   B. Bargaining

   C. Mediation

   D. Force majeure

Module 2

1. When the competitive environment is limited by the lack of qualified suppliers or by intellectual property rights, what type of bidding is unlikely?

   A. Fixed

   B. Competitive

   C. Open

   D. Limited

2. Term that describes the following factors: economic, physical, and political.

   A. Geopolitical

   B. Market forces

   C. Supply and demand

   D. Federal Reserve

3. One of the fundamental keys to employing successful negotiation strategies.

   A. Early involvement

   B. Planning

   C. Decision tree analysis

   D. "What-if" mapping

4. Agency responsible for public company regulations that require public disclosure of important financial data.

   A. Trade Commission

   B. Securities and Exchange Commission

   C. Antitrust Division

   D. Federal Communications Commission

5. Contains information that describes the purchasing team's objectives, its strategy, and the strengths and weaknesses of its position, along with a similar assessment of the supplier's position.

   A. Business plan

   B. Negotiation plan

   C. SWOT analysis

   D. Risk analysis

6. Name the enterprise system primarily used to determine when to place orders for standard materials so that they arrive exactly when it needed.

  A. Just-in-time

  B. Electronic procurement

  C. Material Requirements Planning

  D. Virtual Private Network

7. What is the most widely used electronic process for exchanging data related to procurement between buyer and supplier computers?

  A. Electronic Data Interchange

  B. Public Key Infrastructure

  C. Transmission Control Protocol

  D. Material Requirements Planning

8. EDI that is conducted between trading partners is managed through this.

  A. Internet

  B. Extranet

  C. Value Added Network

  D. Public Key Infrastructure

9. Name of an auction where the award goes to the lowest bidder:

  A. Dutch

  B. English

  C. Reverse

  D. Double

10. Term that describes when the supplier owns the material stored at your facility until you actually use it.

  A. Contract inventory

  B. Outsourcing

  C. Supplier managed inventory

  D. Consignment

11. A measure of the range of deviation from a given number specified within which a product will be acceptable and beyond which it will not.

  A. Acceptance

  B. Upper control limit

  C. Tolerance

  D. Lower control limit

12. Method used for determining if a particular piece of equipment is functioning at the level specified.

    A. Acceptance testing

    B. Fitness for a particular purpose

    C. Value analysis

    D. Merchantability

13. The quality application of statistical techniques to control a process.

    A. Acceptance testing

    B. Tolerance stack-up

    C. Inspection process

    D. Statistical Process Control

14. A statistical measure of the variability or dispersion within a set of data points.

    A. Pareto chart

    B. Tolerance

    C. Standard deviation

    D. Process capability analysis

15. Type of chart that demonstrates the few categories or units that typically account for the majority of the total occurrences.

    A. Pareto chart

    B. Tolerance

    C. Standard deviation

    D. Process capability analysis

16. A tool used to document supplier nonconformance and require necessary steps to correct the noncompliant situation.

    A. Corrective action

    B. Standard operating procedures

    C. Nonconformance report

    D. Breach of contract

17. Name the principle process used to prevent the recurrence of a specific problem in the future.

    A. Corrective action

    B. Value analysis

    C. Root cause analysis

    D. Benchmarking

18. Process of continuous improvement focused on increasing customer satisfaction.

   A. Total Quality Management

   B. Customer service

   C. Root cause analysis

   D. Corrective action process

19. Quality term that means continuous improvement involving everyone as a group or team.

   A. Teaming

   B. Reengineering

   C. Kaizen

   D. Total Quality Management

20. Quality reduction of errors to six standard deviations from the mean value of a process output.

   A. Standard deviation

   B. Variance

   C. Delta

   D. Six Sigma

21. A quality series of international standards on environmental management.

   A. ISO 9000:2000

   B. ISO 9004:2000

   C. ISO/TS/16949

   D. ISO 14000

22. A production function tasked to ensure a given standard of quality.

   A. Quality assurance

   B. Production management

   C. Manufacturing operations

   D. Production control

23. The title of managers who oversee product lines and have broad responsibilities for development of new business opportunities.

   A. Production managers

   B. Business managers

   C. Purchasing managers

   D. Product managers

24. Method of including the Purchasing Department in sourcing and new product introduction activities.

    A. Early involvement

    B. Teaming

    C. Staff meetings

    D. Production planning

25. The group that plans supply requirements and handles purchased materials.

    A. Planning

    B. Production

    C. Purchasing

    D. Materials management

26. The documents that address the "how to" of purchasing, defining the specific tasks required to perform any given operation.

    A. Purchasing policy

    B. Standard operating procedures

    C. Code of conduct

    D. Guidelines

27. Name of practice when there are few or no suppliers available and the buyer must use recruiting and persuasion to develop a source to meet the organization's needs.

    A. Bidding

    B. Reverse marketing

    C. Request for Proposal

    D. Sourcing

28. Process that determines if a particular supplier is capable of handling a specific job.

    A. Sourcing

    B. Request for Proposal

    C. Score carding

    D. Supplier qualification

29. A classification indicating that a supplier has met certain criteria and levels of performance.

    A. Qualification

    B. Certification

    C. Acceptance criteria

    D. Statistical Process Control

30. Form of teaching and guidance that assists individuals and organizations reach a higher level of performance.

    A. Training

    B. Coaching

    C. Benchmarking

    D. Mentoring

31. Term that describes a supplier adding a percentage above cost to the selling price.

    A. Delta

    B. Cost of business

    C. Markup

    D. Profit margin

32. A statistical methodology used to assess where prices are heading.

    A. Linear regression analysis

    B. Trend analysis

    C. Comparative analysis

    D. Exponential smoothing

33. The best fitting straight line calculated from a series of data points.

    A. Trend analysis

    B. Linear regression analysis

    C. Comparative analysis

    D. Exponential smoothing

34. Price analysis that takes a number of forms ranging from benchmarking industry standards to a side by side analysis of prices.

    A. Trend analysis

    B. Linear regression analysis

    C. Comparative analysis

    D. Exponential smoothing

Module 3

1. One of the comparative analysis tools for decision making.

    A. In-source

    B. Make or buy

    C. Outsource

    D. Request for Proposal

2. Process of carefully balancing the specific, expected benefits of the supplier engagement with factors that you may not be able to control.

A. Pareto analysis

B. Gantt chart

C. "What-if" analysis

D. Risk analysis

3. The transfer of a previously performed function from the organizational staff to a third party supplier.

A. In-sourcing

B. Outsourcing

C. Function transfer

D. Consignment

4. Classification of material that goes directly into the product being manufactured.

A. Work-in-process

B. Direct material

C. Finished goods

D. Raw material

5. Method of inventory replenishment that establishes a minimum level of inventory that, when reached, will trigger a reorder.

A. Lot for lot

B. Order point

C. Fixed order quantity

D. Periodic order quantity

6. An automated inventory process that includes elements such as cost information, management reports, and the ability to model situations through "what-if" analysis.

A. Just-in-time

B. Manufacturing Resource Planning (MRPII)

C. Supplier managed

D. Material Requirements Planning (MRP)

7. Process of finding ways to use as few purchased items as possible to perform as many functions as possible.

A. Value analysis

B. Cataloging

C. Standardization

D. Communization

8. Used as a continuous improvement tool to determine the degree of improvement required.

   A. Gap analysis

   B. Delta

   C. Deviation

   D. Benchmarking

9. Term that describes the set of activities performed to lower costs of products and services.

   A. Cost avoidance

   B. Purchase price variance

   C. Cost reduction

   D. Standard costing

10. A buying strategy where minimum amounts are purchased as needed.

   A. Ad hoc

   B. Spot

   C. Individual

   D. Minimal

11. Practice of buying before actual or forecasted needs are known precisely.

   A. Future

   B. Forward

   C. Contracting

   D. Advanced

12. Practice of offsetting the current contracted price by taking the opposite position in the futures market.

   A. Contracting

   B. Future

   C. Hedging

   D. Forward

13. A tool to review the potential outcomes of alternative decisions in a graphical format.

   A. Forecasting

   B. Decision tree analysis

   C. Trend line analysis

   D. Hedging

Module 4

1. Process of defining the organization's long-term objectives and identifying the best methods to reach them.
   A. Long-term planning
   B. Benchmarking
   C. Strategic planning
   D. Best practices

2. Key process used to assist organizations in developing strategic plans.
   A. Benchmarking
   B. Management by objective
   C. Best practices
   D. SWOT analysis

3. Tool for categorizing key areas of spending by cost and associated risk and formulating a strategy for each.
   A. Commodity management
   B. Spend analysis
   C. Supply positioning analysis
   D. Risk management

4. Flows from a department's stated vision and is used to align the development of its goals and objectives with the organization.
   A. Mission statement
   B. Vision statement
   C. Goals and objectives
   D. Standard operating procedures

5. Developed within an organization to ensure that standard methods are employed to accomplish goals and objectives.
   A. Mission statement
   B. Vision statement
   C. Goals and objectives
   D. Standard operating procedures

6. The function requiring the manager or supervisor to control resources and processes within a specific span of responsibility.
   A. Teaming
   B. Management
   C. Supervision
   D. Expediting

7. Theory of management that views the organization as an interrelated, interdependent group of elements that functions as a single entity.

   A. Contingency

   B. Systems

   C. Scalar

   D. Chaos

8. Describes the number of subordinates that report to a specific manager.

   A. Line-Staff Principle

   B. Management by Objective

   C. Departmentalization Principle

   D. Span of Control Principle

9. Management view that holds that organizational goals and individual goals can be mutually compatible.

   A. Theory Y

   B. Flat Organization

   C. Exception Management

   D. Theory X

10. A process designed to assess past behaviors and accomplishments.

   A. Background check

   B. Job analysis

   C. Theory X

   D. Structured interview

Answers to Assessment Test

Module 1

1. **B.** A specification describes your organization's specific requirements for the particular purchase to the supplier.

2. **C.** The requisition must, at a minimum, describe what is being purchased and the quantity, or you will not be able to place it as a purchase order. Other information such as lead time, price, and supplier can be derived through the sourcing process if required.

3. **D.** The BOM contains a listing of each part that goes into the final product, along with its relationship to other parts and where it occurs in the product.

4. **C.** Without this minimal information, a purchase order cannot create a contract potentially favorable to your organization.

5. **C.** Direct costs are the costs of products or services that are included in what an organization physically delivers to its customer.

6. **C.** Many industries rely on performance criteria, composition or measurements agreed to in advance by a professional or testing organization as the standard met by a particular product. Referencing the standard's number in the part description ensures that the delivered product will meet those criteria and saves the time of having to write out extensive detail.

7. **A.** Benchmarking is a method for determining how other organizations or products perform. Properly used, they can provide a guideline for your purchase.

8. **C.** A Letter of Credit is issued by a bank to the seller and guarantees payment for the goods sold. Once the products are shipped, the seller can claim the amount promised in the LC from the issuing bank.

9. **D.** A sole source exists whenever there is no alternative to using the supplier for the product being purchased. A single source describes the situation whereby a company *chooses* to use only one supplier.

10. **D.** In competitive bidding, suppliers submit their best price and terms to the buyer. The buyer then selects the supplier most suitable to its needs.

11. **C.** Technical capability ensures that the supplier has the physical wherewithal and expertise to perform the requirements of the contract.

12. **C.** Supply and demand drive price. For example, as demand increases (or the supply becomes more scarce), the existing buyers will bid up the price.

13. **B.** Quality is often measured in terms of conformance to specifications. High quality, therefore, implies a minimum number of unusable parts.

14. A. The site visit gives employees of the buying organization an opportunity to inspect the supplier's facility. During the visit, for example, buyers can assess the supplier's operations for up-to-date equipment, conformance to environmental regulations, and the general state of their facility. They may also have the opportunity to observe the processes used to control quality.

15. C. A weighted average is the derived score based upon the subjective ratings of team members. It lends credibility to an otherwise subjective choice because it averages (or levels) various disparate opinions.

16. A. Article 2, Sales, governs the sale and purchase of goods only. Services are not directly included in the UCC.

17. C. To be valid under the body of law known as the Statute of Frauds, most contracts must be evidenced by writing.

18. B. Detrimental reliance refers to the principle that *unjust* enrichment can produce substantial damages to the buyer or seller and should not be allowed.

19. D. These are the minimum requirements of contract formation. Mutual agreement means a meeting of the minds, legality refers to conformance to law, consideration is an exchange of value (typically, money and goods), and capacity refers to the individual's mental or physical capacity to make a reasonable decision.

20. B. Bartering is the exchange of goods and services by two or more parties for other goods and services that each respectively owns.

21. C. A warranty assures performance in accordance with the buyer's specification or a standard description of the product or service. If the product or service fails to meet these specifications or does not perform for the stated period of time, the warrantor promises specific action, usually repair or replacement.

22. D. Merchantability is a warranty that requires that the product be able to perform its ordinary function. It is said to derive from agricultural dealings when a merchant, purchasing cartloads of harvested product, was unable to inspect all of it due to the manner in which it was packed but, nevertheless, needed assurance that the goods at the bottom of the cart were equally saleable (merchantable) as those that could be inspected at the top.

23. B. Managing the relationship with the supply community is one of the key functions of the Purchasing Department. This is best accomplished one supplier at a time.

24. C. Management by exception requires reporting of incidents that occur outside the expected range of standards. For example, rather than reviewing a list of all products received, you might want to see only those that arrived late.

25. A. Expediting is a method used to ensure that purchased goods and services arrive as planned and scheduled.

26. C. Breach is a term that describes the condition under which a buyer or supplier is unable or unwilling to perform in accordance with the terms and time limits of the contract. Under the terms of contract law, breach provides the injured party with certain additional rights.

27. D. Since it is typically very hard to determine the financial consequences of a contractual breach, the parties agree in advance to a specific amount of damages to be liquidated to the injured party should the other party default on its obligations.

28. B. Liability is a legally enforceable obligation created by an agreement.

29. A. The UCC does not allow a buyer unlimited time to inspect a product before determining it is nonconforming.

30. C. Mediation can be initiated when a dispute arises in the course of contract performance if it is an option in the contract. Under mediation, parties agree to be reconciled to an equitable solution to their issues by a mutually agreed upon third party. Unlike arbitration, the parties are generally not bound to accept the results of the process and may continue on to court.

Module 2

1. B. For competitive bidding to produce effective results requires several suppliers (or at the very least, more than one) willing to make legitimate offers. When a product has a patent controlled by the manufacturer, only one supplier will be able to sell the product.

2. B. These three elements govern the nature of the market (e.g., highly competitive, ologistic, over-sold, or over-stocked) and provide the foundation for its climate.

3. A. Negotiations have a more positive outcome for the buying organization if the Purchasing Department has early involvement in the acquisition process. Early in the product development cycle, for example, the buyer can have greater influence on the selection of suppliers and the choice of materials to be used which can, in turn, save the organization significant amounts later on.

4. B. The SEC regulates publicly held companies and requires from them the regular submission of reports on their financial condition.

5. B. Prior to engaging in an important negotiation, a purchasing team is often formed. The team develops strategy and assesses the supplier's situation.

6. C. MRP is an automated tool that balances purchasing requirements with incoming customer orders and forecasts.

7. A. EDI has been adopted by approximately 8 percent of U.S. corporations for exchanging procurement and logistics data. EDI uses the ANSI X12 standard as the format.

8. C. The VAN provides network services between trading partners, translating and mapping information from one system to the other so that they are interoperable across various programming platforms.

9. C. In a reverse auction, suppliers compete for the business offered by the buyer, usually in real time, by lowering their respective bids.

10. D. True consignment inventory is 100 percent owned by the supplier until such time as it is taken from inventory and put into operation. Typically, it is received as an incoming product. The receiving process then initiates an invoice for payment.

11. C.   Tolerance is generally expressed as plus or minus. It might appear something like this: Required Diameter $3/32$" $(+/- 1/64$"$)$, meaning you will accept product that deviates from the $3/32$" standard by no more $1/64$". You will thus accept all submissions in the range of $5/64$" to $7/64$".

12. A.   As its name implies, acceptance testing is performed by the buyer to determine if the equipment being purchased meets the contracted specifications. It is also called a "sign-off" and indicates that any final payment can now be processed.

13. D.   SPC is used primarily to control machine processes where deviation from specification occurs. The buyer selects an upper limit and a lower limit as the outside parameters of acceptable variation. Variation outside these limits may result in lot rejection.

14. C.   Standard deviation is a measure of variability or spread within a set of numbers. For data that follows a normal distribution, approximately 68 percent of all data will fall within one standard deviation of the sample mean, 95 percent of all values will fall within two standard deviations, and 99.7 percent of all data will fall within three standard deviations.

15. A.   Also know as the 80:20 rule, the Pareto Principle states that 80 percent of the results can be attributed to 20 percent of the events or, more commonly, 80 percent of the problems are caused by 20 percent of the product.

16. A.   Generally, a corrective action is a report prepared by the buying organization citing non-conformities discovered in the seller's products. It requires the seller to report on immediate actions taken to contain the problem and usually provides an additional 30 days to perform a root cause analysis that can jointly improve the process.

17. C.   Root cause analysis investigates a problem to determine its underlying cause and what measures can be taken to eliminate it.

18. A.   TQM holds as its premise that continuous improvement focused on the customer's satisfaction should drive quality.

19. C.   *Kaizen* is a Japanese term for continuous improvement that involves everyone in the organization. *Kai* translates to change; *zen* translates to good.

20. D.   Six Sigma is a quality approach that requires a reduction of errors to the range of plus or minus three standard deviations.

21. D.   ISO 14000 standards are designed to provide an internationally recognized framework for environmental management, measurement, evaluation, and auditing. The standards address subjects such as environmental management systems, environmental auditing, environmental labels and declarations, environmental performance evaluation, and life cycle assessment.

22. A.   Quality assurance is an internal function tasked with the job of ensuring that product shipped to the customer conforms to specification. Largely due to this role, QA has general responsibility for the quality programs within a manufacturing organization.

23. D.   The product manager's role is to manage the particular line of products from design and marketing efforts through manufacturing and distribution.

24. A.   Early involvement by the Purchasing Department in the new product introduction process can assist in aligning future strategies with sourcing needs and provide a smooth transition to new materials or suppliers.

25. D. Materials management covers all functions related to the planning and internal distribution of purchased product. Subfunctions include production control, receiving, the warehouse, internal material distribution and, in some situations, logistics.

26. B. SOPs are used to describe procedures and how certain tasks are to be performed so that they can be performed uniformly throughout the organization.

27. B. Reverse marketing, as its title implies, is the marketing of the buying company to the supply community to convince those interested that your organization is valuable to them.

28. D. Qualification usually includes a formal audit process to determine if the supplier can meet the specification of the product being purchased. The "qual" is generally conducted by a cross-functional team, typically consisting of staff from Engineering/Design, Purchasing, Finance, Quality Assurance, and Manufacturing.

29. B. Often conducted through field audits, the certification means that the supplier has met all conditions required to do business with your organization. It does not, however, qualify the supplier for any specific business.

30. D. Mentoring is an educational process in which the mentor serves as a role model, counselor, or teacher who provides opportunities for professional development, growth, and support to less experienced individuals in career planning or employment settings.

31. C. Markup is added to the direct costs of production to cover overhead and profit.

32. B. Trend analysis is one form of looking at the past and present to project trends in the future. A strong trend will appear on a graph as a straight line.

33. B. Linear regression analysis is a statistical technique that compresses events composed of two activities into a single line on a graph through a standard formula. Once the formula has been calculated, the user can apply "what-if" values to one number to determine the value of the other. Often used in trend analysis where one variable is time, regression can be used to predict future supply or pricing.

34. C. Comparative analysis is often used to make a buying decision. The process looks at the features and benefits of the item to be purchased and compares (usually side by side) the value of competing products.

Module 3

1. B. Make or buy analysis attempts to compare the cost and benefits of manufacturing product internally or purchasing it from an outside source.

2. D. Risk is an inherent factor in all business dealings. Assessing the risk of an undesirable occurrence requires close observation of key elements and frequent data input to determine the current state.

3. B. Outsourcing has been gaining momentum lately. It is defined as the movement of a service currently performed by the organization's employees to another organization.

4. B. Direct material is the material that actually goes out the door in the form of a product.

5. B. Order point inventory replenishment (sometimes called min/max) determines when to order a part maintained in inventory by setting a minimum safety level that, once reached, requires replenishment. The amount of the difference between the current amount on hand and the maximum limit of stocking suggests the size of the order.

6. B. MRPII expands the capability of MRP by adding modules for financial analysis and additional cost reporting, as well as providing tools for performing "what-if" calculations to determine capacity and mix requirements.

7. C. Part standardization is the process of reducing the number of parts used to reduce handling overhead costs, drive lower prices through consolidated purchases, and reduce the risk of stock outages.

8. A. Gap analysis identifies the quantitative difference between an existing process and a benchmarked best practice, seeking ways to implement improvements that will narrow the gap.

9. C. Cost reduction uses multiple tools such as volume consolidation, negotiations, part substitution, and part reduction to reduce the cost of purchased items.

10. B. Spot buying covers immediate needs during a period of days. It is also known as hand-to-mouth buying.

11. B. Forward buying takes advantage of current low pricing or anticipated shortages by purchasing against potential future demand.

12. C. Hedging is generally used for transactions where currency fluctuations are common. The buying organization, on placing an order, will purchase the currency for payment at the time of the order. In this way, if the value of the currency increases or decreases it will not generate a change in the actual purchased price.

13. B. Decision tree analysis traces the implications and theoretical valuation of the outcome of specific decisions and presents it in the form of a table or chart.

Module 4

1. C. Strategic planning is related to the organization's mission statement and is used to develop a plan for achieving it.

2. D. SWOT analysis lists an organization's strengths and weaknesses as internal data that can be controlled or leveraged and external opportunities and threats that require action to meet the plan.

3. C. Supply positioning analysis divides all purchases by risk and cost, creating four squares into which all categories can be placed.

4. A. The mission statement provides the clarity of direction that enables the Purchasing Department to align its goals and objectives with the rest of the organization.

5. D. SOPs create a written guide so that employees can perform specific tasks uniformly.

6. B. Management *is* the control of resources.

7. B. A system is a combination of related parts organized into a complex whole. The systems approach holds that a synergy develops from these interdependent functional elements that creates a greater whole than the theoretical sum of its parts.

8. D. The Span of Control Principle specifies that individual managers should have no more subordinates than they can effectively supervise.

9. A. Theory Y managers believe that employees are capable of hard work and have cooperative, positive attitudes. This translates to an understanding that the average person learns to accept and even seek responsibility and that individuals have the ability to exercise a relatively high degree of imagination and creativity in the workplace.

10. D. During the hiring process, the interviewing managers probe the applicant for information. This information then can be used to help assess the individual's capability and fitness for the position.

Operational Purchasing Practices

Chapter 1

Procurement and Best Business Practices

THE C.P.M. EXAM SPECIFICATIONS COVERED IN THIS CHAPTER INCLUDE THE FOLLOWING:

- ✓ Employing procurement processes to align with organization's strategy
- ✓ Reviewing user requests
- ✓ Developing requirements
- ✓ Using cost-related analysis tools
- ✓ Developing a tactical approach to order placement

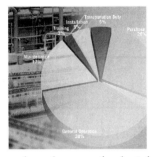

The role of the *supply management* professional is rapidly changing. While in the past the *purchasing manager*'s area of responsibility was clearly relegated to efficient "processing" of purchase orders, the pace of today's business environment has expanded that role to control of the entire sourcing and acquisition process. To be successful in this rapidly changing, dynamic marketplace requires not only the traditionally disciplined approach to managing critical business relationships but also the ability to quickly understand and employ strategic new methods and technology. Purchasing managers today must have the ability to assess and respond effectively to current market conditions and the foresight to envision the future needs of the organization, setting into motion plans that will respond to the changing dynamics of the continually reinvented organization. Indeed, today's purchasing manager must be a master of change. And to facilitate that dynamic of change, the purchasing manager must also be a master of *best practices*—methods shown to provide outstanding results—to continually ensure that change drives improvement in the *business process* and does not simply replace one poorly functioning system with another poorly functioning system. That is why we begin our preparation for the C.P.M. exam by reviewing the key elements of those processes and best practices that are fundamental to excellence in procurement and for which you will have ultimate responsibility.

Understanding Procurement

Effective *procurement* requires the utilization of sound business practices that maximize value to the organization through the acquisition of goods and services. This follows the old adage that the Purchasing Department's role is to deliver the right material (or service) in the right amount to the right place at the right time and at the right price. You can do this by employing well-conceived strategies—a plan to enhance competitive bidding, for example—that leverage clearly defined processes to manage the supply base. As a purchasing manager, you will be expected to conceive and implement strategies that employ best practices.

Employing best practices in procurement ensures that the organization and ultimately the purchasing manager make correct decisions. This means that an organization must develop plans that are in alignment with its goals and best interests. Frequently, these plans evolve from well-defined sourcing strategies developed to help the organization achieve its overall objectives. In turn, sourcing strategies rely on a clear set of tactical procedures to ensure their implementation. At the root of these tactical procedures are the day to day methods the organization employs to convey its requirements to the supplier. Many organizations refer to these processes as *standard operating procedures (SOPs)* and maintain them in formalized document libraries.

Understanding and Conveying Requirements

Sound business practice requires that you understand and can clearly describe to a prospective supplier the requirement of your purchase. Unless you can describe to a supplier exactly what you need, the purchasing process will not be successful. As we will detail below, this description often takes the form of a *specification* for materials or a *statement of work (SOW)* for services. Most commonly, it is the internal user who generates this information—often called a *requirement*—and it is the purchasing manager's responsibility to ensure that it is properly conveyed to the supplier in the purchasing document (such as, the Purchase Order or Contract). In the case where a purchase is particularly complex, the process of stating organizational needs is so critical that you may find a face-to-face meeting with your supplier is in order. That way, you can ensure that there are no misunderstandings or faulty interpretations of the requirement. A well-developed and well-stated requirement describing exactly what it is you expect to receive is the key to successful procurement. For this reason, you must ensure that there are systems in place that accurately convey the needs of your customers to you so that you can formalize them into a contract or purchase order. At the minimum, you should include the following elements in your purchasing documents when stating requirements:

Material or Service   This describes what it is you expect to receive from the supplier. This description can be provided in the form of a specification, a statement of work (SOW), a drawing, a part number, or the nomenclature of an *off-the-shelf* or brand name part. Along with the stated quantity and the quality of the purchase, this can be the basis for approving payment and must be easy for third parties such as receiving personnel, finance, and auditors to understand the transaction after it is completed.

Specification   A specification contains a technical description of the material being purchased. In its simplest terms, it can be a reference to a supplier's stock number or a brand name. It can also refer to an engineering drawing (or a set of drawings) provided by the user that shows the part or assembly with call-outs for the type of materials required and all necessary dimensions to produce the part. Or, in the case of chemicals and other formulated and processed materials, the specification can be tendered as a recipe or in compositional format.

Statement of Work (SOW)   Unlike a specification, the SOW describes the requirements for a service. It may be stated in detailed and prescriptive format, describing not only what needs to be done but the method to be used and how often the service must be done as well. Or it may simply be stated in terms of expected outcomes. Frequently, the SOW also contains a set of metrics describing the level of performance required. These are called *Key Performance Indicators (KPI)* and are often used to determine the level of performance requiring corrective action or, on the other hand, when an incentive bonus may be due.

We'll discuss the SOW in greater detail in Chapter 2, "Sourcing."

Time of Performance This indicates the date when you expect to receive the product or service you're purchasing in the purchasing document. The document must clearly state delivery or work completion dates so that the supplier understands precisely what is required.

Expressions such as "Rush" or "ASAP" are inappropriate because they can be open to a variety of interpretations. It only requires a little more effort to specify an exact date. Consider calling the supplier to determine the earliest possible date and pass that along to your internal customer. If the proposed date is acceptable, it should then be included in your purchasing document.

Price and Payment Terms You'll need to include exactly how much your organization has agreed to pay for the specified product or service in the requirement so that you avoid misunderstandings and can clearly determine your organization's financial obligation.

The purchasing document should also specify when payment is due. This is usually expressed as a net number of days, such as Net 30 or Net 45. A discount period may be included where the supplier specifies the amount of the discount as well as the number of days the buyer can make payments and still earn the discount. The discount period is often expressed as a formula:

2/10 Net 45

This means that if payment is made within 10 days, a 2 per cent discount can be taken, but in any case the total balance is due in 45 days. The annualized discount savings for a 2 percent discount for 10 days (in this example) actually equals 73 percent! (Two times 365 divided by 10.)

Shipping Destination, Method, and Terms If you're purchasing materials and intend to use a specific carrier to transport the purchased material, you should include this in your requirement, as well. You'll need to specify the level of service—overnight air, second day air, ground and so on—and indicate if the supplier is to bill your account, pay for it and then bill your organization, or absorb the freight cost outright. In your instructions, include the exact destination of the shipment and the point at which the ownership of the goods, or title, transfers from the seller to the buyer. Fortunately, there are standard expressions for these terms, which we will introduce in Chapter 3 when we outline transportation terms.

Creating Strategic Plans and Tactics

Virtually all organizations develop a set of key goals and objectives to guide their operations and, typically, formulate a broad plan to achieve them. This plan is usually referred to as a *strategic plan*. It focuses activities to achieve the organization's overall mission. So, as each segment of the organization pursues individual commitments to achieve its goals, it generates the need for materials and services from the supply community. The Purchasing Department, as the interface between internal departments and their suppliers, then formulates its plans based upon meeting these needs and commitments in alignment with the various conditions that drive its supply base.

As you look closely at the various missions within the organization based on their functional roles, specific sets of strategies that determine how and when goods or services must be purchased, become apparent:

Finance Strategies involving finance are critical to the organization's success. Cash position relative to the overall economy often determines when new technology can be acquired or when additional product lines can be launched. In a period of declining prices, organizations may want to postpone major purchases for a period of time in the anticipation of lower pricing in the near future. Business organizations with strong cash positions during weak economic times frequently find acquisitions of other companies an attractive way to expand market position. Obviously, these strategies generate purchasing requirements that must be dovetailed with overall procurement strategies so that they are properly met with appropriate action when it is needed.

Manufacturing and Operations Manufacturing and operational strategies develop from the need to meet customer demand. The influx of orders and the development of new product lines generate purchasing requirements that are critically time phased to meet current market demands. At various phases of the product life cycle significantly different requirements must be met, so it is imperative that the Purchasing Department develop its strategy accordingly. For example, early involvement in the development phase of a new product can be critical since that is when much of the sourcing, supplier qualification, and contracting activity will take place.

Other strategies developed in conjunction with purchasing can similarly support operational strategies. These include *just-in-time (JIT)* delivery, *Supplier Managed Inventory (SMI)*, and a variety of other programs developed to enhance well-run operations and eliminate non-value-added costs.

Sales and Marketing Sales and marketing drive product or service adoption and develop strategies that are critical to the organization's revenue stream. Accurately forecasting anticipated volumes provides critical data to operations and can be the basis for developing supply management strategies. The timing of a new product launch will typically generate requirements for additional capital equipment and marketing material, so it is important that strategic plans be coordinated with the Purchasing Department to the extent that its involvement will be required.

Supply Management While procurement strategies are generally created to respond to the needs of other internal organizations, it is important for Purchasing to develop plans that anticipate changing conditions in the marketplace as well. As a result, you often find strategies for procurement formulated along commodity lines to allow for specific trends that may be affecting one industry more than another. Changes in supply or demand can trigger decisions to hold purchasing plans for later or to accelerate them in the face of temporary opportunity. Prices are rarely in equilibrium, so commodity-specific strategies must be developed to react quickly to changing supply and demand conditions.

Typically, supply management strategies focus on key areas of spending and technology, seeking formularies to balance various needs at any given time. Thus it is important to have well-conceived decision making strategies for favoring one aspect over another. For example, it must be clear to the individual buyer whether the acquisition of advanced technology overrides the need to reduce costs when the organization's strategy seeks to gain greater market penetration of its products or services based on price competition. You can easily see how the interpretation of this strategy can affect supplier selection, favoring a supplier with superior technology over a supplier with best pricing (or vice versa). Supplier selection, therefore, becomes one of the key elements in the Purchasing Department's strategic plan.

The purchaser must understand that strategic planning has a dual aspect: internal strategies that are driven by the organization's mission as it is developed within other departments and external strategies that drive purchasing decisions in response to market conditions. In the final analysis, the key to effective strategy for procurement is the proper alignment of procurement activity with the strategic plans of its internal customers and conditions in the supply base. This will be manifest in both long-term and short-term commodity plans that relate purchasing decisions to individual market conditions and specific internal needs.

Finding Innovative Methods and Exploring Alternatives

Closely linked to the development and implementation of procurement strategy is the traditional role of the Purchasing Department as a strategic tool itself. In most organizations, policy requires the implementation of business processes through purchasing activities that reduce cost and increase life-cycle value. Later in this chapter, we will explore some of these methods in more detail, but for now it would be valuable to point out that the strategies just outlined require specific tactics to ensure favorable results. A program to reduce the purchase prices of a specific set of materials may best be implemented through a competitive bidding process—as a tactical tool—whereas the codevelopment of new technology that requires prodigious engineering costs from a potential supplier might be more easily gained through negotiation.

To be effective, the purchasing manager must continually explore new methods and seek out alternatives that will improve existing processes. In turn, these improvements will spawn new strategies. Tactics and strategies thus feed one another in a cycle of *continuous improvement*.

Providing Purchasing Services

The decision to initiate a particular purchase develops in a variety of ways and from a variety of circumstances. Usually purchases are initiated by an internal user based on some planned and budgeted need that can be justified by a specific operational purpose. For example, new technology may require the purchase of new manufacturing equipment, or the development of a new product line may require building models or ordering special tools. In a manufacturing environment, raw material needs are generated through a formal planning process based on incoming customer orders and forecasts of anticipated production needs.

For the purchaser, it is important to understand the overall needs and responsibilities of the internal customer so that when requirements are generated, they can be fulfilled in the most expeditious manner possible. Often this requires the development of close relationships with those staff members responsible for generating the purchasing requirements you will be handling. It also involves understanding the supplier community and its marketplace, including an in-depth knowledge of industry standards and methodologies, so that you can best advise your internal users on which supplier may be best able to handle a specific requirement or how to develop a requirements statement using language common to the industry. While you are rarely expected to provide technical expertise, your customers should be able to rely on you and your team to find new suppliers, assist in the selection of an existing supplier for a specific job, and advise them on which supplier provides the best business solution in any given situation.

Your customers will frequently have specific goals that relate to how and where purchases are made, such as the development and use of a new source for advanced technology or the use of a supplier who is willing to undertake the codevelopment of new engineering processes, that will enable your organization to develop a better position in the marketplace for its products or services. Occasionally, the need will arise to use *Minority Business Enterprises (MBE)* suppliers, which are classified as minority or disadvantaged businesses or sources within a certain geographical region or national boundary, to enhance your organization's own competitive position in these areas. Your sensitivity to such issues and ability to enhance these positions will help build strong relationships within your customer base that will open further opportunities for your involvement in their business processes.

You and your team will also be responsible for evaluating overall supplier performance and developing ways to work with suppliers to improve that performance. If you can do this effectively, you will add measurable value to your internal customers' mission.

Accepting Orders

Requests to purchase or contract for materials and services can be submitted to the Purchasing Department in a number of ways. However, regardless of the method of submission, a number of common elements define the process and requirements in most organizations:

1. The purchasing staff must have documented evidence that the order has been duly authorized in accordance with prescribed organizational policy prior to processing it for placement.

2. The information outlined in the "Understanding and Conveying Requirements" section that originates with the requestor must be present, along with any required accounting data, user information, and known supplier sources. Briefly summarized, this information includes:

    a. The user's name and department

    b. The cost code, General Ledger (GL) account or budgeting center being charged

    c. A description of the purchase in terms that can be understood by the supplier

    d. The quantity needed (and the amount of acceptable overage or underage, if applicable)

    e. The date required

    f. Estimated cost (if not exactly known)

    g. Suggested suppliers (and justification if a specific *sole source* is required)

    h. The shipping address or location where the materials are to be delivered or where the work is to be performed

3. The order must not have been placed previously without proper procedural due diligence by the Purchasing Department. In most organizations, the Purchasing Department is the only authorized buying entity and purchases made outside the authority of the Purchasing Department are considered unauthorized and are frequently referred to as *maverick purchases*.

Order Approval and Authority

Most organizations designate individuals or job positions within each department that are authorized to approve requests for purchases. Often this authority is hierarchical, requiring increasingly higher approval according to an existing chain of command and depending upon the spending amount represented by the request.

In most organizations, all but a few specialized spending requirements must be placed by the Purchasing Department. Buying through other channels is usually considered unauthorized spending and is strongly discouraged. There are a number of important considerations for this. First of all, spending outside of the recognized purchasing channels cannot benefit from negotiated discounts accorded the larger volumes that are placed within the system, and the volume of these purchases do not count toward further discounts since they are often purchased from noncontractual sources. Secondly, these purchases do not benefit from the trained due diligence performed by the professional buyer and can result in liability for the organization. Thirdly, they are not likely to be properly captured in the budget and so cannot provide visibility for future requirements and expense allocations. And, finally, they are not likely to be placed with the most qualified supplier because the maverick buyer will have few resources or incentives to perform more than the most perfunctory competitive analysis.

Types of Purchase Requests

Purchase requests can be generated in a number of different ways depending upon the organization's level of automation and the nature of the purchase. We'll discuss some of the more commonly used processes, such as requisitions, catalog ordering, MRP, and system-generated orders.

Requisitions

Requisitions are documents generated by the user or user department containing the specific information outlined in the preceding paragraphs. They may be submitted as a paper form through standard internal distribution channels or as an electronic document through an existing computerized system, often linked to the organization's primary data system. Sometimes organizations use e-mail to transmit them.

Paper requisitions usually contain the written signatures of the approving managers, whereas electronic requisitions are signed digitally. In general, today's electronic systems automatically route user requests to the approval authority based upon an existing workflow hierarchy. Approval dates and times are maintained in a workflow database within the system and kept for future audit reference.

Catalog Ordering

The *electronic catalog* is another automated method for ordering standard products. Here, the user accesses a listing of products available for ordering within the organization's electronic requisitioning system (usually available as a distinct section on the organization's internal network or *intranet*). By using a search engine that returns data stored by key words or product categories, users can find products they are authorized to purchase and in some systems perform side-by-side comparisons of pricing, features, and functions from competing suppliers in order to make the appropriate selection.

There are numerous ways to generate and store electronic catalog data, depending on the system being used. However, the Purchasing Department (or a cross-functional team led by Purchasing) generally selects the suppliers in advance; negotiates the prices, terms, and conditions; and processes whatever contractual documents are needed. In many systems, the supplier actually maintains the data, either outside or inside the organization's firewall, depending on security requirements. Changes to the data can be made in real time (that is, immediately) or at periodic intervals and typically require the designated buyer's approval.

Systems are available today that enable users to "punch out" of the existing electronic catalog and access a supplier's website catalog (or a group of catalogs) directly, often through the common tools such as a web browser. Once accessed, items can be captured and moved directly into the user's system and then processed as a normal catalog order. This can be as simple as dragging a desired item into the user's requisitioning system. As convenient as this sounds, there is a catch: the supplier must be prequalified since significant work is required in advance to ensure compatibility between the systems of each party.

MRP and System-Generated Orders

Material Requirements Planning (MRP) systems, typically used in manufacturing operations, generate automated requisitions or special electronic listings of current and planned requirements that can be transmitted directly to a supplier. Overall requirements are based on a combination of incoming customer orders and forecasts of customer order and can be time phased so that material reaches the organization at a specific time. (We will review this in more detail in Chapter 10.)

Each product (or line of products) has a distinct *Bill of Materials (BOM)*, a formulary of the parts that constitute the final product, from which detailed requirements can be quantified and summarized by the supplier. These summaries are usually transmitted electronically.

Table 1.1 contains an exploded BOM, with a brief summary of the combined requirements by the supplier in typical printed format. As you can see in Table 1.1, in a simple listing, parts are grouped by level. In most production environments, the final product is composed of a number of *subassemblies*, sections that must be assembled or manufactured separately before being built into the product being sold, so the order in which they are assembled is designated by a level number. Thus Level 5 parts in a subassembly are put together before Level 4 parts and so on. This table lists the parts by their order of assembly but does not show their relationship to one another. A listing such as this shows the number of common parts being used and their specific order of assembly. Note that Part Number 34009-40023, a hex nut, is listed on both Level 2 and Level 5. Another type of listing would list the BOM by specific part number so that total requirements for the product could be determined.

Table 1.1 shows the format used for a simple listing of a BOM. It shows the assigned part number, the engineering revision number, the quantity (and the unit of measurement), along with their nomenclature and the supplier.

TABLE 1.1　　Bill of Material: Swing Arm Task Lamp Assembly (Listing)

Level	Part Number	Revision	Quantity	Unit of Measure	Description	Supplier
1	15400-10000	A	Parent	Each	Lamp assembly	Make
2	24001-30010	A	1	Each	Lamp switch	Delta
2	25950-40010	B	1	Each	Lamp switch housing	Delta
2	34009-40023	A	2	Each	10-32 hex nut	Omni
2	35010-45098	B	2	Each	10-32 bolt	Omni
3	40900-10000	C	1	Each	Light socket assembly	Delta
4	60902-29845	B	1	Each	40-watt light bulb	Consoli-dated
4	48098-60090	B	1	Each	Lamp cone assembly	Delta
5	89009-34896	D	1	Each	Swing arm assembly	Marsten
5	34009-40023	A	10	Each	10-32 hex nut	Omni
5	35010-45098	B	10	Each	10-32 bolt	Omni

Figure 1.1 shows where the parts from the Table 1.1 BOM are actually used in relation to one another. This view of the lamp assembly BOM shows the relationships between individual parts in their subassemblies and how they roll up into the final product.

Placing Orders

There are two key considerations that must be addressed in any system for placing orders with suppliers: first, the format used to convey the order to the supplier and second, the priority of placement. We'll discuss these issues in this section.

FIGURE 1.1   Diagrammatic Bill of Materials (BOM)

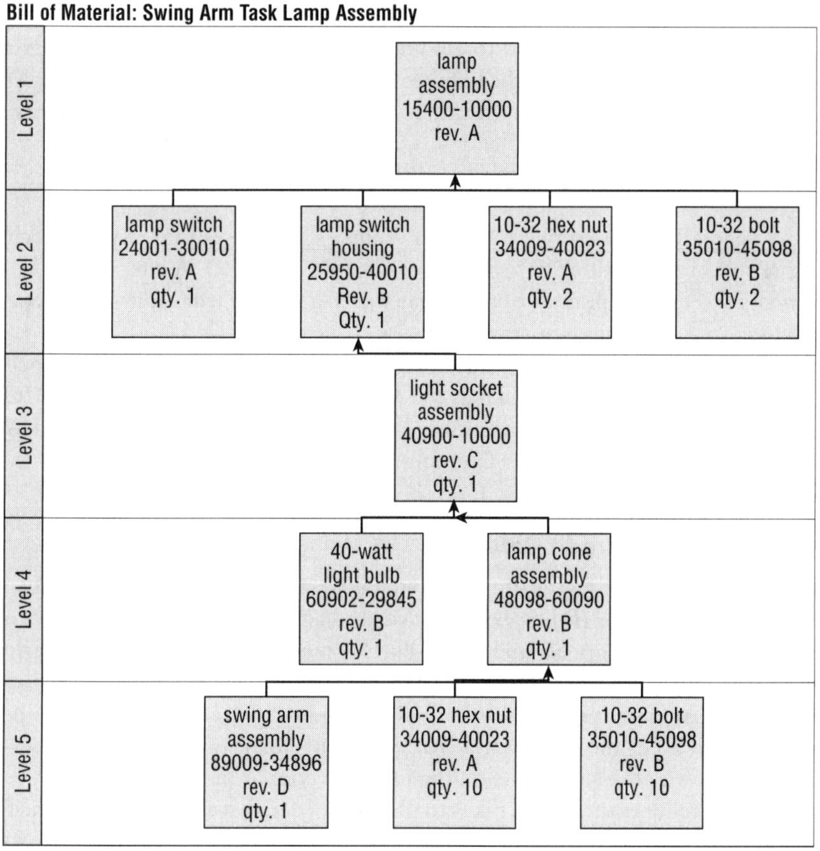

Bill of Material: Swing Arm Task Lamp Assembly

Level 1	lamp assembly 15400-10000 rev. A
Level 2	lamp switch 24001-30010 rev. A qty. 1 — lamp switch housing 25950-40010 Rev. B Qty. 1 — 10-32 hex nut 34009-40023 rev. A qty. 2 — 10-32 bolt 35010-45098 rev. B qty. 2
Level 3	light socket assembly 40900-10000 rev. C qty. 1
Level 4	40-watt light bulb 60902-29845 rev. B qty. 1 — lamp cone assembly 48098-60090 rev. B qty. 1
Level 5	swing arm assembly 89009-34896 rev. D qty. 1 — 10-32 hex nut 34009-40023 rev. A qty. 10 — 10-32 bolt 35010-45098 rev. B qty. 10

Ordering Formats

A number of different formats can be used to convey purchase orders to the supplier, depending upon the circumstances and the nature of the requirement. Each method has its own specific requirements, as you can see from the following: POs, blanket POs, contracts, credit cards and system generated orders.

Standard Purchase Orders

The *purchase order (PO)* is likely the most commonly used form of purchasing document. As a contractual document, the PO contains all of the information we outlined in the requirements section along with the organization's standard *Terms and Conditions* boilerplate. POs are numbered for unique identification and audit control and, in paper format, usually contain a number of copies for distribution to the supplier, the Accounting Department, the original requestor and the files. POs can be transmitted by any common form of mail, by fax, or by a variety of other electronic processes including e-mail.

Blanket Purchase Orders

The *blanket purchase order* covers a purchasing commitment to a supplier for specific products or services at an agreed upon price for a set period of time or for a limited quantity or spending amount. Commonly used to eliminate many smaller orders so as to minimize the amount of paperwork processed, the blanket PO, once placed by the Purchasing Department, can be used by other groups within the organization to set releases as frequently as needed and when needed.

Contracts

A *contract* generally covers services or other complex purchases that require special legal language or terms and conditions beyond the scope of a typical PO. A contract is also used when requirements extend over periods of time longer than a year or when automatic renewal may be required to ensure continuing operations.

Under the broader heading of contracts, we can include a number of similar documents used in the normal course of business, such as the *Memorandum of Understanding (MOU)* and the *Letter of Intent (LOI)*. Many organizations also have specialized *agreements* used for particular purposes, such as an Agreement for Consignment or a Master Supply Agreement. We will discuss these in more detail in Chapter 3.

Purchasing Cards or Credit Cards

Issued to specific users within the organization whose duties require making frequent small purchases, the *purchasing card (P-card)* or credit card can effectively reduce the clutter of low-value requisitions and purchases processed by the Purchasing Department that can interfere with efficient supply management. Used mainly for incidental purchases associated with nonproduction or *Maintenance, Repair, and Operations (MRO)* products, P-card purchases can be controlled through limits placed by the organization for specific products or services (or classes of products and services), or even through limits on the industry type or individual supplier.

The card also reduces the time it takes to place an order as well as the cycle time for payment to the supplier, reducing (or eliminating) the typical cost associated with the buying and payment of POs.

Of course, one of the major drawbacks to use of the P-card is the limited amount of control over where purchases are made. When an organization is attempting to consolidate suppliers for better pricing, Purchasing has no way to ensure that existing suppliers under contract get used.

System-Generated Orders

There are a variety of orders that are generated internally through various planning and scheduling systems such as MRP or other automated inventory replenishment systems. For the most part, organizations using these systems issue documentation electronically as agreed upon with the supplier in advance (and usually according to a contract). MRP and system-generated orders have already been described in this chapter.

Externally managed inventory through a formal SMI program is a relative of system-generated orders, insofar as replenishment signals are controlled by the supplier based on a negotiated level of inventory or the receipt of incoming orders.

Placement Priority

Electronic catalog and system-generated orders are most commonly transmitted in real time directly to the supplier through some electronic media. A manually generated order, however, requires buyer intervention to accomplish several tasks. With a manually generated order, the buyer must determine proper authorization, establish the source of supply, and review requirements for legality and conformance to applicable regulations such as those related to the *Environmental Protection Agency (EPA)* or the *Occupational Safety and Health Administration (OSHA)*. A manually generated order also requires that the buyer convert the requisition to a PO or contract. Because buyers typically have backlogs of multiple orders to place, some process for determining the order and timing of their placement must be implemented.

First In, First Out (FIFO)

Using the *First In, First Out (FIFO)* method, orders received in the buyers' queues are prioritized by order of receipt so that the oldest one becomes the next to be placed. While this sounds fair, it could adversely affect operations if applied too blindly because it ignores the need for urgency in the case of emergencies or critical outages.

Priority System

Using a *priority system* method, priorities are established within the department to address specific needs. For example, conditions that could create a work stoppage in a manufacturing operation or situations that may immediately jeopardize employee health will require immediate attention, and buyers are required to put other work aside to address them. Separate priority will often be assigned to orders with specific lead times so that user needs can be uniformly accommodated. Items with the longest lead time may be placed soonest.

Cycle Time

In some organizations, buyers' performance metrics include the *cycle time* for orders based on the date and time received and the date and time placed with the supplier. Buyers are measured on how long it takes, on average, for a particular to place orders during a specific time period. Obviously, if this becomes the key consideration, it will provide incentives to the buyers to place the easy orders first—the ones requiring the least amount of sourcing or negotiation—to reduce the average turn around time in the queue. However, as a measure of internal service, cycle time and customer satisfaction with the purchasing process go hand-in-glove.

Mastering Procurement and Business Tactics

Procurement tactics naturally follow the course established by organizational and departmental strategies. Indeed, you might well consider that tactics are the methods and processes through which we implement effective strategies. A buyer may develop the most appropriate and innovative strategies, but unless they can be effectively executed through practical measures, the organization may never realize their benefits.

In this section, we will explore how business and procurement strategies are generally applied.

Budgets and Expense Allocation

Most organizations implement critical strategies through some form of spending. Typically, this spending comes in the form of the purchase of capital equipment or the hiring of additional staff and their accompanying support materials and services. It may also be reflected in larger spending on new product development or through additional marketing and advertising. All of these are strategic efforts that are usually implemented through Purchasing.

A budget can be viewed as an organization's spending plan. Usually, budgets get allocated (or funded) to specific departments or functional areas, cost centers, or projects, and incoming goods and services are charged against those accounts. To a large extent, an approved budget may be the final authorization to proceed with expenditures.

Because adherence to an established budget can mean the difference between profit and loss in a business organization, or the continuation of operations in a nonprofit, management takes the budget seriously and pays close attention to individual areas of conformance. This may explain the sensitivity that internal users often manifest when ensuring that expenses are charged to the correct cost code.

The Finance Department usually manages the control and allocation of expenses and is responsible for categorizing and reporting actual expenditures. Finance is also responsible for paying suppliers and requires that specific criteria are met prior to disbursing the organization's funds. For materials, accounting practice typically requires that a duly authorized PO and a Receiving Document, along with the supplier's invoice, are in place prior to payment. (In the case of services, usually a sign-off on the supplier's invoice by the budgeting manager or department head indicating satisfactory completion of the service is required in lieu of a Receiving Document.) This is commonly referred to as a *three-way match*.

Finance, along with internal and external auditors, verifies that purchases are made in accordance with approved policies and procedures. To the extent that Purchasing implements (or at least touches in some significant manner) most of these procedures in its dealing with suppliers, it becomes an instrument of the organization's financial apparatus and undergoes periodic audits to ensure proper conformance. Public companies must meet regulatory audit requirements under the *Sarbanes-Oxley Act of 2002 (SOX)*. SOX determines that corporate management is responsible for establishing and maintaining adequate controls and procedures for financial reporting. Maintenance of purchasing policies, procedures, and records is included among these responsibilities.

 The Sarbanes-Oxley Act was passed to ensure that senior corporate executives would be held responsible for any financial misconduct within the organization. It also requires that organizations develop and implement reporting processes that safeguard financial integrity. You can find out more about the Sarbanes-Oxley Act of 2002 by visiting http://frwebgate.access.gpo.gov/cgi-bin/getdoc.cgi?dbname=107_cong_bills&docid=f:h3763enr.txt.pdf.

Establishing Procurement Methods

Many systematized processes exist for placing POs, as outlined earlier in this chapter. But far more important than simply determining the appropriate document or format for a particular purchase, the Purchasing Department also has responsibility for actually driving the deal. By this we mean that the purchasing manager has a fiduciary obligation to ensure that goods and services are acquired in accordance with the best interests of the organization. This can be accomplished either through negotiations (bargaining) or through some form of competitive bidding process.

Procurement Negotiations

Negotiation, in its simplest form, can be a way of striking a deal through a process of give and take. Buyer and seller each have specific objectives in developing the bargain, and generally accepted best practice indicates that, in a successful negotiation, each party achieves an equal measure of satisfaction. Techniques and methods for accomplishing this, so critical to maintaining a competitive, motivated supply base, will be discussed in Chapter 6.

Competitive Bidding

Another common way to strike a purchasing agreement with a supplier is through the competitive bidding process. The typical objective of competitive bidding is to ensure that the buying organization receives the lowest market pricing for a given purchase, with all other terms and conditions remaining equal. To do this, the buyer needs to ensure that a number of conditions are present:

Competition The marketplace contains a reasonable number of qualified or qualifiable suppliers who are willing to compete. The more suppliers available (within manageable degrees), the greater the competition will be. Competition is the buyer's best friend.

Value The goods or services have significant enough value to make the bidding process worthwhile.

Savings The bidding has the potential to result in lower prices.

Requirements A clear specification or SOW (or industry standard) is available to all bidders.

Contract The suppliers have the capability and are willing commit to furnishing the goods or services at the price bid and under.

Time There is sufficient time to conduct a fair and impartial process.

Corrections and Clarifications A process exists to provide suppliers with answers to questions or corrections to specifications. Answers to questions asked by one supplier must be shared with all others.

We'll discuss competitive bidding in more detail in Chapter 2.

🌐 Real World Scenario

Caveat Emptor: Buyer Beware of Competitive Bidding Traps

Unscrupulous suppliers have developed an onerous repertoire of dirty tricks to circumvent the competitive bidding process. We refer to these as traps.

One competitive bidding trap occurs when a supplier intentionally bids for a new product without including associated tooling or startup costs, thus providing a price that the more forthright competition cannot possibly meet. However, the price offered is usually somewhat above the normal cost associated with production. In this way, the supplier can gradually recover the tooling costs over a period of several years, while at the same time always excluding competitors who will be unable to match the price without absorbing the tooling or startup costs that are continually rising due to inflation. As the years go on, the supplier not only recovers the full cost of the tooling, but can also charge a significantly higher price for the materials as long as it stays just below the next lowest bid (which includes tooling).

Another competitive bidding trap occurs when the supplier realizes that the specifications will require further change after the bid is awarded. This is often the result of improperly designed products or an ill-conceived SOW, although it sometimes results from a simple mistake made by the buyer. The supplier makes the original quote at below cost and reasonable market prices. However, the inevitable changes are then quoted on a substantially higher basis than would ordinarily be justified (since there will be no other bidders at that point) and thus the supplier can recover the difference and earn a handsome premium as well.

Reverse Auction

A recently popular automated process known as the *Reverse Auction (RA)* has enabled the acceleration of bidding from what formerly took months to a mere few days. It is called a "reverse" auction because it allows suppliers to bid (usually bidding is conducted on behalf of the buyer) and the lowest price, rather than the highest price, wins the bid. The RA provides an electronic marketplace where prequalified suppliers can bid on a buyer's requirements in real time instead of through a delayed process and, most importantly, can determine their position in the overall bidding process so that they can improve their bids as they feel appropriate. An auction serves the additional benefit of ensuring to the buyer that a fair and reasonable price has been established.

Internal Cost-Related Analysis Tools

A number of tools and methods are used internally to track the performance of the Purchasing Department relative to the nature of the organization's *costs*. For the purchasing manager to effectively manage this critical area requires a detailed knowledge of the various aspects of costs and how they are calculated.

Defining and Determining Costs

Costs are categorized and defined both in terms of their method of calculation and their relationship to the organization's balance sheet. Here are some of the more common ways accountants characterize them.

Direct Costs

Direct costs are those expenditures directly incorporated into the product or service being delivered to the end customer. Typically, these costs are generated only when there is a product or service being sold, or when *finished goods* inventory is being built in the anticipation of future demand. This implies that without sales there will be no direct costs.

In most manufacturing operations, it is common to account for and distribute the total company *overhead* (see the next section) as a percentage *burden* added to each separate product or product line. That way, the total cost of producing a specific product can be calculated on a stand-alone basis.

Indirect Costs

The elements of cost that are associated with the organization's operation but not directly with a specific product or service are classified as *indirect costs*. These costs can be further subdivided into three other categories: fixed, variable, and semivariable.

Fixed Costs   Costs that remain relatively constant within a specific range of operations, regardless of changes in production or service volumes, are considered *fixed costs*. When calculated on a per-unit-produced basis they increase and decrease with corresponding variations in volumes. Examples of such expenses include rent, facilities maintenance, nonproduction related service contracts, and administrative support from Information Technology providers. They are usually expenses committed by management as part of the general planning process and are often reallocated to various departments based on a standard financial formula.

Variable Costs   *Variable costs*, on the other hand, are costs that increase or decrease in relation to production or service volumes. When calculated on a per-unit-produced basis they remain relatively constant regardless of the organization's output. Examples of these expenses would include consumable materials and spare parts used in manufacturing. Variable costs are typically incurred in relation to some specific reaction to a change in demand and so are accountable at the consuming departmental level.

Semivariable Costs   *Semivariable costs* are costs that change in response to changes in operational levels but not necessarily on a uniform basis. They exhibit qualities of both fixed and variable costs, having elements of both. Managerial bonuses might be considered as an example.

Overhead

Overhead costs, usually called *General and Administrative Expenses (G&A)* on the *Profit and Loss Statement (P&L)*, are those costs generally connected with the operation of the organization as a whole and cannot be directly connected with any specific operational activity. Examples include equipment depreciation, utilities, interest expense, outside auditing, and legal fees. Commonly, overhead and indirect costs are kept separate.

Overhead expenses are usually allocated back to the various operational units or product lines on a percentage basis. Some organizations use direct labor for the method of calculation, while others may use direct materials or even machine hours.

Total Cost of Ownership

The total cost of acquiring and using a material or service is sometimes called the *total cost of ownership (TCO)*. Total cost methods typically track all the additional costs beyond the purchase price that are associated with the life cycle of the materials or services purchased by an organization. This can include the cost of transportation and customs duties—called the *landed price*—to acquire the product; installation and maintenance (in the case of equipment); training; rework; inventory carrying and storage costs; handling; and finally, disposal at the end of life, as illustrated in Figure 1.2. As you might surmise, the typical life cycle costs far outweigh the simple purchase price. Figure 1.2 illustrates what a typical breakdown might look like for capital equipment. Notice that the actual purchase price accounts for just over one-fourth the total life-cycle costs.

Standard Cost and PPV

Standard costs are the planned costs to manufacture specific products or to provide a unit of service, as defined for a specific time, either at the present time or for some specific date in the future. In the case of a newly introduced product or service, they are often based on engineering estimates. Standard costs typically determine the selling price of an item or to determine operating budgets and projected cash flow. They are also used as benchmarks and to set goals for cost reduction efforts.

The *Purchase Price Variance (PPV)* is the reported difference between the actual price paid by the organization and the standard cost shown in the Bill of Materials. Despite the fact that it is widely used to measure purchasing performance, there are numerous, often indeterminate reasons for a typical PPV, many of which are the result of market conditions or engineering changes that are beyond the control of the purchasing manager.

FIGURE 1.2   Total cost of ownership build-up

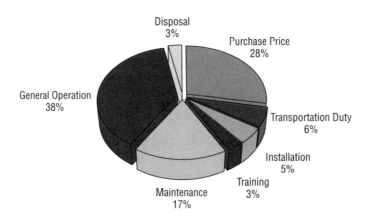

Hard and Soft Costs

Internal savings are frequently calculated on the basis of reduced labor requirements or the elimination of certain building space. Unless these savings actually result in the elimination of cost—that is, reduced head count or lower rent—they are considered *soft costs*. Soft costs may or may not result in a benefit to the organization. On the other hand, savings that are actually reflected in a lower price paid for an item or the elimination of specific head count are considered *hard costs*. In the calculation of a savings contribution to the organization, the purchasing manager must consider the relevancy of the cost.

Accounting Systems

Virtually all organizations use an accounting system to maintain its financial records. The system usually incorporates a *Chart of Accounts* to classify expenditures and determine how to allocate individual purchases. The Chart of Accounts simply lists the names and numerical designations of the various expense codes such as Office Supplies, Telephone, Travel, or Equipment. When combined with a specific *cost center* (the designation for a section or department within the organization) the expenses can be clearly categorized and allocated to a specific department or individual.

Budgets are ordinarily created along these lines and so actual expenses can be rolled up into the same categories for comparison. Individual accounts are then rolled up into the P&L statement on the same basis. This method enables organizations to control spending and to evaluate performance to original budgets.

One method for allocation in common use today is *Activity Based Costing (ABC)*. This method allocates expenses from a company-wide cost center—Utilities, for example—to the actual project or operation using it. Often these allocations are based on a business unit so that management can determine the profitability of one unit compared to another.

Utilizing Financial Tools

When we refer to financial tools, we typically mean the methods used to analyze the financial performance of the organization or a particular activity within the organization. These methods are often expressed in terms of a specific ratio. Here are some common examples you should understand:

Return on Investment (ROI)   *Return on Investment (ROI)* describes the effectiveness of a particular investment in terms of how long it takes to recover (or earn back) the initial funding. ROI can be calculated as the *Net Present Value (NPV)* of the revenue created divided by the initial investment.

ROI = (Savings × Time) − (Discount Rate × Time)

Return on Total Assets (ROTA)/Return on Net Assets (RONA)   *Return on Total Assets (ROTA)* and *Return on Net Assets (RONA)* are measures used to determine how effectively capital is deployed within the organization. Here, net income (that is, revenue less expenses) is divided by the value of assets in operation to determine effectiveness.

ROTA = Net Income / Total Assets

Net Operating Margin   *Net Operating Margin* reflects the profitability of the organization by calculating the percentage of its *total operating income* (sales less direct costs) to its overall sales.

NOM = Net Operating Income / Revenue

The purchasing manager uses these measures both internally for gauging the organization's performance and externally for assessing the performance of suppliers. Often these measures help select or qualify suppliers on the basis of their financial strength and leverage.

Keeping Supplier Information

One of the key responsibilities of the Purchasing Department is the maintenance of ethical and sound business relationships with the organization's suppliers. In this pursuit it is especially important to note the adage that "perception is everything." In ordinary dealings with suppliers, the purchasing manager must always ensure that there is not the least compromise of integrity or even the perception of impropriety. (We will cover this more in the section covering ethical principles in Chapter 3).

Confidentiality

Confidentiality is a mutual responsibility and a critical obligation, both legal and ethical, that buyer and supplier owe one another. Maintaining confidentiality becomes especially important when the information one has received or is divulging can affect the organization's competitive position and result in financial loss. Typically, organizations sign a contractual document—called a *Non-disclosure Agreement (NDA)*—legally binding them to maintaining one another's intellectual property (IP).

The purchasing manager must ensure that no one in the organization discloses information about one supplier to another, such as bids, pricing, manufacturing methods, designs, plans, formulas, nonpublic measures of performance, or any other form of intellectual property. Both Purchasing and Legal have an obligation to instruct and inform all personnel in the organization who come into contact with suppliers or the general public about these obligations and to conscientiously protect supplier information from compromise through special care and diligence.

Business Reports

The Purchasing Department maintains a variety of reports covering supplier performance, such as cost profiles, quality records, and on-time delivery performance. It is important that the department uses this information properly and confidentially. Internal users with access to this information should be similarly informed.

Samples and Returns

Samples should only be accepted from suppliers when there is a specific need for evaluation, and following evaluation, they should be returned. If there is no immediate need or internal request for the particular sample, it should not be accepted in the first place. The organization should pay for any samples that it keeps.

It is also good business practice and the Purchasing Department's responsibility to ensure that rejected or excess goods for which credits have been issued by the supplier are properly returned. Many times credits are taken by Purchasing and sent to Accounts Payable before the supplier has authorized returns. This practice simply messes up the books of the respective organizations and creates a great deal of ill will. For continued good business relations, it is important that organizations keep their financial accounts in proper order.

Summary

In purchasing, best practices generally cover the creation of strategic and tactical plans for the acquisition of goods and services that align with the organization's mission, as well as implementing those plans in a manner that provides added value. Best practices in procurement also cover the processing of user requests to purchase goods and services.

In order to meet their responsibilities effectively, the purchasing manager must be an enabler capable of matching the needs of internal customers with what is available to purchase in the marketplace. The Purchasing Department requires effective and efficient operation through its interface with suppliers, to ensure that critical requirements are conveyed properly and in a timely manner.

The purchasing manager should also demonstrate the ability to use the tools available to obtain the best value for organizations in dealings with suppliers. These tools include methods for financial analysis and determining total cost of ownership, as well as processes to develop competition that results in greater purchased value to the organization. The purchasing manager also needs to have a strong understanding of accounting methods and techniques so as to add further value to internal customers and to make sound judgments in the application of fiduciary responsibilities.

In addition, the purchasing manager must ensure that all personnel in the organization honor the dictates of good ethical practices and that information furnished by suppliers is maintained in confidence This dovetails with the regulatory requirements you will review in the next chapter.

For additional reading on topics related to this chapter, please see Appendix A.

Exam Essentials

Be able to describe the mission of the Purchasing Department.   It is important to understand the nature of effective procurement and how to employ best business practices.

Understand and convey user requirements to suppliers.   This requires an understanding of the various classes of purchases and methods available to convey a clear set of requirements. It is the Purchasing Department's responsibility to correctly format POs so that they can be properly understood by suppliers.

Be able to formulate a specification or statement of work. Knowing when to use either of these methods is critical. They convey the work needed in clear and precise terms. You also must know what other elements, such as price, shipping destination, and payments terms, must be included with the PO.

Be able to create strategic plans and tactics. Various strategies are used within the organization to align with the organization's mission. Purchasing not only has its own strategic plan but must also support the strategic plans of its internal customers through effective procurement.

Be able to develop and implement new processes. The purchasing manager must know how to add value to the organization through innovative methods and the creative use of new technology applications in supply management.

Know the requirements of a properly prepared request for purchase. Requisitions must be properly authorized and contain specific information needed to properly fulfill the actual order. Auditing processes require adherence to specific policies and procedures, and it is your responsibility to understand and implement them.

Understand the various types of purchase requests. Know when each of the various kinds of requests are used, such as requisitions, catalog orders, and demand-driven automated MRP, what they should contain, and the systems used to convey them.

Be able to select the proper order format. You must be able to use the various kinds of order processes established by the organization and understand when to use them. These methods include using standard POs, BPOs, electronic orders, contracts, and purchasing cards.

Be able to identify priorities for the placement of orders. There are various methods for prioritizing orders so that the critical needs of the organization can be met. You must know the different methods available and when to use them.

Understand the tactical application of procurement strategies. You must be able to identify the key methods for effecting a deal with suppliers. You must be able to decide when you should negotiate terms and conditions and when you should use competitive bidding or reverse auctions.

Be able to analyze costs. Costs are broken into multiple categories for accounting purposes, and each has its own nature. You must understand how these systems work so you can properly categorize purchases and know the implications of maintaining budgetary requirements.

Understand the requirements for confidentiality. It is not acceptable, and sometimes even illegal, to compromise trade secrets or intellectual property held on behalf of your suppliers. You should be able to understand what is confidential and how to protect it.

Be able to manage supplier sampling practices with integrity. You must understand when it is appropriate to accept supplier samples and how to deal with them with uncompromised integrity. This also applies to handling other supplier-owned material, including products being returned for credit.

Review Questions

1. Day to day tactical purchasing procedures support supplier sourcing strategies. These procedures are sometimes called:

    A. Standard operating procedures

    B. Supplier sourcing procedures

    C. Strategic buying procedures

    D. Tactical supplier support procedures

    E. Procedural issues

2. A statement of work is always related to a:

    A. Specification

    B. Service

    C. Requirement

    D. Purchase order

    E. Work order

3. Which of the following items is not always required on a purchase order?

    A. Price

    B. Quantity

    C. Description

    D. Payment terms

    E. Statement of work

4. Effective purchasing procedures and strategies create a cycle of:

    A. Just-in-time

    B. Continuous improvement

    C. Strategic planning

    D. Supply management

    E. Customer satisfaction

5. When working with internal customers, the Purchasing Department's contribution _____ includes technical expertise: (Select the word that best fits.)

    A. Rarely

    B. Always

    C. Sometimes

    D. Never

    E. Often

6. The term "maverick purchase" means:

 A. A requisition from a disgruntled internal customer

 B. Negotiating with a very upset supplier

 C. A lack of Purchasing Department involvement

 D. A purchase requirement without a cost

 E. A California real estate deal

7. A purchase requisition *must* include all of the following items *except*:

 A. Internal customer's name

 B. Charge to cost center code or budget center

 C. Description of the material or service

 D. Date required

 E. Name of a specific supplier

8. Competitive bidding can be used as a procurement method when all of the following exist *except*:

 A. Sufficient time

 B. Many suppliers

 C. A complete specification or scope of work

 D. Nominal purchase value

 E. A supplier question and answer process

9. Which type of cost is associated with finished goods inventory?

 A. Indirect costs

 B. Fixed costs

 C. Variable costs

 D. Direct costs

 E. Overhead costs

10. The financial ratios of Return on Investment (ROI), Return on Total Assets (ROTA), Return on Net Assets (RONA), and Net Operating Margin measure an organization's:

 A. Liquidity

 B. Profitability

 C. Financial activity

 D. Capital structure

 E. Market valuation

Answers to Review Questions

1. A. Tactical activities are covered in standard operating procedures, which outline the specific steps taken to accomplish a process or task.

2. B. A statement of work describes a service, whereas a specification describes the properties of a product or material.

3. E. A statement of work is generally too complex to be included in a PO.

4. B. Continuous improvement processes built-in to sound purchasing procedures and strategies ensure an ongoing cycle of increasingly effective performance and greater value to the organization.

5. A. The Purchasing Department's role covers business operations and processes, not the technical aspects of the product or service being purchased. That is best left to experts in other departments.

6. C. Without Purchasing involvement, there is no assurance that the procurement will fall within the scope of an existing contract. Thus, "maverick" refers to a purchase outside the typical confines of good business practice.

7. E. The Purchasing Department, while capable of determining the preferred source for any particular purchase based on historical activity or good sourcing practices, has no way of obtaining the other data unless it is included in the requisition.

8. D. Since the competitive bidding process requires a great deal of effort, it is not often a good use of the buyer's time when the purchase is of low value.

9. D. Direct costs are directly related to finished goods. All other costs listed related to work in process or overhead costs.

10. B. The ratios (ROI, ROTA, RONA, and Net Operating Margin) reflect various aspects of an organization's profitability and effectiveness.

Chapter

2

Sourcing

THE C.P.M. EXAM SPECIFICATIONS COVERED IN THIS CHAPTER INCLUDE THE FOLLOWING:

- ✓ Developing specifications, statements of work, and acceptance and performance criteria
- ✓ Identifying and selecting suppliers
- ✓ Developing and soliciting quotations, proposals, and competitive bids
- ✓ Complying with applicable laws and regulatory elements
- ✓ Developing and managing internal classification of qualified suppliers.

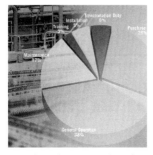

In this chapter, we'll introduce you to some of the most valuable tasks performed by the Purchasing Department: developing bids and proposals, evaluating suppliers' responses, and selecting the supplier that provides the greatest value to your organization. The purchasing manager is expected to ensure that this process results in fair and consistent supplier selection that is fully aligned with organizational objectives.

To manage this effectively, you will also need to know how specifications, statements of work, and performance criteria are commonly developed, along with your role in properly conveying them to the supplier. Since you will also have responsibility for ensuring compliance to laws and regulations throughout this process, you will be required to have a working knowledge of how they affect the selection and contracting process. Additionally, we will review the various supplier classifications and their general requirements and how this information is maintained for internal use.

Establishing Requirements

As noted in Chapter 1, a description of the organization's detailed needs for any purchase consists of a number of elements, including terms and conditions, lead time, and technical requirements. In order for the organization's procurement team to select the most appropriate source for any specific purchase or for any potential supplier to submit an accurate bid or proposal, these elements must be available for documentation. In this section, we explore how to generate and document requirements, convey them to suppliers, and use them in your supplier selection process.

Creating and Organizing Requirements

In most organizations, new requirements are developed by the *using department* (the department that will actually receive the goods or services) in conjunction with other interested parties. Similarly, existing specifications are periodically reviewed by the using group, and any changes generated are conveyed to the Purchasing Department prior to any subsequent purchases. Specifications and subsequent changes for standard products and services are usually documented and filed by the *Document Control* section responsible for physically maintaining the organization's specifications. However, when there are no formal processes within the organization for developing specifications, it is the responsibility of the *requisitioner*, the individual initiating the request, to supply sufficient information to the Purchasing Department so that the correct product or service gets procured.

Roles and Responsibilities

The responsibility for creating and maintaining specifications generally resides with the user or the using department. For direct materials used in a manufacturing organization, that usually means an engineering group or research and development group closely associated with making the product being shipped to the organization's final customer. In other cases, the department responsible for the budget is also responsible for the specifications. When a statement of work (SOW) for a service used by the entire organization is being purchased, for example, travel, consulting services, or telecommunications, most commonly an administrative department, such as Finance, Human Resources, or Information Technology will take responsibility.

Project Team

The development of complex requirements often takes on a project–oriented nature and a cross-functional team is chartered with the responsibility to define and document the organization's specific need in that particular situation. This team is composed of technical experts, users, and of course, the Purchasing Department. On occasion, outside information sources may be required, and consultants may be engaged to assist the project team. Frequently, it is this team that actually makes the final supplier selection.

Customer Inputs

In situations where the components or service being performed are critical to the operations of the organization, customers may play an important role in the development of specifications. It is not uncommon in high tech industries, for example, where speed of product development and time to market introduction can be critical for success, to have representatives of the organization's final customer participating in the development of specifications. Occasionally, customers will actually determine the specifications themselves if they are felt to be critical to their product's success.

Other Inputs

Besides the internal user or engineer, the most common sources of additional information detailing the specification or SOW come from existing or potential supplier(s) of the item to be purchased. Based on the degree of collaboration, it is common to find suppliers participating actively in the development of specifications. While this may sound like a conflict of interest, the supplier is usually in the best position to help formulate requirements, especially where there is no internal core competency in a particular commodity area. This collaboration often leads to a more complete understanding of the user's requirement on the part of the supplier and substantially lowers the risk of receiving inadequate product or service quality.

It is also not uncommon, as noted previously, for organizations to engage third party consultants who are experts in a particular industry or commodity to assist with the development of requirements and the writing of the specification due to their unique domain knowledge, especially when there is insufficient expertise within the organization, and where cost or overall risk is substantially high.

In addition, there are many third party organizations that provide industry standards for products or services in common use. Such standards exist for a large number of commodities—fasteners, lubricants, and grades of ore, to name a few—and can be used to speed the development process or align specifications with commonly employed definitions. Standards are often in place for an entire industry, making the specification process fairly straightforward.

Developing Specifications and Formats

Detailed requirements are typically described by a written specification (in the case of materials) or a statement of work (for services). These describe the precise parameters or standards that a supplier must meet in order for the purchase to be accepted by the buyer. Having a "tight" specification, that is, one that clearly and completely defines the organization's intended purchase, helps prevent problems later on. First of all, it creates the need to fully develop and define the purchase requirements internally so that they can be clearly documented by the Purchasing Department on orders or contracts. Secondly, it enables the supplier to have a full understanding of what your organization expects to receive so that the supplier can properly meet your requirements. In both cases, documentation is important in avoiding future conflict because a clear, unambiguous description is difficult to dispute after the receipt of the goods or services.

Specific formats vary from organization to organization and can range from a variety of written descriptions to detailed drawings or even actual samples. The key is to convey your requirements so that they cannot be misunderstood by the supplier. The old carpenter's adage, "Measure twice, cut once," also applies to the value of well-developed specifications. It is far less costly to develop a clear description of your requirements in the first place than to have to go through the return and repair process because the specifications were not specific enough or presented clearly.

Specifications

There are two elements to consider when developing a specification. First, there is the actual description of the product or material in terms of its physical characteristics, what it looks like, or how it functions. Second, there is an element of quantification that evaluates the level of performance. Certain measures of quality, such as the frequency or *mean time between failures (MTBF)* for equipment and the allowable number of rejected *parts per million (PPM)* for purchased parts, are typically systematized into an inspection process for determining acceptance at delivery and subsequent payment.

Specifications are typically created using one of three approaches, depending upon the organization's objectives:

Technical Specifications   *Technical specifications* describe the physical characteristics of the material or product being purchased, such as dimensions, grade of materials, physical properties, color, finish, and any other data that defines an acceptable product. Written technical specifications may be supplemented by drawings or samples. Table 2.1 demonstrates an example of a technical specification.

TABLE 2.1   Sample Technical Specifications

ITEM	SPECIFICATION
Display area (mm)	170.9(H) x 128.2 (V) (4.5-inch diagonal)
Number of dots	640 x 3 (H) x 480 (V)
Pixel pitch (mm)	0.267 (H) x 0.267 (V)
Color pixel arrangement	RGB vertical stripe
Display mode	Normally white
Number of colors	262,144
Contrast ratio	450
Optimum viewing angle (contrast ratio)	6 o'clock
Brightness (cd/m^2)	450
Module size (mm)	199.5 (W) x 149.0 (H) x 11.5 (D)
Module mass (g)	360 (Typ)
Backlight unit	CCFL, 2 tubes, edge-light, replaceable
Surface treatment	Antiglare and hard-coating 3H

Functional Specifications   The function of a product can be defined in terms of its actual role and what it is intended to do. *Functional specifications* define the job to be done rather than the method by which it is to be accomplished. Typically, functional specifications do not limit the supplier to providing a specific solution, as in the case of a technical specification, thus enabling the supplier to create the best possible solution. For example, a functional specification may require "the safe and efficient movement of passengers from Zone A to Zone B" at an airport.

Functional specifications are typically used to solicit suppliers' proposals for further evaluation by the purchasing organization when a specific solution is not known. They are often combined with performance specifications, outlined next, to create a more detailed requirement.

Performance Specifications   While technical specifications define the product's physical characteristics, and functional specifications describe what role the product plays, neither describes just how well the product must perform. This is the purpose of a performance specification, which describes the parameters of actual performance the item or service must meet. With a performance specification you are primarily interested in results rather than in method.

In the example just given of passenger movement at an airport, a performance specification might call out just how many passengers must be moved in any particular time period, or it may state the number of hours the device must be operational in any specific period.

Performance specifications can be described by a virtually unlimited choice of criteria. However, they must be capable of being expressed by some clearly stated metric. Some of the more common parameters include:

Speed   Product must travel at 20 miles per hour.

Output   Product must produce 400 acceptable parts per hour.

Quality   Product must be capable of 2000 operational hours before failure.

Efficacy   Product must reduce rejected parts by 20 percent.

 Be sure to keep the specification types clear in your mind. There are subtle differences that may be confusing. For example, performance characteristics *can* be included in a technical specification and technical data *can* be included in a performance spec. The purpose of the specification must be made clear.

Standards

Using pre-established standards is another way of describing specifications or supplementing the description when that is appropriate. Literally dozens of organizations provide published standards available for general use, including The American National Standards Institute (ANSI), the National Institute of Standards and Technology, and the Society of Automotive Engineers (SAE), to name just a few. A detailed listing of Military and Industry Standards and Specifications has been assembled by the Los Angeles Public Library and can be found on the Internet at `http://www.lapl.org/guides/standards.html`.

Benchmarking

In its simplest form, a *benchmark* provides a measurement as a guide for establishing a specific requirement. However, benchmarking can also be a detailed process for determining how one organization is performing in relation to other organizations. For example, your organization's cost for packaging a particular product is 12 percent of its total cost, which seems to be somewhat high. Are you over-specifying your packaging requirements? Obtaining data or finding a benchmark from others in your business sector might validate your spending or indicate an opportunity to save cost by reducing specifications to less expensive alternatives. The organized use of methodologies that focus on the function of a material, process, or service in providing value to the customer is also called *value analysis*.

Quality Control

Most people readily agree that quality is less costly when controlled within the initial process itself rather than through some form of inspection at a stage following manufacture or shipping. Prevention is less expensive than finding a full-blown cure.

Methods of *quality control* typically include automated controls to measure compliance to specification and site inspection at the point of manufacture where corrections can be made. It also includes control of the process through a continual sampling and measurement discipline known as *Statistical Process Control (SPC)*. This process relies on a variety of data collection and measurement systems, reports using run data and flow charts, and diagrams showing the actual distribution of measures in relation to process control limits. Figure 2.1 shows the actual time taken to process a work package in relation to the *Upper Control Limit (UCL)* (the highest point of measurement at which performance is acceptable) of 17.5 days and the *Lower Control Limit (LCL)* (the lowest point of measurement at which performance is acceptable) of 1.5 days. The average for the period shown is described by a line at 9.4 days. Whenever a statistically significant number of occurrences fall outside this range—1.5 to 17.5 days—the process being used is out of control and will need to be reengineered.

One of the more commonly used tools in SPC is the measurement of *process capability* (C_{pK}). This compares the actual process range of the supplier's manufacturing capability with the buyer's acceptable range of variation. A C_{pK} of 1.00 means that the supplier's actual variation range and the buyer's allowable variation range are the same. A C_{pK} of more than 1.00 indicates that the supplier's process is in better control than the buyer requires, while a C_{pK} of less than 1.00 indicates that the supplier will produce greater variation than the buyer will allow. Ideally, the process yields a C_{pK} of 1.33.

FIGURE 2.1   Statistical Process Control chart

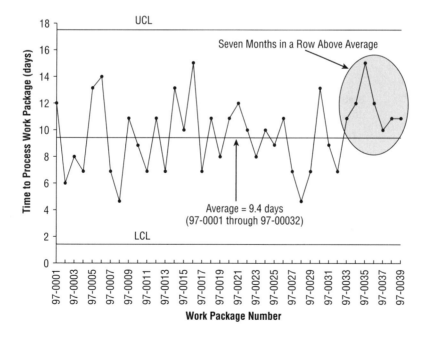

Statement of Work

A *statement of work (SOW)* outlines the requirements for a purchase of services rather than a product. Nevertheless, like a specification, it defines exactly what is needed in enough detail so that disputes will be avoided when it comes time for payment for the services performed.

All SOWs, whether simple or highly complex, usually contain a number of common elements. They often include:

Description of the Work to Be Performed   This is often task oriented and provided in sequential terms following some logical, defined process of workflow. For example:

1. Generate a detailed design for the lab work area.

2. List all work to be performed by the nature of the subcontract required.

3. Submit work specification to at least three applicable subcontractors for each major trade.

Timeline   Each section of the work must be completed within a specific time. The timeline details the expected completion times of each element in the workflow and ensures that the project finishes on time. Often the timeline specifies the points at which approval is required before proceeding further to ensure that requirements for one section are met before proceeding on to another. Timeline approval points may also trigger payment to the suppler for acceptable work performed.

Performance   The SOW must clearly define the parameters for acceptable quality and performance and the metrics by which they will be determined. Subjective terms such as "good" or "best" should be avoided whenever possible and replaced with more objective measurements such as "100 percent" or "within two hours of notification" so that it is clear to both parties if (or when) the requirements have been met.

Statement of work and *scope of work* are interchangeable terms. You might notice the use of both in other books and materials about purchasing.

Terms and Conditions

As an adjunct to both specifications and statements of work, terms and conditions, which we discussed at length in Chapter 1, define the contractual obligations of the supplier and the purchasing organization. To the extent that your organization's standard terms and conditions will be included in all solicitations for quotations, they should be considered an integral part of the specifications.

While terms and conditions naturally vary from organization to organization, each generally uses a set of standard terms and conditions for purchase requirements, modified from time to time by terms and conditions tailored specifically for a given purchase. Typically, these are included in the boilerplate on the reverse side of a purchase order or in the standard library of contracts prepared by the Legal Department.

Standard terms and conditions usually include sections covering warranties, liability, indemnity, payment terms, legal jurisdiction, intellectual property ownership, contingencies, cancellation, shipping requirements, and inspection. For a more complete picture, you may want to look at the back of one of your organization's purchase orders or one sent in by a customer. Terms that are customized for a particular purchase and tend to apply uniquely to that specific purpose may include such provisions as installation, acceptance criteria, training, and timelines. These are typically added as amendments to the standard contract or in the wording on the face of the PO.

On the face of a PO, special terms and conditions are usually included as a subset of the item's description. For example, you might have a description in the PO such as "Valve, pneumatic as described in the attached specification." And then following that description, you might see a list like this in the PO:

The following additional terms and conditions apply:

1. Approval by Robert Johnson required prior to payment.

2. Delivery no later than July 23.

3. Call 24 hours before delivery: (234) 555-1212

Specification Traps

There are a number of traps that purchasers unknowingly build into their specifications. Some increase cost unnecessarily while others unwittingly ensure that the best solutions are not accepted. We'll discuss these traps in this section.

Customization Assumptions   This trap arises from the mistaken assumption that the product being purchased must be customized to conform to user requirements. *Customization* typically adds cost so the purchaser is well-advised to investigate if this is truly required. An internal change in process with little or no resulting cost can often eliminate the need for customization. The term *standardization* also refers to the methods used to reduce or eliminate custom, one-time, and seldom-used components and processes that introduce variability and can potentially create added cost and quality problems.

Disregarding Performance Requirements   Specifications unnecessarily stricter than actual performance would simply add cost without adding benefits. They may also eliminate potential suppliers who are unable to perform to the higher requirements and thus eliminate price-reducing competition.

Conversely, specifications that are too open or loose, or with important details missing, tend to invite unacceptable quality and can create costly mistakes. The supplier can provide a product or material that meets specification precisely but will not perform in its intended function. Often, a supplier will "low-ball" an initial bid, purposely bidding well below market price to buy the business, knowing that a *change order* request will follow. Having already received the contract, the supplier is then relatively free to charge any amount it wishes and thus recover its loss on the initial bid.

Brand Name   Specifying a brand name limits competition and thus increases the likelihood of higher prices. Brand names may or may not improve the chances of receiving better quality; nevertheless, they typically cost more as a result of higher advertising costs to create the brand name in the first place and because of the perception that users have that substitutes will not perform as well. One way to avoid this trap is to specify the brand name and include the verbiage "or equivalent" to allow for greater competition. This means that any product meeting the same specifications as the brand name will be acceptable to the purchaser.

Locating and Developing Sources of Supply

In its traditional sense, *sourcing*, the identification, evaluation, and development of potential suppliers, has been the fundamental strategic role of the procurement activity. Today, this role has expanded to a broader level and includes the understanding and analysis of the specific marketplace from which the purchase is being made, as well as developing and employing various processes to enhance competition. In this section we will examine the basic elements of finding potential sources.

Source Types

The nature of the source from which the purchase is made can vary widely and be dependent upon the nature of the purchase, the nature of the industry in which the purchase is being made, and the size of the purchase. The purchasing manager must develop an understanding of how various supplier types can affect sourcing decisions.

For instance, a buyer needs to know whether to use a local source as supplier or whether location is irrelevant. The buyer should also be concerned with the size of the supplier; perhaps the organization would receive better service from a smaller supplier, where the volume of business might be more significant for the supplier and the buying organization would have more leverage. The buyer should also determine whether the organization should use a distributor or a manufacturer.

The Hidden Cost of Using Brand Name Products

Companies spend a great deal of effort and money creating a brand name that is indistinguishable from the actual process being performed. A case in point is Xerox. So common has this name become, that we use it as though it were a verb: "Please xerox five copies for me."

We once received an order for several testers that were called out by brand name. Checking with the user, we discovered that he was simply using a shorthand for the function and that there were many brands that would perform as well and be equally acceptable. Subsequent bids from competitors produced a savings of $70,000 on an original request for $300,000.

Local, Domestic, or International

Sourcing decisions based on the suppliers' location can often provide distinct advantages in specific situations. A local supplier, for example, may feel a greater obligation to maintain higher levels of service because it shares the same community as the buyer. And buying organizations may have the same preference for supporting other members of the immediate community. Local suppliers, too, can frequently provide faster response time as well as lower freight costs.

On the other hand, the buying organization can develop greater competition simply by expanding the geographical range of its sourcing to national sources that may provide better pricing and wider choices.

Similarly, there are numerous trade-offs to consider when making a decision to source domestically or internationally. Typically, communications and delivery are more reliable with domestic sources, whereas international sources can usually provide lower prices due to reduced labor costs.

There are also payment methods to consider when evaluating offshore or domestic sources. Commonly, sellers will want overseas buyers to guarantee payment through some form of bank document, such as a *Letter of Credit (LC)*. An LC usually contains provisions triggering an automatic payment from the buyer's bank upon documented proof of shipment or at some specific predetermined time intervals. This can be a relatively costly process and can tie up cash or credit lines for an inordinate period of time.

In addition, considerations regarding additional risks due to fluctuations in currency exchange rates must also be taken into account when purchasing internationally, and long term contracts often contain a clause that adjusts the selling price based on any significant change in the exchange rate at the time of delivery.

Finally, you should also take into account logistical issues such as customs duties, taxes, *tariffs*, and added shipping costs.

Duties   Most governments, including the United States, charge taxes for the import and export of certain types of goods. The C.P.M. exam requires you to distinguish between three major types of duties:

Ad Valorem   *Ad valorem* duties are duties charged as a percentage of the shipment's value (e.g., 10 percent). Ad valorem is the most commonly assessed form of tariff.

Specific Duties   *Specific duties* are duties imposed as a flat rate for some specified measure of goods, for example $6.00 per ton.

Compound Duties   *Compound duties* combine both ad valorem and specific duties, such as $6.00 per ton *and* 10 percent of the total value of the shipment.

Shipping   The purchasing manager has to consider the additional costs of shipping as well as the potential delays and risks of conducting business along an extended supply chain when making a decision to source overseas. Goods that are sensitive to environmental conditions or are needed in a reliable and timely manner are often shipped by air since the alternative, ocean freight, can be very slow. This can add significantly to shipping costs.

Inventory   Longer supply chains typically require higher levels of inventory to buffer the long lead times and potential fluctuations in demand. The longer pipeline may also contain several weeks of inventory in various stages of manufacture or shipment if it is a regularly used product. Because most products are paid for at the time of shipment, this can tie up significant amounts of the organization's cash and can result in increased costs for carrying the inventory.

Documentation   Goods traveling across international borders often require special documentation and licenses or must comply with certain restrictions. The most common of these include export and import licenses, commercial invoices, certificates of origin, insurance certificates, and international bills of lading. The *Convention on Contracts for the International Sale of Goods (CISG)* establishes uniform regulations in an attempt to standardize the rules governing international commerce but has not yet found universal acceptance. The *United Nations Commission on International Trade Law (UNCITRAL)* publishes an updated list of countries that have adopted the CISG at `http://www.uncitral.org/en-index.htm`.

Size

As a purchasing manager, you should consider the size of the organizations you are sourcing from before making a final decision to choose a specific source. Smaller–sized organizations often have a greater incentive to provide more customized and personalized service than larger ones since they rely more heavily on individual accounts. Larger organizations, however, may have greater technical resources and may be better able to respond to wide swings in demand.

Original Manufacturer or Distributor

Distributors frequently service the spot buying market and typically maintain substantial inventories in order to better service their clientele. As a result, they must often charge somewhat higher prices than the original manufacturing sources. Consequently, the purchasing manager's decision should take into consideration the volume of the purchase. The greater the volume, the more likely you are to obtain lower prices directly from the manufacturer. However, if you need small quantities of many different products (such as hardware), your advantage may lie with a local stocking distributor.

Types of Competition

Supplier selection is also determined to a large extent by the nature of competition, whether that competition is established directly by the buyer as an offshoot of an organizational policy or as a result of conditions prevailing in the industry. In the following section, we will define the various competitive conditions that you may encounter.

Open Competition

Open competition is said to exist when there are multiple suppliers available to fill your specific requirements and they are willing to vie for your business. When strong competitive factors exist in the marketplace, the buyer's negotiating position is stronger, and there are greater opportunities for gaining concessions in price as well as in payment terms, service, and support. To continue to foster robust competition, the buyer will want to avoid customization so that as many companies as possible can easily supply the product or service and maintain the widest possible area of source selection to keep the number of competitors high.

Sole Source

What if only one source is capable of meeting the buyer's needs? Then, you have a *sole source* situation—the exact opposite of open competition. Sole source situations are often the result of a government-created monopoly, such as a local utility, and there is little the buyer can do to gain concessions. Typically in this kind of situation there is formal oversight by some governing body to ensure customers get fair treatment, but beyond such public regulation, there is sometimes little incentive on the part of the sole source to negotiate.

Single Source

A *single source* situation is similar to the sole source but is a condition created by the buying organization, either through product customization where only one supplier is capable of producing the product, or through some predefined collaborative relationship that by its nature excludes competition. In this case, the benefits of the relationship itself provide a competitive advantage—such as a supplier managed inventory program or joint development of new technology—that outweighs the benefits of open competition.

Technical or Limited Competition

Technical competition (also known as *limited competition*) is created when only a limited number of suppliers are available for a particular product due to patents or limited production capability. Competition in a particular industry can also be limited to only a few suppliers within a geographical area, commonly due to the existence of franchises or large initial investments required to enter the business, and the buyer can find it financially impractical to extend procurement beyond the limited area.

Partnership/Joint Venture

On occasion, organizations will form a joint venture to create a source of supply when none exists or to jointly share the expenses of developing new technology. While not specifically limiting competition, the investing organizations have little or no incentive to purchase outside the bounds of this partnership because the costs of development have already been invested and there are no other ways to recover the investment.

Multiple Sources

Multiple sources are sometimes used by the same organization, either to foster competition or because no single supplier is capable of fulfilling 100 percent of the requirements. Frequently, multiple sources will be maintained to reduce the risk of interrupted supply, and there are also situations where some percentage of the business may be set aside for small or minority enterprise.

Requirements Integration

Sometimes organizations will choose to combine the requirements of a class of products or services—MRO, for example—and source them through one supplier. Doing so can consolidate and leverage spending in many commodity areas that would ordinarily produce little discount and marginal service. By integrating supply, buyers can often provide service benefits, such as desktop delivery for office supplies or online purchasing.

Locating Suitable Suppliers

There are so many ways to locate potential suppliers, it is hardly possible to list them all. Our methods have ranged from using online search engines and business directories to calling colleagues and attending networking activities at our local ISM affiliate. There may also be sources of information available to you through the technical staff within your own organization, and that is often the best place to begin your supplier sourcing activity.

In this section, we'll discuss some of the more common methods of locating sources.

Directories and Industrial Guides

The most traditional means of locating potential suppliers is through industry-focused directories and buyers' guides. These are typically published in conjunction with a trade magazine or an industry association and contain listings of suppliers grouped by specialty or geographical location. These directories also often contain information about the supplier's products or services, capabilities, and size and market segment, along with contact names and telephone numbers.

One of the most commonly used directories is the *Thomas Register*, a general directory covering several hundred industries and hundreds of thousands of suppliers. Other directories are focused more specifically on one particular industry, such as those published by *Ceramic Industry* magazine directed at the ceramic manufacturing industry and the Buyers' Guide published by *Electronics Weekly* magazine.

There are also the ever-popular telephone directories such as the local yellow pages. These provide listings of businesses for a local calling area by category but typically provide no specific information beyond the advertising paid for by the organization. Regional business directories published by local newspapers to promote business in the readership area are also popular, as well as membership directories published by the local chamber of commerce.

Internet Search Tools

Today, it is common to use the Internet to search for suppliers. Using easily accessed search engines such as Google or MSN Search, you can locate multiple suppliers for any product or service simply by entering product key words in the search. The problem, as you may have already experienced, is that there is so much information available on the Internet that it can be impractical to search through it all. For example, a Google search for the term "paper cup manufacturer" returned 120,000 entries in less than one second.

Trade Associations/Trade Shows

Trade organizations typically sponsor magazines and online directories that help the buyer find sources. More importantly perhaps, these organizations sponsor local or national trade shows that bring together all of the significant suppliers within a specific industry for several days of workshops and exhibits where buyers can effortlessly contact a significant number of suppliers in one location. An example is WESCON, an annual exhibit held on the west coast for electronic component suppliers. This is a trade show that brings together hundreds of established and newly organized companies that supply the electronics OEM marketplace and is cosponsored by several professional organizations, including the *Institute of Electrical and Electronic Engineers (IEEE)*.

Governmental Agencies

Many governmental agencies provide information and directories that can be used for sourcing. The most commonly available are those published by the U.S. Department of Commerce and the U.S. General Services Administration's Federal Supply Service.

Minority Supplier Directories

For those seeking minority suppliers, there are literally dozens of minority business directories available, many through local minority business councils. One of the most useful directories is released by the U.S. *Small Business Administration (SBA)* online at `http://www.sba8a.com`.

Consultants

When a significant or critical need arises and there are no internal resources to provide adequate sourcing activities, Purchasing managers often reach outside the organization for proven expertise. Engaging consultants that are industry experts can save the time it takes to find and prepare detailed studies and comparisons of sources since they already have substantial knowledge of suppliers and can leverage their expertise to shorten the time it takes to develop the best supplier fit. While this might appear to be an expensive approach, in the long run it can save valuable time and expense.

Determining Changing Marketplace Factors

One of the most significant determinants of sourcing decisions generates from the ever-changing nature of the marketplace. Supply and demand continually interact to produce varying pricing profiles. When product is in short supply or production resources come under threat (e.g., oil and the Middle East), prices can rise dramatically and capacity limits may, in addition, create supply *allocations*. Organizations wishing to continually work with the most price competitive suppliers who stay up to date on the latest technological advances and business methods must maintain an aggressive review process that periodically surveys the market as conditions change.

Economic Conditions

Supply and demand continually drive prices up and down. As economic conditions change, demand increases or declines, generating shortages or excesses in supply at any given time. As previously noted, increased supply or decreased demand (or combinations of both) generally lead to reduced prices. What drives these fluctuations can be a mystery. However, the astute purchasing manager can take advantage of these conditions by seeking increased competition during periods of abundant supply and declining prices when suppliers are more anxious to seek new business or, conversely, by locking in prices through contracts when facing periods of shortage or inflationary pricing.

Market Complexity

The extent to which an organization's economic strategy can be employed—for example, when to lock in prices through extended contracts or when to pay more for higher quality levels—depends somewhat significantly on the complexity of the market. Markets with few suppliers and little potential for product substitution tend to offer only limited opportunities for the buyer to use competition to advantage. On the other hand, markets in which widely competitive forces exist and shortages in one product can be easily offset by substituting another—that is, markets with greater complexity—provide the buyer with a great deal of leverage to gain improvements. Cost reduction efforts can produce the greatest results in industries with broadly diverse alternatives, so the buyer's sourcing effort should always begin by determining the nature of the marketplace.

Nature of Competition

The nature of competition in any particular market varies. Are there many technical solutions available or only one or two? Is the market characterized by geographical limitations with very high transportation costs? If, for example, the product being purchased is covered by a patent or controlled by patented manufacturing technology, competition will be unlikely. Similarly, when startup costs are high, such as those that occur in the development of proprietary tooling, competition tends to become constricted once the initial sourcing decision is made. It is always wise to understand the nature of competition in this regard before committing to generating short term cost reductions since the sourcing effort will likely require major engineering efforts.

When dealing with sources of critical supplies or services, the buyer needs to maintain continual vigilance for potential traps that will unknowingly limit the nature of the competition for that particular product or service. The buyer must also develop strategies for dealing with such traps in the future.

Technology

When technological change drives conditions in the marketplace, new sources of supply must always be under consideration. New technology frequently generates new opportunities for capital investment, and emerging businesses tend to spring up everywhere. The buyer should be sensitive to these opportunities but be able to balance them with the need for maintaining long-term relationships that produce value beyond price or the latest fad in technology.

With critical supplies and services, one should always monitor the supply base to ensure that existing sources are keeping abreast of technology and adding improvements as necessary. Suppliers that do not constantly upgrade their processes to take advantage of new technology could easily become obsolete. The buyer should consider ways to continually monitor existing suppliers and their technological position relative to their competitors so that ongoing changes do not adversely affect their organization's own competitive position.

Performance

As economic conditions change, so can supplier performance. Suppliers under continual pricing pressures due to emerging global markets, for example, may tend to sacrifice some of the quality that qualified them for business in the first place. Delivery delays, cuts in services, and quality failures are often the early signs of declining performance due to economic hardship. Companies providing critical supplies and services need to be continually measured against industry performance standards. Initial signs of deteriorating performance should be met with clear improvement projects and, depending upon the rapidity of decline, additional sourcing activities.

Obtaining Bids and Proposals

Bids and proposals are integral elements in the procurement process. When a clear specification or SOW exists, the buyer will typically solicit a competitive bid or a *Request for Quotation (RFQ)*. When specific information does not exist or when there are a number of potential ways to meet the user's requirements, proposals are often requested, often through a formal *Request for Proposal (RFP)* process. How the buyer structures the bidding or proposal strategy depends on a number of factors outlined in the next section.

NOTE   The collective process of RFP, RFQ and RFI is often referred to as an "RFx" where the small "x" is used to indicate any one of the formats.

Bidding Guidelines

Bidding is a competitive process that enables the buyer to leverage several potential sources of supply through a single activity to obtain the most favorable business terms. In order for this process to be successful, a number of conditions, such as those outlined here, must be met.

Provide Clear Content   A solicitation for bid should provide sufficient information about the requirement so that a supplier will be able to offer exact pricing and provide whatever other detailed information is required to successfully obtain the purchase order. Typically, this will include facts such as the exact specification of the required goods or a SOW for a service, the quantity required, payment terms, the expected time of performance, necessary quality levels, and shipping or performance location. The solicitation must also include the deadline for submission.

Determine Compressible Spending   Before engaging in the solicitation process, the buyer is responsible for determining if market conditions will support a reduction in price or an improvement in terms. Unless favorable market conditions are present, competitive bidding will not be worthwhile. While there is no precise way to ensure this under all conditions, benchmarking industry trends, whenever possible, might provide some guidance.

Ensure Responsive, Responsible Competition   When selecting potential suppliers or candidates to which bids will be sent, it is important that the buyer prequalify them to ensure that the bids returned will be responsive to the organization's needs. This means that the supplier has the means to fully understand the buyer's needs and can, under normal business conditions, fulfill the requirements.

The buyer should ensure that the suppliers are in a position to meet any purchasing requirements; that, for example, they have the necessary financial means to produce the product being specified or that they have the equipment needed to meet the requirement in a timely manner. If tooling is required, the buyer must be careful to ensure that the supplier is not applying the bidding trap by absorbing the cost of the tooling as a way of buying the business.

Enable Fair and Ethical Bidding Processes   As a buyer, your job is to properly ensure ethical conduct in the solicitation and acceptance of bids, making sure that all suppliers are provided with exactly the same information and have an equal amount of time to respond. Answers to questions submitted by one supplier need to be distributed to all suppliers bidding to further enhance the competitive process.

Suppliers should also be made aware of the process for awarding the business by the buying organization, whether it is the lowest price or some combination of terms, as well as the criteria for making the final selection. Many organizations use a weighted average scoring process developed by a cross-functional internal team to select suppliers for complex services since it can be extremely difficult to unilaterally evaluate and select the best supplier.

Hold an Open Pre-bid Conference   A pre-bid conference, where all potential suppliers have the opportunity to receive a briefing on the bid package from the organization's staff, may be used when the requirement is relatively complex. Usually, this is held for all potential suppliers at one time and provides an opportunity to review the specification, time frames, drawings or blueprints, and to meet the staff. The pre-bid conference also provides an opportunity for suppliers to become familiar with the organization's policies and procedures, payment practices, and code of conduct, as well as any special requirements that relate to the particular procurement.

Although this practice in the bidding process can enhance competition through personal contact and expedite the process through real time resolution of questions, it can also be time consuming for both parties. For this reason, it is important to schedule the conference far enough in advance so that all parties may attend and so that you can have the right personnel available to provide answers. This is especially relevant when the pre-bid conference is mandatory or when the requirements are particularly complex.

Formulating the Bid or Proposal Type

There are a number of procedures that can be used in the solicitation of bids and proposals, depending upon the nature of the requirements and the objectives of the bidding process. Some widely used solicitation types include sealed bids, offers to buy, Requests for Proposal (RFP) and Requests for Quotation (RFQ). Each of these have a variety of potential applications, so choosing the optimal method for obtaining a specific bid requires a clear understanding of its advantages and limitations. The section that follows will provide the background for making the best selections.

Sealed Bid

Typically used in government-related contracting, the *sealed bid* is an offer submitted in a sealed envelope that is opened with other bids at a previously designated time and place. This method is used when the buyer does not wish to publicly reveal any of the bids prior to a specific deadline to prevent others from leveraging it to unfair advantage. There are two types of sealed bids that are used frequently in procurement: *open bidding* and *restricted bidding*.

The bidding process may be open to any qualified supplier that wishes to enter a bid. In most cases, qualification takes place at an earlier date and the supplier must be approved by the time the bids are sent out. On the other hand, the bidding process may only be open only to a specific group of suppliers due to the requirements of a regulatory process (e.g., minority or small business set asides) or to ensure that sensitive information does not get into the wrong hands. The former process is referred to as "open" bidding, while the latter is called "restricted" bidding.

Posted Offer to Buy

Government contracting requirements are often posted in a public bidding document or online. This ensures that the general public has open access to the process. In common usage, this notice is referred to as a *posted offer to buy*. This process is not used by commercial organizations much, although notices on Purchasing Department websites open to the supplier community are now becoming more common. Figure 2.2 illustrates a typical online posting as an invitation-to-bid from the Bureau of Financial Management at the City of Harrisburg, Pennsylvania. Notice that some of the business requirements, such as the due date and required format, are posted outside of the actual specifications as a way of calling particular attention to them.

Automated Bidding

It is common today to generate automated bids using a number of computer-based processes. In addition to submitting and receiving bids and proposals directly through the Internet, many organizations are turning to the *reverse auction* process to enhance competition.

A reverse auction is typically an event that enables prequalified suppliers to submit many bids in sequence with the objective of outbidding their competitors and thereby winning the business. Outbidding in this case means submitting real time offers that go below the prices submitted by their competition. The bidding process ends at a specific time, and usually the lowest bidder obtains the order. On occasion, the business may be divided between several bidders on a percentage basis, with the lowest bidder receiving the largest allotment.

FIGURE 2.2   A sample invitation-to-bid

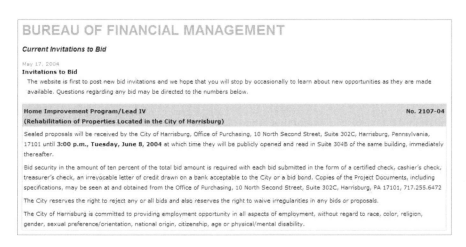

Request for Information (RFI)

The *Request for Information (RFI)* is used by organizations seeking to develop a bid list or prequalify potential suppliers. Generally, the RFI asks suppliers to submit general information about their companies, such as size, financial performance, years in business, market position, product lines, and a variety of other information that can determine the supplier's suitability for participating in some future competitive event. Of the three requests we discuss in this section, the RFI is used the least because of the advent of the Internet and how easy it is to gather information now.

Request for Proposal (RFP)

The Request for Proposal (RFP) is used when a specification or SOW has not yet been developed, or when the buyer has a general requirement and wants to solicit various ideas on how that requirement can best be met. Included in the RFP are typical objectives of the future contract and as much of the background behind the requirement as is already known. The language of the RFP usually allows the supplier some freedom in determining the most effective solution and often enables the supplier to actually establish the specifications. Sometimes prices are requested along with the proposal, and sometimes suppliers are specifically requested not to submit price quotations.

Request for Quotation

The Request for Quotations (RFQ) is virtually no different than the second part of the two-step bidding process just described. It is used when a specification or SOW has already been formulated and the buyer needs only to obtain price, delivery, and other specific terms from the suppliers in order to select the most appropriate source. The specifications are sent to prequalified suppliers soliciting price and other terms and conditions.

 Real World Scenario

Two-step Bidding

When RFPs are not used to solicit price quotations, the buyer may use a two-step process. In this procedure, the buying organization generally assembles a specification or SOW based upon the collective responses of the suppliers (or a modification of the most agreeable solution) and then submits the requirement back to the suppliers for a price quotation.

The time required to fully implement this process is often a factor limiting its use. In a complex RFP, it is not uncommon to allow suppliers three to four weeks to respond, so it is easy to see that the overall time to progress through a two-step process can take several months, considering the time it takes to formulate the initial proposal, then work it into a specification and resubmit it for quotes.

Managing Sourcing Data

Most organizations maintain listings of suppliers with whom they have established some form of business relationship. These listings provide other users with both the current status of a particular supplier and whatever historical data may be available. Referencing historical data is particularly useful as a method of avoiding duplication of effort, since the organization's prior records can tell a buyer if the supplier is qualified for a particular purpose. This prevents having to gather the usual information needed to qualify that supplier.

There are numerous ways to designate and list suppliers. Outlined next are a few of the more common ways.

Types of Sourcing

To enhance their usefulness, supplier listings are usually developed according to some form of commodity categorization—in addition to the product or service they supply—indicating their current supplier status. Some of the more common listings in use include the commonly used *approved supplier list (ASL)*, along with listings of certified, qualified, preferred, and disqualified suppliers. These lists are usually developed and maintained by the Purchasing Department but are considered an integral part of the quality control process. Let's describe these in more detail.

Approved Supplier List

One type of list the buyer keeps is an approved supplier list (ASL), which contains a listing of suppliers who have met the organization's compliance criteria and are qualified to provide specific *direct materials*, *controlled materials*, or manufacturing-related services to the organization. ASLs are usually used in manufacturing environments where technical and quality control requirements are necessary. Suppliers are often expected to pass on-site inspections and to maintain pre-established levels of quality, service, and on-time delivery. Suppliers listed on the buyer's ASL are considered first-tier suppliers.

Certified Suppliers

When the need to integrate the quality standards and systems of multiple organizations exists so that inspection and training costs can be held to a minimum, purchasing departments often establish a listing of suppliers that have met these particular requirements. *Certified suppliers* are suppliers that do not furnish direct materials and are, therefore, not appropriate for inclusion on the ASL. They might apply to suppliers removing hazardous waste or specially licensed consultants, as well as companies supplying certain types of telecommunications or network hardware.

Qualified Suppliers

Qualified suppliers are those that have successfully completed a formal screening process but may not yet have been qualified for the ASL or that may be supplying a product or service that does not require the stringent supplier site inspection criteria used to establish eligibility for the ASL. These are usually suppliers who meet all of the business requirements of the organization and are approved by the Purchasing Department for future business as it may arise.

Preferred Suppliers

A *preferred supplier* listing generally includes suppliers who have proven capabilities that make them especially valuable to the buying organization. Often they are suppliers who provide exceptional service or favorable pricing. They may be suppliers already under contract to provide particular products or services so the Purchasing Department will encourage their use.

Preferred supplier listings may also include minority- or woman-owned and disadvantaged businesses, companies that are engaged in contractual (or similarly formalized) partnerships, as well as good customers or clients of the buying organization.

 Watch out. Subtle differences in terminology usage regarding the supplier's actual status may confuse you. Remember that the approved supplier list is used in audit-controlled environments.

Disqualified Suppliers

On occasion, a supplier will be unable to meet the organization's requirements, have a contract terminated for violations, or consistently fail to maintain acceptable performance or quality levels. Under these circumstances, suppliers will often be banned from conducting further business and will be added to a listing of *disqualified suppliers*. This listing may be further reinforced by a reference stating "Do Not Use" following the supplier's name in the buying organization's computer system.

Maintaining Sourcing Lists

To take full advantage of the value inherent in maintaining sourcing lists, the buyers must take special efforts to keep them up to date. Fortunately, computerization and *Enterprise Resource Planning (ERP)* software has greatly aided this process. Keep in mind that some listings, such as the ASL, are auditable for compliance with ISO certification. Some of the other considerations you may want to keep in mind include:

Electronic Tools   Most computer-based purchasing systems in use today enable the buyer to include special status in the *Supplier Master Record*, the database that maintains information about the supplier such as their address, key contact personnel, and payment terms. Reports can then be run listing suppliers by specific sourcing list status. This can be extremely useful when sourcing requirements dictate using suppliers from one of these categories.

Contracts Database   Organizations that do a substantial portion of their business through contracts often maintain a database where they are centrally stored. This is useful not only in providing historical guidance to the buyer but in assisting with future sourcing decisions and avoiding duplication of effort.

Regulatory Factors Governing Purchasing

As you may imagine, numerous laws and governmental regulations—federal, state, and local—affect purchasing activities to one degree or another in the United States. Many of these play key roles in the way business organizations can function, while others establish the legal framework for buying and selling.

In your role as purchasing manager, you will not only need to understand how laws and regulations affect business conducted domestically, but you will also need a thorough understanding of how the laws governing businesses in other countries vary widely from those in the United States. What is taken for common business practice in one country may be unheard of in another.

In this section we've outlined the laws and regulations that you might stumble across frequently as purchasing manager.

Uniform Commercial Code

The *Uniform Commercial Code (UCC)*, especially Article 2, the section governing sales, is perhaps the regulation most commonly used by purchasing departments in conducting day-to-day business. The UCC was developed by the legal community early in the last century as trade between the states began to accelerate and the need for uniform laws became evident. It has subsequently been adopted and ratified by 49 U.S. states and Washington, D.C.

UCC applies in every state except Louisiana. Louisiana operates under a legal system more closely tied to French law than the English legal system that formed the foundation of law in the other states.

The UCC governs a variety of commercial areas, most importantly the sale and purchase of goods. It does not generally apply to services except in the case of combined purchases of goods and services: if the product represents more than 50 percent of the total transaction value, the UCC covers the purchase.

You can find out more about the UCC by visiting http://www.law.cornell.edu/ucc/ucc.table.html.

Antitrust Legislation

While the system of conducting business in the United States requires open and fair competition to ensure economic justice, many individual assaults have been made on this system in an attempt to gain personal advantage. These have typically been met with appropriate legislation by the U.S. Congress. For instance, you'll recall from U.S. History class what happened when railroad monopolies began selective pricing of freight to favor businesses in which they held an interest. They were able to effectively reduce competition by charging exorbitant freight rates to competing companies, resulting in higher prices for their products compared to those in which the railroad owners had an interest. The result of these unethical business practices is government regulation, which we'll discuss in depth in this section.

Sherman Antitrust Act (1890)

In response to increasing public concern over the formation of monopolies in the U.S. and their negative impact on commercial trade, Congress passed the Sherman Antitrust Act in 1890. The act banned business contracts made in the form of a trust, or those created under unethical circumstances such as through bribes, graft, or coercion. The act restricts "every contract and combination in the form of trust or otherwise, or conspiracy, in restraint of trade or commerce." The law was accompanied by sharp teeth in the form of criminal penalties and treble damages for violations. Included in the outlawed practices were conspiracies to fix pricing and to require reciprocal buying.

The Sherman Act has seen several amendments over the years designed to further refine its prohibitions, most significantly the Clayton Antitrust Act of 1914.

Clayton Antitrust Act (1914)

The Clayton Antitrust Act of 1914 was designed to bolster the provisions of the Sherman Act and further reduce monopolistic practices. It made certain corporate practices illegal, including price cutting to freeze out competitors, exclusive pricing arrangements, and tying contracts (where the purchase of specific goods and services by the buyer is contingent upon the purchase of other goods or services as a package). It also outlawed the holding of stock by one company so that it could gain control over another, thus reducing or eliminating competition, and the practice of interlocking directorates where a few influential individuals controlled an industry by sitting on the boards of related companies.

Robinson-Patman Act (1958)

The key element of the Robinson-Patman Act of 1958 is that it barred direct or indirect price discrimination that reduced competition. This Federal legislation prohibits suppliers from exclusively charging lower prices to certain customers simply because they purchase in larger quantities than other customers. While some specific exceptions apply, quantity discounts for exactly the same quality of like material (or services related to the purchase of the material) are basically illegal under this law unless all competing buyers are eligible for the same discount.

In addition, the provisions of Robinson-Patman prohibit the *purchaser* from knowingly receiving a discriminatory price or forcing the supplier to provide one. It also forbids the seller from providing, and the buyer from accepting, any commission related to the sale.

The law, however, does allow the seller to match the prices of its competitors and to lower prices when there is a valid justification——for example, when there are differences in distribution costs or when perishable goods have reached the end of their shelf life.

For the act to be enforced (which, by the way, it rarely is), it must be proven that the alleged price discrimination produced an adverse effect by limiting competition and at least one of the alleged discriminatory sales crossed state lines. In addition, the act applies only to goods and materials of a predominantly physical nature rather than intangibles such as services (unless related and subordinate to the goods being purchased), and the goods in question must be of "like grade and quality." Altogether, there are some ten provisions that must be violated concurrently for enforcement to take place.

Federal Trade Commission (FTC) Act (1914)

The Federal Trade Commission Act (FTC), also created in 1914 along with the Clayton Act, established the Federal Trade Commission as the watchdog agency for restraint of trade activities and to investigate any alleged improprieties between buyers and sellers. The agency is empowered to root out and prosecute instances of illegal, unfair, or deceptive business practices. However, buyers rarely have dealings with the FTC, so it's unlikely that as a purchasing manager you'll have much to worry about in this regard.

OFPP (Office of Federal Procurement Policy) Act (1974)

Though it's been through several amendments, the OFPP (Office of Federal Procurement Policy) Act of 1974 established the official *Federal Acquisitions Regulations (FAR)*, the U.S. government's procurement policies, which are overseen by the OFPP.

OFPP oversees several statutes related to acquisitions for such government organizations as the Department of Defense, the General Services Administration, and the National Aeronautics and Space Association.

For more information, including full versions of the FAR, please go to `http://www.arnet.gov/far`.

Defense Acquisition Regulations (DAR)

This set of regulations, essentially an extension of the FAR (see the previous section), is used specifically for purchases by the Department of Defense.

Other Governmental Legislation

Most governmental regulation affecting commercial business dealings is focused on eliminating collusion and conspiracy to fix pricing. However, a purchasing manager should be aware of a number of other laws enacted by Congress that impact the conduct of routine purchasing activities, such as the Small Business Act, the Davis-Bacon Act, the Walsh-Healey Public Contracts Act, the Service Contract Act, the Prompt Payment Act, the False Claims Act, and the Buy American Act.

The Small Business Act (1953)   The Small Business Act represents an effort by Congress to foster the participation of small, disadvantaged, and woman-owned businesses in federal contracting. It requires federal purchasers to assign a designated volume of purchasing to small businesses (called "set asides") and to allow some contracts to be split between large and small businesses, where the small business has the opportunity to share part of the contract, providing they can match the bid terms.

The Davis-Bacon Act (1931)   The Davis-Bacon Act and its amendments require that federal construction projects over $2,000 contain a clause establishing the minimum wages to be paid to various classes of workers employed under the contract. Under the provisions, contractors and subcontractors are required to pay workers employed under the contract wages at least equal to the locally prevailing rates and fringe benefits for similar projects.

The Walsh-Healey Public Contracts Act (1936)   Closely related to the Davis-Bacon Act, the Walsh-Healey Act applies to government purchase and contracts exceeding $10,000. Going beyond requiring minimum wage, the act limits the work week to 40 hours and attempts to ensure safe and sanitary working conditions. There is also a provision that, in effect, blackballs violators by making them ineligible for further government contracts for three years and distributing a list of their names to federal contracting agencies.

The Service Contract Act (1965)   This act empowers the Employment Standards Administration to predetermine the prevailing wage and benefit rates to be paid for federal service contracts that are over $2,500. It also provides the enforcement mechanisms for the Davis-Bacon and Walsh-Healey acts that include safety standards and record-keeping requirements.

The Prompt Payment Act (1982)   This act ensures that federal agencies pay suppliers and contractors in a timely manner and even allows for the assessment of late payment penalties and interest.

The False Claims Act (1863)   Under the False Claims Act, those who knowingly submit, or cause another person or entity to submit, false or fraudulent claims for payment of government funds can be held liable for treble damages plus civil penalties.

The Buy American Act (1933)   The Buy American Act of 1933 was passed to ensure that the federal government supports domestic companies and domestic workers by buying goods manufactured in the U.S. that are made from materials mined or produced in the U.S. The law provides exceptions for items not commercially available in the U.S. or if the price is more than 6 percent higher than comparable foreign products. It also allows exceptions for purchases under $100,000 or by department head waiver.

Foreign Trade Regulations

In addition to numerous domestic laws governing trade, Congress has enacted several key pieces of legislation affecting foreign trade, and the U.S. government has been signatory to a number of others that were negotiated internationally. Some of the more significant of those include:

General Agreement on Tariffs and Trade (GATT)   This international agreement, first signed in 1947, has now become a significant element of the World Trade Organization (WTO). Affecting trade in goods only, the agreement was designed to help reduce restrictive tariffs and encourage international trade. Approximately 110 countries now participate.

North American Free Trade Act (NAFTA)   This treaty was designed to enhance trade between the U.S., Mexico, and Canada, offering favorable tariffs and removing import and export barriers for goods that primarily originate in one of the three countries.

Real World Scenario

Should the U.S. Waive the Buy American Act?

How important is it to ensure that the U.S. government support U.S. businesses during poor economic times and in a time of military conflict? You'd assume it was very important, especially during the recent conflict in Iraq. But during the summer of the Iraq conflict, the State Department decided to waive requirements that the military purchase U.S.-made cars and trucks for the post-war effort. This led to a strong complaint to the Secretary of State from a leading minority congressman stating that if U.S.-produced cars were good enough to win the war, they should be good enough to win the peace.

Do you agree? Is a law passed in the Depression of the 1930s to protect U.S. jobs still appropriate for the U.S. to follow in 2004?

United Nations Convention on Contracts for the International Sale of Goods (CISG)   Ratified by Congress in 1986, this treaty was initiated to provide uniformity to global sales and automatically applies to commercial sales between the signatory countries. It does not apply to trade for services only. The full text of the agreement can be found on the Internet at `http://www.uncitral.org/english/texts/sales/CISG.htm`.

Trade Agreements Act of 1979   One of the stated purposes of this act is "to foster the growth and maintenance of an open world trading system." It was also enacted to expand opportunities for U.S. international commerce and to support and enforce the rules of international trade.

Foreign Corrupt Practices Act   This law is primarily know for its anti-bribery provisions that make it illegal for any U.S. citizen to bribe a foreign official in order to obtain or sustain business. It is somewhat confusing because it applies only to officials and does not include payments made to facilitate routine duties (sometimes called "grease").

Summary

Sourcing is one of the most important functions performed by the Purchasing Department. The purchasing manager with a thorough knowledge of how to effectively find, develop, and manage sources of supply will truly add value to the organization.

A key activity in sourcing is to ensure that your internal users establish and effectively communicate their requirements to the suppliers. When obtaining quotations or proposals, it will be your task to objectively analyze supplier responses so that when a decision is made to use a particular source, the organization can be assured it will obtain optimal value in the procurement. This often involves gaining a thorough understanding of the marketplace and the economic factors that prevail. It also requires that you fully understand the various methods for obtaining information and competitive bids from suppliers and when to use them.

The purchasing manager is also responsible for ensuring the development and maintenance of sourcing lists so that others within the organization will have access to up-to-date information about which suppliers are qualified for any particular purchase.

Closely related to sourcing activities are regulations and laws governing the conduct of business, such as the Uniform Commercial Code and the various antitrust acts. It is important that you understand how these laws affect the sourcing decisions you make and how they may impact ongoing relationships with suppliers so that you are able to minimize the risk of the negative impact a violation would have on your organization.

 For additional reading on topics related to this chapter, please see Appendix A.

Exam Essentials

Be able to organize and convey user requirements to suppliers.   When placing orders or obtaining quotes and proposals from suppliers, it is the Purchasing Department's responsibility to ensure that the organization's needs are clearly and concisely documented.

Be able to apply the appropriate format when specifying requirements.   There are various formats available to convey your organization's requirements to the supplier, including technical specifications (defining the parameters of individual attributes), functional specifications (defining the job to be done), and performance specifications (defining the metrics required for acceptable operation) for products and the SOW for services.

Be able to select the appropriate sourcing type for any given procurement.   You should know the available tools for locating potential suppliers, such as Internet search engines, industry directories, and historical records, along with the pros and cons associated with using each of them. You should select the method that produces the needed results in a manner aligned with the size and nature of the purchase.

Be able to identify the various types of competition.   The nature of competition in the particular marketplace—open or limited—usually determines the selection criteria for the supplier. You should know how to identify the common competitive factors governing selection criteria.

Understand how to use available tools to locate suppliers.   There are a number of listings (such as those maintained by local chambers of commerce), directories (such as the *Thomas Register*), search engines (such as Google), and trade publications that you can use to locate appropriate potential sources of supply.

Identify key factors determining marketplace conditions.   Sourcing is often a matter of timing, so the purchasing manager should understand the various economic and competitive conditions affecting the supplier's industry at any given time. Be aware of the supply and demand situation as well as the status of developing technology.

Be able to formulate and obtain bids and proposals.   You should be familiar with the various competitive bidding formats—such as sealed bids or open postings—as well as the methods for obtaining information, quotations, and proposals from potential suppliers (referred to collectively as the "RFx" process).

Understand the regulatory factors governing purchasing.   The purchasing manager should be familiar with the various laws and regulations governing business to business procurement in order to eliminate the possibility of placing the organization in conflict with them. Especially important is the Uniform Commercial Code (UCC) and the several antitrust laws.

Review Questions

1. Creating specifications may include input from which of the following parties?

    A. Using department

    B. Specification project team

    C. Organization's final customer

    D. Existing or potential supplier

    E. All of the above

2. Technical specifications include which of the following characteristics?

    A. Physical

    B. Technical

    C. Functional

    D. Performance

    E. Quality

3. Statistical Process Control measures:

    A. The acceptable quality range limits

    B. Number of rejects over a time period

    C. Quantities of acceptable units over a time period

    D. Process mapping via the Internet

    E. Statistical deviation of suppliers

4. Terms and conditions define what type of obligations?

    A. Services

    B. Financial

    C. Contractual

    D. Delivery

    E. Acceptance

5. Purchasing costs typically increase when specifications include all of the following *except* for:

    A. Customization

    B. Brand name

    C. Performance requirements

    D. Methods of standardization

    E. Firm deadlines

6. Which supplier characteristics can affect sourcing decisions?

   A. Location

   B. Domestic or international

   C. Size of company

   D. Original manufacturer or distributor

   E. All of the above

7. The type of supplier that is the only source capable of meeting the buyer's needs is called a:

   A. Single source

   B. Technical source

   C. Sole source

   D. Limited source

   E. Open source

8. The type of bidding used in government-related contracting is called:

   A. Automated bid

   B. Two-step bid

   C. Sealed bid

   D. Closed bid

   E. No bid

9. A method for an organization to develop a bid list or prequalify potential suppliers is called:

   A. Request for Quotation

   B. Request for Bid

   C. Request for Qualification

   D. Request for Information

   E. Request for Proposal

10. The legislation that prohibits the purchaser from knowingly receiving a discriminatory price from a supplier is called the:

   A. Clayton Antitrust Act

   B. Federal Trade Commission Act

   C. Davis-Bacon Act

   D. Robinson-Patman Act

   E. Sherman Antitrust Act

Answers to Review Questions

1. E. Input for specifications comes from many locations that include the department requesting the purchase (the using department), the team involved with specifications, the end customer of the product, or the supplier.

2. A. Physical characteristics are the core element of technical specifications.

3. A. The measurement of upper and lower control limits is the essential element of Statistical Process Control.

4. C. In purchasing, terms and conditions (often in boilerplate details) proscribe the legal and contractual elements of the buying transaction.

5. D. Standardization assists in *lowering* procurement costs driving larger volumes within a smaller framework of parts. All the other options typically increase cost.

6. E. All of these elements affect sourcing decisions since each of them can influence key factors in the ongoing procurement relationship.

7. C. When only one source can possibly fulfill a procurement requirement, it is considered the sole source. A single source situation occurs when the buyer chooses to use only one source.

8. C. Legislation calls for bidding in the government sector to be sealed in order to protect the integrity of the bidding process and to ensure a fair and equitable outcome by preventing one bidder from gaining access to another's bid and enabling that supplier to undercut the other.

9. D. The RFI is used to solicit and gather information about the supplier that can help eliminate supply sources that do not meet the minimum supplier standards of the organization.

10. D. Robinson-Patman is the only one of these acts specifically focused on fair pricing practices. It was enacted in part to outlaw the practice by some companies of underpricing their smaller competitors by selling at prices far below fair market value and thus eliminating them as competitors.

Chapter

3

Selecting Suppliers and Measuring Performance

THE C.P.M. EXAM SPECIFICATIONS COVERED IN THIS CHAPTER INCLUDE THE FOLLOWING:

✓ Comparing and evaluating supplier offers for products and services

✓ Qualifying and selecting appropriate suppliers

✓ Measuring and rating ongoing supplier performance

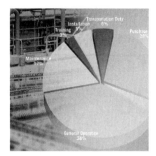

Since the Purchasing Department may be expected to lead the process of evaluating competitive offers and selecting the supplier for any particular contract, the methods used for selecting them are some of the most important elements of the purchasing manager's skill set. Indeed, effective supplier management, one of Purchasing's most vital functions, truly begins with establishing the proper initial selection criteria and ensuring that the right supplier gets chosen. However, far too often inadequate preparation and effort goes into this process with predictably disastrous results: disappointing performance. Even worse, in too many organizations a weak and poorly trained buyer has virtually no input into supplier selection and contract awards in the first place, yet is expected to manage ongoing supplier performance. That is why it is critical that you clearly understand the methods available and employ them professionally.

This chapter introduces you to evaluating and selecting suppliers for specific contracts and some of the methods available to measure and manage a supplier's ongoing performance.

Selecting the Supplier and Awarding the Contract

You cannot make a silk purse out of a sow's ear. To produce a specific result, you must choose the correct mechanism. The supplier is the fundamental resource employed by your organization to meet its requirements, and if you do not select correctly, you will never achieve satisfactory results.

Proper supplier selection, despite requiring a strong measure of distinctly human intuition, must be performed systematically and to the most objective criteria you are capable of developing. As you read the steps to selecting the right supplier outlined in this section, think about how your organization might benefit from a more rigorous approach to this discipline.

Evaluating Offers

Before selecting an offer, every buyer should employ some process of evaluation to ensure adequate consideration that all aspects of the organization's needs are being optimized. Evaluating a supplier's offer means not only evaluating its bid or proposal from a cost perspective, it also means evaluating the supplier's ability to perform to the required level of speed and quality. You need to evaluate offers in terms of potential risk as well as potential benefits. In providing incentives to obtain the contract by reducing the price, for example, will the supplier continue to maintain the level of quality the organization requires? Issues such as this will be merely one among the many you will have to consider.

In contract law, the term "offer" has a specific legal meaning. We will discuss some of the legal aspects of contracts in Chapter 4, "Forming Contracts." For our purposes here, we are using the term more loosely to mean any bid or proposal submitted by a supplier.

In performing proper *due diligence*, the buyer reviewing an offer evaluates three key criteria before reaching a decision to award the contract to a specific supplier: responsiveness, capability, and competitive value. Because of the inherent subjectivity of much of evaluating suppliers, there is strong evidence to show that a thorough review process produces the most reliable results when it involves several individuals from a cross section of functional departments. In fact, we generally find that the evaluation process can be best performed in a cross-functional team environment where individuals perform separate evaluations but come together to develop a consensus.

Here, then, are the guidelines for determining responsiveness, capability, and competitive value that you will want to consider when awarding a contract.

Responsiveness

Most obviously, the basic criteria for receiving the award will be the supplier's ability to perform to the specification or scope of work contained in your request. In high value or high profile contracts, it is wise to actually visit the supplier's facility and physically inspect the facility (we'll discuss qualifying when we discuss site visits later in this chapter) to qualify the supplier and determine its ability to meet your requirements.

In many situations, however, site visits may be physically or financially impractical, so other methods to confirm the supplier's ability to respond should be used. For instance, you might consider contacting a supplier's references to ask about similar work performed in the past. This is frequently an effective way of determining overall supplier competency. You may also want to review the response document to ensure that the supplier has answered all the questions in your bid proposal and successfully addressed any mandatory requirements you have set forth. While oversights sometimes occur, it is not a good sign to discover that some of the key elements of your requirement remain unaddressed. Offers that do not answer your specific questions should be considered *nonconforming* and rejected.

The thoroughness of the supplier's response and the level of detail the supplier provides generally signifies the supplier's level of understanding of your requirements and its expertise in providing workable solutions, services, or conforming parts.

You should also determine the extent to which the supplier's proposal conforms to your organizational business and ethical policies and procedures. Does the offer appropriately address warranty issues? Does it conform to your organization's policy regarding commercial liability and *damages*? Is it signed by the proper authority? Are the correct documents, such as insurance certificates and copies of applicable licenses, attached?

Perhaps even more significantly, how closely do the supplier's terms and conditions match those of your organization? You may want to keep in mind that reconciling conflicts in terms and conditions can require a great deal of negotiation effort and typically requires participation by the legal organization.

Capability

While many capable suppliers may respond to your proposal, your task will be to determine which supplier is the most qualified for this *particular* contract. In your evaluation, you should consider several critical factors, which we'll discuss in this section.

Operational Capacity

One of the key considerations in award determination will be the supplier's physical capacity to meet your needs as promised. You do not want to select a supplier that could have difficulty meeting the required volume due to capacity constraints or conflicts with the scheduling of other jobs. A simple ratio of current output to capacity can provide a valuable indication of this ability. Your risk of on-time delivery failure increases when a supplier's loading for your produce or service exceeds 90 percent, especially in industries where skilled labor or production capacity can be difficult to obtain.

You will also need to ensure that the supplier has the ability and systems to properly schedule orders and keep track of current operations to meet its commitments. With little or no technology to assist in the scheduling process, the supplier may have difficulty keeping track of its obligations and may prove unreliable. You should be able to benchmark this through the customer references the supplier provides.

Past performance, while not necessarily a clear predictor of future performance, can provide some further insight into the supplier's operational capability. You may be able to develop data on this from your own organization's internal records. If not, you may need to perform some benchmarking activities and, certainly, check with as many referenced accounts as possible.

Technical Capability

Another key capability to be evaluated is the supplier's technology and technical ability. Does it have the necessary equipment, tools, and talent to meet your requirements? This can be determined not only through site visits but through historical performance records and active participation in industry events. How many patents does the company hold in comparison to its competition? How often does it lead the market with the introduction of new products?

You might also consider certification as an adjunct to technical enablement. Does the supplier have the necessary licenses, insurance, and certifications required to ensure regulatory compliance? This not only reduces the supplier's liability, in many cases it may reduce the liability of your own organization too because lawsuits directed at your supplier while they are performing your contract will potentially bring your organization into the fray as well.

Financial Ability

A key indication of the supplier's ability to service your needs is its history of profitability. When a company's profit trend spirals downward at a faster rate than its competitors, it is usually an indication that it will soon begin to experience financial strain. This may also affect its ability to meet current schedules, to effectively invest in new equipment, to employ new technologies for future efficiency, or to hire the best talent.

Avoiding the Obvious

We recall a situation when our contract award team prepared a recommendation to select a particular supplier for a molded plastic part. High quality was critical since this particular part held a key function in the assembly, and its failure in the field could create enormous problems. This supplier produced far and away the best quality we could find for this particular material. Pricing was competitive, and the company agreed to all our terms and conditions.

It was just prior to issuing the PO that one of our team members discovered a startling fact. Our annual volume for this part was approximately $3 million. The company chosen had sales in the prior year of just over $7 million, putting in question the supplier's capacity to handle this award in an orderly manner. Upon further questioning, we learned that it was the supplier's intent to subcontract a good deal of the work to another shop, one we had previously declined to qualify for this particular project since it did not have the ability to meet the exceptional quality requirements needed for this part.

We decided to award the entire contract to the runner-up, although there was much discussion about using the first supplier we selected for part of the contract so that we could include them on our list of approved suppliers. However, we chose not to do so since we did not want to dilute the volume by awarding business to two suppliers and thus potentially increase the price.

From this exercise, we learned to include a clause in future RFPs indicating that subcontracting would not be allowed without our express written permission.

Competitive Value

Most of all, buyers should expect to gain the greatest value possible through the award of business. Value, as illustrated in Figure 3.1, can be considered the optimal combination of a number of factors. Most importantly, these factors include price, service, technology, and quality.

FIGURE 3.1   Elements of value

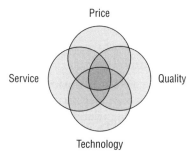

Price

Price is driven by a number of factors, not the least of which is the current supply and demand situation in the particular marketplace. While there is in general an identified tendency for supply and demand to seek equilibrium, the condition where one exactly matches the other, it is rarely the case that markets ever reach this condition for long. More often, the two factors are in continual flux.

When supply of available goods or services exceeds the demand generated by willing buyers, prices usually drop. Conversely, when demand exceeds supply, that is, when many buyers are chasing fewer available products, prices traditionally rise. However, faced with declining prices, suppliers usually move away from marketing the product or service and on to other, more profitable, offerings. Similarly, faced with rising prices, consumers tend to move to less costly alternatives. Keep in mind though, in today's economy conditions are rarely uniform from industry to industry or cycle to cycle. In addition, in the more complex industries, such as electronics, numerous factors beyond supply and demand come into play. This makes price trend predictions virtually impossible.

Price, of course, is relative to other considerations as well. As buyers analyze price, they should consider two factors: competition and Return on Investment (ROI). First, how does the price offered by the supplier compare to prices commonly found in the open market for other products or services of a similar nature? A buyer, negotiating price, wants to achieve at the very least a *fair and reasonable* price. Second, does the price paid provide a reasonable ROI? That is, does the price paid reduce costs substantially enough to justify the initial expenditure? Organizations typically look for an ROI that returns the value of the investment in less than one year or adds profit at a rate above what is traditionally earned.

When considering price, the buyer may also want to consider overall life cycle costs which include all of the costs associated with purchasing and using the product for the duration of its useful life. This consideration is also known as total cost of ownership (TCO) and includes various other costs such as maintenance or storage that might affect the comparison of suppliers' offers. At the very minimum, an analysis of the cost of materials should include the expense of transportation. The cost of goods which include transportation is known as landed price.

Service

When you evaluate service, you will look at a number of factors:

- Full support for just-in-time delivery
- The flexibility to accommodate rush orders
- Strong engineering and design support
- An accommodating return policy or a guarantee of satisfaction

Buyers also evaluate how well the supplier responds to unexpected situations, such as accepting return of slow moving or obsolete parts. From the customers' perspective, service is the element that bonds the organization to the supplier. In developing relationships with customers, the supplying sales team generally strives to develop a perception of responsiveness to problems and issues. But in your evaluation, you should evaluate the selling organization's proactive efforts in avoiding problems in the first place.

Technology

In any consideration of value, two questions regarding the use of technology are important: First, how effectively does the proposed technology meet current requirements? Second, how long into the future will the technology continue to be viable? In answering these questions, your evaluation should rely heavily on input from engineering and other user groups familiar with the technical qualities in the requirements.

Always keep in mind though, that technological innovation can provide your organization with a competitive advantage. So your evaluation will also want to take into account the reputation of the supplier as a technical leader in the market.

Quality

The evaluation of quality involves both the supplier's ability to conform to specifications and the perceived satisfaction of the user. This concept parallels the argument that a Ford or Nissan is as functional as any of the luxury automobiles, yet buyers are willing to pay substantial premiums to own the latter. Clearly, variations in such intangibles as comfort and appearance can be hard to evaluate mathematically, yet consumers continue to value and pay for them.

Key to any supplier evaluation will be an analysis of the systems the supplier has in place to control the quality of its output, such as Statistical Process Control (SPC), which we discussed in Chapter 2, "Sourcing," and the programs it utilizes to maintain continuous improvement. Effective application of process improvement programs such as *Six Sigma* or *Total Quality Management (TQM)* can have a tremendous impact on the long-term quality of a supplier's product or service and should be regarded as a form of insurance. Certifications, such as those issued in accordance with the standards of the *International Organization for Standardization (ISO)*, also provide assurances that the supplier has programs in place that will reasonably ensure continued levels of quality.

For more information on Six Sigma and Total Quality Management visit: www.asq.org and www.isixsigma.com. Finally, for more information on the International Organization for Standardization, check out: www.iso.org.

Applying Selection Criteria

Qualifying a supplier requires the disciplined application of an objective process. This typically includes a set of criteria appropriate for that particular supply segment to which some form of measurement can be added. Evaluation is most commonly performed by a cross-functional team with members chosen from the various departments or *stakeholder* groups affected by the choice of supplier. It is the team's job to develop the final supplier selection through some method of achieving consensus. Commonly, consensus is generated through the application of a scoring matrix that averages the inputs from each of the team members. We'll discuss consensus matrices and other methods for supplier selection in this section.

Site Visit

The site visit is one of the more common tools used to develop an evaluation of a supplier. While not every member of the team will attend the site visit, it is important that at the least representatives of the user group, the quality group, and supply management attend.

In addition to performing an inspection to audit the supplier's facilities (and perhaps records), the site visit provides an opportunity to establish or further develop working relationships with staff that you may not get to know under arms-length circumstances. If you use this effectively, it may save time in the future when you need a problem solved quickly.

Qualifying the Supplier

Clearly, the site visit is conducted to qualify or continue the qualification status of a particular supplier. It is a formal process and should be well prepared for in advance. And since it can be somewhat costly considering travel expenses, the team should develop a process that will enable it to come away with as much information as possible.

By way of a checklist, here are several key areas you should cover during the site visit, which we will discuss here in this section.

Order Processing and Fulfillment

Order processing and fulfillment covers the methods by which the supplier receives, processes, and schedules incoming customer orders. It includes shipping and tracking records. Some of the specifics you should cover include the efficiency and effectiveness of:

- Systems employed for entering and verifying customer orders; level of automation and reliability
- Methods used to prioritize orders
- Processes used to schedule orders and monitor delays
- Comparative length of backlog
- Cycle times
- Flexibility in meeting spikes and valleys of incoming orders
- Training and expertise of the staff

Operations

The areas of operations you should consider reviewing for a supplier audit include manufacturing, engineering, facilities management, and procurement. Specifically, you should be concerned with:

- Capacity (the current level of operation as a percentage of the maximum level of operation)
- Degree of automation and technological enablement
- Complexity of the product line
- Flexibility to fulfill additional requirements
- *Work-in-process (WIP)* tracking and lot tracking ability

- Inventory management
- Preventative maintenance
- Record keeping
- Production flexibility
- Reliability of suppliers and methods used to improve performance
- Training and expertise of the staff

Quality Systems

Quality systems generally consist of the methods used to ensure current quality and the processes employed for longer term improvement. A buyer performing a supplier audit should review the following in regard to quality systems:

- Systems used to evaluate and control quality (including testing)
- Management commitment to quality improvement
- Processes employed for continuous improvement
- Record keeping
- Compliance control
- Internal audit
- Measures and methods used to determine customer satisfaction
- Supplier quality engineering
- Communications programs
- Training and expertise of the staff
- Training programs for employees

Cost Control

The method used for controlling costs is one of the key elements that should be covered in a site visit, largely because the suppliers' ability to manage cost will indicate its future viability as a partner. To a large extent, your organization's ability to compete with others in your market depends upon the effectiveness of your suppliers and their ability to keep pace with market pricing. Some of the most important areas you should review include:

- Ability to properly account for cost by job
- Systems used to allocate costs by task
- Effectiveness of cost control initiatives
- Process documentation
- Engineering support
- Performance of value analysis
- Adherence to accepted standards of cost accounting
- Establishment of aggressive company-wide goals

Finance

How an organization manages its finances generally determines how long it will stay in business. Today, the U.S. government sets strict rules for financial accountability, and site inspections can effectively determine the efficacy of government regulations. Look for evidence of:

- Effective profitability management
- A strong balance sheet
- Excellent credit ratings
- Sarbanes-Oxley compliance (for public companies)

For publicly held companies, you can use a number of reports (some of which are available online) to determine an organization's financial condition, including:

- Annual statements and reports, some of which are available for free online at `http://www.prars.com/`.
- *10-K reports* filed with the *Securities and Exchange Commission (SEC)* are available online at `http://www.sec.gov/edgar.shtml`.
- Ratio of current liabilities to current assets (also called *current ratio*) are available online through any financial report search engine, such as `finance.yahoo.com`—just enter the ticker or company name.
- Earnings per share of stock. (Found on any financial report search engine, such as `finance.yahoo.com`—just enter the ticker or company name.)
- Return on net assets (RONA). (Found on any financial report search engine, such as `finance.yahoo.com`—just enter the ticker or company name.)
- Ratio of debt to assets. (Found on any financial report search engine, such as `finance.yahoo.com`—just enter the ticker or company name.)

Management

You should evaluate the management team and its style of management to determine an organization's compatibility with that of your organization. Some things to consider in relation to management include:

- Management policies, for instance, whether they reflect honest dealing and strong adherence to an ethical code of conduct
- Management's commitments to other customers and to suppliers
- Management's maintenance of long-term and short-term needs

Quantitative Analysis

There's an old adage: "If it's worth doing, it's worth measuring." (Or sometimes alternatively expressed: "Nothing that can't be measured is worth doing.") This measurement process is called *quantitative analysis* to indicate that the analysis is provided in mathematical terms. With quantitative analysis you will use statistics and analytical matrices to suppliers.

Well in advance of any site visit, the team should establish the criteria it will use to evaluate and select a supplier. To the extent possible, you should conduct this evaluation using objective, quantitative methods so that you can easily present data that requires minimum amount of interpretation.

Weighted Average

When evaluating a supplier, you may often use a rating matrix called a *weighted average*. A weighted average defines critical areas and attempts to develop an objective, average score based upon the opinions of the various team members. Table 3.1 shows you an example of a typical weighted average evaluation chart. Although the category titles and values will vary widely depending upon what is being evaluated, the format will likely always look similar.

TABLE 3.1   Supplier Evaluation Matrix Example

Category	% Value	A*	B*	C*	D*	E*	Average Score	Weighted average
Cost	**35%**							
Relative bid	15%	4	4	3	4	5	4.0	.60
Contain-ment tools	8%							
Tracking system	4%							
Market leadership	8%							
Quality	**30%**							
Historical defect levels	10%							
Incoming insp.	08%							
Six Sigma	06%							
SPC	06%	5	3	3	4	2	3.4	.204
Technology	**15%**							

*Rating Scale: 1 = Poor, 3 = Average, 5 = Excellent

TABLE 3.1   Supplier Evaluation Matrix Example *(continued)*

Category	% Value	A*	B*	C*	D*	E*	Average Score	Weighted average
Road map alignment	7%							
Market leadership	4%							
R&D budget	4%							
Service	**20%**							
24x7 Customer service	4%							
Scheduling flexibility	8%							
Design assistance	5%							
Automatic status updates	3%							
TOTAL	100%							

*Rating Scale: 1 = Poor, 3 = Average, 5 = Excellent

During the initial development of the weighted average matrix, the team assigns percentages to each of the major sections. In the example shown in Table 3.1, these major categories are cost, quality, technology, and service. The categories are then broken down into subsets composed of each of the individual elements being scored. Each is assigned a portion of the total percentage allocated to the broader category. In a simple analysis, there may be only two or three subsets, while in a complex analysis there may be dozens.

Each member of the team, represented by letters A–E on the table, prepares a separate rating, evaluating any of the categories they are qualified to assess. Assessment is made on a sliding scale and scored accordingly. Some scales use a 1–3 rating system; others use 1–5. Occasionally you see scales of 1–10, but that gets far more complex than necessary. Some users prefer scales with even numbers (such as 1–6) so that individuals are forced onto one side or another and cannot select a midrange score to remain neutral. All relate the numbers to some measure of judgment, for example, 5 = excellent and 1= inadequate.

Individual scores are then tallied into a master score sheet, averaged by subset, and then weighted by the percentage allocated to it. As an example, let's say that the team decides quality should be given an overall value of 25 percent and one of its subsets, SPC measurement systems, should be given 6 percent. The five individuals (A–E) rate the subset on a scale of 1–5, as shown here:

1. A. 5
2. B. 3
3. C. 3
4. D. 4
5. E. 2

Average = 3.4 (17/5)

As you can see, the average of their ratings comes to 3.4. This is then multiplied by 6 percent (.06), the amount allocated to the subset, to determine its total value: $3.4 \times .06 = .204$.

The sum of the subsets equals the total percentage score for each category. The total scores for each category then add up to the supplier's total rating.

However, a word of caution is in order: Regardless of the number of team members used to develop the rating, it will still be a subjective rating. As a result, you should consider a wide margin of error when evaluating scores, and only when the order of magnitude clearly separates one supplier from the rest should you consider using this as an absolute selection criterion. If, for example, your team evaluates six suppliers, five of which score in the 50–60 point range and one that scores 87 points, you have a clear mandate. On the other hand, if three score in the 50–60 point range and three score in the 75–85 point range, you may simply have developed a short list of suppliers in the top range for further evaluation.

Weighted Bid Analysis

Another method for comparatively evaluating suppliers' offers can be implemented through the use of a *weighted bid analysis*, or *cost-ratio analysis*. This method is also known as *transformational bidding* because it weighs one supplier's bid in comparison to others by transforming the value of their offer to some equivalent percentage based upon their demonstrated performance or added value.

In simple terms, let's say you know from past experience that Supplier A's billing process results in more errors than Supplier B. You have been able to measure the additional cost and found it adds about 1 percent to the cost of all the products you purchase from Supplier A. You also know that it costs 2 percent more for shipping from Supplier A than from Supplier B. Therefore, you transform their bids to equivalency by adding 3 percent to Supplier A's bid.

Here's the math for this example:

Supplier A's Total Bid = $142,000

Supplier B's Total Bid = $144,000

Supplier A's transformed bid (adding 3%) = $146,260

Supplier A's bid is actually higher than Supplier B using this method.

Reviewing, Approving, and Issuing the Contract

Once the scoring or other method for determining supplier selection has been completed and approved by the team, the contract may need to be reviewed and approved by other internal groups or individuals according to company policy. If the contract is for tangible goods covered by the UCC, chances are good that the organization's standard PO terms and conditions will apply and the issuance of a PO will be all that is required. In this case, any further approvals needed depend upon the PO value. Some organizations require a purchasing manager's approval prior to the issuance of a PO if it exceeds a certain value. Since the budgeting manager has already approved the expenditure, the purchasing manager reviews the PO for its conformance to organizational policy and good business practices.

In the case of contracts for services not covered by the organization's standard terms and conditions, the buyer may have to write up a special contract. Typically, organizations rely on a previously developed set of contracts for each particular category of service—construction or consulting, for example. These contracts will have already had legal review. However, should the supplier wish to change any of the clauses in the contract that may impact its legal value, a further legal review will be required.

Depending upon company policy and procedure, most purchase orders can be signed by an authorized buyer. Contracts, however, are usually signed by an officer of the company or a senior manager as a means of ensuring one last sanity review. A purchase order must often be issued even with a contract in place so that it can be recorded on the organization's financial system for payment.

Administering the Contract

Once the contract has been approved and implemented, the purchasing manager is in charge of providing continuous supplier evaluation and performance improvement in relation to the contract. Your objective is not only to measure current performance, but also to identify areas for improvement and collaboratively develop programs to implement improvement. Let's discuss some of the ways in which you will do this.

Implementing Performance Standards and Rating Systems

Managing supplier performance is one of the most valuable functions performed by the Purchasing Department. While this responsibility by its nature must be shared with technical and quality groups, it is generally expected that the purchasing manager will assume overall responsibility for the relationship with a supplier. This especially applies to ensuring that key suppliers receive timely input regarding their performance from the customer's perspective.

While there are many ways to evaluate a supplier's performance, two of the more common methods, tracking performance and customer surveys, are outlined in this section.

Tracking Performance

Many organizations monitor supplier performance using a weighted average matrix similar to the one used for the initial selection (see Table 3.1, earlier in the chapter). Some of the specific criteria will change, of course, but it lends the credibility that comes with consistency to continue to use the same or closely related evaluation data.

As an alternative, you may consider using a matrix with similar criteria but have it relate to agreed upon levels of service. To do this requires that you attach a *Service Level Agreement (SLA)* to the original contract that outlines the expected level of performance in quantitative terms. Incorporated into the contract, these metrics then become the agreed upon guide for evaluating performance.

As an example, under Cost in the matrix, you might include a target price that produces a 4 percent decrease in each quarter. A supplier that achieves only a 3 percent decrease will receive a score of 75 percent since only 3/4 of the goal was reached. Similarly, a quality metric might establish the number of lots rejected in a particular period, and a supplier would be rated according to actual performance. Be certain to have the individual subsets rated only by qualified individuals that are members of the team, and average the scores if there is more than one person performing the rating for any subset.

In the example of a quarterly performance evaluation shown in Table 3.2, we've included only the cost data for illustration purposes. While the four major categories remain the same as in the original selection matrix from Table 3.1, and their total percentage is the same, the corresponding subsets have changed to more objective criteria which are based on the signed SLA. In this example the supplier achieved a score of 26.5 of a possible 35 something just above a 75 percent score. Accordingly, this leaves much room for improvement.

TABLE 3.2   Quarterly Performance Evaluation Example

Category	Target Score	Actual	%Value	Actual Weighted Score
Pricing	40	30	15%	
Inventory reduction	30	20	8%	
Packaging	20	20	4%	
Competitive benchmark	10	8	8%	
TOTAL SCORE/COST	100	78	35%	27.3%

The formula for calculating the actual weighted score is a little bit tricky, so we're providing it here for you. Simply put, you take the amount under Actual divided by the amount under Target Score and multiply that number by the % Value. In the example shown in Table 3.2, the Actual Weighted Score is:

$$\% \text{Value} \times (\text{Actual} / \text{Target}) =$$
$$35\% \times (78/100) =$$
$$35\% \times .78 =$$
$$27.3\%$$

Customer Survey

In situations where uniform metrics may be difficult to establish, it is possible to use a customer evaluation instead. This is typically conducted in the form of a periodic survey, as shown in Figure 3.2. The results of this survey then provide the data for an element (or perhaps all elements) of the evaluation. Surveys are more commonly used for service providers.

Following Up and Expediting

In addition to ongoing evaluation of standard contract terms, a purchasing manager must carry out a number of other internal duties when problems occur during the performance of the contract. These typically include such activities as expediting delayed orders, tracking lost shipments, resolving accounting discrepancies, and returning defective product. To the extent that these problems recur, you should establish uniform processes to ensure that they are eliminated so that the internal customer perceives a well-managed supplier. If these problems become issues (rather than isolated occurrences) through nonperformance, they should be included in the evaluation matrix and reviewed with the supplier on a regular basis.

Developing Good Practices

Compliance with good business practices goes a long way to cementing the relationship between two organizations. To that end, the buyer must be continually aware of how well the supplier sticks to its stated policies and how conscientiously its management values ethical principles and strict adherence to legally responsible behavior. Let's discuss policy, law and principles for a moment.

Conformance to Policy

Many organizations develop policy statements regarding ethical and legal conduct. They do this so that there can be no misunderstanding by employees, customers, and suppliers of their intentions to manage in accordance with community accepted principles.

These policies need to be aligned with the actual practices of the supply base and compliance enforced to the extent possible. While it would be useless for you to expect each and every supplier to adopt the precise wording of your organization's policy, you should obtain copies and review the actual policies of your suppliers and, at the same time, ensure they have read copies of yours.

FIGURE 3.2   Customer Evaluation Survey

Customer Evaluation Survey			
Supplier Name:		Date:	
Summary Supplier Evaluation	Excellent	Average	Poor
CORPORATE/SALES	☐	☐	☐
COST MANAGEMENT	☐	☐	☐
QUALITY	☐	☐	☐
DELIVERY	☐	☐	☐
RESPONSIVENESS	☐	☐	☐
TECHNOLOGY	☐	☐	☐
Supplier Performance Factors	Excellent	Average	Poor
CORPORATE			
Billing processes	☐	☐	☐
Sales support	☐	☐	☐
Personnel turnover	☐	☐	☐
Timely response to inquiries	☐	☐	☐
Employee knowledge	☐	☐	☐
Employee courtesy	☐	☐	☐
COST MANAGEMENT			
Price reductions	☐	☐	☐
Peripheral costs	☐	☐	☐
Warranty administration	☐	☐	☐
QUALITY			
Quality and process control	☐	☐	☐
Continuous improvement	☐	☐	☐
Errors and omissions	☐	☐	☐
Corrective measures	☐	☐	☐
Incoming inspection requirements	☐	☐	☐
DELIVERY			
Meets customer requests	☐	☐	☐
Accuracy	☐	☐	☐
Documentation	☐	☐	☐
Advance delay notification	☐	☐	☐
RESPONSIVENESS			
Timely implementation of spec changes	☐	☐	☐
Manages complaints expeditiously	☐	☐	☐
Customer focused attitude	☐	☐	☐
Continuous improvement processes	☐	☐	☐
TECHNOLOGY			
Provides timely technical assistance	☐	☐	☐
Engineering support	☐	☐	☐
Maintains roadmap	☐	☐	☐
Communicates changes	☐	☐	☐
IT systems	☐	☐	☐

Conformance to Law

In Chapter 2 we reviewed applicable laws and regulations that would likely apply to supplier relationships. This is by no means an exhaustive list. There are literally thousands of additional laws governing environmental regulations, working conditions, health and safety, equal opportunity, and financial practices. If your organization is global, it is likely there are local variations for all of them. No individual can possibly be knowledgeable about all of them.

For this reason, and for a variety of other practical reasons, you should rely on both the spirit of the supplier's desire to conform and its actual history of doing so. You can audit the former by reviewing documents and questioning their staff; you can audit conformance history through public records.

This is important, believe us. You never want to see the CEO of one of the suppliers *you* have chosen appearing on the evening news being led away to prison in handcuffs. If you have any doubts whatsoever about the supplier's compliance, you should contact your legal counsel immediately.

Ethical Principles

Would you recommend doing business with an organization that utilizes child labor? Would you recommend doing business with a supplier that evades taxes by hiding revenues in another country? Would you approve a supplier that pays substandard wages? Some of these actions may not actually violate a law, but they may violate the law of your conscience.

So how do you regulate conformance to a set of moral expectations that may or may not violate any laws? You can do so by establishing a set of ethical principles governing your expectation of how suppliers will behave. These, if you like, are the rules *buyers* expect suppliers to meet.

Ethical principles are usually issued in the form of a document, such as an *Ethical Code of Conduct*, outlining the organization's expectations for employees and suppliers. Sometimes this document is the same for both groups; sometimes organizations will write them separately.

The Ethical Code of Conduct is usually organized by specific subject matter such as legal compliance, working conditions, financial accounting practices, and so on. There is no clear formula, and different organizations emphasize different elements.

Here are URLs for two examples of organizations with Ethical Codes of Conduct that you might find useful. HSBC is a globally positioned bank headquartered in the U.K.: http://www.hsbc.com/hsbc/purchasing/ethical-code-of-conduct. Hewlett-Packard is a well-known global supplier of computers: http://www.hp.com/hpinfo/globalcitizenship/environment/.

Managing Records and Data

Most organizations have policies regarding the management and retention of records. Some of these policies are based on legal requirements (e.g., the Internal Revenue Service requires documents relating to taxes be stored for seven years), and others are based on good business practices, such as keeping journals of engineering activity to limit future liability and to prove the development history of a particular patent.

Those policies notwithstanding, it is important that you maintain historical data indicating supplier performance so that there can be no misinterpretations and disputes in the conduct of the evaluation process.

Summary

Supplier evaluation and selection is one of the key organizational functions led by the Purchasing Department. It is critical, therefore, that the purchasing manager develop and implement effective processes for qualifying suppliers and determining the award of business. We have explored how supplier responsiveness and capability can be evaluated and how these attributes need to be combined with the elements of value to ensure that your organization receives the best return for its expenditure.

There are many ways to evaluate supplier performance, but we strongly recommend using a quantitative approach. This approach generally requires team input to gain appropriate objectivity and, in the case of key suppliers, data should be gathered from physical visits as well as from the evaluation of written offers. Most commonly, supplier selection data is put into a weighted average matrix as a means of comparing various suppliers and their offers.

Ongoing contract administration requires the use of continuous improvement methods to generate greater value for your organization. Here too the use of a weighted average method for evaluating performance is strongly recommended. You will also find that customer surveys can provide important feedback when measurement is not altogether practical.

Organizations must strive to develop sound business practices that conform to applicable law as well as fundamental ethical principles. It is a key function of the purchasing manager to ensure that there is alignment between the requirements of their organization and that of the supplier.

In the next chapter, we will look at how these methods are best applied in day-to-day operations.

For additional reading on topics related to this chapter, please see Appendix A.

Exam Essentials

Be able to evaluate supplier offers.   To effectively compare offers, you will need to evaluate the suppliers' responsiveness to the requirements in your request, their capability of performing to your needs, and the competitive value they offer.

Understand and apply the elements of value to an analysis of suppliers' offers.   The wise organization selects the supplier that offers the best value, not just the best price. Value can be described as the confluence of four elements: price, technology, quality, and service.

Be able to qualify a supplier.   Prior to any award, key suppliers should be qualified by a site visit conducted by a cross-functional team. During the visit, a number of areas that impact performance need to be audited to ensure that the supplier can meet its commitments. Areas of critical concern are operations, quality, cost control, financial viability, order processing, and the management team.

Be able to quantitatively evaluate a supplier.   To objectively compare several suppliers requires the use of some form of mathematical evaluation. The most commonly used method is the weighted average, where performance in various areas is assigned weights and an overall evaluation score can be calculated.

Obtain necessary contract review and issue the contract.   You should understand that internal requirements exist for formal contract approval and ratification, such as legal and safety reviews. You also need to know how to issue the contract, and only contracts for tangible goods should be issued in the form of a purchase order.

Be able to effectively administer the contract.   You are required to implement an ongoing supplier evaluation program by developing a weighted average performance and rating system. This system is similar to the one used in the supplier selection process with the substitution of actual performance history for potential capability. You may also use a supplier performance evaluation survey in cases where you are unable to apply actual metrics.

Be able to ensure conformance to law and good ethical principles.   Investigate the history of the supplier's legal violations and internal policies to ensure maximum compliance. You also need to determine alignment with your organization's ethical principles and policies through the exchange and review of written policies.

Review Questions

1. Besides costs, what is the major reason for evaluating a supplier's offer?

   A. To determine the supplier's ability to perform

   B. To measure the supplier's position in the marketplace

   C. To provide delivery lead time

   D. To provide specification tolerances

   E. To determine transportation methods

2. Supplier offers that do not answer the buyer's specific questions are considered:

   A. Nonresponsive

   B. Unethical

   C. Out of tolerance

   D. Rejects

   E. Nonconforming

3. The ratio of a supplier's actual output to its total production capacity is called:

   A. Leverage ratio

   B. Profitability ratio

   C. Quick ratio

   D. Operational capacity utilization

   E. Capacity ratio

4. A supplier's competitive value includes all of the following *except*:

   A. Price

   B. Quality

   C. Location

   D. Service

   E. Technology

5. "Work-in-process" is an element of which of the supplier's functional areas?

   A. Order processing and fulfillment

   B. Quality systems

   C. Finance

   D. Cost control

   E. Operations

6. A buyer-created weighted average supplier evaluation rating matrix is used to:

    A. Measure supplier performance

    B. Gauge production output

    C. Rank industry position

    D. Select supplier offers

    E. Forecast future performance

7. A document attached to a supplier contract used to detail the expected level of performance is called a:

    A. Contract rider

    B. Performance evaluation

    C. Service Level Agreement

    D. Customer Evaluation Survey

    E. Quarterly Performance Evaluation

8. Compliance to good business practices includes all of the following *except*:

    A. Corporate Policy Statements

    B. Applicable laws and regulations

    C. Statement of work

    D. Ethical principles

    E. Codes of conduct

9. An assessment of the ratio of current assets to current liabilities is related to which of the following supplier functional areas?

    A. Order processing and fulfillment

    B. Quality systems

    C. Finance

    D. Cost control

    E. Operations

10. Life cycle costs are also known as:

    A. Cost of goods sold

    B. Landed costs

    C. Production costs

    D. End of life costs

    E. Total cost of ownership

Answers to Review Questions

1. A. Core to the evaluation of any potential source is an assessment of the supplier's ability to perform. The best price has no value unless the supplier can actually deliver quality goods or services on time and at the quality needed.

2. E. The technical term "nonconforming" is the term used to describe a supplier's offer when it does not answer the buyer's specific questions. In this case, nonconforming means it does not conform to the requirements of the bid.

3. D. This ratio informs the buyer of approximately how much additional capacity exists.

4. C. Location is not a key issue in assessing a supplier's competitive value.

5. E. Work-in-process describes the goods during the manufacturing process. Manufacturing is an element of operations.

6. D. The purpose of a weighted average supplier evaluation rating matrix is to select suppliers based on their perceived performance in critical areas.

7. C. A Service Level Agreement is the primary document used to record agreed upon metrics for performance.

8. C. A statement of work describes the organization's requirements and is not relevant to establishing good business practices.

9. C. The ratio of current assets to current liabilities, called the current ratio, is a financial measurement tool indicating the organization's solvency.

10. E. Total cost of ownership is another term associated with life cycle costs for a particular purchase.

Chapter

4

Administering Contracts

THE C.P.M. EXAM SPECIFICATIONS COVERED IN THIS CHAPTER INCLUDE THE FOLLOWING:

- ✓ Creating and issuing purchase orders and contracts
- ✓ Reviewing contracts for conformance to legal requirements
- ✓ Aligning contracts and purchasing practices with organizational policy
- ✓ Maintaining purchasing documents, records, and data

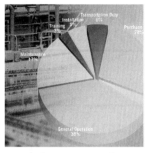

In this chapter, we will focus on reviewing key aspects of creating and managing various types of purchasing contracts and documents. As a purchasing manager, you will be required to understand the nature and purpose of contracts and what constitutes a legally binding obligation. You will also need to become familiar with a variety of standard elements that are required for contracts and what types of contracts should be used in any particular procurement transaction.

As you probably know by this time, forming and administering contracts covers a broad range of the Purchasing Department's responsibilities and constitutes a major investment of required talent. Problems with document verbiage, issues regarding unclear specifications, lack of supplier performance and unseen financial obligations plague many organizations. The vast majority of these contractual problems, however, can be reduced or even eliminated by establishing clear process requirements for developing them and ensuring that they receive appropriate approval and legal review.

Properly administering POs and contracts also requires close attention to detail so that the supplier's compliance with the terms and conditions adds the full measure of value that was originally intended by the organization. This often involves resolving discrepancies and expediting deliveries, as well as handling disputes and contractual violations. Establishing purchasing policies and practices that conform to ethical behavior and enhance the organization's integrity are keys to the Purchasing Department's effectiveness in performing these obligations.

Contract Essentials

The Purchasing Department is responsible for the issuance and management of a variety of purchasing contracts and documents. Since they generate both legal and financial obligations for the organization, the buyer needs to apply due diligence to their formation and management.

 In its basic form, a contract represents a legally binding agreement made by two or more parties to complete a specified action at a specific point in time. It represents a *bargain* that is valid in a court. Contracts may be generated to cover the purchase of either goods or services.

In this section, we will review the basis for forming contractual obligations and the key elements that provide their validity.

Contract Essentials

Contracts cover the purchase of both goods and services. Services are generally covered by state laws (known as common law or case law), which establish precedents that can help resolve disputes. Goods are considered personal property and are covered by Article 2 of the Uniform Commercial Code (UCC). You will recall from Chapter 2 that the UCC was developed to provide a measure of standardization in the laws of commerce between the states and has been adopted by 49 U.S. states (all states except Louisiana) and the District of Columbia. One other body of law, known as *statutory law*, covers acts and regulations enacted by the U.S. Congress and state legislatures.

Written Contracts

In broad terms, contracts can use either written or oral formats. While from a purchasing point of view, written contracts pose the least amount of risk, it is important to understand that oral contracts can be equally enforceable if they meet a common set of conditions. However, the *Statute of Frauds*—laws designed to prevent fraud—requires certain types of contracts to be validated in written form:

- Contracts for goods sold under the UCC exceeding $500 that are not specifically manufactured for the user. (This amount will likely increase to $5,000 under pending proposals.)
- Contracts for the sale or transfer of real estate.
- Contracts to assume the debt or duty of another.
- Contracts that cannot be completed within one year, either by their own terms or because they are objectively impossible to complete.

Agreements required to be evidenced in writing (such as those just listed) do not have to take a specific contractual form. However, at the least, the writing must contain:

- Identification of the other party as the individual responsible for the contract
- Some form of signature of the above
- A clearly identified subject of the contract
- Specific terms and conditions
- Identification of the consideration (as an exchange of value)

There are a number of exceptions to the written requirements of the Statute of Frauds under which an oral contract will be enforced, including the partial completion of an oral contract up to the point of performance. If, for example, a contract to buy $10,000 worth of parts has not yet been committed to writing and is cancelled by the buyer after $2,000 worth of parts has been received and accepted, will the seller be able to force the buyer to honor the entire contract? The answer is no. Since the value of the remaining portion of the contract exceeds $500 and there is no evidence in writing of any contract, the buyer is under no obligation to honor the original agreement. Similarly, the seller would not be responsible for delivering any more than that already shipped.

Oral Contracts

The principle of *detrimental reliance* applies when it can be shown that reliance on the oral promise will produce substantial or unconscionable injury to the promisee or will unjustly enrich the promisor. The fact that the promisee relies on the oral promise to its detriment is generally not considered sufficient reason to entitle it to enforce an oral contract. However, when customized products are made for a buying organization under an oral agreement and cannot be sold to any others, the contract is enforceable by the seller.

If an oral contract not required to be in writing (e.g., for goods under $500) is modified to the extent that it falls within the Statute of Fraud, then the contract must be in writing to be enforceable. For example, if $200 worth of goods is added to an oral contract already totaling $450, it's required that the entire contract be put in writing since the total amount ($650) exceeds the limit of $500 for an oral contract.

Also considered in the formation of a contract is the law of Promissory Estoppel. An oral contract unenforceable under the Statute of Frauds may be enforced under the doctrine of Promissory Estoppel if one party made an oral promise and the other party relied upon that promise and performed part of or its entire obligation. Under these conditions, the oral promise cannot be rescinded simply because it is not evidenced in writing.

Contract Requirements

In order for a contract to be legally enforceable, it is commonly agreed that four key elements need to be demonstrated: mutual agreement, legality, consideration, and capacity. Let's discuss each of these in more detail.

Mutual Agreement   As evidence of a "meeting of the minds," *mutual agreement* includes an *offer* and its *acceptance*. When a buyer places a purchase order, for example, it is considered an offer to buy, and the seller's acknowledgment is generally considered an acceptance. An acceptance can also be demonstrated by actual performance, such as a shipment of materials or some constructive action of service that indicates such acceptance. This is called a *unilateral contract*, whereas a contract containing both an offer to sell and an agreement to buy is considered a *bilateral contract*.

If a seller extends an offer in the form of a quotation but the buyer requests modification to some of the terms, it is considered a *counteroffer* rather than an acceptance. By requesting modification, the buyer, in effect, rejects the original offer and proposes a new one.

If a buyer issues a solicitation for a certain quantity of materials and a seller provides a quotation, does it signify that a contract exists? No, because a solicitation is not necessarily an offer to buy.

Legality   A contract requires a legal purpose. Contracts that violate a legal statute or are against public policy are invalid.

Consideration   Consideration means an exchange of anything of value. To be valid, a contract has to show evidence that an exchange of some value for a promise is part of the agreement. Consideration does not necessarily have to be exchanged in the form of money. It can also be in the form of various types of services rendered.

The Trouble with Electronic Purchasing

Electronic purchasing is a relatively new process that has yet to be fully recognized under the UCC or the Statute of Frauds. The primary issue concerns the ability of one party to fraudulently alter a document after agreement has been reached. While faxed signatures and documents, along with Electronic Data Interchange (EDI) transactions, are generally considered reliable evidence of contractual obligations, other forms such as e-mail have yet to be fully accepted as legal. Parties using electronic transmission for business are usually counseled to initiate some contractual documentation, such as a formal trading partner agreement, outlining the processes and obligations that will govern them.

 One way to think of consideration is by referring to the Latin term *quid pro quo.* Translated literally quid pro quo means "this for that" or "something for something." While we generally consider this to mean something of equal value, it is also generally considered that value is subjective and must be determined by the parties to the exchange.

Capacity   Parties to a contract need to be legally *competent* to enter into it and perform its *obligations.* Minors, for example, are not considered legally competent. A person who is legally insane cannot be a valid party to a contract.

Contract Types

Typically, a Purchasing Department will use a wide variety of contractual documents during the normal course of business. The exact document you choose will largely depend on the business needs of your organization and the type of purchase being made. Outlined in this section are the contracts that are most commonly used and which you will need to become familiar with.

Purchase Orders

In almost all environments, the PO is the most common purchasing document available, and is in effect, a contract. As a standard form, it is the easiest way to order purchased materials and services and provides the most commonly required audit trail. A standard PO can be used for recurring or repetitive purchases as well as one-time purchases. In addition to stating the specific requirements for the purchase, the PO usually conveys your organization's standard terms and conditions, sometimes termed a *boilerplate.*

The PO can be both an offer and a means of acceptance, depending upon the existing circumstances. When issued in response to a solicitation for bids, it can be considered evidence of contract formation. On the other hand, when sent to a supplier without having previously received a quote or proposal, it may be considered simply an offer to buy.

In addition to standard terms and conditions covering remedies, warranties, liabilities, rights of inspection and rejection, ability to cancel, and other typical clauses (usually transmitted by the fine print on the reverse side of the PO), the PO will generally describe on its face what is being purchased, the price being paid, the terms of delivery, and any other instructions needed to describe the specific requirements of that particular order.

Blanket purchase orders are variants of the standard purchase order, commonly used in two formats:

Requirements or indefinite delivery contracts   *Requirements contracts* or *indefinite delivery contracts* are blanket purchase orders used when the buyer wishes to lock in pricing or lead time in exchange for a commitment to purchase all of the organization's requirements (or at least some described minimum and/or maximum amount) but specific quantities and delivery dates are not yet known. Sometimes, the requirements contract will be used to make commitments to a supplier for a certain line of products (for example, office supplies) in exchange for a specified discount level or for some other consideration such as setting up an automated, online ordering program.

Definite Quantity Contracts   A *definite quantity contract* is a blanket purchase order that specifies the amount being purchased during a given time frame but not the specific delivery dates. This type of contract is also known as a *take or pay* contract because the buying organization cannot cancel it and must pay for it at the end of the contractual period even if it is not used.

Fixed-price Contracts

Fixed-price contracts are the most commonly used contracts in typical business environments. Most fixed-price contract types are defined in the Federal Acquisitions Regulations (FAR) as they apply to government purchases; however, they are commonly adapted for commercial use by Purchasing Departments. Essentially, they are contracts where prices are agreed to in advance of performance. There are five types of fixed-price contracts that we will discuss in more detail here.

Firm-fixed-price

A *firm-fixed-price contract* is exactly what its title states: the price is not subject to adjustment. The buyer and seller agree to performance at the stated price, and the risk of profit and loss passes solely to the supplier.

Fixed-price-with-incentive

For the *fixed-price-with-incentive contract,* a profit formula is established based upon target cost and target profit within an agreed upon maximum price. The final price is established by adjusting the actual profit the supplier receives based on the difference between the final cost agreed to by the parties and the original target cost. Typically, the amount saved by reducing the cost is shared by both parties. In other words, this contract type provides an incentive to the supplier to hold down the costs and thereby increase its profit.

Fixed-price-with-economic-price-adjustment

The *fixed-price with economic price adjustment contract* allows pricing to be adjusted upward or downward based on established contingencies such as escalating labor and material rates. Changes in actual costs beyond the supplier's control or reasonable ability to foresee, above or below the contract's baseline, can lead to an adjustment reflected in the supplier's pricing. This method is frequently used for multiyear contracts or when economic conditions are unstable. Often, this is a standard contract with the inclusion of a clause allowing *escalation* or *de-escalation* of prices under agreed upon conditions. When it is difficult to calculate actual prices, adjustments are sometimes based on some readily available business or financial index.

Fixed-price-with-price-redetermination

Similar to the economic price adjustment contract, the *fixed-price with price redetermination contract* is used when prices are anticipated to change over time but the extent of those changes cannot be predicted, such as during startup operations. Generally, the specific time for redetermination will be included.

Fixed-price, Level-of-effort

The *fixed-price, level-of-effort* method of pricing, although relatively uncommon, is usually used in situations when the precise amount of labor or materials is unknown but the parties can agree on a standard level of effort (such as the type and quantity of tools to be used or the rated proficiency of the employees) and a given price. Thus the fixed-price, level-of-effort contract is similar to the concept in the time and materials contract, which will be discussed shortly.

Cost Reimbursable Contracts

Cost reimbursable contracts are primarily used by government organizations and large corporations as an inducement for supplier participation in situations where the initial research and development engineering or capital investment may be very high and the financial risk great. These contracts assure the supplier that the buyer will cover, at a minimum, agreed upon costs up to an agreed upon monetary ceiling. The supplier may not exceed that amount without prior approval, unless it wishes to go forward at its own risk. Cost reimbursable contracts are used in a variety of ways, as you will see in this section.

Cost-plus-fixed-fee   The *cost-plus-fixed-fee contract* is a cost-reimbursement contract that allows the supplier to recover actual costs plus a fee negotiated prior to the contract's inception. The fee is considered fixed because it does not vary from the amount of the cost, although further negotiation of the fee based on changed conditions can be considered.

Cost-plus-incentive-fee   The *cost-plus-incentive-fee* is another reimbursable contract which, like the fixed-price-with-incentive contract outlined previously, provides an initially negotiated fee with a formula-based adjustment that reflects the relationship of total allowable cost to total target cost.

Cost-plus-award-fee   The *cost-plus-award-fee* provides additional incentive for the supplier to produce excellent results by enabling the buyer to make a financial award in addition to the cost and negotiated fee. It is designed to provide the supplier with a financial incentive for excellent performance.

At one time the federal government used a *cost-plus-percentage-of-cost* contract. For obvious reasons, this provided the supplier no incentive whatsoever to hold down costs. Recently, the *Government Accounting Office (GAO)*, the Federal watchdog agency, caught on and banned this practice in November of 2002.

Cost-sharing   A *cost-sharing contract* is generally used in a partnering relationship where all parties share the cost and the accruing benefits according to a negotiated formula. The costs are typically limited to a specific amount or an *in-kind exchange* that is defined at the contract's formation. In many ways, this type of contract is similar to a *joint venture* where all parties own a portion of the operation.

Cost-only   Used primarily between universities and other not-for-profit and research organizations, the *cost-only contract*, as its name implies, covers reimbursement only for actual costs, without including a fee. This contract typically supplements one organization's capabilities and enable full utilization of the other's resources that might otherwise remain idle.

Time and Materials Contracts

Time and materials (T&M) contracts are used when there are no acceptable ways to determine what a fair and reasonable price may be for a particular project, such as a well-digging contract where the exact depth of the water and the composition of the soil may be unknown. With this type of contract, the rates for labor and the markup for materials are initially negotiated with a cap, or *not-to-exceed (NTE)* amount, specified as a limit. In most ways, T&M contracts are similar to cost-reimbursable contracts.

Letters of Intent

A Letter of Intent (LOI) can be useful when parties are seriously working toward a final contract and wish to proceed with some of their preliminary efforts under a formal agreement. Letters of Intent can outline the broad intent of the contract regarding some terms that have not yet been specified or agreed upon. Depending on how complete LOIs are, they can be a legally binding contract between buyer and supplier. They can also induce the supplier to perform some specific action such as reserving production scheduling time or ordering materials in advance of an actual contract. Some of the most common elements of an LOI include:

Price and Terms   This may include projected costs and how they will be determined. It may also broadly outline the terms and conditions that will apply under a given set of assumptions. In some instances the LOI may specify the accrual of payment to the supplier for work performed in the development of the contract, such as research needed to validate a statement of work. It may also include payment terms.

Obligations   A section covering obligations is also typically included. This section generally outlines what each party must do prior to proceeding with a contract and which party will pay for what activities.

Incentive Contracts

We have outlined two commonly used incentive contracts in this section, the fixed-fee-with incentive and the cost-reimbursable-plus-incentive contracts. These are based primarily on cost reduction. However, there are often other reasons to provide incentives to the supplier, such as when accelerated delivery may be highly valuable (such as in development work) or when specific elements of performance (quality, for example) are needed. Typically, such contracts fall into the fixed-price or cost-plus categories but contain clauses calling for additional payments for improvements in the negotiated level of performance.

Confidentiality   Generally, an LOI binds the parties to the same level of confidentiality as a standard contract. This enables the free exchange of proprietary information so that certain elements of the contract can be predefined.

Exclusivity   This section outlines the length of time the parties are bound to an exclusive relationship. Following this period, the parties may enter into agreements with others under pre-established confidentiality conditions and protection of any intellectual property developed.

Structure   Often the nature of the relationship needs to be stated prior to beginning even basic aspects of the work. This includes defining the nature of the final agreement—e.g., the type of contract or the disposition of intellectual property—and what the nature of the relationship will be subsequent to a contract.

Time and Conditions   The elements related to time and specific conditions express the parties' intent to form a final agreement by a specific date and under described conditions. These reflect the known conditions that must be present at that time in order to proceed and without which either of the parties are not obligated to form a further contract.

Binding or Nonbinding Clauses   Included in most LOI documents are statements indicating which portions of the agreement shall be binding and which shall not. For example, the parties may agree to be bound by an intellectual property clause granting the rights to any IP developed to one or the other of the parties.

Licensing Agreements

When another party has secured ownership rights to specific intellectual property—such as an invention or a software program—through a *patent* or *copyright*, your organization will need to obtain permission to use it. Usually this permission is given in the form of a *licensing agreement*, a contract for which the licensee will pay either a fixed fee or a *royalty* based on usage. A royalty is similar to a commission insofar as it is generally calculated as a percentage of gross sales. There are a number of different formats you may encounter, but the more common ones you will likely come in contact with include:

Exclusive License   This grants usage rights to only one party so that no others may be so licensed.

Nonexclusive License   This grants usage rights to a party but does not limit the number of others that may be similarly licensed by the owner.

Partially Exclusive License   This grants exclusive rights to use the patent within a geographical area or for specific products.

End-User License Agreement   The *End-User License Agreement (EULA)* is a three-way contract between the manufacturer, the author, and the *end user* written to cover proprietary software. It is often attached to a program that requires you to check a box indicating acceptance of the terms prior to being able to use it.

 Real World Scenario

Intellectual Property

In general, intellectual property is protected in the U.S. by specific law and a number of registration processes. The more common of the processes are outlined below:

Patent   A patent is generally considered a set of exclusive rights granted by a government to an inventor for a specified period of time. In the U.S., this is usually for 20 years. For the period of time covered by the patent, the patent holder owns a monopoly, and others wishing to use it must obtain a license. Patents are granted for inventions and processes, as opposed to copyrights, which are granted to written documents, designs, and software; or trade-marks, which identify products.

Copyright   Copyrights grant ownership of various forms of expression such as works of art, literature, software programs, or audio/visual material (and similar forms of expression). Ownership enables the exclusive right to publish, sell, or license it.

Trademark   A trademark is a word or symbol that identifies a particular brand, product, or business. Like a patent, it can also be registered with the U.S. Patent and Trademark Office so that exclusive ownership can be reserved.

Service Mark   A service mark is similar to trademark, except it is used to identify a service rather than an actual product.

Here's an example you might recognize:

- Serial Number: 71347272

- Filling Date: Feb. 12, 1934

- Registration Number: 0313765

- Design Search Code: 030906 030926

- Word Mark: Mickey Mouse

Consigned Goods Contracts

It is becoming increasingly common for organizations to require suppliers to stock inventory at the buyers' sites in order to support rapid delivery. These arrangements are called Supplier Managed Inventory (SMI) and are included in a contract covering specific conditions, such as when and under what conditions the transfer of ownership from the supplier to the buyer takes place, which party bears the financial liability of loss during storage or potential obsolescence, and the general payment terms.

Other Contract Types

During your career you will doubtless encounter a wide variety of contracts that are employed in special circumstances or broadly outline the terms and conditions of ongoing relationships outside of any specific statement of work. There are so many types that it would be impossible (and beyond our scope) to list them all. For reference, here are just a few:

Master Purchase Agreement   A *Master Purchase Agreement* covers special terms and conditions for the purchase of critical materials. You may also find this listed under *Master Supply Agreement* in directories of legal agreements.

Master Services Agreement   The *Master Services Agreement* addresses terms and conditions related to the purchase of nontangible goods. Since the UCC does not cover services directly—except when the major portion (greater than 50 percent) of the contract is actually for goods—it is always a good idea to have an overriding contract in place for each significant service purchased by your organization.

Construction Contract   A *construction contract* is used for significant building and facilities improvement contracts where special risks of performance and liability exist.

Non-disclosure Agreement (NDA)   A Non-disclosure Agreement (NDA) or *Confidentiality Agreement* protects sensitive information from disclosure to third parties or the general public. An NDA can be unilateral, that is, binding upon only one party, or mutual and binding on both parties.

Commercial Lease Agreement   *Commercial Lease Agreements* form contracts for equipment owned by one party and used by another for a fee. Leases are essentially rental agreements that outline the responsibilities and liabilities assumed by each of the parties. Terms generally state which party is responsible for maintenance and upkeep as well as the conditions for use and warranties.

Methods of Exchange

As we discussed earlier in this chapter, a contract requires both an offer and acceptance in order to be legally enforceable. Questions often arise regarding how to handle disparities between the form of the contract and the form of its acceptance, one issued by the supplier and the other by the buyer. If the terms of the two differ, which should prevail? This brings up the topic referred to as the "battle of the forms."

Battle of the Forms

Typically, for low value goods orders, the buyer will issue a simple PO containing the organization's standard terms and conditions in the form of a boilerplate on the reverse side. The supplier acknowledges the order, issuing its own form with a corresponding boilerplate on its side. In common practice, neither party reads the other's boilerplate. But what happens when the two sets differ?

The answer to this gets rather complicated and has created some confusion. Section 2-207 of the UCC looks at this from three different perspectives:

1. Do the conflicting forms establish a contract?

2. If a contract does exist, what terms are then enforceable?

3. If a contract does not exist, but the parties have performed anyway, what are the terms of the contract established by their performance?

While many courts have ruled on these questions, there seems to be no uniform conclusion. For material goods, what appears to emerge is the concept that if one party *says* it accepts an offer, a contract exists even though the terms may be different or additional terms are included in the acceptance. But how are the additional terms or conflicting terms handled?

To complicate the answer to this question, Section 2-207 indicates that additional terms included by the seller in its acknowledgment become part of the contract unless the buyer's contract expressly prohibits such additions or if they materially alter the original contract. If not, the added terms become part of the contract unless the buyer specifically objects within a reasonable time frame. Thus the additional terms are added to the buyer's contract.

Conflicting terms, on the other hand, are generally considered as self-canceling, that is, they do not apply. Instead, standard terms contained in the UCC become the default provisions.

The Mirror Image Rule

Because the UCC does not expressly apply to services, the battle of the forms does not arise when services are contracted. Instead, the *mirror image* rule applies under the Statute of Frauds. (The Statute of Frauds is originally an English law c.1677 and was adopted under the U.S. constitution, and the UCC is used as a reference for interpreting the statute: specifically it is in the UCC: Article 2: 2-201.). This requires that offer and acceptance match exactly, that is, be mirror images of each other, before a contract can be enforced. If the acceptance differs from the offer, it is considered a counteroffer. However, if either of the parties initiates performance following such counteroffer, it is considered an acceptance.

WARNING   Careful: actions speak louder than words. Initiating any act that indicates the existence of a contract can be tantamount to accepting the other parties' terms.

Acceptance of an Oral Agreement

Under the terms of the UCC, oral agreements require written confirmation by way of a memorialization of the agreement if they are for material goods with values greater than $500. If they are and the confirmation has been offered, the party receiving the written confirmation has 10 days from the receipt of such confirmation to object. Otherwise the contract is considered accepted.

Other Contract Elements

As you may imagine, numerous important legal elements are included in every contract. Each of these varies with the nature of the particular situation for which the contract is being written. Let's discuss some of the more common ones.

Revocation

In most cases, an offer may be revoked by the party making it any time before it is legally accepted by the other party. The revocation can take any form that expressly or implicitly indicates that the party making the offer is no longer willing or able to enter into a contract. A clear example of this would be the incapacity of the seller to perform as a result of a fire that destroys its facility or the sale of the item being offered to another party.

An action inconsistent with the offer is also considered a revocation if notice of the action is provided to the other party prior to acceptance. If, for example, we offer to perform a service for your organization next week and, before you can accept, leave you a voice mail that we have gone on vacation, we have then revoked the offer.

Change Orders

Common in construction projects and other services, change orders present another issue. Having established a contract with your organization, is the supplier required to accept changes to the SOW? Most service contracts include appropriate criteria for making unilateral changes, including the method of pricing them. Without such protection, the supplier is under little obligation to accept changes or to price them in relation to its initial contract pricing. Change orders are subject to the same requirements of writing as the original contract.

Dispute Resolution

Most contracts, including POs, contain legal remedies should a dispute arise. Many contain mediation or arbitration clauses or some other method for resolving them, such as a formal appeals process. In commercial transactions, disputes may ultimately come to a court for resolution.

Section 2-207 of the UCC can be a handy reference for more detail regarding contract modification, rescission, and waiver.

Legal Authority and the Buyers' Responsibilities

In dealing with contracts, there are some specific principles you will need to keep in mind so that you fully understand your role and responsibilities, as well as the limits of your authority. Consider agency, authority, and financial responsibility, discussed in this section.

Agency

An *agent* is an individual with the authority to act on behalf of a principal, in most cases an employer. This means that your organization may be legally bound by the terms of any contract you have signed. The law of agency covers the legal principles governing this relationship and the buyer's relationship to the supplier. As an agent, however, *you* will not be held *personally* liable for such acts, providing you have not violated the law or your organization's express business and/or ethics policies.

Authority

As an agent, the buyer is required to perform certain duties. Within the scope of these duties the buyer is given certain authority, both by role and by specific designation.

Apparent Authority

Apparent authority comes with the role of buyer. It differs from *actual authority* insofar as no specific charter is given to perform designated duties other than those typically associated with buyers' duties through common business practice. In effect, it is an implied authority but one that third parties may legally rely upon. The title of buyer (or any similar association) will generally be taken to mean that authority has been granted to contract and buy goods and services for the organization. The buyer's spending limit is technically only controlled by internal policy, meaning that a supplier may rely on the buyer's authority even if it exceeds the amount allowed by the organization.

WARNING   If you place or authorize an order in an amount that exceeds your authority, your organization will likely be bound by the amount since, in your role, you have apparent authority. However, your organization may hold you personally responsible for any amount exceeding your designated authority should any liability arise.

Limited Authority

Limited authority means that the agency may be limited within the scope of an individual's responsibility. Most commonly, in commercial environments, the agency of a salesperson is specifically limited. Sales representatives are hired to solicit business and coordinate activities between the respective organizations and thus have limited authority. They are not empowered through the agency to commit their company to any specific obligations. For this, you will need to find an individual who is at least designated as a manager.

Ratification

When an agent acts beyond the designated scope of its responsibility, the contracting organization, may nevertheless choose to ratify the action. This ratification thus binds the obligations created by the contract and releases the agent from personal liability.

Financial Responsibility

At all times, the buyer as an agent holds a position of *fiduciary* trust, as well as business responsibility, toward the principal. Thus the buyer is expected to act prudently and with the best interest of the organization, especially in carrying out financial duties. This responsibility covers conformance to legal, as well as ethical, principles. Needless to say, the exercise of good judgment and integrity are paramount to meeting this responsibility.

Reviewing Contracts for Legal Requirements

Legal decisions are typically based on historical precedent: how prior cases regarding the same circumstances have been resolved by the courts. Unfortunately, as a purchasing professional you are not always aware of the most recent decisions and how they might affect your contract since you are primarily focused on the business issues. Before issuing a contract, therefore, you should ensure that it conforms to appropriate legal requirements in addition to the business needs of your organization. To this end, it is best to obtain legal input prior to its writing. In fact, many organizations have policies requiring that only their legal department can draft contracts.

In some organizations, standard contracts drafted by legal counsel are available for your use when needed. Whenever possible, you should use these rather than the contracts submitted by the supplier since they likely offer more specific protection in your circumstances. It is never a good idea to simply sign a contract presented by the supplier.

Legal counsel provides assurance that the contract conforms to applicable law and regulations and that your organization's liability is minimized. In addition to this, you may also want to employ counsel for a number of specific circumstances, such as those listed below:

Intellectual Property Rights   As just discussed, you need to be certain that your organization does not infringe on any IP rights legally granted to others and that you have properly protected its own IP rights through proper disclosure processes.

Legal Venue   Your legal counsel will require language in the contract to determine which state's laws will be considered and in which state's court action will be taken should litigation be required.

This can be quite difficult when dealing with international suppliers. Some countries recognize the rules established by the United Nations Convention on Contracts for the International Sale of Goods (CISG) as discussed in Chapter 3, but others do not. Your counsel may wish to obtain advice from a local attorney in the country in which you are conducting business.

Assignability   Legal review may also be required to ensure that the contract will be transferable to any future business interests your organization may acquire (such as through acquisition, merger, or the creation of a subsidiary) and, at the same time, limit the supplier's ability to transfer the contract without prior approval.

Insurance   For some contracts, you will want to be certain that the supplier carries the proper insurance, such as workmen's compensation, so that additional liability does not accrue to your organization. Legal counsel will often require that you obtain copies of the supplier's certificate of insurance as evidence that it is in place. In some cases, in addition to insurance, a performance bond may be required. These bonds are usually purchased to insure against the buyer's loss should the supplier default in providing the agreed upon services.

Reviews and Claims   Under certain circumstances, you may wish to include a process for review should there be a dispute regarding the contract. This benefits both parties. Reviews are generally a form of mediation and often simply refer questions and decisions to more senior management or to corresponding company counsel. In government environments, however, the process is generally more formal and will often involve an actual review board convened for the express purpose of reviewing supplier protests and claims.

Parol Evidence   The rule of *parol evidence* prevents the use of oral testimony to alter a written contract. This means that any oral promises made by the supplier during the contracting process must be put in writing or they will not apply. Only the written contract can be used as evidence of an agreement. As a result, it is extremely important to review the deliverables with legal counsel to ensure that all commitments are accurately reflected in the document.

You should be certain that this is clearly written into your contract to avoid disputes when field personnel become involved and begin to make *ad hoc* changes.

Reservation of Rights   Your legal counsel will also want to similarly review any clauses that specifically limit your organization's rights to the full performance of the contract. This will include a requirement that no changes can be made in the contract without the express consent of the buyer.

Liability Limitations   Suppliers typically want to limit liability to replacement of a product or service under the terms of the warranty. Depending on the circumstances, however, this may limit your organization's rights to claim *incidental damages* such as transportation or special handling costs. In some cases, *consequential damages*—including lost revenue or profit, damage to property, or injury to persons—may be in order. Clauses covering these conditions are often contentious and best left in the hands of your attorney.

Liquidated Damages   It will often be impossible to calculate the actual monetary damage or loss suffered under certain circumstances. In such situations, the parties will agree to a predetermined amount—known as liquidated damages—to be paid in the event of default. This is also a contentious process and so requires input from legal counsel. It is important to determine a reasonable amount for damages in any particular case so that it will be upheld if the argument goes to court.

Regulated Materials   Laws governing the transportation, use, and disposal of regulated and hazardous materials, such as the Toxic Substances Control Act (1976) and the Resource Conservation and Recovery Act (1976), require special attention since these substances can create exceptional liability for your organization. Special legal and technical expertise is definitely required when dealing contractually with any material that might fall under these regulations. These are high risk areas and, at the minimum, require that the roles and responsibilities of the parties be clearly defined.

Force Majeure *Force majeure* identifies acts or events that are outside the control of the parties involved, such as wars, natural disasters, strikes, and the like. Typically, either one or both parties to a contract are relieved of performance when such uncontrollable actions occur and are not held liable for damages. It is important, however, to be certain proper legal language is included in your contract since there are no automatic provisions covering this.

Aligning Contracts and Practices with Policy

Most organizations maintain a set of documents governing the practices conducted by the Purchasing Department. These usually take the form of written policies or operating procedures. They are designed to provide effective guidance in the conduct of activities so that employees understand their obligations to the organization. In scope, these policies and procedures vary, but they typically cover elements such as purchasing authority, supplier management, quality standards, record retention, conformance to law, and good business and ethical practices.

The purchasing manager is expected to bring to the job sufficient expertise to interpret and enforce these policies and may expect to be called upon for input when they are being created or revised. In some organizations, the purchasing manager will have the additional responsibility of actually writing and maintaining the purchasing portion of organizational policy.

Conformance to Law

At the minimum, organizations are required to conform to antitrust, environmental, and health and safety laws. As you will recall, antitrust regulations were covered in Chapter 3, and some of the laws covering environmental and health and safety processes were outlined above. In addition, there are numerous laws governing intellectual property (which we discussed earlier in this chapter), and there are rules governing confidentiality such as the *Uniform Trade Secrets Act (UTSA)* that define rights for particular trade secrets. As a purchasing professional, you will be required to have a working knowledge of all of these laws and regulations.

In addition, you should become familiar with the activities and regulations of certain governmental agencies that are empowered to protect the rights and welfare of the general population. One of these organizations, the Environmental Protection Agency (EPA), is charged with enforcing federal laws relating to hazardous materials, clean air and water, and waste disposal. Many of the regulations and laws enforced by this agency carry criminal charges if violated, so you should become very familiar with their overall requirements.

The Occupational Safety and Health Act (OSHA) gives rise to a variety of rules and regulations governing safety in the workplace. Under certain circumstances, your organization will want to include a clause in its contracts that essentially shifts the burden of compliance to the supplier. A clause in the contract requiring compliance with applicable laws is generally sufficient protection, but it must be crafted by legal counsel since regulations are quite formal in this area.

Ethical Principles

The Institute for Supply Management (ISM) maintains a set of ethical standards for the supply management profession titled Principles and Standards of Ethical Supply Management Conduct. These are excellent guidelines to use as a basis for your organization's business ethics policy and as individual guidelines for the purchasing staff. In light of continuing scandals involving the questionable integrity of corporate officers and the subsequent U.S. requirements for reporting imposed by the Sarbanes-Oxley Act, we cannot emphasize enough the importance that you understand, adopt, and strictly adhere to the covenants of viable code of ethics.

Here are some areas that should be of particular concern:

Conflict of Interest   A conflict of interest occurs when purchasing employees conduct the organization's business in such manner as to further their own personal gain or that of their families and friends. This includes providing insider tips on activities that would affect the price of stock, or buying and selling from relatives. It also includes owning a share of any organization that conducts business with the organization that employs you.

Bribes   It is illegal to accept *bribes* and *gratuities* in the form of money or any other valuable goods or services with the intent to influence decisions. You probably understand this. However, it is important to also understand that even the perception of unethical conduct must always be avoided. This includes accepting frequent meals and entertainment from suppliers or any gifts that could be considered to have even nominal value. In a position of financial trust, one must exercise impeccable judgment.

Similarly, it is also illegal for the buyer to offer bribes to others. Although in some countries, gratuities are customary for work performed in the normal course of duties, it is clearly a violation of U.S. law to offer a bribe to any government or business official to influence a decision, regardless of the country in which it takes place.

Personal Purchases   Be certain that any purchases you make for your personal use from a supplier conforms to the organization's policy and that it is fair to the supplier and others in your organization. Some organizations encourage this as a means of supporting valued suppliers and gaining benefit for their employees; others look upon it as a conflict of interest.

Proprietary Information   You will be expected to maintain confidentiality at all times and to protect the *proprietary information* in the possession of your organization, regardless of its ultimate ownership. This includes maintaining the confidentiality of plans and intentions. If you must disclose information to a supplier or other third party in the normal course of your business, be certain that you obtain a signed confidentiality agreement or non-disclosure agreement before so doing.

ISM provides excellent references for codes of ethics in their Principles of Social Responsibility and Principles and Standards of Ethical Supply Management Conduct. You can find these documents on the ISM website at www.ISM.ws.

Maintaining Purchasing Documents and Records

To comply with standard records retention programs and legal processes, you are required to know how to maintain certain documents and for what specific period of time they must be retained. Some of the requirements are mandated by law (such as those outlined by the IRS) while others are based on organizational policy and sound business practices. Keep in mind that it is equally important to know when *not* to keep documents as it is to know when they should be kept. There is no inherent value to storing records that will never require access if it is not a legal or regulatory requirement. You must ask if the records are worth the cost and space of storage and if you want to keep them on site or at a third party storage facility. You must also determine if they should be kept in printed format or in electronic media.

Not all documents related to contracts and POs will be maintained by the Purchasing Department. In some organizations, it is common for the Legal Department to hold all documents related to written contracts. Also, equipment records and related drawings are often kept by the using department. However, it is more typical to find that most of these are stored by the Purchasing Department if they are related to purchasing activities.

Examples of the kind of records generated and maintained by the Purchasing Department include:

Purchase Orders and Contracts   This includes quotes and acknowledgement history. POs and contracts are typically filed by *open orders* (those that are still active) and *closed orders* (those that have been fully received or have expired). Today, of course, many of these records are being maintained electronically and require no filing space.

POs are kept for a six-year period (following their expiration) as required by most taxing authorities, including the U.S. Internal Revenue Service (IRS). The UCC, it should be noted, only requires that POs for goods be kept for a four-year period.

Supplier Qualification Records and Periodic Reviews   These are historical records containing the original qualification data and supplier ratings and reviews. They are typically maintained as long as the supplier is active. Also included here might be the records of previous negotiations. All of these records are retained in accordance with organizational policy.

Catalogs   These are generally maintained in a central library, although it is becoming less common for organizations to keep printed catalogs because so many are available online or in electronic format. This media certainly reduces the storage and filing requirements and is preferred since it is typically more up to date. Electronic catalogs also do not vanish, as do some of their more popular paper counterparts.

Inventory Records   These records, such as traveling requisitions and historical ordering data by part, are also likely to be found in many Purchasing Departments. Commonly today, these records are maintained on computer systems. These are kept for a relatively short period of time and only as required by organizational policy.

Project Files   These files are kept when appropriate and when they are for projects led by the Purchasing Department, such as cost reduction or quality improvement programs. These are also kept for a relatively short period of time and only as required by organizational policy.

It may be worth mentioning that records are stored in a variety of formats, including paper and electronic media such as tape, floppy disks, and CDs. In some environments, they are also stored on microfilm (or microfiche). From a record retention and legal perspective, the media should make little or no difference to the storage policy.

Summary

One of the primary responsibilities of the Purchasing Department involves creating and issuing purchase orders. Since contracts (and, of course, POs) are considered legally binding documents, the purchasing manager must become familiar with the basic principles of contract formation. These principles are founded on the basic requirements that are needed in order for a contract to be legally binding: mutual agreement, legal purpose, consideration, and the capacity to enter into a contract.

There are numerous types of standard purchasing contract types available based primarily on payment schema. Contracts generally fall into two major categories, fixed price and cost reimbursable. To a large extent, the payment method selected determines the way that risk is shared between the contracting parties. In addition to these major categories, agreements are commonly developed for licensing intellectual property, maintaining confidentiality, leasing buildings and equipment, and consigning goods.

Buyers, as agents, are granted certain legal authority to commit the organization to a contract, but with this authority also generates a measure of fiduciary responsibility to the employer. It is important, therefore, that in complex situations you seek legal review and proper approval prior to signature. It is also important that you align your contracts to conform to applicable law and organization policy. Today, ethical behavior is one of the key issues in business and it is critical that you understand your obligations. A good reference point is the Principles and Standards of Ethical Supply Management Conduct, a set of ethical standards published by the *Institute for Supply Management (ISM)*.

Finally, you are also responsible for maintaining and retaining files and records commonly associated with purchasing activities. You should become familiar with your organization's policy regarding records retention.

For additional reading on topics related to this chapter, please see Appendix A.

Exam Essentials

Be able to prepare and execute purchase orders and contracts.   You will need to know what constitutes a contract and when a contract is required by the UCC or the Statute of Frauds. You will also need to know the differences between various types of POs and contracts and the requirements for selecting specific types.

Understand the basic elements required for contract formation.   For a contract to be legally enforceable, it must demonstrate the presence of specific principles, including mutual agreement, legal purpose, consideration, and the capacity to enter into a contract.

Know the principles governing legal authority and the buyers' responsibilities.   As an agent of the organization, you will be required to know the principles of agency and the authority of the buyer with respect to conducting typical purchasing activities. You should also understand how this authority creates a fiduciary responsibility to your organization.

Determine when to obtain legal review.   Because you are not a practicing attorney, you may not be familiar with the nuances and precedents of the law governing commercial contracts. A host of special clauses must be carefully worded and included in contracts under specific circumstances. Thus it is important you seek legal review of any contract not already approved by legal counsel.

Understand when legal requirements govern your purchases.   At the minimum, you should be aware of a number of legal requirements that, in addition to the UCC, the Statute of Frauds, and antitrust laws, govern the activities that may be associated with purchasing goods and services. These include the Uniform Trade Secrets Act, EPA regulations, and the laws governing hazardous materials, as well as those associated with OSHA.

Know the ethical principles that govern purchasing activities.   You are required to know the ethical principles governing conflict of interest. In addition, you need to understand the rules regarding bribery and issuing gratuities as well as those covering the disclosure of proprietary information. Two excellent references are the Institute for Supply Management's codes of ethics, Principles of Social Responsibility and Principles and Standards of Ethical Supply Management Conduct.

Be able to distinguish record types and maintain records retention policies.   You are required to know the various types of records generated and received by the Purchasing Department, what organizational policies and legal requirements cover them, who maintains them, and for what period of time they must be kept.

Review Questions

1. Issuance and management of purchasing contracts and documents generate what type of obligations?

   A. Uniform Commercial Code

   B. Audit trail

   C. Business and economic

   D. Time and materials

   E. Legal and financial

2. Records required by the IRS should be kept by your organization for a period of:

   A. Six years

   B. Five years

   C. Four years

   D. Forever

3. The Statute of Frauds requires certain types of contracts be validated in written form for all of the following *except*:

   A. Sales or transfers of real estate

   B. Goods sold under the UCC exceeding $1,000

   C. Contracts that cannot be completed within one year

   D. Goods sold under the UCC exceeding $500

   E. When assuming the debt or duty of another

4. When written contracts are required at a minimum, all of the following elements are required *except*:

   A. A clearly identified subject of the contract

   B. Specific terms and conditions

   C. Identification of the consideration

   D. Delivery dates

   E. Some form of signature

5. When it can be shown that reliance on an oral promise will produce substantial or unconscionable injury to the promisee or will unjustly enrich the promisor, it is an example of:

   A. Mutual agreement

   B. Promissory Estoppel

   C. Unilateral contract

   D. Detrimental reliance

   E. Bilateral contract

6. Four key elements must to be included in a contract for it to be legally enforceable. They include all of the following *except*:

   A. Mutual agreement

   B. Counteroffer

   C. Capacity

   D. Consideration

   E. Legality

7. Indefinite delivery contracts are also called:

   A. Blanket purchase orders

   B. Open purchase orders

   C. Purchase orders

   D. Take or pay contracts

   E. Flexible contracts

8. Legally protected intellectual property includes all of the following *except*:

   A. Patents

   B. Contracts

   C. Copyrights

   D. Trademarks

   E. Service marks

9. Which of the following are considered illegal under U.S. law?

   A. Cost reimbursable contracts

   B. Payment to obtain a contract

   C. Incentive contracts

   D. Fixed-price with economic price adjustment contracts

   E. Tips and gratuities

10. If a buyer approves a purchase order significantly in excess of their spending authority, the order must be:

   A. Ignored by the supplier

   B. Declared null and void

   C. Rescinded by your organization

   D. Revoked by the UCC

   E. Honored by your organization

Answers to Review Questions

1. E. Procurement contracts and documents are used to evidence the parties' agreements and to establish the agreed upon basis for payment, so they affect legal and financial issues.

2. A. The Internal Revenue Department regulates that organizations maintain records for six years for auditing purposes.

3. B. Contracts for goods that exceed $500 must be in writing. If a contract is for real estate, the assumption of a debt or duty of another, or a contract that cannot be completed within one year, the contract must be in writing to meet the Statute of Frauds.

4. D. Delivery dates are not a required item for a written contract to be valid, although they are typically included within a Purchase Order document.

5. D. Detrimental reliance indicates a promisee's reliance to an oral contract that will cause substantial or unconscionable injury. All other items are elements or types of contracts or are not issues relative to a promisee's reliance to an oral contract. Promissory Estoppel indicates reliance on an oral promise, but that reliance will not produce substantial or unconscionable injury to the promisee.

6. B. A counteroffer is a modification of the original offer by the offeree and has nothing to do with the elements of a contract.

7. A. Blanket purchase orders, also known as indefinite delivery and requirements contracts, are used when the buyer wishes to establish set pricing and terms but does not yet wish to place orders for specific quantities or delivery times.

8. B. Contracts, while at times considered confidential, are not considered intellectual property by the U.S. Patent and Trademark Office.

9. B. Payment to obtain a contract is considered bribery. Bribery is illegal under U.S. law.

10. E. Under the rule of apparent authority, the buyer has the authority to issue binding purchase orders. Spending limits are an internal matter to be determined by organizational policy.

Chapter 5

Administering Contracts for Supplier Compliance

THE C.P.M. EXAM SPECIFICATIONS COVERED IN THIS CHAPTER INCLUDE THE FOLLOWING:

- ✓ Managing contract compliance
- ✓ Tracking and expediting deliveries
- ✓ Handling supplier-related deviations

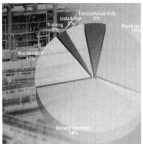

Administering contracts to ensure supplier compliance is a very important responsibility of the Purchasing Department.

The central focal point for contract compliance is meeting the requirements of the internal customer. Purchasing departments do not usually have the resources to closely manage the hundreds of suppliers to the organization, nor would it make sense for its staff to even try to do so since rarely will the Purchasing Department be staffed with the same level of expertise as the using or customer department. Instead, you can be best served by relying on your internal customers, those employees and departments directly responsible for the supplier's performance, for day-to-day operational information such as quality evaluations and on-time delivery reports. Using this information, you will be able to conduct periodic business reviews with key suppliers to help them understand areas for improvement and how they can best achieve stronger performance. This is the essence of *Supplier Relationship Management (SRM)*, a term recently coined to describe the activities related to monitoring and improving supplier performance. Integrated with the broader picture will be the Purchasing Department's daily tactical activities that revolve around tracking and expediting deliveries as well as responding to supplier-related discrepancies.

In this chapter, you will review the broader concepts of contract administration including how the purchasing manager can establish proactive measures to ensure supplier compliance and internal customer satisfaction within the framework of existing contracts. In doing so, you will also review how to deal with problems relating to supplier payments and how change orders can affect contract terms and conditions.

Managing Contract Compliance

The purchasing manager routinely oversees the management of contract administration and supplier relations. Part of this responsibility is to ensure that the terms and conditions of the contract are followed, especially where they may diminish the value of the contract to the organization. Another part involves the continuing effort to improve supplier performance and to maintain strong business relationships. While no purchasing manager can be an expert in all areas of the profession, you should constantly strive to provide solid advisement and purchasing authority to your organization's suppliers. Handling potential problems early and in a proactive mode will go a long way to diffusing problems before they become major issues.

Post Purchase Order Administration

Much of the Purchasing Department's responsibility lies in the ongoing management of the purchase order or contract after it has been negotiated and placed with the supplier. This is very much of an organic process that takes on a life of its own, which often involves lots of routine work that generally fills much of the buyers' day. To be successful, the purchasing manager must set a firm, proactive approach to monitoring day-to-day activities within the context of continuing fiduciary due diligence, ensuring that internal users receive the benefit of the bargain in good faith. Success will also depend in large part on the effective involvement of the using department and those most familiar with the specific requirements of the contract.

In the following section, you will review many of the routine duties associated with the activities of managing supplier performance to ensure that their contractual obligations are being met.

Ensuring Supplier Performance

Administering any contract can be a complex, dynamic process requiring skillful attention to detail and thorough familiarity with its objectives and terms and conditions. Therefore, it is important for your internal customers to understand that it is their responsibility to inform you or your staff of any discrepancies or areas of dissatisfaction. You may be able to help them understand this process by reviewing some key contract administration principles with them prior to the contract's actual implementation:

- Clearly define roles and responsibilities in advance so that you can work as a coordinated team.

- Read and understand the contract's requirements. Be certain that the actions you take are in line with its terms and conditions.

- Develop a checklist of areas for periodic review to avert potential problems early.

- Maintain a sound, business-like relationship with the supplier, instituting clear lines of communication and conflict resolution and avoiding reactive positions.

- Anticipate areas that may require change, and develop an understanding of potential cost implications.

- Resolve problems quickly before they escalate or create major issues.

During the course of the contract, and for supplier performance in general, you and core members of the cross functional Supplier Management Team will likely want to monitor a number of key deliverables for specific performance. Some of the elements critical to successful contract fulfillment include compliance with cost objectives, on-time delivery performance, adherence to quality requirements, and accurate reporting. Specifics on how these elements can be controlled and periodically reviewed by the affected groups are covered in the section on Supplier Relationship Management later in this chapter.

Often, a project management approach to contract compliance can establish a framework and timetable to monitor performance, providing a useful reporting mechanism as well. Figure 5.1 shows a simple timeline approach using a *Gantt chart* that graphically tracks the progress of the project by illustrating on a calendar when events are scheduled to take place, how long they will take and when they are expected to complete. The Gantt chart also shows the relationship between events, especially which events must complete first before others that are dependent upon them can start. for monitoring contract development and initial performance phases. You may also find this method useful for monitoring improvement programs.

FIGURE 5.1 Timeline for contract development

	❶	Task Name	Duration	Start	Finish
1		− Finalize SOW	30 days?	Wed 5:18:05	Tue 6/28/05
2		Organize existing RFP material	5 days	Wed 5/18/05	Tue 5/24/05
3		Determine RFP Structure	2 days?	Wed 5/25/05	Thu 5/26/05
4		Refine language and create SOW	5 days	Fri 5/27/05	Thu 6/2/05
5		Finalize SOW	5 days	Fri 6/3/05	Thu 6/9/05
6		Develop SLA and KPIs	5 days	Fri 6/10/05	Thu 6/16/05
7		Submit budget	4 days	Fri 6/10/05	Wed 6/15/05
8		Legal review	5 days	Fri 6/17/05	Thu 6/23/05
9		Management approval	3 days	Fri 6/24/05	Tue 6/28/05
10		− Implementation Planning	17 days?	Fri 6/10/05	Mon 7/4/05
11		Identify process steps	3 days	Fri 6/10/05	Tue 6/14/05
12		Identify transition steps	3 days	Wed 6/15/05	Fri 6/17/05
13		Identify additional scope	1 day?	Mon 6/20/05	Mon 6/20/05
14		Develop full transition timeline	5 days	Tue 6/21/05	Mon 6/27/05
15		Management Approval	5 days	Tue 6/28/05	Mon 7/4/05
16		Finalize Contract and Issue PO	1 day?	Thu 8/21/03	Thu 8/21/03
17		− Performance Management	23 days	Tue 7/5/05	Thu 8/4/05
18		Finalize SOPs	3 days	Tue 7/5/05	Thu 7/7/05
19		Manage/Monitor Performance	20 days	Fri 7/8/05	Thu 8/4/05
20		Establish Performance Review to Goals	7 days	Fri 7/8/05	Mon 7/18/05

Maintaining a complete file of reports and correspondence covering actual supplier performance will be useful for conducting subsequent business reviews and for resolving any disputes should they arise. Include in these files progress reports, notes from important meetings, change and amendment history, a log of issues and customer feedback. In the case of ongoing supplier monitoring, records will include the history and details of periodic reviews and documentation of ongoing improvements.

Processing Change Orders

Having to process change orders is a typical event during the course of any contract. Formal change orders involving revised specifications or additional requirements are monitored and documented through processes known by a number of names, such as *Engineering Change Order (ECO)* or *Specification Change Order (SCO)*. Usually, these changes are tracked and recorded by the Document Control Department or through the Quality Engineering Group. However, your responsibility will likely include negotiating the cost implications and effect on the delivery timetable with the supplier.

In addition to engineering-generated changes, amendments to the contract are sometimes required to reflect an additional scope of work, such as adding new areas of responsibility to the supplier's duties or redefining a completion timeline.

A seasoned procurement practitioner is aware of the likelihood of ongoing changes to the contract and negotiates the process in advance, maintaining an awareness of the competitive bidding trap (discussed in Chapter 3, "Selecting Suppliers and Measuring Performance") where the supplier under-prices the initial contract with an expectation of added profit margin from the inevitable change orders once the contract has been agreed to by the parties. Generally, the mechanics of implementing changes, including allocating their financial impact, can be outlined in the initial contract so that the process works smoothly. To a large extent, this is the responsibility of the Purchasing Department representative leading the contract negotiation team and is well facilitated when following the guidelines for internal customer review just provided.

Price Adjustments

Firm-fixed-price-contracts require pricing adjustments only when changes in the specifications or scope of work occur. However, many contracts—especially those developed in government procurement—require price adjustments and fee payments based upon a wide range of conditions and the nature of the contract. (We outlined contract types in Chapter 4, "Administering Contracts.") Most common of these are the economic price adjustments required by escalation contracts or changes in the rates determining baselines in the cost-plus contracts. You will have already defined how and when such changes can be applied in the initial contract and will have linked them to a change in a specific index or a predetermined cost factor.

In most circumstances, escalation changes will be documented by changes in predetermined pricing such as the cost of labor (in union environments) or materials. Often fluctuations in these cannot be known in advance and so a contract clause will allow for increases (rarely decreases) to the cost basis beyond a preset trigger threshold. Similarly, when purchasing through international sources, contracts will allow for cost fluctuations based on a predetermined currency exchange rate.

Sometimes the cost basis will be adjusted by increases or decreases in specific published indices governing labor or materials. Transportation rates, for example, are often based on fuel pricing from a published index and passed through to the buyer as a fuel surcharge.

Warranty Claims

A *warranty* is a seller's guarantee to the buyer that if the product or materials being sold does not perform as specified, the seller will take a particular remedial action. Most frequently, the remedy will be to replace the products at the seller's expense. The buyer should be aware of the contractual rights granted by a warranty and practice diligence in exercising those rights.

Warranties and limitations of liability are generally the source of much negotiation during the contract formation process. To reduce their unknown financial exposure, suppliers will generally want to limit their warranties to a specific (and narrow) set of conditions and for a limited time. Often, warranty clauses are taken for granted and not specifically negotiated, becoming additional grist for the battle of the forms.

The UCC specifically allows a seller to disclaim any or all warranties, but it does not provide any specific rules or guidelines as to how the warranty should be disclaimed. Because of this, the buyer must be aware of the actual language being used to reference or convey the warranty in any particular case. Generally, the seller is required to include a statement specifically disclaiming an actual warranty, such as all goods are sold "as is." Terms such as "no warranties, express or implied" are generally insufficient to disclaim a specific warranty.

Sections 2-312 through 2-318 of the UCC cover commercial warranties for goods and products. Under the UCC, warranties fall into two classifications: express warranties and implied warranties. Let's discuss the more important aspects of each of these in more detail.

Express Warranties

Express warranties provide specific assurances regarding the performance of a product or service. Typically, they are explicitly spelled out within the framework of the contract or purchase order. Created by the words or actions of a seller, an express warranty can be provided either through a specific promise or the description of the product. An affirmative statement or a sample of the product can be considered as the basis for a warranty.

Implied Warranties

An *implied warranty* is provided by rule under the UCC simply by offering goods or products for sale, even when there is no mention of how the product will be expected to perform. As its title suggests, the warranty need not be stated; rather it is implicit in the offer or acceptance by the seller. The intent of this warranty is to allow buyers to purchase goods and products with reasonable assurance that they will meet certain inherent and basic requirements.

The UCC creates two distinct types of implied warranties: merchantability and fitness for a particular purpose.

Merchantability   *Merchantability* means that the seller implicitly warrants that the product is fit and suited to be used for the ordinary purposes for which it would be purchased. It also implies that it is of average quality and performs the basic functions that may be stated by the manufacturer.

The UCC does not intend for a seller to create an implied warranty for goods not normally sold in its regular course of business. For example, a manufacturer of molded plastic parts does not create an implied warranty when it sells one of its obsolete molding machines to another business.

Fitness for a Particular Purpose   *Fitness for a particular purpose* means that if the seller knows (or has reason to know) the intended use by the buyer for the goods being sold, the seller then warrants that the goods will be suitable for that purpose. A seller, therefore, may not knowingly sell a product that will not do the job and then refute responsibility. In effect, this means that the buyer may rely upon the seller's expertise in selecting a suitable product and seek remedy should the product not perform as intended.

As in the case of merchantability, the seller need only warrant goods that it would convey during the usual course of its business.

Disclaimers

As noted earlier, sellers may disclaim warranties in writing if the writing is specific enough to describe the conditions not being warranted. In addition, the disclaimer needs to be conspicuous and stand out from other portions of the contract. That is why you will often see disclaimers written in bold or capital lettering. However, the UCC indicates that a buyer must have some recourse if the goods received are defective or unusable, and so the seller cannot enforce a clause that takes all the rights away from the buyer.

Figure 5.2 illustrates a liability disclaimer from the State of California's Department of Consumer Affairs web page. Under the area titled Disclaimer of Warranties/Accuracy, you'll notice it disclaims express and implied warranties by specific reference. This disclaimer also uses capital letters that stand out conspicuously to state the legal requirements of the warranty.

FIGURE 5.2   Sample disclaimer of warranty and language

Disclaimer of Warranties/Accuracy and Use of Data/Computer Viruses
Although the data found using the Department of Consumer Affairs' Home Page access systems have been produced and processed from sources believed to be reliable, no warranty expressed or implied is made regarding accuracy, adequacy, completeness, legality, reliability or usefulness of any information. This disclaimer applies to both isolated and aggregate uses of the information. The Department of Consumer Affairs and the Department of Consumer Affairs' Home Page provide this information on an "AS IS" basis. All warranties of any kind, express or implied, including but not limited to the IMPLIED WARRANTIES OF MERCHANTABILITY, FITNESS FOR A PARTICULAR PURPOSE, freedom from contamination by computer viruses and non-infringement of proprietary rights ARE DISCLAIMED. Changes may be periodically added to the information herein; these changes may or may not be incorporated in any new version of the publication. If the user has obtained information from The Department of Consumer Affairs' Home Page from a source other than The Department of Consumer Affairs' Home Page, the user must be aware that electronic data can be altered subsequent to original distribution. Data can also quickly become out-of-date. It is recommended that the user pay careful attention to the contents of any metadata associated with a file, and that the originator of the data or information be contacted with any questions regarding appropriate use. If the user finds any errors or omissions, we encourage the user to report them to the Department of Consumer Affairs' Home Page Webmaster.

©2004 State of California

Supplier Relationship Management (SRM)

Contract management also requires the use of Supplier Relationship Management (SRM) methodology, as well. SRM is the broad process of aligning the goals of your organization and the supplier community, one supplier at a time. Often, this is a process of tactically aligning the typical variation in processes between several organizations using analysis, collaboration, and jointly developed action plans.

In its automated format, SRM can be seen as a way of gathering information from multiple procurement systems in order to develop metrics that measure and evaluate supplier performance. Inherent in the measurement process, however, is the discipline of continuous improvement, the methodology for developing and implementing ongoing improvements in business and operational processes to achieve a specific goal. Let's discuss the elements of SRM in more detail.

Monitoring Performance

Expected supplier performance levels are generally included in the general terms and conditions, product specifications (in the case of goods), or in the statement of work (in the case of services) for any given purchase. Often referred to as service levels, they can also be included in a separate addendum to the contract known as a Service Level Agreement (SLA). Within the SLA, *metrics* (sometimes referred to as Key Performance Indicators, or KPIs, as we discussed in Chapter 1) are included to define the expected performance of the supplier.

Performance measures by themselves have little intrinsic value, so they are generally reviewed in terms of actual progress toward a specific goal or compared with a stated baseline standard. For example, if you are measuring cost reduction, you might indicate a KPI in terms of dollars per part or dollars per hour. Your goal would likely be stated in these same terms or perhaps as a percentage reduction. In this way, data and assessments can help reduce spending and risk and to improve operations in quality, delivery, and service—the key goals of the supply management process.

In many organizations, supplier performance monitoring is automated through the use of some software system. Organizational procedures generally define what types of monitoring techniques are to be used and the frequency of reporting. The purchasing and quality teams then implement a supplier review process through regular meetings, site visits, product testing, and customer surveys to determine where gaps exist in reaching the desired objective. Once gaps are identified, the next phase of enhancing supplier performance is the execution of corrective action plans.

Managing Supplier Activities

In general, a fairly wide variation exists within the scope of typical supplier activities, and you may find that in your organization only the key elements of their duties are actually being measured on a routine basis. Yet, as a buyer or purchasing manager, the responsibility for ensuring that all supplier commitments are met will be yours. With hundreds of suppliers and thousands of events taking place daily, how can you possibly manage them all?

There are several ways you might consider for managing a broad scope of activities such as the following:

Management by Exception   One method of managing supplier activities relies on an automated reporting system and alerts you only when exceptions to the required standard occur. This is called *management by exception*. You receive notification only when events occur outside of the expected range of possibilities. For example, if you use a computer-based system for documenting receipts, you may be able to get notification of late deliveries whenever shipment are overdue by a specific amount of time.

Input from Internal Users   You might solicit regular input from your internal users, either through surveys or through direct reporting methods. Or you might consider spending time with the users of the materials and services you purchase. This way, you observe the problems when they actually occur and from the perspective of your customer. It helps you understand the impact of actual failures (or successes) and enables you to better communicate them to your supplier.

Site Visits   It is not uncommon to find buyers monitoring activities directly in the supplier's facility so that they can become more actively involved in resolving issues. As Yogi Berra, the retired coach of the New York Yankee baseball team, once said, "You can observe a lot just by watching."

Reviewing Performance

Performance reviews are generally presented in a report format, outlining the supplier's actual performance to goal or standard for a specific period of time. Often these are conducted in a formal meeting environment and within the framework of a standard predefined agenda. Since extensive reviews are typically very time consuming, it is common to them to critical suppliers and to hold them on a quarterly basis, especially when the supplier's team must travel a long distance to visit your facility. Use of your organization's business review process, in fact, is probably one the most widely accepted formats. Often, these are supplemented with an annual *executive review* where senior managers come together to exchange forthcoming *business plans* and *technology roadmaps*.

The use of a performance *scorecard* is a popular communication method for delivering supplier reviews. The scorecard is a compilation or summary of the supplier's performance to the pre-established metrics called for in the Service Level Agreement. It is common to generalize performance into categories such as quality, cost, on-time-delivery, and service on the scorecard, touching on the high points and low points of actual results.

It is important that you also allow time to obtain supplier feedback on problems from the supplier's perspective and to garner ideas on how your organization can better align their processes. While you want to avoid reducing the process to a sales presentation, you should also consider asking for feedback on how the supplier feels it can better serve you.

Developing Performance Improvements

While many variations of continuous improvement exist, the basic steps are fairly well-defined:

1. Analyze existing conditions.
2. Determine the gaps that exist between the actual conditions and the desired state.
3. Develop plans to eliminate (or reduce) the gaps.
4. Implement the plan.
5. Measure improvements.
6. Repeat the cycle.

These steps are generally conducted within the framework of a *commodity management* team that is sponsored by the *business unit* leader. We've found it useful to manage improvement initiatives as projects, using Gantt charts and assigning specific actions and timelines to individual team members. This creates both accountability and a sense of understanding of all the elements that are required to make the project successful.

The identification of business process gaps that have a financial ramification to an organization, along with the identification of a plan to remedy the gaps, is a key element of the Sarbanes-Oxley Act of 2002, Section 404, which we discussed in Chapter 1.

Tracking and Expediting Deliveries

In the normal course of daily routine, supplier shipments will not meet their required delivery dates. Sometimes this is due to errors or damages in shipments; other times it is due to factors such as production delays, miscommunication of requirements or just Murphy's Law. In any event, as a supplier manager you will be required to assist in resolving them and to handle the communications between the supplier and your internal customers. Two of the most frequent situations that will require your intervention, dealing with shipments and expediting orders, are described in this section.

Tracking and Monitoring Shipments

Fortunately, today most shipping agencies have automated tracking tools that can immediately report the status and whereabouts of virtually any worldwide shipment. Many of these tools can even be accessed through the Web and likely many of you have already used the FedEx or UPS tracking systems to locate parcels.

Lost and damaged shipments require the submission of a claim in order to obtain reimbursement. You will likely find this process takes several weeks, so it is best to reorder immediately, keeping in mind that unless you specifically requested shipping terms that require the supplier to maintain ownership title of the goods until actual delivery, your organization will take ownership of the goods at the time of shipment and it will be your organization's responsibility to file the actual claim with the carrier. In most organizations, however, it will be the Traffic or Receiving Department's responsibility to handle the paperwork, and you will only become involved to the extent that corrective action or expediting is required.

Expediting Orders

Expediting refers to the process of following up with suppliers (through some form of direct contact) to accelerate the shipment of orders or to determine the current status of a particular order and when it will be ready for shipment. It may be counter-intuitive, but expediting provides no additional value whatsoever to the product or service and simply increases the associated overhead cost.

Expediting, however, can be required as the result of numerous circumstances and is fairly commonly used. In case you are wondering why it is necessary, some of the typical reasons for expediting include:

Late Production   You will expect your supplier to communicate with you in situations where your order has not been shipped (or delivered) as expected. You will need to re-establish a delivery date with the supplier, communicate with your internal customer, and determine if there is any way to mitigate the potential damage to your operations. Some situations may require you to follow up further on subsequent shipments to avoid the situation in the future.

Rush Orders   There are times and circumstances that will require you to request shipment in less than the normal time cycle. You may be required to negotiate this with the supplier—offering some future value or additional fees as compensation. We once called a supplier to request a rush status be placed on an existing order. When we made the request to the supplier's customer service representative, she broke out in laughter. We asked what was so funny and she replied, "Which of these six rush orders I have for you would you like me to do first?".

Back Orders   There are occasions when a supplier is only able to ship part of the order by the requested time. This is called a *split order*, and the remaining balance is called a *back order*. While your contract or purchase order may prohibit such practice, you may be willing to bend the rules when you need something urgently rather than see the entire shipment arrive late. You will likely want to flag the order so that you can follow up with the supplier prior to the promised date for shipping the balance to be sure you avoid any further delays.

You may want to consider the methods your organization uses to perform the expediting to ensure you are using the least costly and most effective method. *Status checks*, for example, may

---

Who's Responsible for Expediting Orders?

Although it is most typical for the Purchasing Department to handle expediting as part of the supplier management process, you may want to keep in mind that it is not always the responsibility of the Purchasing Department to handle every circumstance that requires expediting. In some organizations, it is up to the using department to manage this, while in others it may be handled by the inventory planners or the Production Control Department, depending upon their level of involvement. However, the stand-alone job function and title of expeditor is rapidly disappearing from contemporary organizations since we are coming to recognize that prevention is more effective than cure.

---

be performed today through some form of electronic media, such as e-mail, that will use fewer personnel resources, reserving personal contact for the more critical conditions. When expediting seems to become a way of life, it is important to develop a continuous improvement program to reduce or perhaps eliminate it altogether.

Handling Supplier-Related Deviations

There are many circumstances—serious and minor—when you will find suppliers are unable to perform adequately or are creating errors that require corrective action. In some cases, issues can be resolved amicably with little lasting effect on the relationship; in others, legal recourse and a permanent parting of the ways may be in order.

In this section, you will find a review of some of the most common situations involving deviations and the typical ways of handling them.

Dealing with Inadequate Performance

Inadequate performance stems from a wide variety of conditions, some easily remedied while others are more critically serious. The simpler issues can be dealt with by the Purchasing Department; the more complex ones may require the intervention of legal counsel. Most performance issues that we've encountered are a result of a lack of clarity in the contract language and expectations that are not incorporated into writing.

Contract Breach

Typically, a supplier's *breach of contract* will occur when it is unable or unwilling to perform to the terms and conditions required by the contract within the agreed upon time frame. In the case of a shipment of nonconforming goods, however, the supplier has the right to *cure* or remedy the failure in a reasonable amount of time.

The UCC gives the buyer the right to ask the supplier of goods for adequate assurance that it can perform to the contract, should the buyer have reason to suppose that it will be unable to do so. If the supplier does not respond within 30 days, the buyer may then cancel the contract under the principle of *anticipatory breach*.

Similarly, *anticipatory repudiation* occurs in situations where, prior to the time the performance is required, the supplier informs the buyer that it will be unable to perform. This gives the buyer the right to consider the contract breached and act accordingly.

Purchasers' Remedies

When a supplier breaches the contract, it is quite likely that the buyer will suffer some form of damage. Under the UCC, the buyer has the right to be "made whole" for its loss. Several common categories of damages may be appropriately claimed by the buying organization as a result of loss:

Actual Damages   *Actual damages* cover compensation for the real losses that have been incurred in specific circumstances covered by the contract. However, to be recoverable (and enforceable) they must be capable of precise measurement. Actual damages might cover, for instance, the loss of an injection molding tool owned by your organization but stored at the supplier's facility.

Consequential Damages   The legal definition of consequential damages refers to those losses that arise not from the immediate act of the party but in consequence of such act.

Liquidated Damages   *Liquidated damages* provide for a predetermined fixed payment amount in the event of a breach of contract. They typically apply only when the actual damages would have been very difficult or impractical to determine and when the amount of the liquidated damages is reasonable. Courts have generally not enforced a liquidated damages clause when it is intended to be punitive or when it is significantly in excess of a reasonable amount of damages that may have been incurred.

Incidental Damages   Incidental damages cover the reasonable expenses or costs that result from loss or harm, such as the cost of transportation for replacement products.

Cover Damages   Cover damages may be claimed when a contract is breached (in the case of late delivery, for example) and the buyer must purchase replacement goods at a price higher than that contracted with the supplier. In this case, the buying organization may claim the difference between what it would have paid under the contract and what it actually paid.

Purchasers Breach

In addition to the supplier's breach, the UCC also covers the purchaser's breach. The purchasing organization can breach the contract in a number of ways. For example, breach may occur if the buyer wrongfully rejects a conforming shipment upon receipt or later rejects the shipment having first accepted it. In the case of *latent defects* that do not show up on original inspection, the buyer is obligated to provide adequate time for the supplier to fix the problem once it has been discovered. The buyer may also establish anticipatory repudiation when it informs the supplier that it will be unable to accept the goods.

In the case of a purchaser's breach, the seller may also apply for remedies. Typical remedies available to the seller include:

Contract Recovery   The supplier may claim the entire contract value should the buying organization breach, providing that it makes a reasonable and diligent effort to sell the goods to another buyer. Whatever value the supplier may obtain through scrap is discounted from the total amount claimed.

Market Value   The seller may claim the difference between the sale at current market value and the sale to the purchaser.

Recovery of Lost Profits   The supplier may include lost profit in any legal action to recover damages as a result of the purchaser's breach.

Costs   The seller may recover the cost of selling or disposing of the goods to another party in the event of a purchaser's breach.

Liability Issues

Liability in a commercial environment generally refers to the legal responsibility for the cost of damages. It is the Purchasing Department's responsibility to reduce the risk to the organization whenever potential liability exists.

Potential financial liability can be a significant factor for the purchaser when evaluating risk and should be carefully considered during the contract formation process. It is always advisable, when there appears to be potential for significant liability to arise from a contract, to defer to legal counsel for review and the crafting of proper contract language. Similarly, when issues surrounding liability or potential liability actually do arise, it is always advisable to obtain legal advice.

Actual liability can generate from a number of conditions, including, for example, damage to goods during transit, damage from faulty equipment or workmanship, loss of revenue due to associated production delays, loss or damage due to field failure, loss due to the cessation of the supplier's operation or inability to perform, and legal responsibility for violation of public laws and regulations—just to list a few.

Mitigating Loss

The intent of legal language and the UCC is generally to provide for the recovery of actual losses from transactions involving goods and to compensate the party bearing the loss to the extent that it can be made whole again, or restored to its original position. However, documentation becomes critical in order to prove the value of the damages and to ensure adequate recovery.

In this section, we'll highlight some specific factors you should be aware of regarding mitigation of loss.

Limitations

The supplier has the right to limit liability for consequential damages and incidental damages in the contract). You need to be certain that the limitations specified are favorable to your organization.

Hold Harmless

A common clause in contracts is designed to protect the parties from the responsibilities for damages incurred through the violation of any laws or regulations. The term *hold harmless* refers to the language that places the liability for damages on the other party. Supplier contracts will often require that the buyer hold them harmless from any third party suits arising from the performance of its obligations. This is especially contentious in cases where product liability due to loss or injury is involved and where each party has an obligation to indemnify the others when they do not contribute to the liability. It is not uncommon for parties to determine in advance the extent of each party's responsibility and subsequent liability.

Manufactured goods are also subject to the *Consumer Product Safety Act*, which requires reporting of any hazards to the public and to the Consumer Product Safety Commission. It also requires the recall of potentially unsafe products, so the buyer needs to be sure that there is adequate financial compensation when any recall is necessitated by a supplier's defective parts or material.

The supplier should also be required to hold the buyer harmless from any liability arising out of its violation of patent or copyright laws. Since this is an area of great complexity and potentially great financial liability, it is critical that the buying organization obtain maximum indemnification, including the requirement that the supplier defend it from any infringement suits.

Indemnification, Insurance, and Bonds

Another way to limit liability is by requiring suppliers to carry and show proof of adequate insurance when the potential for loss is very high so that your organization receives proper *indemnification* should a loss occur. Most important, of course, is the coverage for worker's compensation, and it is common for buyers to require suppliers that work on site to maintain certain levels of coverage.

Chances are good that your company carries insurance coverage for its property in the event of fire, theft, or loss due to certain natural disasters. You should determine if this coverage applies to property owned by your organization but stored at a supplier's facility (tooling, for instance) and if not, you should require that the property be insured in your organization's favor in the event of loss or damage.

Numerous forms of bonds (a form of insurance) are also available to ensure against contract performance failure, such as when the supplier fails to pay its subcontractors for labor or materials or when the supplier fails to meet the terms of the contract altogether.

Risk of Loss During Transit

The burden of risk resulting from loss or damage during the transportation of goods from the supplier generally depends upon when the title (or ownership) to the goods passes to the buyer. Title passes when the goods are relinquished to the buyer or consigned to a buyer's agent such as a trucking company or a freight forwarder. Transfer is evidenced by a *Bill of Lading* (or similar document) that conveys ownership and describes the goods and their value.

Buyers often confuse the issue of title transfer with the terms of payment for shipping so you want to be certain your purchase orders designate them properly. These are two separate issues. For example, the widely used shipping term *FOB* (literally, Free on Board) indicates that the shipper pays to have the goods transported to the point of shipment. If the goods are transported by water, this is the point at which the goods cross the ship's rail. Thus shipping terms might be designated as FOB Factory, indicating that the buyer will accept the goods at the shipper's factory. This means that title will transfer to your organization when the goods are picked up by the carrier and you will have to pay for the full cost of shipping. Or it might be designated as FOB Destination, meaning that the supplier pays to have the goods shipped to the final destination. If, however, the transportation is by the buyer's freight company, the title will pass when the goods come into their hands. If the transportation is through the seller's transport, the title will pass when the buyer receives the goods. In either case, the seller will pay the freight up to the destination specified on the purchase order.

The general rules covering ownership of materials in transit are specified in Incoterms, the widely-accepted criteria for defining the passage of title in international trade. Purchasing departments are generally aware of these terms and designate them on the face of their purchase orders. The Incoterms website, shown in Figure 5.3, provides an outline of how these terms affect title and thus risk of loss. For more detailed information, you may want to visit the International Chamber of Commerce (ICC) website at `http://www.iccwbo.org`.

FIGURE 5.3   The Incoterms Preamble Webpage

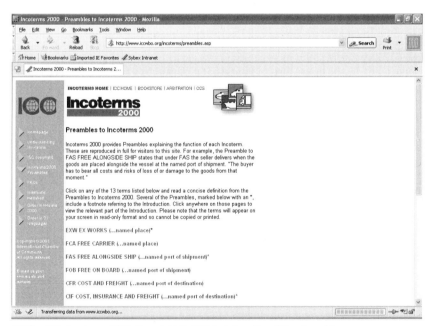

ICC No. 560, Incoterms 2000, Copyright © 1999 by International Chamber of Commerce. All Rights Reserved. Reprinted with the permission of the International Chamber of Commerce through ICC Publishing, Inc., New York, NY.

Resolving Errors and Omissions

There are a myriad of problems that arise during the life of a typical purchase order or contract, generating a significant amount of supplier management duties for the Purchasing Department. Here are some of the more routine problems you will encounter and be required to resolve.

Mistakes

Most errors in order fulfillment come as a result of inaccurate, incomplete, or erroneous descriptions on the PO. When you consider the sheer volume of manual transactions performed by the Purchasing Department, this should come as no surprise. How to eliminate these errors has plagued purchasing managers around the world. Seemingly, the only cure will arrive when all routine transactions are automated through computer-based systems.

While mistakes are part of human nature, the UCC does not recognize the concept of an honest mistake. Case law dealing with court decisions regarding mistakes does not appear to provide a unanimous and clear set of guidelines. However, there a few principles that might be useful to understand:

- For the most part, the courts do not seem inclined to review mistakes that are not considered *material* to the purchase.

- When a supplier acts in reliance of a purchase order that is erroneous, by manufacturing the wrong item, for example, the buyer will likely not be granted any relief. This is called a *unilateral mistake.*

- If a mistake made by the buyer is so obvious that it reasonably should have been discovered by the supplier, relief will usually be granted.

Shipment

Losses due to shipment errors or damages are so common in most organizations that it is often considered a standard element of cost. Indeed, in some organizations thefts during shipment can create a major problem. Despite the efforts of the best minds in logistics, it appears that this issue will continue.

However, there are some specific ways that you can minimize the risk of loss or damage in shipment. They include:

- Use a third party logistics provider to leverage greater volumes for improved service and faster delivery.

- Specify terms that pass title to your organization only upon delivery to your facility. Keep in mind that the passage of title and who pays the freight are two separate specifications.

- Specify your own packaging requirements.

- Require shipment of the entire order prior to payment.

Pricing and Payment Issues

It has been said that the best way to maintain good supplier relations is to pay them on time. It has also been said that the more an organization owes to another, the greater the importance of servicing it becomes. Clearly, we are dealing with a double-edged sword.

It is equally important to pay suppliers in accordance with the contract as it is to refuse unwarranted and unjustified advance payments. Payments should always be made in accordance with some clearly defined event, such as receipt of goods or achievement of a specific milestone. Keep in mind that it is typical practice to invoice buyers upon shipment. If the shipment takes ten days to arrive and you are on payment terms of Net 30 Days, you can improve your organization's cash position by as much as 33 percent through payment terms predicated on the receipt of the goods and not just the invoice.

In many organizations, the rework generated by inaccurate or incomplete invoices can result in horrendous added costs. Eliminating these problems should be a key focus for continuous improvement. One company we know of rejects about 30 percent of the incoming invoices due to errors in pricing or in simply failing to include the PO number so that payment can be tied to a specific order. With volumes in excess of 5,000 invoices per month, you can just imagine the additional cost this generates.

It is standard practice in most organizations to pay suppliers for returned materials and then wait until a credit memo is issued to the buyer. Unfortunately, many organizations fail to recognize who needs to do the follow-up to ensure that the credit is actually issued. If you are in a position to write purchasing procedures, be sure to include this step, otherwise you may have no assurance that the credit has actually been issued.

Overages can also present billing problems. Does your organization have a clearly defined policy for the percentage or value of overruns that are acceptable? Is it prominently displayed on the face of your purchase order? If not, you are an easy target for cost overruns due to an overly aggressive sales agent.

Here are some of the other issues with payments you will likely encounter:

- Late payments that generate credit holds. Payments are often delayed by a manual sign-off process or invoices are incorrectly entered into the accounts payable system or, worse, lost.

- Purchase order and receiving documents cannot be matched. Often, the supplier uses one nomenclature or part number while your organization uses another. Aligning the two systems can pay off for both.

- Invoices and POs do not match due to price variations. This can be avoided through the use of automated catalogs and through buyer diligence in obtaining quotes prior to placing the order.

Resolving Supplier Conflicts

Conflicts are normal in any relationship. How you resolve your conflicts, however, can determine the quality of your relationship with suppliers. Through the judicious use of continuous improvement processes, you may be able to significantly reduce them and so foster even better relationships with your suppliers.

Best practices in contract compliance require a highly evolved, proactive approach to conflict resolution. To accomplish this, you must have precise and legally compliant documentation of your processes. You should review a number of key areas regularly to determine how well actual processes conform to standard operating procedures and legal requirements. Some specific areas for your attention such as contract modifications, rejection of non-conforming goods, termination and dispute resolution are outlined in the following section.

Contract Modifications

Modifications and changes to a contract will likely occur throughout its life to fit changing requirements and market conditions. A modification, under the UCC, is typically treated differently from the original contract formation and does not require the presence of some of the key factors, such as consideration, that must be evident during the initial formation phase.

In the event that both parties are at general odds regarding the terms and conditions of a particular contract, they may simply decide to rescind it and renegotiate a new one. If it is discovered that a mutual mistake or fraud has occurred, the court may decide that reforming the contract is in the best interest of both parties.

Evaluation and Acceptance or Rejection of Goods

The buyer typically reserves the right to inspect all goods and to accept or reject them in accordance with the terms of the contract. Once the buying organization accepts the goods, however, it is generally not allowed to later reject them for quality or for quantity. However, payment for goods does not evidence acceptance, so the buyer that subsequently rejects material in accordance with the contract has the right to recover payment.

Goods that are received and subsequently rejected may be returned. However, once accepted by word or deed (e.g., actual usage), then the goods cannot be subsequently rejected. As noted earlier in the chapter, a supplier generally has the right to remedy (through rework or replacement) nonconforming goods within a reasonable period of time and at its own cost. The buyer also has a duty to help mitigate the loss if there is a reasonable way of using the goods in another application or at a downgraded price.

The UCC requires that the buying organization provide the seller with timely notice of its intention to reject nonconforming goods and, if the seller does not act within a reasonable period of time, gives the buyer the right to return the goods freight collect or to store the goods in a public warehouse and charge for storage fees.

Contract Termination

Typically, contracts are terminated when both parties have fulfilled their obligations. However, contracts can also be terminated for the convenience of the buying organization (if such rights exist in the contract) but usually require that all reasonable costs incurred by the seller up to the cancellation point are borne by the buyer.

Contracts can also be terminated for cause and cancelled as a result of breach. An inexcusable delay can result in contract termination, unless the delay was caused by uncontrollable events (force majeure). There are also occasions when one party can be excused from a contract because performance becomes commercially impracticable, such as when raw material supplies are unavailable. To be so excused requires some relatively stringent conditions, and these are probably best reviewed by legal counsel. However, the simple fact that a supplier is losing money is not sufficient cause to terminate a contract.

Often a buyer will discover that a particular supplier is having deep-rooted financial problems. If these problems continue, they are quite likely to result in service cuts and diminished quality. It is possible that the buying organization may be willing to assist by offering progress payments based on the level of completion of the products or services or even to pay for and take ownership of the material prior to their completion.

Federal bankruptcy laws do not allow for a buying organization to cancel its contract simply on the basis of the bankruptcy filing, so the rules covering anticipatory repudiation do not apply. The law, however, does allow the supplier to choose which contracts it intends to complete and which ones it will cancel.

It is also not unusual for a contract to be terminated by mutual agreement or suspended for specific periods of time. As long as both parties agree, it is perfectly acceptable to do so.

Dispute Mediation and Arbitration

When parties are unable to reach agreement on how to administer a particular aspect of their contract, they often turn to third party sources for resolution. Many of these avenues are outside the formal court system,

Mediation is the most commonly used method outside of the court system for reaching settlement in a dispute. Contracts often contain a clause requiring mediation when the two parties cannot agree on a solution. Generally, the mediation is conducted by a facilitator selected with the approval of both parties. Keep in mind, however, that mediation is not legally binding on the parties.

Arbitration, on the other hand, is a similar process but one that does render a binding judgment that can be later enforced in court. Typically, arbitrators have either a legal background or a strong technical and business background in the matter being submitted. Arbitration tends to be less expensive than court systems since the same rules of evidence will not apply.

Choice of Law

When a dispute requires resolution, the question of jurisdiction becomes important: what law or rules should apply? What specific court and location should hear the case? Obviously, this could have a significant impact on the outcome or decision, so *Choice of Law* or legal venue is typically cited as part of the terms and conditions. Warning: since only a small fraction of purchases actually end in court litigation, you may think including this clause is unimportant. But be careful, if you use the supplier's terms and you *do* encounter a dispute requiring third party resolution, you may be traveling to the supplier's location.

Summary

Forming and administering contracts is one of the key competencies of the purchasing manager. In this chapter we reviewed how you can best manage contract compliance and what potential value this brings to the organization. Post-purchase-order monitoring goes a step beyond the simple administration of the contract and includes ensuring compliance by working to achieve continuous improvement and an atmosphere of collaboration with your suppliers.

There is, of course, much routine work to be dealt with, as well. In administering contracts, the Purchasing Department is also responsible for processing change orders and the daunting task of negotiating the additional pricing for those changes when the supplier already has been awarded the business. In addition, the Purchasing Department is responsible for administering price adjustments on cost-plus contracts and reviewing claims for additional fees or increases in percentages.

Monitoring warranties, filing claims, and processing returns is another of the Purchasing Department's routine tasks which, under common circumstances, adds a great deal of value and support to the internal customer. Along with this, the Purchasing Department handles the tracking and monitoring of the ongoing processes for expediting deliveries and maintaining on-time delivery performance,

There are a number of circumstances where suppliers will be likely to create contract breaches, and the Purchasing Department is charged with resolving them. Along with this goes the task of resolving conflicts through a variety of avenues such as arbitration and mediation.

 For additional reading on topics related to this chapter, please see Appendix A.

Exam Essentials

Be able to ensure post-contract compliance.   Ensuring compliance often involves leading a cross-functional team and taking a project management approach to performance reviews.

Process change orders, price adjustments, and warranty claims.   These tasks drive to the heart of the Purchasing Department's value-added responsibilities by managing the ongoing cost changes and keeping the escalations typically attendant with them to a minimum.

Be able to manage and facilitate the improvement of inadequate supplier performance. Many things can go wrong during the course of a contract, and often strong remedial action is required. The purchasing manager will typically monitor supplier performance for signs of contract breach and must be ready to recover value and mitigate loss.

Be able to resolve product discrepancies and pricing variations.   The purchasing manager should develop a proactive approach to resolving day-to-day issues that result from improperly filled orders and lost shipments.

Be able to initiate and manage corrective action.   Your duties will include contract termination, along with administering a variety of dispute resolution methods such as mediation and arbitration.

Review Questions

1. Continuous improvement refers to the process of:

   A. Developing new processes

   B. Monitoring performance

   C. Managing supplier activities

   D. Implementing ongoing improvements

   E. Reviewing performance

2. The Document Control Department tracks:

   A. TDGs

   B. TTIs

   C. ECOs

   D. SRMs

   E. UCCs

3. A manufacturer's warranty of fitness for a particular purpose provides assurance that the product:

   A. Will work properly

   B. Will be fit for ordinary usage

   C. Will be fit for a specific purpose

   D. Will be required

   E. Will last for a set time

4. Contracts for the commercial purchase of goods may generally be terminated for all of the following reasons except:

   A. Convenience

   B. Bankruptcy

   C. Non-performance

   D. Inexcusable delay

   E. Impracticality

5. When a seller indicates that it will not be able to produce the product purchased, the term to describe this is:

   A. Anticipatory repudiation

   B. Unilateral error

   C. Anticipatory breach

   D. Liquidated damages

   E. Bankruptcy

6. Two of the more commonly used warranty types are:

    A. Breach and cure

    B. Express and implied

    C. Express and specific

    D. Merchantability and implied fitness

    E. Implied and stated

7. SRM refers to the process of:

    A. Managing supplier activities

    B. Tracking warranties

    C. Developing contract compliance

    D. Expediting orders

    E. Measuring liability

8. Expediting adds little or no value *except* when:

    A. Automated

    B. Tracking orders

    C. Ensuring delivery

    D. Processing POs

    E. Tracing back orders

9. Which of the following processes is binding?

    A. Mediation

    B. Continuous improvement

    C. Dispute resolution

    D. Arbitration

    E. Acceptance of goods

10. Contracts can be terminated by the buyer for all of the following reasons *except*:

    A. Inexcusable delay

    B. Buyer's convenience

    C. Bankruptcy

    D. Breach

    E. Commercial impracticability

Answers to Review Questions

1. D. While the other choices are all processes, only continuous improvements, as its name implies, is focused on producing improvements.

2. C. Engineering Change Orders (ECOs) are used to document changes to specifications and are usually tracked by a Document Control section within the manufacturing organization. ECOs are the only items in this list that are actually documents.

3. C. Fitness for purpose means exactly what it implies: the product will work for its intended purpose.

4. B. Federal Bankruptcy law prohibits the termination of a commercial contract simply because the buyer or the supplier files for bankruptcy.

5. A. Anticipatory repudiation occurs when a supplier declares it is unable to fulfill the contract. Anticipatory breach, the only other possible answer, is declared by the buyer when the supplier is unable to submit proof that it can meet the contract requirements.

6. B. Express and implied are the only pair of terms that refer to warranty types; none of the other sets contain valid warranty types.

7. A. SRM is an acronym for Supplier Relationship Management. The other processes do not relate to the key objective of managing suppliers.

8. A. The functions listed in options B–E add cost but virtually no value but when fully automated, an expediting system can add much value at virtually no cost.

9. D. Arbitration is binding. The other processes can be considered dynamic.

10. C. Federal bankruptcy laws do not allow for a buying organization to cancel its contract simply on the basis of the bankruptcy filing and so the rules covering anticipatory repudiation do not apply.

Managing Systems and Relationships

PART

II

Chapter

6

Managing Negotiations

THE C.P.M. EXAM SPECIFICATIONS COVERED IN THIS CHAPTER INCLUDE THE FOLLOWING:

✓ Formulating strategies and plans in preparation for negotiations

✓ Negotiating with suppliers to achieve the highest value for your organization

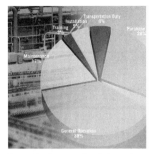

Your organization naturally seeks to obtain the maximum value for its investment in goods and services. Not surprisingly, so does your supplier; both organizations seek to gain the highest possible benefit from all of their business transactions. So when there is much value at stake, both parties generally come together to reconcile their positions. This process is referred to as *negotiations*.

As you have learned in previous chapters, any business transaction involving commercial buying and selling requires both a valid offer and acceptance. Between these two elements, however, there typically lies a gap of expectations and requirements: your budget, for example, allows a certain amount of spending for a particular purchase, but the supplier's offer contains a significantly higher amount. Obviously, this creates a gap. How do you reconcile these two seemingly oppositional positions so that each organization can achieve its respective goals? In these circumstances it is critical to engage the supplier in some form of negotiations.

A major portion of the buyer's time will be spent conducting negotiations with suppliers to obtain more favorable terms for their organization. That is not to say that you continually engage in petty haggling with your suppliers. However, when the outcome of a procurement activity is critical to the organization's goals, a successful conclusion can never be in doubt: You will need to meet the goals and expectations of your organization as well as ensuring that the supplier continues to value your business. Negotiation is most likely to occur when the conditions for competitive bidding (see Chapter 3, "Selecting Suppliers and Measuring Performance") are not present, such as when there is a sole- or single-source situation. It may also be required even when competitive bidding has taken place. Despite the fact that you have issued an RFP and selected the most appropriate supplier, there may still be gaps in filling all of your organization's needs. Negotiation, therefore, requires much additional planning, research and, most importantly, precise execution in order to achieve a successful outcome and meet your organization's objectives. How this is accomplished and the sequence in which it logically progresses is the subject of this chapter.

Assessing the Negotiating Environment

It is important that you first assess the current situation prior to conducting actual negotiations. Assessing the negotiating climate typically involves gaining an understanding of market conditions for the particular commodity or service being purchased and the position of the supplier in that market. Market conditions generally refer to circumstances such as the availability of supply in relation to actual demand or the number of suppliers in the marketplace available to create a competitive situation. What is the market share for each of the major players and how aggressive is the battle for market share? How profitable are companies in the industry and what constitutes a typical profit? What is the economic outlook for this particular segment of the economy?

In addition, it is important for you to assess the relationship you have with the supplier. Often, this can determine the atmosphere during the negotiation and have an important impact on how you and your team develop your negotiation strategy. With this information come insights into the supplier's objectives and, as a result, many clues that tell you what supplier strategies to expect during the negotiations.

In this section, you will explore the nature of the competitive environment and how your understanding of it can assist you in your negotiations.

The Competitive Environment

When the competitive environment is limited by the lack of qualified suppliers or by intellectual property rights, competitive bidding is unlikely. In this circumstance, negotiations may be the only way to achieve organizational objectives. You can assess the likelihood of conducting competitive bidding by using the checklist in Table 6.1. This table describes the specific circumstances in the marketplace and the degree to which their presence fosters competitive bidding. Keep in mind that, as mentioned in the table, there can be no bidding if only one supplier can meet your requirements.

TABLE 6.1   Understanding the Competitive Environment

Competitive Condition	Competitive Bidding Degree
Multiple *qualified* or *qualifiable* suppliers	High
Contracting is feasible	High
Competitive environment is regulated	Medium
Contract recently negotiated	Medium to low
Product or service is covered by patents	None
Clear specifications or SOW exists	High
Government-controlled resource	None
Attractive volume	High
Only one source of supply	None

Nature of Competition

Competition is available in virtually all markets for goods and services. What you have to assess is the nature of that competition so that you can effectively formulate your procurement strategies. Higher competition generally results in lower prices and a greater willingness by suppliers to provide additional services.

Competition can be evaluated from a number of perspectives:

The Number of Qualified or Qualifiable Suppliers in the Market   Higher numbers generally foster greater competition.

The Impact of the Buyer   Greater purchasing volume encourages vigorous competition for your business in markets where competition exists.

The Barriers to Entry for the Particular Product or Service   The lower the cost to establish new businesses in the particular market, the greater the competitive pressure.

Capacity   Often related to the number of suppliers, higher levels of unused capacity within an industry fosters greater competition.

Dominant Brand   Effective branding strategies that make one supplier or one product more desirable than others result in less vigorous competition.

Ability to Substitute   Products or services that are easily substituted by those from other industries are more highly competitive.

Role of Market Forces

When analysts speak of market forces, they generally refer to factors—economic, physical, and political—influencing and affecting buying and selling at a particular time. These factors may exist within a specific industry or a geographical location or over the course of an entire economy. To some extent, the very nature of competition itself is dynamic and in continual flux so that when you evaluate a given set of conditions—capacity or barriers to entry, for example— at any specific time, you do little more than freeze a frame in a never-ending film.

From the point of view of purchasing function, supply and demand are two of the most important market force factors, and you need to pay very close attention to them. Often in flux, supply and demand influences prices in many different ways. While supply and demand will theoretically reach equilibrium over time so that the supply of a given item exactly matches the demand for it, in reality this is rarely the case. More often than not, the ratio of supply and demand continually moves higher and lower, with fluctuating prices reflecting any imbalance. Figure 6.1 shows how prices can increase as a result of reduced supply because buyers tend to bid up prices to meet their requirements. Buyers compete with one another to obtain scarce goods and services. Keep in mind, however, that as prices increase, with all other factors remaining constant, new capacity will usually enter the market to take advantage of the perceived profit, eventually creating additional supply that once again brings prices lower. The ratio of supply to demand always affects prices. When supply is more plentiful than demand, suppliers must lower prices to make buying more attractive; when demand outstrips supply, buyers compete for the few available resources and prices rise.

FIGURE 6.1   The effect of supply shortage on price

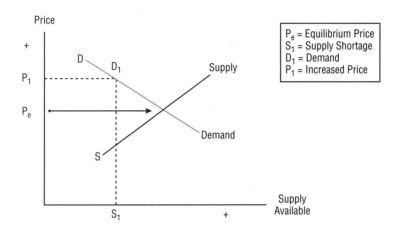

 Supply shortages can also result from an unexpected increase in demand or some physical situation such as a plant shutdown that severely limits production.

In Figure 6.1, the point P_e represents the equilibrium point at which supply and demand are equal—shown by their intersecting lines. When the available supply decreases along the line S to the point S_1, well below the demand line, prices rise to P_1.

Early Involvement

Early involvement by the purchasing group is one of the fundamental keys to employing successful negotiation strategies. The later the involvement of the Purchasing Department in sourcing decisions, the less leverage will be available for negotiating favorable terms. In other words, the greater the supplier's certainty that it will receive the order, and the less likely it will be to engage in serious negotiations.

Early involvement is essential to avoiding being locked into a single source prematurely without sufficient negotiating leverage to influence critical terms of the contract. This is especially true during the new product development cycle and when engaging a new supplier. Figure 6.2 depicts graphically how the influence of the Purchasing Department diminishes as the course of the supplier engagement progresses. As you can see, involvement during the initial phases of the engagement allows the Purchasing Department to exercise greater influence and incorporate more robust processes than it can when it is engaged later in the development process. Furthermore, the actual impact of that engagement also diminishes with later involvement.

FIGURE 6.2   Factors influenced by the Purchasing Department's early involvement

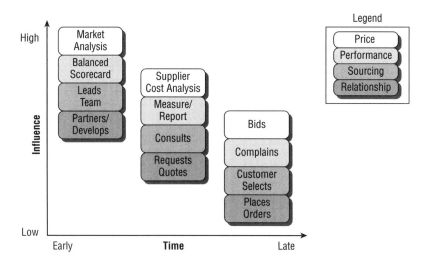

Gathering Information and Analysis

Information, as they say, is power. Having the right information available when needed is always critical to a successful approach to strategy formulation. It is important to know at least as much (and perhaps more) about the conditions that may influence the negotiation as the supplier. By being informed, your team will be able to develop realistic and workable strategies and avoid the embarrassment of establishing unreachable goals. Having the right facts can also preclude the supplier from springing surprises.

Each team member should be responsible for gathering a portion of the information that is needed to adequately prepare for both developing strategies and actually participating in the negotiations. Price analysis and market conditions, noted previously, are just a few aspects of your analysis, but there are many more outlined next.

Analyzing the Supplier's Situation

In gathering information, you might first want to consider looking at the situation from the supplier's point of view: what motivates their position and what are they likely to value the most? Conversely, what concessions might they be willing to make to achieve their goals?

Financial Needs

It is relatively easy to assess a U.S. corporation's financial condition if it is *publicly held* (with stock trading on an open stock exchange) since the Securities and Exchange Commission (SEC) regulations require public disclosure of important financial data. From publicly accessible reports such as those filed with the SEC and from the reports of market analysts tracking its stock performance, it will be possible to gain some relative understanding of the supplier's financial picture and insight into its level of motivation to obtain your business. Obviously, the greater the financial need, the greater the supplier's incentive to offer concessions.

With a privately held organization, gathering this information may be difficult. You will often need to obtain information available through an industry organization or professional association or through other sources familiar with the supplier's operations. The supplier's competitors will often have comparative data to share with you based on marketing surveys they have conducted, but you will naturally want to take into account the source and the simple fact that suppliers are not in the habit of passing along good news about their competition.

Existing Relations

There are many reasons a supplier wants to maintain its favored position with you. Replacing a valuable customer can be costly and the supplier has already "sunk" the costs of acquiring your business. Prior to negotiations, your team should completely analyze the motivational factors that will likely drive concessions to you. Some of the questions you might want to ask in this regard include:

- How much does a supplier value the status of its existing relationship with your organization? Are you a reference account?
- How does your business impact the supplier's bottom line?
- How does your volume affect the supplier's position in the marketplace?
- Does your organization require more or less customer service than others?
- Are your business needs relatively easy to forecast?
- Are your volumes consistent?
- Do you pay your invoices in an acceptable time frame?
- Are your organizations engaged in joint product development?

Analyzing Your Organization's Position

You will likely know a great deal more about your organization and its specific needs than you will about your supplier's, so the exercise of gathering and analyzing your own position will encourage your team to more clearly identify areas where concessions may be required. This exercise should flag those concerns for further research into the supplier's situation so that you enter the negotiation with at least some understanding of its likely position. This is really the first step in planning the negotiation process and developing a strategy. You will want to cover some of the same areas we discussed in the preceding section on the supplier's needs and will certainly want to review some of the following requirements:

Urgency

When does your organization need the product or service you will be negotiating? If it is needed urgently, you may want to prepare to negotiate accelerated delivery by trading concessions in other areas such as price or transportation methods. On the other hand, if the requirement can be met over a period of time, allowing the supplier to fulfill it when time and resources are not being otherwise used, this might prove a useful concession to achieve better prices.

Priority of Needs

When you initially evaluated a key supplier, you may have measured its performance on a weighted average matrix to help in the selection process. If you recall from the previous chapter, we actually developed a hierarchy of importance by assigning values to each of the categories: Cost, Quality, Technology and Service.

In establishing the priority of needs for a particular negotiation, you will want to review your selection matrix to help determine the approximate priority of the organization's needs. Table 6.2 shows an evaluation matrix similar to the one we developed in Chapter 3. If we assigned the following values to our selection process, then we would likely want to assign a similar set of values to our negotiation priorities:

TABLE 6.2   Supplier Evaluation Weighting

Category	Percentage
Cost	40%
Quality	25%
Technology	20%
Service	15%

In terms of concessions, then, we would likely trade elements of service (the lowest value on the list) for pricing concessions (the highest value on the list).

Internal Constraints

Unknown conditions within your organization may preclude your team from fully leveraging its negotiating position, and they need to be identified prior to establishing a strategy. For example, it may be impossible to precisely define a scope of work for a construction project renovating an existing building. Contractors rarely know what they will find when opening a wall or ceiling. As a result, you will likely be unable to develop a firm fixed price for the project. Other contracts may be similar, where quality, delivery, and liability are dependent on a set of conditions that are not known at the time of negotiation.

In addition to unknowns, there may internal management pressures to achieve certain goals beyond the value that they may conceivably add. Using a proprietary architectural design to beautify the lobby of the headquarters building may hamper your ability to negotiate with the contractors; nevertheless, it would be unrealistic for a buyer to consider altering an architect's design.

You may also want to consider situations where trade-offs will require an additional investment by your organization. For example, if shortened lead times are critically necessary and the supplier has no flexibility in its manufacturing processes, you may need to develop longer range forecasts. This may require the addition of a staff planner or a more sophisticated software system. With this knowledge, you will be able to properly evaluate the costs of items that will not be effectively negotiated.

Preparing for the Negotiation

Once you have reviewed the general negotiating climate and have a relatively clear understanding of the forces operating behind the scenes, so to speak, you need to prepare for conducting the negotiation itself. This involves a great deal of planning that builds your confidence through a keen understanding of the circumstances you will likely encounter during the actual negotiation. It is also a continual process of fact finding and analysis that leads and guides your strategy.

In preparation, you will likely want to select and orient your cross-functional team to ensure that you are all working together toward common objectives. With your team in place, the primary focus of your planning will be to carefully review the supplier's proposal from the perspective of your organization's needs. To what extent are your needs being addressed and where are there critical gaps that fall short of your objectives? The more you know about the contents of the proposal, the less likely you will be caught off guard by any omissions or issues that have not been clearly thought out. Planning for negotiations, in a way, also involves understanding the needs and objectives of your supplier, anticipating its most likely position on any key issue in relation to yours. If you and your supplier can avoid creating surprises with unexpected issues both during and after the contract negotiations, the chances are that the actual performance will run smoothly.

This section will guide you through the processes normally conducted in preparation for negotiations. We will cover some of the ways you might select and assess the team and how you will formulate objectives and develop strategies.

Selecting and Leading the Negotiating Team

In any significant negotiation, you will first want to form a support team composed of technical experts, the financial group, and members of the user groups—likely the same people that participated in the preparation of the RFP and the supplier selection. This team should always be led by the senior representative for Purchasing who is participating in its activities to ensure that business objectives are met and that the negotiations are conducted in an atmosphere conducive to continued collaboration. The purchasing representative will also be responsible to ensure the negotiations are carried out with integrity and in an ethical manner.

Selection Criteria

It is naturally important that key members of the user group—the stakeholders, as they are sometimes called—actively participate in the negotiation process for a number of reasons. First, there are technical issues that will arise during the course of discussions that only they will be qualified to answer. Second, as the users, they are in the best position to understand the importance of the various elements of the offer and so can determine when specifications can be relaxed as well as the value of certain trade-offs. Third, as *subject matter experts (SMEs)*, the users are in the best position to evaluate what service levels should be established and the metrics to evaluate performance. And last, the users are the successors of the bargain—the group that must live with the resulting conditions—and they will inherit not only the wins but the losses as well.

In addition to members of the user group, you should ensure that you have representation from the various business units such as Finance or Facilities. These are the support staff that can provide additional skills—based on their functional roles—to the team when needed. You should select team members according to their behavioral skills as well. Behavioral skills include such qualities as decisiveness, intelligence, problem-solving abilities, drive to achieve, patience, and the ability to communicate. It will be up to you, as leader, to determine what behavioral skills will be needed and who within the broad stakeholders community best demonstrates them.

Assessing the Team's Strength and Weaknesses

It is a good idea for the members of the team to jointly assess its collective strengths and weaknesses in advance. By doing so, team members will develop a more realistic understanding of the constraints they are operating under and what technical skills are available to effectively maneuver to a favorable concession. Externally imposed deadlines can often generate situations that create bad decisions, or the lack of authority to make a decision can lead to a stalemate.

Communicating with Team Members

One of the most important roles the team leader has is that of the communicator. The team leader is responsible for seeing that participants know what factual information is needed and who should be gathering it. Information should have a clear distribution channel so that everyone can be updated on relevant information as it becomes available. Exercise caution, however, to ensure that there is not so much information generated that it inundates the team and creates data overload.

The team leader also needs to define the individual roles that may be necessary during the course of the negotiation and to help assess which members are best suited to each specific task. This is likely to include deciding who will become the team's spokesperson and how decisions to accept or reject offers will be made. Signals need to be developed that can indicate to other members when offers are acceptable and when they are not, similar to the way they might be used in a sporting event when the coach wants to send a specific play to team members. The team also needs to know who will make the final decisions and the authority level of each of the negotiators.

Formulating Objectives and Developing Strategies

Once the team has been selected and is operationally in place, your next step is to lead the development of a plan for the actual negotiation. It is always best to put this plan in writing so that you and your team members can use it as a future guide.

As a first step in developing the plan, team members should list their objectives and the anticipated objectives of the supplier. Objectives can be based on the identified gap between initial expectations in the sourcing process and those actually achieved. Under each objective, indicate the likely impact of not achieving the objective. Then rank the objectives on this list by priority, focusing on developing a strategy for those that are most critical. The strategy will outline what initial offer you can expect and what you can counteroffer. (You might call these "take-aways" and "give-aways.") You will also need to determine a position at which you would be willing to accept the offer and one where you would be willing to walk away altogether for each of the key objectives. Your assessment of the situation, such as current market conditions, will play a critical role in this process, for without it you will likely not be able to understand the supplier's needs and motivation.

Team Negotiation Advice from Peter B. Stark and Jane S. Flaherty

Peter B. Stark and Jane S. Flaherty, authors of *The Only Negotiating Guide You'll Ever Need*, explain that there are times when negotiating as a team is a wise decision:

1. Having more than one team member can provide access to more expertise. Of course, this is only an advantage if each team member truly has something essential to add to the negotiation process.

2. Generally, when more people are thinking about alternative ways to generate win-win outcomes, success is more likely.

3. There is strength in numbers. Presenting a case as a unified group packs considerable power.

4. The focus is less likely to be on one individual's personality.

If you decide to negotiate as a team, the following guidelines will prove helpful:

-   Determine what types of expertise are needed to support your side of the negotiations.

-   Find people who have the needed expertise; are good, confident communicators; and work well as a team.

-   Hold planning meetings prior to the negotiation to agree on team goals, strategies, and tactics.

-   Ensure team members will be available to provide their expertise throughout the negotiation.

-   Select a lead negotiator or team captain.

-   Select a scribe to keep accurate notes during both the planning meeting and the negotiation.

-   Assign roles and responsibilities for each team member.

-   Practice! Pull together another team of people to represent the counterpart and then rehearse your negotiation. A dry run can be extremely helpful in raising the confidence level of all team members.

Reprinted with permission from The Only Negotiating Guide You'll Ever Need *by Peter B. Stark and Jane S. Flaherty. For more information, visit:* www.everyonenegotiates.com.

Gap Analysis can be viewed as the process of assessing (measuring) the difference between the current condition and the desired outcome.

It is sometimes helpful to go one step further and have your team run through a mock negotiation exercise where you set the stage by reviewing general market trends and ask some of the team members to assume the supplier's role. What objectives are they likely to have? What concessions are they likely to make? At what point in each of the elements do you feel the supplier will concede and at what point simply walk away?

As you answer these questions for your own position and then compare them to the answers you come up with for the supplier's anticipated position, you will gain a preview of how the actual negotiations may develop and how you can best respond to specific offers or demands. This is much like scripting a football play book where time, field position, score, and other key elements in the game are assessed using a *decision tree* to determine what play should be logically called next. Indeed, you should consider having this script put into written form so that each member of your team has the opportunity to review it periodically during the course of the negotiations.

Objectives

When your supplier selection team established its initial requirements and began the process of determining the most qualified supplier, it also developed a set of expectations. These expectations were based on your organization's needs. Whatever needs are not fully satisfied in the supplier's response, even when that response is the best one received, will need to be further negotiated. You will likely have performed a gap analysis prior to constructing your negotiating plan, so you can compare what you have to what you actually wanted. This can form the basis for determining what you will want to negotiate and your negotiating objectives.

In this section, we'll discuss the few elements you might want to consider including in your checklist such as price, quality, service levels, capacity or volume, the length of the contract, and managing specifications.

Price

Despite the fact that you understand the nature of value and the concept of total cost of ownership, the focal point of any negotiation is usually price. The seller wishes to reasonably maximize profit and the buyer wishes to obtain the best possible price. In most cases, the ideal position for both is a fair and reasonable price. For the most part, the best way to determine a fair and reasonable price is through the current pricing in an open market, such as a commodities exchange. On an exchange, commodity prices fluctuate openly in response to supply and demand so the trading price at any given time reflects the current price a buyer is willing to pay and the current price at which a seller is willing to sell.

In the absence of a public exchange, however, the buyer can turn to the competitive bidding process. When properly executed, the competitive bidding process can approximate an open market exchange. But even when the competitive bidding process is used, there may be some further need to negotiate price. For example, while a specific contract may have an agreed upon fixed price, the buyer will also want to fix the rates for changes and perhaps prenegotiate the conditions under which the contract may be extended for an additional period of time. This may or may not have been addressed in the initial proposal or competitive bid.

When evaluating and negotiating price, you also need to consider some of the auxiliary elements that immediately and directly affect price, such as shipping costs and disposal costs, and the terms of payment. Insofar as these can be directly associated with a clearly measurable price factor, they can be evaluated as part of the price package. Conceding a point or two on the price list in exchange for more favorable payment terms (e.g., Net 30 extended to Net 45) can be calculated as a cash value.

Price Analysis

It is important for you, as the lead negotiator, to understand when a quoted pricing represents an acceptable offer. The reasonableness of a particular price can be established through an analysis of a number of factors such as market conditions, volume of the purchase, overall volume given the supplier, nature of the specifications, and risk. It can also be determined through benchmarking and whatever other comparative analysis is available to the buyer. Always keep in mind, however, that price is not necessarily directly related to the supplier's cost. In fact, the process of price analysis typically evaluates price without regard to its components of cost and, in most commercial environments, without consideration of the supplier's net profit or operating margin.

Quality

As negotiations progress, you will likely find that increased quality specifications result in higher prices and that relaxing some of the noncritical specifications may result in lower prices. To the extent possible, the technical group on your team should review the specifications as part of the planning process. Knowing where specifications and tolerances can be relaxed and where they cannot needs to be determined largely in advance and should be included in the negotiation plan.

Service Levels

In many cases, service levels are included in the statement of work in the form of a Service Level Agreement (SLA). As with quality specifications, service levels too can be relaxed and traded off as a concession to receiving some other benefits in exchange. Required lead time that can be extended through some improved planning on your end and early placement of orders may prove beneficial to the supplier and could result in a greater commitment to on-time delivery. Or you may be willing to make some pricing concessions in order to obtain just-in-time delivery (JIT) or the benefit of establishing a Supplier Managed Inventory (SMI) program.

Service levels can also be evaluated in terms of engineering support provided by the supplier and the impact of this support on your operations. If one of your organization's key objectives calls for being the first to market, engineering support from the supplier can be a crucial factor in getting you there.

Capacity/Volume

Whenever the potential for limitations in a supplier's production or service levels exists as a result of forecasted changes in market conditions, you will need to address it contractually. During periods of constrained capacity and shortages when supplier's cannot keep up with demand, you will want to ensure that your organization has the protection it needs by locking in specific commitments from the supplier for certain amounts of its capacity or specific volumes based on your anticipated needs. This, of course, is always a trade-off, since in exchange for guaranteed capacity, the supplier usually wants a guaranteed volume of business.

Length of Contract

Another point of negotiation occurs when there may be considerable risk involved in the fluctuation of prices and you (or the supplier) wish to lock in pricing for a given period of time. If your team sees prices rising, you will want a longer term for the contract at the current pricing; the supplier, seeing the same trend, will want to shorten the contract period, hoping that increased prices will result in additional revenue. The opposite is true, of course, when prices appear to be falling.

There are many other reasons for negotiations to occur around the length of the contract. The supplier naturally wants to be assured of your organization's business—all other things being equal—for as long as possible. You may want a longer contract period to avoid the additional cost of switching from one supplier to another.

Managing Specifications

The technical users on the team are generally responsible for determining the specifications. Often, you will find that the tighter the specifications are (in terms of typical industrial capabilities), the more you will have to pay. Tighter specifications may also mean additional inspection time (and cost) that interferes with the smooth operation of the supplier's production. It is always advisable, in situations where specifications are critical, to maintain a *want* position, a *need* position, and a *can accept* position so that you are flexible enough to earn concessions for more critical factors.

Establishing Priorities

As previously described, organizing the priority of your team's objectives can be one of the most important aspects in any negotiation planning process. Based on team discussions and consensus, it is possible to organize each of the stated objectives into a priority list or, at the least, indicate if they are high, medium, or low. During the actual course of negotiations, you will want to be certain to maintain these priorities to avoid wasting time by negotiating for relatively unimportant objectives.

Establishing priorities also relates to determining the amount of time devoted to the actual negotiations. Setting deadlines and the number of sessions reminds everyone that there is an objective to be reached. With this in mind, little time should be devoted to minor issues until the major ones are resolved. However, the order in which you negotiate specific items, critical or minor, can be varied to meet the team's overall strategy.

Preparing Psychologically

Psychological preparation generally means preparing well enough to develop a high level of confidence in the validity of your position. As mentioned earlier in this chapter, confidence develops from having a firm grasp of the conditions in the marketplace and understanding the position of both parties relative to their competitors. Gathering facts and analyzing the supplier's position, as well as your own, leads to a clear understanding of what concessions are required and what concessions are going to be impossible to obtain. Attempting to achieve that which is impossible can only lead to disappointment and confrontation. On the other hand, lowering expectations below what is truly possible can lead to demoralization and a sense of loss following the negotiations. The best practices today have buyer and supplier teams working collaboratively so that both achieve the fullest benefit of the bargain.

Planning Your Agenda

As part of your psychological preparation, you will want to have your agenda set up in advance. This provides your team with a sense of direction and sets your own pace for the negotiation. The timing of the negotiation is always a critical factor in establishing a strong base for leverage. Timing means not only when the negotiations start and end, but when individual items will be open for discussion. This gives you the opportunity to achieve key objectives first before relinquishing key concessions. Negotiations often move much like card games, where one player can use cards discarded by the other.

Conducting Practice Sessions

Finally, it can be quite useful to have your team practice for the actual negotiations by holding some realistic practice sessions. During these sessions, team members can take turns in the anticipated role of the supplier and gain some insight into the situations that are likely to occur during actual negotiations. You can make the process even more realistic by bringing in participants from other groups and creating a somewhat competitive environment by offering relatively substantial prizes.

Conducting the Negotiation

When it is time to actually conduct the negotiation, you will employ a myriad of techniques and tactics. For example, one of the best practices in preparing for and actually conducting negotiations is to continually ask questions whose answers provide a better understanding of the situation and the needs of both parties. Asking questions also helps to control the pace and direction of the negotiations, which can be especially useful when you need to bring the discussion back to its key points.

To a large degree, your tactics will depend upon the overall strategy you and your team developed during the planning phase. Implementing your strategy essentially amounts to how you approach the negotiations—cooperatively in a *win-win* mode or win-lose in an adversarial mode. Win-win modes tend to encourage collaboration in the negotiation process. Win-lose strategies tend to rely on power to control the negotiation process.

The following section reviews many of the more traditional tactical aspects of conducting negotiations that you will probably use. Although it is unlikely that they will all fit your personal style of negotiating, keep them in mind and include them as part of your playbook. You never know when you might need a special effect.

Creating the Climate

Establishing the climate is one of your first concerns just prior to and during the negotiation process. Climate refers to the physical aspects of where the negotiations are taking place, as well as the general mood of those conducting the negotiations. It encompasses both the physical atmosphere and the nature of the personal interaction.

Supplier representatives often understand this all too well and have been taught to do as much as possible to keep the lead negotiator or decision maker in a good mood. However, it is generally no longer considered acceptable to conduct serious business negotiations over an expensive lunch or dinner with wine.

Location

There is a maxim in sporting events that the home team has the field advantage. Most of the spectators are fans of the home team, and the team likely plays the majority of its games on that particular field. It's hard to say how true this is, but there are some related aspects to consider when choosing the location where you will conduct negotiations. Typically, negotiations are held at the buyer's office, although there is no hard and fast rule about that. If negotiations are conducted at your site, you may be subject to more interruptions by routine business matters than you would be at some other place. On the other hand, you will have the comfort of familiar ground, as well as the convenience of having support staff and records nearby.

In times past, it was thought that there was a critical psychological advantage to holding negotiations in a familiar environment, and you may have heard that the seating arrangements around the conference table can provide an advantage. There may be some truth to this when high-stakes international political outcomes are at stake, but such details rarely influence the kind of business negotiations you will be routinely conducting. This is not to imply that some element of cat-and-mouse intrigue will not be present during your negotiations, since there is often a strong desire on the part of participants to "ink the deal" with favorable terms. It is more important, however, that regardless of where you are, you consider any potential negative impact the environment may have and take whatever steps necessary to counter it.

As part of an awareness of your surroundings, you must also be aware of the body language and the physical actions of those in the negotiations. Learning to read these signs can be useful in determining the mood and status of your supplier's team.

It is universally accepted that the crossed-arm posture (usually sitting with arms folded across the chest, but sometimes seen with the hands held behind the head) represents an unwillingness to listen or to accept what is being said. See what you can do to get your suppliers to open up their posture and demonstrate they are becoming more receptive to your proposals.

Developing a Collaborative Atmosphere

A collaborative atmosphere, it is felt by many, is the most conducive to negotiating in environments where long-term relationships are important. While the popularity of win-win negotiations rises and falls with time, there can be little doubt that positional or adversarial contact rarely produces the best results. If your team takes a competitive stance, it is likely the supplier's team will do the same. You should have already developed your priority list of objectives prior to your first session, so you might want to consider that the supplier has done the same. If your discussions are congenial and nonconfrontational and you listen well, you will come away with an understanding very early in the negotiations of what exchanges of value can take place.

That is not to say there is any reason to pretend you and the supplier are bosom friends. However, you will benefit from good relations if you consider that the supplier's representative is as anxious as you are to do a good job.

You should also keep in mind that sales personnel have generally been given a great deal of training in the tactics of negotiations. Any "tricks" you have learned are likely to be known by one or another member of your supplier's team. Remember the objective of any negotiation is to reach an agreement, so there is little value in playing games. If your position is firm, let that be known. If you are not clear about the implications of a concession, ask questions and hold a caucus with your team.

An important part of developing a collaborative negotiation is to avoid imposing artificial deadlines. If there are absolute time constraints, you should indicate so at the beginning of your negotiation and stick to them. By the same token, you should not let deadlines be imposed upon you, either. To maintain your future credibility, it is critical that you honor your commitments. Do not make decisions before you feel completely ready, regardless of the circumstances.

Allowing for Cultural Differences

When conducting negotiations with personnel from nations other than your own, the most important rule to remember is that cultural differences will invariably have an impact. Even when the parties are speaking the same language, the native speaker may have a different conception of the terminology than the person speaking a second language. Similarly, body language and expressions take on different meanings in different cultures. The only certain way for you to understand this is to do your homework diligently and become familiar with as many of the nuances of the supplier's culture as you can. Sometimes, it helps defuse this potential problem if you take the initial step (sensitively, of course) of informally discussing these differences together.

Travel guides, such as those published by Fodor and Lonely Planet, are excellent tools for helping you to understand the business and cultural customs in various countries (www.fodors.com, www.lonelyplanet.com).

Adopting a Negotiating Style

While there is an endless array of negotiating styles, and small libraries can be filled with the texts describing them, there are two basic types of negotiators: collaborative negotiators who seek to develop outcomes that enhance the sense of accomplishment of both parties (win-win) and power (or positional) negotiators who seek to prevail in achieving their objectives regardless of the impact on the other party. Even after you spend many years in purchasing, it is unlikely you will consistently use one or the other.

Tactics

The tactics you will likely use for negotiations are closely related to the specific style you adopt, and there appear to be endless compendiums of them strung along like so many pejorative proverbs. Here are a few of the more common tactics:

- Generally, more can be gained by listening than by talking. Accordingly, take copious notes and review them frequently.

- Question how your statements will align with your objectives—pronouncements can be pointless or even counterproductive.

- Avoid accepting the first offer.

- Always ask questions, especially when there is useful information to be learned.

- Do not make concessions without receiving equal consideration. This does not necessarily mean that each and every concession need result in some consideration...but do keep track.

- Attend to deadlines; establish them sparingly and only when necessary.

- Keep your wits about you and avoid reacting emotionally.

- Issues need to be prioritized. When reaching an impasse on one, park it for a while and go on to the next.

- Take breaks whenever you feel the need. Do not attempt to fight fatigue.

- Refrain from bluffing and use only data you can prove. Imagine the embarrassment and loss of face that could result in being discovered.

- Last and final offers should mean exactly what they say.

- Understand and use body language as a communication tool to your advantage.

Sole Source Tactics

Negotiating with a sole source can provide a measure of challenge. As long as your organization is able to maintain its objectives from a marketing perspective, you will likely find little to negotiate. Typically, sharing the risk in new product development or distributing the burden of inventory will produce some benefit to both parties. However, if profitability becomes significantly impacted through changing market costs or products reaching their end of life, your organization may want to initiate steps to avoid financial loss prior to discontinuation. In this case, you and the supplier will need to work closely together to monitor the profitability for both sides and make recommendations regarding the timing of any changes in terms and conditions.

Documenting the Negotiation

It is important to properly document negotiation activities so that personnel unfamiliar with the specifics of the project will be able to clearly understand what occurred, should the need arise. Documentation should be approached from two points: first, by documenting the negotiation plan and its objectives and comparing the objectives to actual outcomes as a way of determining the team's effectiveness and, second, by providing an executive summary of the actual negotiation so that auditors will be able to assess its impact, and approving authorities will be able to understand what you are requesting.

The negotiation plan should contain information that describes, at a minimum, the team's objectives, its strategy, and the strengths and weaknesses of its position, along with a similar assessment of the supplier's position. Often, it is useful to include an opening position and bottom line (least acceptable) position for each of the key objectives. Your team should also prepare likely scenarios for the supplier's position. When the negotiation has concluded, you should review the original planning document and describe where the objectives were met and where they fell short.

The executive summary should describe the objectives of the contract and the negotiation, what was achieved in relation to initial goals, the cost and benefits to the organization, and any alternative courses of action that may be possible. Any future follow-up action should also be included in this summary.

Summary

Conducting successful negotiations requires careful planning and organization. As a first step in your planning process, you should prepare an assessment of current market conditions for the industry and organizations with whom you will be engaged. Assessing the negotiating environment includes developing an evaluation of the competitiveness of the particular industry and what impact you and your supplier have in that market. Be sure to consider aspects such as overall industry capacity, pricing trends, availability of substitute products, and other factors that will help establish an understanding of the competitive forces potentially influencing the outcome of your negotiations.

You will also want to look closely at the supplier's situation to assess elements of its current condition that might affect its motivation. What are its financial needs and how does your organization fit in with them? Similarly, you will want to have a full understanding of the factors influencing your organization. Establish the urgency of the requirements and a prioritized set of needs and understand any significant internal constraints. Early involvement in the contracting process will assist your efforts to affect a favorable outcome.

If the outcome of the negotiation will significantly impact your organization, you will likely want to form a support team composed of key internal users, a finance representative, and someone from the quality assurance group. With the help of the team, you can then formulate your guiding objectives and strategies using many of the same criteria you used during the supplier selection process.

When it comes time for the actual negotiation, your team should have completed a detailed plan prioritizing needs, outlined roles and responsibilities, selected a location, and discussed the likely scenarios that might occur and how you will deal with them. You should also consider what negotiating style might produce the best results and what tactics you can use to enhance it.

All of the planning and strategy development should be documented so that others will be able to understand what occurred. Using an executive summary to describe objectives and outcomes will help you gain internal approval and describe any follow-up actions that will be required.

For additional reading on topics related to this chapter, please see Appendix A.

Exam Essentials

Be able to identify the information needed to develop an understanding of the negotiating environment. Actionable information regarding market conditions and the supplier's position in that market will help you better understand motivational factors and circumstances driving its specific needs.

Be able to gather specific information and analyze and prioritize the current needs of your organization and those of your supplier. Obtain factual data and develop an understanding of the needs of both organizations so that you can better formulate your strategy.

Know how to plan for actual negotiations. Identify and prioritize your organization's needs and the likely needs of your supplier. Determine where they align and where they are going to clash. Establish a support team and define the roles and responsibilities of its members

Be able to conduct negotiations to achieve a successful outcome. Establish effective strategies, determine appropriate styles and tactics, and develop a well-thought-out plan prior to the first session. Maintain an objective attitude throughout the negotiations and continually focus on achieving results.

Understand what documentation will be required. Include your planning and strategy documents in the contract records so that those coming after you will be able to understand what occurred. Be able to provide the approving authority with an executive summary of what was achieved.

Review Questions

1. The process where buyers and sellers come together to reconcile their positions is called:

   A. Offer and acceptance

   B. Mirror image rule

   C. Give and take

   D. Negotiation

   E. Mediation

2. In assessing the negotiation climate, the availability of supply in relation to actual demand is what is generally referred to as:

   A. The breakeven point

   B. The buy-sell ratio

   C. Market conditions

   D. Supply and demand

   E. The economic outlook

3. Which condition would be the least likely to use for competitive bidding?

   A. A sole supply source

   B. An attractive volume

   C. Clear specifications or scope of work

   D. Multiple qualified suppliers

   E. Contracting is feasible

4. One of the fundamental keys to employing successful negotiation strategies is:

   A. Supplier assessment

   B. A specification document

   C. The caliber of negotiation team members

   D. Early purchasing department involvement

   E. Financial objectives

5. What is typically the first step in planning the negotiation process and developing a negotiation strategy?

   A. Developing a negotiation timeline

   B. Understanding the supplier's position

   C. Analyzing your organization's position

   D. Identifying fall-back positions

   E. Planning negotiation tactics

6.   Employees in the best position to evaluate what service levels should be established and the metrics to evaluate supplier performance are known as:

   A. Knowledge workers

   B. Requestors

   C. Customers

   D. Subject matter experts

   E. Quality managers

7.   Who defines individual roles that may be necessary during the course of the negotiation and helps assess which members are best suited to each specific negotiation task?

   A. The purchasing manager

   B. The team leader

   C. A user

   D. The buyer

   E. The supplier

8.   When a negotiation team develops a written plan for the actual negotiation, the first thing the team should list is its:

   A. Needs

   B. Wish list

   C. Objectives

   D. Specifications

   E. Expectations

9.   The most common focal point of negotiations is usually:

   A. Delivery

   B. Quality

   C. Quantity

   D. Price

   E. Service levels

10.   When the negotiation team organizes its negotiation objectives as high, medium, or low, it is called a:

   A. Ranking

   B. Priority list

   C. Weighted average

   D. Position plan

   E. Issue matrix

Answers to Review Questions

1. D. Negotiation is the process employed to develop an agreement between parties through an exchange of view.

2. C. Market conditions include all economic factors that might influence the course of a negotiation, including availability.

3. A. Competitive bidding requires at least two parties.

4. D. Studies have shown that the earlier the purchasing department becomes involved the greater its leverage in assuring a successful outcome.

5. C. Unless you clearly understand your organization's position, you will not be able to create an effective plan and strategy.

6. D. The employees in your organization who actually use the goods and services you purchase will be in the best position to determine requirements and to know when they are being met.

7. B. It is the team leader's responsibility to assign tasks to individuals on the team according to their organizational role and capabilities.

8. C. An understanding of the overall objectives of the organization should drive the team's strategy.

9. D. Negotiations seek to resolve differences, and the most common difference is price.

10. B. A priority list is used by the negotiation team to rank in order the priority of its objectives so that members can remain focused on those of greatest importance.

Chapter 7

Using Computer-Based Systems

THE C.P.M. EXAM SPECIFICATIONS COVERED IN THIS CHAPTER INCLUDE THE FOLLOWING:

- ✓ Understanding and using procurement-specific computerized software tools
- ✓ Maintaining computer-based data
- ✓ Sourcing and selecting procurement applications

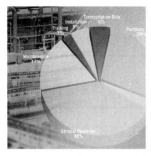

The supply management landscape has changed rapidly over the past several years, largely as a result of computerization. Procurement departments are becoming increasingly inclined to move routine transactional processes, such as placing purchase orders, to computer-based platforms to gain efficiency and better utilization of employee time. This *reengineering* process has paralleled, for the most part, the widespread acceptance of automated systems across the entire spectrum of our organizations and the increasing use of the Internet for business.

Today, organizations are increasingly turning to computerized tools to integrate all of the elements in the *procure-to-pay* process. By doing so, they are realizing the financial benefits of increased productivity and reduced cycle times generated through the automation of routine processes such as requisition and purchase order generation, quotation, bidding, order tracking, expediting, supplier payment, and procedural compliance. Today, tools are widely available to assist purchasing departments in timing their buying decisions based on market trends in pricing and availability. Indeed, the current trend to *web-based sourcing*, using tools that automate and speed up many of the more tedious procurement processes such as RFIs and RFPs, has enabled organizations to improve their supplier selection and reduce prices through standardization methods that would otherwise be cost prohibitive. Using these tools, organizations have even been able to manage their buying power in some of the smaller spending areas, such as MRO (Maintenance, Repair, and Operations expenses), that would have been impossible several years ago.

Buyers and sellers have shared equally in these benefits through the transparency of supply capacity and product demand, producing greater collaboration and alignment between their organizations. Partners are now able to share supply and demand data in real time, and the result has been savings for both. This has been especially apparent in the recent trend to Supplier Managed Inventory (SMI) programs (or *consigned inventory*), where inventory is stored at the buyer's site and paid for only as used. Widespread adoption of methods such as this has freed up enormous resources across the *supply chain*. Just as buyers have benefited from the ability to find more sources more easily, suppliers have benefited from the ability to reach larger markets without additional cost.

In this chapter, we will review the most commonly used computer-based technology applications and their function in the organization. We will also cover the computerized systems tools being used in supply management and how they link to the organization's broader *information technology* structure.

Using Basic Information Technology Processes

Before delving into the specifics of procurement applications, and by way of an introduction to the subject matter, it is worthwhile to go over some of the fundamentals of computerized systems by looking at the basic terminology, along with the types of *platforms* in use and the nature of the *software applications* developed for them.

Computer Basics

As computer systems evolve, the language describing their individual elements naturally changes too. However, you will need to be familiar with some of the basic terminology to effectively manage your internal systems, regardless of their brand or configuration. In this section, we will discuss some of the most commonly used terms.

Data Processing Terms

Basic data processing terms describe the fundamental principles of information technology:

- *Bits/bytes* are the basic building blocks of computer technology. A bit is one binary digit—the smallest unit of computer programming—taking the form of a one or a zero. A byte is a grouping of eight bits that make up a single character.

- *Data* represents the basic information assembled from bits and bytes that is put into a computer.

- A *record* consists of an individual set of data, such as a name or an address.

- A *file* contains a set of related records that are usually stored in one place.

- A *digital system* is a system in which information is conveyed as data in a series of bits and bytes.

Hardware Terms

Computer hardware refers to the elements of a computer system that you can actually touch. The major terms that describe computer hardware include:

- The *central processing unit (CPU)* is the brains of the computer and is responsible for performing most of the computational work.

- *Storage media* consists of a variety of products, such as hard disk drives, memory chips, magnetic tape, CD-ROMs and DVDs, on which data is stored either optically or magnetically.

- *Input devices* are the hardware tools that enter data into the system. They include keyboards, scanners, readers, memory devices, and disks.

- *Output devices* are the hardware components that store or display information, such as printers, monitors, and the storage media listed previously.

- *Communication devices* transmit data between computers and across networks. They include modems, broadband routers, switches, and wireless receivers.

Computer Types

Today, virtually all appliances and automobiles use imbedded computers to one extent or another, so the list that follows is incomplete to the extent that it does not attempt to describe all computational devices. However, it does list the traditional set of computer types that buyers commonly refer to when they describe the kind of devices they commonly use.

- The *personal computer (PC)*, desktop or laptop is the most visible computer in use today and makes up the majority of devices purchasing managers employ.

- The *minicomputer* is one step above the PC and is designed for limited multi-user applications, such as those that might be found in smaller organization.

- The *mainframe* runs major applications that require a great deal of computational power and storage capacity. They also run large networks that communicate with thousands of terminals, sometimes located around the world.

- *Workstations* are devices that generally consist of dumb terminals that access data on a mini or mainframe computer in a client/server environment. However, in today's networking systems, PCs are quite frequently used as both stand-alone systems and as workstations.

- The *Personal Digital Assistant (PDA)* is a relatively small, portable device with only limited processing capability that connects to a computer to obtain information from calendars, address books, and lists of project items. PDAs are often combined with cell phones to provide maximum utility.

Network Terms

Computer networks consist of a series of computers linked together to exchange information. Some of the more common terms that reference computer networks include:

- A *local area network (LAN)* is a geographically restricted network, most commonly contained in one building.

- A *wide area network (WAN)* is a network that covers a large geographical area.

- The *Internet* is the largest computer network in the world, connecting millions of computers

- *TCP/IP (Transmission Control Protocol/Internet Protocol)* is a networking standard. TCP refers to that segment of the standard that moves data between applications; IP refers to the standard governing the movement of data between host computers.

- A *virtual private network (VPN)* is a data network that uses telecommunication lines and the Internet to exchange information but is secured by a *tunneling protocol* and firewalls.

- The *network operating system (NOS)* is the software that operates the network.

- *File Transfer Protocol (FTP)* is a standard that moves information across a network or the Internet.
- A *firewall* is a specialized software application that prevents unauthorized access to the network at the point where it connects to public systems.

Platforms

The term *platform* refers to the various underlying elements of a computer system: the software being used (such as the *operating system*), the hardware being used to run the software, and the method of storing and distributing data. This section addresses the latter usage and describes the fundamental configurations used in automated procurement systems.

Centralized Systems   A *centralized computer system* is a single computer—often called a *mainframe*—operating from one location but usually serving many users. These are most commonly used in a *client/server* configuration, where a workstation (or "dumb" terminal) without any processing capability is linked to a mainframe that does all the computational work. This model, in its simplest form, is shown in Figure 7.1. The major advantage of the centralized system is that it can be maintained and operated by fewer personnel since it is located in one place.

Distributed Systems   A *distributed system* is a collection of computer systems (both hardware and software) dispersed across several sites but operating as one cohesive unit. The systems' interaction is generally transparent to the users.

Networks are a form of distributed system that consists of a group of computers linked together electronically so that their users can share information. The most common types of networks are the local area networks (LANs) in which computers are geographically close to one another (typically, at the same location) and wide area networks (WANs) in which they are further apart and generally linked by some form of telecommunications media. This model is shown in Figure 7.2.

The major advantage of the distributed system is that it is modular and can be built or reconfigured fairly easily over large distances.

FIGURE 7.1   Client server system

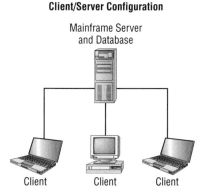

Client/Server Configuration

Mainframe Server
and Database

Client   Client   Client

FIGURE 7.2 Network system

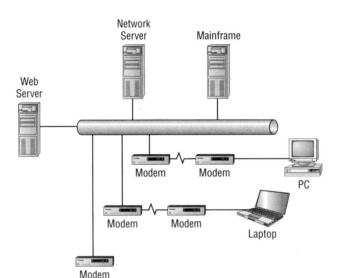

Software Applications

Software is a program or set of instructions that make the computer run or perform specific functions. As you know, software can be purchased as off-the-shelf items (sometimes referred to as "boxed") or as customized applications. Typically, the more common software applications such as word processing or spreadsheet software will be purchased in its packaged form through distributors or directly from the manufacturer. However, buyers usually have the option of downloading the software directly from the producer's website or can have it preinstalled on their computers by the hardware supplier. In some states, boxed software is taxable while the same software downloaded from a website is not, making downloading the software an attractive way to save money.

When buying mission critical applications—such as financial or manufacturing software—organizations often find that the "packaged" version does not meet all of its needs. Consequently, applications are typically modified—customized—by the original or third party programmers so that the software can meet these special needs.

It is sometimes helpful to categorize software types so that you can understand where a particular program fits in the computing process. There are two basic types of software:

Systems Software *Systems software* provides the instructions that make the computer run. Utilities and operating systems such as Microsoft Windows, MacOS, and Linux are typical examples. Systems software also manages the communications and interface aspects of the network.

Applications Software   *Applications software* enables the user to carry out specific tasks such as writing letters with word processing programs or performing financial analysis with spreadsheets programs. The term *applications* also applies to the broader, more scaleable systems such as Enterprise Resource Planning (ERP) applications that can manage an entire organization.

Using Software for Procurement

You will likely find that while much of the software in procurement applies to processes used by everyone in the organization, some of it is naturally dedicated to the procurement process only. As a purchasing manager, you will need to become familiar with virtually all the software used by the organization because your team will be responsible for its purchase, but you should also understand that your roll requires particular expertise in applications used primarily for supply management. When your organization seeks to acquire new or upgraded programs that impact your area, you should expect to be called upon for your knowledge of software tools dedicated to the purchasing function.

This section outlines the software applications most commonly used by various organizations, grouping them by general applications and applications specific to procurement operations.

General Business Applications

General software applications encompass a broad spectrum of software in today's organizations.

Desktop Applications

So-called *desktop applications* include a variety of commonly used software programs, many of which are released and sold in bundled configurations called suites. Microsoft Office is an example of this because it contains word processing, spreadsheets, e-mail, database, and presentation software—all typically designed to be used by the general public as well as the experts. In addition to the traditional office suites, there are numerous other types of applications available to manage files, scan documents, keep track of appointments and contacts, and manage finances. Some of the more commonly used include:

Word Processing   Programs such as MS Word or WordPerfect enable the creation and editing of text materials for letters, documents, reports, and tables.

Spreadsheets   Allow the user to organize, analyze, and manage numerical data; create graphs and charts; and generally provide powerful number crunching capability, including sorting and conversion of data through formulas.

Contact Management   Programs enable users to store and keep track of extensive lists of people. Typically, these tools are used in sales to manage customer relationships by maintaining records of contacts, projects underway, and customer preferences.

Database Management   This type of software allows for the management of relatively large amounts of data through powerful sorting and classification processes, enabling the user to organize and aggregate information logically. Typical *database management systems (DBMS)* in use today are those using relational models that organize data into rows and columns showing the relationship between elements. Two of the most common relational databases are Microsoft SQL and Oracle. The relational database has largely facilitated rapid access to large amounts of information, replacing the slower method of hierarchical databases that stored information in tree formats where data had to be accessed through its corresponding root element.

Project Management   These tools allow users to track complex projects by individual task and timeline. Project management software is often used as a "game plan" to ensure that all participants are aware of their responsibilities and to inform management of the timely progress of the project.

Web Access and E-mail

Web browsers such as Internet Explorer or Netscape provide yet another dimension to software applications, enabling users to effectively access the vast amount of information available through the Internet. As an adjunct to networks, the browser also provides the key user interface to the *World Wide Web*, where information and profiles on just about any organization can be found.

Networks leverage the Internet through the use of a single, common standard: TCP/IP). It is the basic communication language or protocol that allows computers to exchange information over the Internet.

Combined with browsers, *search engines* such as Yahoo! and Google provide some of the most powerful resources for the buyer. Search engines allow the user to quickly find and consolidate information on the Internet on just about any specific subject, product, or service. Today, these tools have become so efficient that they can (and frequently do) return thousands of *hits* for a search objective in a fraction of a second.

Perhaps more than any other tool, *e-mail* has revolutionized the way we communicate in computer-enabled societies. E-mail allows the immediate transmission of individual messages across the Internet and instantaneously enables individuals or groups to communicate vast amounts of information in real time.

WARNING   Tools such as these have vast potential for enhancing and accelerating business processes, but a particularly unpleasant downside also occurs: *Information overload.* Simply stated, this phenomenon occurs when individuals receive more information than they can process or absorb. While no official studies have yet been made public, information overload appears to be largely counterproductive and stress inducing.

Graphics Applications

Graphics tools include programs for creating and viewing illustrations, photography, diagrams, and blueprints. For example, we commonly use Adobe Acrobat Reader, a free application by

Adobe Systems Incorporated, to enable users to open and view document files that have been converted to a specific format that does not require you to have the original application in order to view it. Our engineers use AutoCAD to design and document manufactured parts, and we typically use programs such as Visio to document process flows in graphical format.

Security Applications

Ensuring that computer systems and files are maintained securely has become a major issue for organizations today. There has been a serious proliferation of malicious software distributed surreptitiously—such as *viruses*, *worms*, and *spyware*—that can have devastating effects on an organization's operations. Firewalls have been developed that allow limited access to a particular internal system by blocking material and users coming from systems outside the organization that do not have preauthorization to enter. In addition, software to filter viruses and worms is commonly deployed across networks to help block these attacks.

Additional common security devices include *encryption* and *digital signatures*:

Encryption   This involves the coding (or scrambling) of messages or data so that only the designated recipient can access them. The most common method in use is the *encryption key*. To decipher an encoded message, both the sender and receiver use the same code. In *public key encryption*, there are two keys: a public key that is available to anyone and a corresponding private key that only the sender can access. Using this method, any party can send a message encrypted with the subscriber's public key, but only the subscriber has the private key needed to decrypt it.

Digital Signatures   These consist of encryption technology and a *Public Key Infrastructure (PKI)* that determines the authenticity of a message and the identity of the sender to ensure that it has not been changed. Often, third parties are used as the certificate authority to manage and certify the authenticity of the signature.

Supply Management Applications

In addition to familiarizing yourself with those general applications and processes described in the previous section, you will need to develop a basic knowledge and understanding of the specific applications available for procurement and supply management. These applications, described next, primarily address transactional uses such as requisitioning and purchase order placement, but they also include planning and strategic management tools.

MRP/ERP

Material Requirements Planning (MRP) and *Manufacturing Resource Planning (MRPII)* systems, either as standalone applications or as elements of the larger Enterprise Resource Planning (ERP) system, are some of the most powerful tools available to organizations that need to plan and manage manufacturing operations and control inventory. In supply management, MRP systems primarily determine when to place orders for standard materials so that they arrive exactly when it needed. This helps to reduce the levels of inventory held by most manufacturing organizations and thereby improves cash flow.

Part of the MRP process involves forecasting demand for individual parts so that they can be ordered in advance of receiving actual customer orders. This complex process is generally handled by computer software programs through decision support models using calculated algorithms to predict future requirements. These requirements are, in turn, matched with the capacity of manufacturing centers using *Computer Aided Manufacturing (CAM)* software that controls the capacity and scheduling of equipment.

EDI

Electronic Data Interchange (EDI) is the most widely used process for exchanging data related to procurement between computers. Supported by the American National Standards Institute's (ANSI) *X12* process, basic EDI has been in use in manufacturing organizations for more than 25 years. The ANSI X12 standard defines the data exchange process currently in use, defining terms and specifying the sequence and character length of each *field*. Figure 7.3 describes the organization of this process, showing how individual elements (fields defined in a special dictionary) are rolled into functional segments. An example of a segment would be a "Ship To" address, where SHIP TO NAME, SHIP TO CITY, and so forth represent individual data elements. Segments are then incorporated in transaction sets (such as purchase orders) and then rolled up in functional groups and transmitted in an electronic "envelope."

X12 also specifies the format of processes through a system of numerically designated forms (14 in use by purchasing), each of which provides for a specific function. The following list of purchasing-related CNSI X12 documents provides some idea of the processes included in its scope:

- 840 Request For Quotation
- 997 Functional Acknowledgment
- 843 Response to Request for Quotation
- 832 Price/Sales Catalog
- 850 Purchase Order
- 855 Purchase Order Acknowledgment
- 824 Application Advice
- 860 Purchase Order Change
- 836 Contract Award Summary
- 865 Purchase Order Change Acknowledgment
- 838 Trading Partner Profile
- 869 Order Status Inquiry
- 864 Text Message
- 870 Order Status Report

FIGURE 7.3   The ANSI X12 EDI process

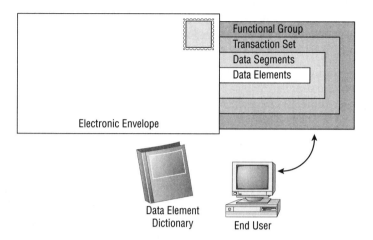

EDI processing is conducted between trading partners who have already negotiated contracts with one another. It is managed through a *value added network (VAN)* provider whose system translates the machine language from one trading partner's data processing system to another's, interconnecting the entire trading group. Setting up these systems can be quite costly, often in the range of $300 to $400,000, so it is understandable that only large organizations have found it cost effective to participate. Recently, however, ANSI has undertaken the conversion of its X12 standard to *XML (Extensible Markup Language)* for use on the Internet. This should provide a far less costly alternative to VANs.

E-procurement

Electronic procurement, or *e-procurement*, refers to exchanging various purchasing related information between organizations using the Internet as the data transfer tool. The Internet is, in part, a collection of networked parties known as the World Wide Web that use the TCP/IP standard to access and transfer data between one another. The Web uses *hypertext markup language (HTML)* as the standard code through which website displays are enabled and a *uniform resource locator (URL)* for identifying individual websites.

Since the World Wide Web is essentially a public system, parties often wish to connect privately to one another using an exclusive network called an *extranet* or virtual private network (VPN). Basically, these use the same protocols as do the public networks, but general access is restricted through the use of passwords and other forms of coding to exclude unrecognized visitors. Similarly, organizations often establish procurement networks within the confines of their firewall, called *intranets*, to maintain internal security and control of information until it is ready to be transmitted to the supplier.

Some of the more common applications using e-procurement processes are described next:

Requisitioning   Automating the requisitioning process is one of the most logical steps to reducing the transactional processing load in the Purchasing Department. Since the user has to complete the requisition anyway, this electronic process begins by converting the organization's paper requisitions to electronic ones. Often, these are created within the bounds of an existing system such as an Oracle or SAP ERP application. However, once the requisition has been submitted, it can be approved electronically by authorizing parties (leaving a clear, auditable trail) prior to submission to the buyer.

Upon receipt, the buyer can automatically convert the requisition to a purchase order and transmit it electronically to the supplier. Typically, *electronic purchase orders (EPOs)* are transmitted via e-mail or an electronically created fax, although companies using EDI can transmit them through their VAN.

Electronic Catalogs   The basis of an electronic requisitioning system is often an electronic catalog, typically maintained by the supplier and stored on either its website or the client's intranet. An electronic catalog is similar in organization to a paper catalog but is stored and accessed through the computer. Typically, users access the catalog for selection. Once the item they wish to purchase has been identified, it can be submitted directly for approval. Following approval, it is routed directly to the supplier, bypassing Purchasing altogether since Purchasing has already approved the catalog's content and negotiated the pricing with the supplier. Except for its automatic transmittal to the supplier, an electronic catalog order is treated in exactly the same manner as any other order.

By simplifying the ordering process for end-users, the Purchasing Department can often save significant cost by driving purchases through a single supplier under a contracted discount rather than using a variety of suppliers selling at list.

Automated RF*x*   In addition to automating the purchase order process, many organizations have tied their RFPs, RFIs, and RFQs to automated systems as well. This enables buyers to construct them from pre-existing templates and transmit them electronically to a much wider supply base than would be possible under traditional methods. The electronic method also allows for automated scoring of the suppliers' responses, removing the tediousness of detailed analysis by the buyer and enormously speeding the process of selection. This also helps avoid maverick purchasing of high-price items by using the excuse that the process just takes too long. It has been shown that an electronic RFP process can reduce the time it takes to go to contract from several months to only a couple of weeks.

Competitive Bidding Events and Reverse Auctions   Automated methods for submitting bids have proven quite effective in obtaining cost reductions because the widest possible supply base can be easily accessed from the computer. With increasing popularity, competitive bidding has turned to the reverse auction to drive substantial price reductions.

The *reverse auction* is conducted in much the same manner as a traditional auction except that suppliers are bidding the price *down*. Buyers have the ability to set the highest acceptable bid (or reserve price) prior to the auction and disclaimers typically give them the right to award to any party, regardless of their position in the bidding.

Inventory Management/Supplier Managed Inventory

In addition to the inventory management processes created by MRP that have enabled significant reductions in the volume of inventory, today there is a trend toward Supplier Managed Inventory,

---

⊕ Real World Scenario

Does the Indifference of a Reverse Auction Hurt Relationships?

"What about our existing relationships and special service we always receive from our supplier?" is the typical question coming from the user. Well, studies have shown that while auctions provide significant savings, they typically result in the incumbent winning the bid by nearly a 4 to 1 ratio!

Reverse auction companies have also developed ways to automatically transform bids from suppliers weaker in service or quality to the same level as their better counterparts, adding the extra cost to their bids by a predetermined factor. This results, for example, in adding a price factor to a supplier whose lower quality may result in 10 percent fewer usable parts of a 10 cents per dollar bid to make it equal to the supplier who has perfect quality.

---

whereby the supplier owns the material stored at your facility until you actually use it. This process is frequently combined with *evaluated receipts settlement (ERS)*, whereby payment is initiated by the pull order, rather than a supplier's invoice. The advantage to the supplier is automatic payment, typically without delay, and the elimination of the need to initiate an invoice. Combined with an *electronic funds transfer (EFT)*, which automatically transmits payment to the supplier's bank account, this system has led to tremendous reductions in transactional processing.

Contract Management

Software that tracks and maintains updates to contracts can be extremely useful to larger organizations in which individual divisions may not be aware of existing contracts at other divisions and thus not able to take advantage of lower pricing. This also prevents one division going through the tedious process of contracting for something already under contract by another division and resulting in enormous time and energy drains with no payback.

Cost Management and Spending Analysis

One of the keys to cost savings is through consolidating spending volumes going to several suppliers under one contract to obtain the greatest discount. Cost management software helps *rationalize* an organization's spending by analyzing the exact categories and suppliers of actual spending during a particular period. From this data, you should be able to formulate a strategy for combining purchases to leverage volume. Many organizations, unfortunately, have no idea what their spending by category or commodity is, since an analysis through manual processes would be nearly impossible. That, however, is changing, and one of the most rapidly growing categories of software is in this area.

Supplier Scorecards

Another of the key benefits of automation is the maintenance of *supplier scorecards*. These are typically the basis for the periodic business review and the ongoing evaluation of supplier performance.

They normally require a great deal of clerical time in tracking and recording specific data, but automated tools, combined with a centralized processing system such as ERP, enables buyers to pull period reports for on-time delivery, pricing trends, and returns at the touch of a key.

Asset Tracking

Asset tracking is usually maintained by the Finance Department, so Purchasing has only limited ability to determine when assets are approaching the end of their useful life and to efficiently plan for replacements. In addition, organizations often find themselves purchasing new equipment for one location when surplus exists in another so maintaining a widely accessible database or a website where obsolete equipment can be listed makes good sense. Currently, greater effort is being given to enabling the involvement of Purchasing in the management and sale of surplus assets so that expenses can be further reduced by recycling excess equipment within the organization.

Preventative Maintenance

In environments where equipment is frequently used, the ordering of spare parts has placed heavy burdens on the Purchasing Department. However, software is becoming increasingly available that ties the scheduled replacement of parts directly to an electronic ordering system, eliminating the need for buyer involvement on a day-to-day basis.

Impact of Automation on Procurement Organizations

The overall impact of current trends toward automation of the transactional processes has led to a recent transformation of the procurement function itself. With the burden of processing purchase orders largely removed from the buying team, organizations are beginning to find more use for their staff in the strategic functions of cost reduction, risk mitigation, and supplier development. This has resulted in a general trend toward upgrading the quality of the Purchasing staff, which places more of a burden on the purchasing manager to recruit talented staff and to reengineer existing process to enable a more strategic, proactive approach. In today's organizations, the enlightened purchasing manager is given more and more responsibility as an overall business manager charged with ensuring that best practices are implemented throughout the supply community.

Sourcing Supply Management Tools

The Purchasing Department plays a dual role in the selection and acquisition of supply management software: providing domain expertise for the development of the statement of work and the typical support role in supplier selection. Generally, the IT group will handle the actual specification development since their team will be providing ongoing support and maintenance for any software installed.

The next section reviews some of the basic aspects the purchasing manager should consider when engaged in this process.

Software

As outlined in the previous sections, the software requirements for supply management generally include systems related to MRP processes and systems related to e-procurement. From a sourcing standpoint, organizations generally opt for inclusion of new or additional modules in their existing ERP framework. However, many of the applications for e-procurement have been developed only recently—spending analysis, for example—so organizations find that they are faced with a number of issues. Should they create applications themselves, or should they acquire third party systems that may not be compatible with their existing systems? Or should they postpone acquisition for the present time and wait until the provider of their existing software platform gets around to developing the process as an additional module?

Make or Buy

The make-or-buy decision for software largely depends on the immediacy of the return on investment and the availability of market-based applications that suitably meet the organization's requirements. In addition, you must also assess the risk factors that may be involved. Use these questions as a brief checklist:

Expertise Available	Can you successfully engage commercial resources that will be able to develop applications to meet your organization's needs?
	How well you can define your requirements?
Potential Risks	What issues are related to the successful implementation of the project?
	What potential risk exists down the road?
Costs	Are the costs fully understood?
	What potential exists for unknown costs surfacing during the project?
	Will customization add significantly to the overall cost?
	What are the ongoing costs for maintenance?
	How do licensing fees compare?
Fit	To what extent will customized software better fit the organization's specific needs?
	How easy will it be to migrate to your platform?

Customized versus Off-the-Shelf

Similar to the make-or-buy decision is the consideration to customize purchased software to meet the perceived special needs of your organization. The temptation, of course, is to bring in the new system to operate exactly as the old system to increase the comfort level of the users.

However, you should consider not only the initial cost to customize but also the ongoing cost of maintenance since the publisher's upgrades to existing software may eliminate the customization already installed or require additional work prior to deployment. You should also keep in mind that there will be ongoing support required and consider the impact of potential turnover of the supplier's staff.

Training

During the selection process for software, training issues should not be overlooked. At the least, you will want to determine the overall cost of training and if it will be held in-house or at a remote location requiring travel. You should also determine the impact to existing operations during the training as a result of lost time.

Outsourcing

Outsourcing IT applications has become relatively common today, especially favoring suppliers who manage networks, help desks, and websites. Most organizations feel that it is no longer part of their core competencies to manage the complex infrastructure required to support fully developed systems. In addition, the coming of age of *Application Service Providers (ASPs)*—software providers who, in effect, rent software that they then maintain on their site—has lent additional credibility to the improved ROI of leasing as these suppliers move into supporting essential functions for the organization. As the IT function moves off-shore to find less expensive labor, the outsourcing formula becomes even more attractive.

While outsourcing continues to remain a risk-focused decision, organizations are increasingly finding that where core competencies are not involved, the benefits of dedicated expertise and reduced cost far outweigh the loss of control.

Summary

Automation is becoming a way of life for today's procurement professional as the variety of tools available for transactional processing expands. As a result, the purchasing manager has to learn new skills to manage technology, including a basic understanding of how computer technology works. The purchasing manager's vocabulary should include standard data processing terminology and a familiarity with the hardware and network requirements common in contemporary organizations. In addition, it is more and more accepted that the purchasing staff will have adequate facility with the more commonly used business software applications such as word processing and spreadsheet management.

Supply management applications are changing rapidly as well, and virtually every function has seen some form of automation. Organizations are increasingly turning to ERP to ensure process uniformity across operations to supplement their original implementations of financial and human resource programs. MRP and EDI are now becoming modules in a broader spectrum of applications. The recent trend to web-based processes has also affected procurement, and buyers are learning that the automation of traditional methods such as competitive bidding provides significant advantages. However, along with the benefits these processes offer is the downside of potential information overload.

One of the side effects of this process is that the purchasing manager is increasingly becoming the organization's domain expert when it comes to selecting software and systems that automate supplier management. As a result, you will find that you are now applying the same decision-making processes (such as make or buy) to your own department that you previously applied to your customer.

For additional reading on topics related to this chapter, please see Appendix A.

Exam Essentials

Understand the basic systems in information technology.   Know the essentials of computer terminology, common hardware types, and software application types. You will also need to understand the basics of network operations and their commonly used terms.

Understand the basic platforms used by computer systems.   Recognize the differences between centralized and distributed systems and where each fits in the organization's scope.

Be able to select the proper tools for purchasing functions from commonly used software applications.   Become familiar with a wide variety of applications used by organizations, including database management, project management, graphics, security, and e-mail software.

Understand the types of systems commonly employed in making purchasing decisions.   Become very familiar with MRP and ERP applications and how they integrate into the purchasing process.

Be able to define and implement e-procurement programs.   Obtain a working knowledge of web-based applications, as well as electronic requisitioning tools, electronic catalogs, and automated RFx processes. In addition, you should understand the automation processes applied to competitive bidding and how they can benefit the organization.

Be able to select the proper software tools for improving purchasing operations and effectiveness.   Become familiar with automated applications that support improved operations, such as tools that analyze spending and assist with cost management and tools that are used for contract and inventory management.

Perform make-or-buy decisions for purchasing software.   Familiarize yourself with the questions that must be answered to determine make-or-buy and software customization decisions. You should also be aware of the implications inherent in outsourcing IT operations.

Review Questions

1.   A geographically distributed network is known as a:

  A. LAN

  B. TCP

  C. WAN

  D. VAN

  E. FTP

2.   In information technology terminology, a set of data such as an address is called a:

  A. File

  B. System

  C. Information

  D. Record

  E. CPU

3.   A network is an example of a:

  A. Distributed system

  B. Virtual private network

  C. Software application

  D. Centralized system

  E. Database management system

4.   The standard governing the flow of data across a network is called:

  A. CPU

  B. TCP/IP

  C. WAN

  D. DBMS

  E. WWW

5.   The system used to plan and time purchases is called:

  A. ERP

  B. EDI

  C. ANSI

  D. MRP

  E. RFQ

6. The process known as Electronic Data Interchange uses which standard?

    A. ANSI X12

    B. TCP/IP

    C. VPN

    D. CAD

    E. PKE

7. SAP is an example of which of the following systems?

    A. CAD

    B. HTML

    C. CPU

    D. ERP

    E. EPO

8. An electronic catalog:

    A. Does not require maintenance

    B. Converts requisitions to purchase orders

    C. Is used to develop an RFQ

    D. Can reduce cost

    E. Requires EDI

9. The decision to buy "off-the-shelf" software applications or create them independently depends mostly on:

    A. Availability of expert resources

    B. Level of automation

    C. Network availability

    D. Security

    E. Customization

10. Automating the RFP process:

    A. Eliminates unwanted suppliers

    B. Reduces negotiating

    C. Increases prices

    D. Improves supplier relations

    E. Reduces contracting cycle time

Answers to Review Questions

1. C. A geographically dispersed network is called a wide area network and is known by the acronym WAN.

2. D. A record consists of an individual set of data, represented by the basic information assembled from bits and bytes.

3. A. A distributed system is a collection of computer systems dispersed across several sites. This also describes a network.

4. B. Networks leverage the Internet through the use of a single, common standard: TCP/IP, which stands for Transmission Control Protocol/Internet Protocol. It is the basic communication language, or protocol, that allows computers to exchange information over the Internet.

5. D. Part of the MRP (Material Requirements Planning) process involves forecasting demand for individual parts so that they can be ordered in advance of receiving actual customer orders.

6. A. The ANSI X12 standard defines the electronic data exchange process currently in use, defining terms and specifying the sequence and character length of each field.

7. D. SAP, like Oracle, is a supplier of ERP (Enterprise Resource Planning) systems.

8. D. By simplifying the ordering process for end-users, the Purchasing Department can often save significant cost by driving purchases through a single supplier under a contracted discount rather than using a variety of suppliers selling at list.

9. A. An important question that should be answered in the decision making process relates to the availability of expertise is can you successfully engage commercial resources that will be able to develop applications to meet your organization's needs?

10. E. It has been shown that an electronic RFP process can reduce the time it takes to go to contract from several months to only a couple of weeks.

Chapter

8

Managing Quality

THE C.P.M. EXAM SPECIFICATIONS COVERED IN THIS CHAPTER INCLUDE THE FOLLOWING:

✓ Managing and measuring quality performance

✓ Ensuring quality performance

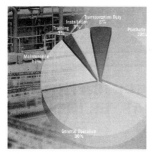

Virtually all organizations strive to improve the quality of their products and services. In fact, quality is often the most critical aspect of the product or service you buy, so it is not surprising to learn that a great deal of effort is spent identifying the degree to which your purchase conforms to the established quality requirements.

In its supplier management role, one of the key responsibilities of the Purchasing Department is to ensure that the organization's quality requirements are being met consistently in order for it to maximize the value from its purchase. But "quality" itself seems to be so broad a subject that purchasing managers are often at odds as to what exactly they mean when they speak of it.

We turn, therefore, to a review of the basic concepts of quality management in this chapter to ensure you understand what quality means, how it is measured, and how you go about achieving its full value. Here you'll look at how you will generally manage your quality activities, how you will measure your suppliers' performance, and how you will go about ensuring that your organization's overall quality objectives are being achieved.

Managing Quality Performance

Managing quality performance has a number of aspects: First of all, you must define what you mean by quality and how it fits into your overall organizational strategy. Second, you need to understand where your organization is currently operating in the range of acceptable performance, and third, you need to determine how you intend to improve it.

Quality Assurance

Quality assurance plays a significant role in the Purchasing Department's daily activities. To a large extent, it drives many of your fundamental processes. Taken in its broadest functional terms, quality assurance is a set of activities through which you define, measure, evaluate, and accept the products and services you purchase, often within the structure of the organization's policies and standard operating procedures. Quality assurance also includes the formal process of identifying and correcting specific problems and deficiencies and the methodology used to do so.

Larger organizations usually have separate departments called quality control or quality assurance, and they often have special job titles that accompany the function, such as quality engineer or supplier quality engineer. Supplier quality and manufacturing quality sections are typically distinct, with the supplier quality function generally included within the purchasing organization. In addition to maintaining incoming inspection processes, Supplier Quality Engineering groups are responsible for identifying, monitoring, and correcting quality problems originating with suppliers.

Defining Quality

In purchasing, when purchasing professionals refer to quality, they usually mean the contractual obligation they have formed with the supplier to provide products or service that conform to a given specification or statement of work. Generally speaking, there are two aspects to this conformance: first, you should consider how closely a product or service matches your requirement, referring to your specification as the baseline metric. In this aspect, you measure the precise deviation (or allowable *tolerance*) from a given number to determine if it meets specification. Second, you consider the actual frequency with which a product or service meets the specification. Here you want to know how often individual elements in a given lot of goods fall outside the acceptable limits.

As an example of how you might look at conformance to specifications, please consider this: if the wall of an aluminum tube is specified to be 1/32 of an inch thick (0.03125) with a tolerance of +/−.0001 of an inch, a tube measuring between 0.03124 and 0.03126 would be within an acceptable range. One measuring 0.031265, however, would not. So in this particular case, any submission outside the specified range would not meet your requirements.

However, purchasing managers must recognize the fact that there are inherent variances produced in the manufacturing of aluminum pipe that prevent the absolute conformance to this specification all the time. Therefore, you measure how often within any given shipment you can expect to find individual tubes that do not meet this tolerance. You might specify this by requiring that 99.5 percent of the material sampled fall into the =/− range. If it does, you accept the entire lot; if it does not, you reject the entire lot.

Employing Quality Systems

Measuring and sampling incoming material, then, is one way to control and manage your suppliers' quality, especially in a product focused, manufacturing environment. A system usually used for this is Statistical Process Control (SPC), and it will be discussed in some detail later in this chapter. However, for your reference, some other commonly used quality system tools are discussed in the following sections.

Certification

Supplier certification is one way of reducing (or eliminating altogether) the need for incoming inspection. In certifying a supplier, the buying organization typically determines that the supplier's internal system for measurement and control of quality is sufficient to ensure it will meet the minimum quality level required without performing further incoming inspections. Certification is often provided on a part-by-part basis rather than as an overall blanket endorsement, so suppliers will need to "qualify" or recertify for each new part they produce.

When a supplier has been certified, it means that your organization will rely solely upon their internal controls to produce acceptable quality. This process usually works fine, but there is one significant caveat: because certification is based on the supplier's current processes (and equipment), your organization will need to know in advance when a supplier changes any production processes so that you can either recertify the process or reintroduce incoming inspection. The need for a proactive, compliant communication system to monitor these activities is evident, and you should carefully include this as a requirement in your supplier certification agreement.

You should also understand that the UCC requirement to inspect incoming materials in a reasonable period of time after receipt will still apply, and your organization will assume responsibility for the goods even if no incoming inspection is actually performed. In your agreement, you should extend liability for nonconforming parts to the supplier until the materials are actually used.

Acceptance Testing

Used most frequently when purchasing capital equipment, *acceptance testing* is a method for determining if a particular piece of equipment is functioning at its expected output level. This usually requires an engineering or manufacturing sign-off and a formal acknowledgment of acceptance (or rejection) communicated to the supplier.

The acceptance testing process is also commonly used to test the first article submitted for approval prior to the supplier's actual manufacture and may represent a step in the certification process.

Inspection Process

The inspection process usually specifies a range of inspection frequency, extending from 100 percent inspection of all products to no inspection at all or any level in between. In most cases, the buying organization may specify routine lot sampling on a random basis or at specific lots or time intervals, or it may require actual on site audits of the process used by the supplier to measure quality.

The location of the inspection is important, too. It is generally agreed that the earlier in the process the inspection can take place, the less costly the corrective action will be. As a result, requirements may specify that the inspection will take place on the supplier's manufacturing line or at final assembly or even as a separate process prior to shipment. Inspection may also be called for at your plant at various operational stages, as well: at the receiving dock, upon release to manufacturing, or even at your final assembly stage.

Similarly, in a service environment, the results or output of the service can require inspection at a variety of times and places. While it is not usual to perform acceptance testing as one might for equipment, there may be a requirement within the SOW that calls for some method of services inspection as part of gathering the metrics for a service level agreement.

Measuring Quality Performance

It's an old adage that you tend to get what you measure for, since professionals have a known tendency to work toward specific goals. For this reason, the ongoing measurement of quality performance becomes critical to the success of any serious effort to generate improvements, keeping in mind, of course, that there are numerous methods for measurement in common use today. Choosing the right measurement depends, to a large degree, on what you intend to accomplish.

Testing for Quality

Most of the time, the measurements you receive relating to quality performance will be based upon some specific testing. These measurements will tell you if the material you are receiving conforms to your specifications or if the process being used to produce the products has the capability of doing the job. In the section that follows, we will examine briefly those methods you are most likely to encounter.

Statistical Process Control (SPC)

SPC was previously defined in Chapter 2, "Sourcing," as a system that measures the actual distribution of events from the beginning to the end of a given process. It is a method of monitoring, controlling, and ideally, improving a process through statistical probability analysis. Its four basic steps include measuring the process, eliminating variances in the process to make it consistent, monitoring the process, and improving the process to its best target value.

When applied to quality measurement, SPC allows you to determine if the output of your process is within the desired range of control. As you will recall, two key measures are used in SPC: the Upper Control Limit (UCL)—the highest point of measurement at which performance is acceptable—and the Lower Control Limit (LCL)—the lowest point of measurement at which performance is acceptable. Between these two points, events are considered acceptable and the process is considered to be in control.

Buyers generally use SPC to measure the tolerances of products produced during rapidly repeating operational cycles, such as the output from automated machinery. In this environment, you determine the range of tolerance mathematically as three *standard deviations* above or below the average of the process. Standard deviation is a statistical measure of the variability or dispersion within a set of data points. It is calculated from the deviation or mathematical distance between each data value and the sample statistical mean, and is usually represented by the Greek letter "S" for sigma. The more dispersed the data is, the larger the standard deviation.

> For data that follows a normal distribution, approximately 68 percent of all data will fall within one standard deviation of the sample mean, 95 percent of all values will fall within two standard deviations, and 99.7 percent of all data will fall within three standard deviations.

Tolerances

By definition, *tolerance* refers to the amount of deviation from the specification data points you are willing to accept. Tolerance is usually given in the same unit of measure or dimension as the specification, as we noted in the example given earlier in the chapter in the section "Defining Quality."

Tolerance stack-up measures the cumulative variations of each of the items in an assembly that goes into a final product. Tolerance stack-up analysis determines if a form, fit, or function problem exists when manufacturing tolerances combine in a finished part or assembly. Tolerance stack-up analysis is typically performed either by assuming worst-case allowable dimensions, or by using statistical analysis of tolerances.

Pareto Charts

The Pareto chart is a type of quality analysis that determines if a few categories or units account for the majority of the total occurrences. The chart simply displays events in the order of their frequency.

> The commonly used Pareto Principle (or 80/20 rule) was originally defined by J.M. Juran in 1950 and named after Vilfredo Pareto, a nineteenth-century Italian economist who studied the distribution of the world's wealth. Pareto concluded that the majority (80 percent) of the world's wealth was in the hands of a minority of its population (20 percent).

Figure 8.1 represents an example of a Pareto chart showing the percentage by category and the cumulative percentage of defects in a hypothetical failure analysis.

FIGURE 8.1   Pareto analysis chart

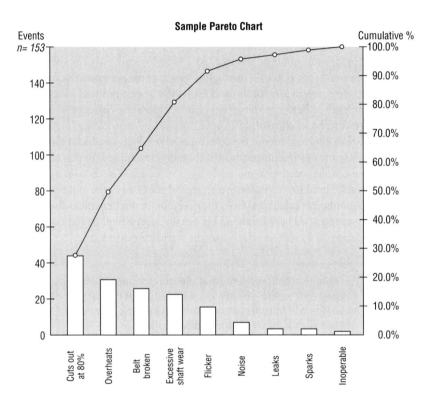

C~pk~

C_{pk} is a process *capability index*. Process capability analysis entails comparing the performance of a process against its specifications. A process is capable if virtually all of the possible variable values fall within the specification limits. This is measured numerically by using a capability index, C_p, with the formula:

$$C_p = \frac{USL - LSL}{6s}$$

In the preceding formula, USL stands for Upper Specification Limit, and LSL stands for Lower Specification Limit. S means standard deviation.

This equation indicates that the measure of process capability is how much of the observed process variation (USL minus LSL) is covered by the process specifications. In this case, the process variation is measured by 6 standard deviations (+/– 3 on each side of the mean). If Cp is greater than 1.0, then the process specification covers almost all of the process observations.

However, the *Cp* index does not account for a process that is off-center. This equation can be modified to account for off-center processes to obtain the *Cpk* index as follows:

$$Cpk = \min \left[\frac{USL - \bar{x}}{3s}, \frac{\bar{x} - LSL}{3s} \right]$$

This equation takes the minimum distance between your specification limits and the process mean and divides it by three standard deviations to arrive at the measure of process capability.

Benchmarking

As it relates to quality considerations, benchmarking is the process of measuring your organization's performance against others within the same business sector or industry to determine what constitutes *best-in-class performance* and how it has been achieved. This comparison can form the basis for a quality improvement program targeting those areas where quality gaps or deviations exist. Benchmarking is also frequently used in conjunction with strategic *value analysis* and planning to help establish goals and allocate resources according to an overall organizational system of priorities.

Philosophically, benchmarking can be considered simply as the search for better methods. It is a way of identifying areas that need reengineering, change, and improvement. It is also a blend of qualitative and quantitative research that can be tedious and painfully difficult to gather, consuming a great deal of resources. For this reason, many organizations turn to consultants and research organizations that are in the business of gathering this information as a way of accelerating the improvement process.

Ensuring Quality Performance

Doubtlessly, one major compliance issue in most organizations involves the notion of getting full value for the price paid. So it is not surprising that ensuring quality performance from suppliers is generally an excellent way to improve the value of purchased goods and services. You should continually ask the question, how do I know that my organization is receiving the full value of its contractual spending? Ensuring quality performance is certainly one proven way.

Let's examine, then, some of the concepts and tools relating to ensuring quality performance from your suppliers.

Enforcing Quality Requirements

The process that *enforces* quality compliance is the key to successfully ensuring your organization's quality policies and requirements are met by your suppliers. In most organizations with a formal quality program, the central tool for this is the *corrective action process*. Surrounding this process is the accurate documentation of quality standards and their conveyance to the supplier, as well as the development of an analysis of the root cause of the issue so that ongoing progress toward resolution of the problem can be properly monitored.

Documenting Quality Requirements

Without proper documentation, quality requirements are rendered virtually meaningless. In most cases, documentation will be related to supplier conformance issues and incoming inspections, but don't overlook the need to maintain accurate records of supplier site visits (when performed) and the history of the supplier's qualification or certification process. The qualification process establishes the supplier's level of capability, and it is important that you refer to this as a baseline when assessing the supplier's ongoing level of support. In many organizations, quality reporting is required on a periodic basis and is usually incorporated into the formal supplier review process.

Conveying Standards

As part of the documentation process, your organization needs to have a system in place that defines the standards of conformance so that all parties will have a baseline point of reference when reviewing quality performance. These often take the form of a set of written specifications and a system for organizing them, usually some body of standard operating procedures (SOP), where the measures of conformance you use are typically referred to as Key Performance Indicators (KPI).

Corrective Action Process

Many organizations employ the *corrective action* process whenever standards of quality conformance are not met by suppliers. This process traditionally documents and conveys notification of supplier nonconformance and similarly documents the requirements and steps necessary to correct the noncompliant situation. The goal of the process is to eliminate the cause of the problem.

Many organizations have robust and well-defined procedures for handling corrective actions. As one example, see the 20-page document used by the Los Alamos National Laboratory, which can be found at http://erproject.lanl.gov/Common/Procedures/QPs/QP-3%204R3.pdf.

ISO 9000:2000 defines corrective action as an action to eliminate the cause of a detected nonconformity or other undesirable situation. Accordingly, the component steps for the process include:

1. Recognize the problem and its effect.

2. Determine the root cause.

3. Determine and implement a short term action plan (often called the "containment" phase).

4. Determine and implement a comprehensive action plan.

5. Determine and implement a preventive action plan.

6. Follow up to ensure compliance.

7. Audit to ensure the plans are effectively eliminating the problem.

Developing Root Cause Analysis

Before you can fully resolve any quality discrepancy, you need to identify and understand its root cause. A *root cause* is the element (or sequence of events) that, if corrected, will prevent a recurrence of the problem in the future. What is the underlying and fundamental element or chain of events that gave rise to the problem in the first place? For tracing the causal relationship of quality issues you'll use process called *root cause analysis*. Root cause analysis thus provides a structured methodology for determining the causal relationships of various elements in the process that may be ultimately responsible for the problem.

As with the corrective action process, root cause analysis also follows a sequential methodology that includes:

1. Data collection. This procedure should take place as close in time as possible to the initial discovery of the problem to minimize the loss of information.

2. Assessment. The assessment phase includes analyzing the data to identify causal factors, summarizing the findings, and organizing them according to logical categories.

3. Corrective action. Identify and implement viable solutions. This means finding answers to several questions, including:

   a. How will the corrective action prevent recurrence?

   b. What new risks will this action introduce?

   c. Does the action fit in with overall objectives?

   d. Are resources available to properly implement the correction?

   e. What are the secondary consequences of implementation?

   f. Can the corrective action be implemented within an appropriate time frame?

   g. Will the results be measurable?

4. Follow-up. Determine if the corrective action has had the desirable effect in resolving the problem. If the problem recurs, the original instance should be reinvestigated to determine if it was properly analyzed.

Other Corrective Action Options

When suppliers are responsible for nonconforming goods or other quality issues, there are a number of options open to you.

Return   Nonconforming goods can be returned to the supplier for further action. (Keep in mind, your organization may be responsible for any further damage while the goods are in its care.) Under the UCC, both the buyer and the supplier have a number of options regarding correction including repair or replacement. If services are involved, however, the likely remedy will be to redo the work or accept some form of discount.

Rework   Under some circumstances, the buyer may be authorized to rework nonconforming goods or services at the supplier's expense. While this requires a negotiated settlement with the supplier, it might prove less expensive than having the products returned or redeploying personnel to correct the deficiency.

Renegotiate   In the case of nonconforming goods or services that are partially usable, the buyer may choose to accept the existing performance and negotiate a reduced rate.

Retrain or Remove   Ultimately, you will need to decide how the nonconformance, or continuing nonconformance, affects your organization's relationship with the supplier. Should you consider having the supplier retrain its employees as part of the corrective action or should you simply find another source for your purchase?

Total Quality Management

Total Quality Management (TQM) is an enduring process of continuous improvement focused on increasing customer satisfaction. As a philosophy, TQM requires the active participation of all members of the organization in working toward the improvement of processes, methods, and services and the culture in which they are fostered.

 Real World Scenario

The Power of TQM

In 1993, the Boeing Corporation was placed on a limited production status (a form of probation) by the Air Force as a result of quality problems, late deliveries, cost overruns, and an adversarial relationship. Boeing's leadership stepped in and implemented TQM with the stated goals of total customer satisfaction, incorporating quality in everything they did and involving the entire team in the optimization of processes. The team focused on the systematic and integrated framework of TQM.

So successful was this approach that in 1998 this team was the winner of the Malcolm Baldridge National Quality Award given by the President of the United States, and today they are contenders for yet another Malcolm Baldridge Award.

Deploying TQM in Purchasing

The most commonly used implementation of TQM in purchasing is likely the use of the supplier scorecard combined with the supplier business review. It is through this process that purchasing has the opportunity to address ongoing product quality or quality of service issues in a meaningful way. By measuring and monitoring performance on a regular basis and by utilizing the dynamics of a cross-functional team, continuous improvement processes can become extremely effective tools for developing greater customer satisfaction.

Kaizen

Kaizen is a discipline closely related to TQM. Kaizen generally means "improvement." Originally a Buddhist term, Kaizen comes from the Japanese phrase, "renew the heart and make it good." Closely related to the western concepts of TQM and continuous improvement, adaptation of the

Kaizen concept also requires changes in "the heart" of the business, corporate culture, and structure, since Kaizen enables companies to translate the corporate vision in every aspect of a company's operational practice. Thus, in the workplace Kaizen means continuous improvement involving everyone as a group or team, from the CEO to the delivery van driver. Proponents of this way of thinking believe that continuous development and improvement is critical to the organization's long term success.

Quality Functional Deployment

Quality Functional Deployment (QFD) is another adjunct of TQM. As a system, it links the needs of the customer or end user with the design, development, engineering, manufacturing, and service functions. The concept develops from a consideration that in today's industrial society there is a growing separation between producer and consumer. QFD is meant to help organizations discover both spoken and unspoken needs, translate these into actions and designs, and focus various organizational efforts on achieving a common goal of customer satisfaction. QFD thus seeks to create a culture where organizational goals are formulated to exceed normal expectations and provide a level of enthusiasm that generates both tangible and perceived value.

Employing Quality Systems

Two major quality standard systems are in use today that, in many ways, complement one another and enable organizations to provide greater customer focused quality assurance. The key elements of these systems, Six Sigma and ISO, are briefly outlined in the sections that follow.

Six Sigma

Six Sigma is a quality movement and improvement program that grew from TQM. As a methodology, it focuses on controlling processes to +/– six sigma (standard deviations) from a centerline, which is the equivalent of 3.4 defects per million opportunities (where an opportunity is characterized as chance of not meeting the required specification). Six Sigma fundamental tenets include reducing the variation within a process, improving system capability, and identifying essential factors that the customer views as crucial to quality.

Six Sigma methodologies incorporate six steps corresponding to the acronym *DMAIC*:

D = Define customer requirement and improvement goals

M = Measure variables of the process

A = Analyze data to establish inputs and outputs

I = Improve system elements to achieve performance goals

C = Control the key variables to sustain the gains

You can obtain further information about this process by visiting the American Society for Quality's website at www.asq.org.

ISO Standards

ISO, the International Organization for Standardization, was established in 1947 as an effort to consolidate widely dispersed methods of approaching quality standards. Its stated goal was to facilitate a means of coordinating, developing, and unifying industrial and technical quality standards. Based in Geneva, Switzerland, ISO is staffed by representatives from standards organizations in each of its member countries, working through committees that establish standards for industry, research, and government.

ISO 9000

In 1987, ISO issued a series of quality management and quality assurance standards as the ISO 9000 series that today, has been adopted by more than 500,000 organizations in 149 countries. This body of standards now provides a framework for customer focused quality management throughout the global business community and has been widely acknowledged as providing the paradigm of assurance that customers will consistently find uniform quality in the products and services they purchase. Organizations are today certified as having achieved the standard through examination by an ISO registrar and may then use that certification as an assurance that standardized methods are being employed.

The 1994 editions of ISO 9001, ISO 9002, and ISO 9003 were consolidated into a single revised document, which is now represented by ISO 9001:2000. ISO suggests that the greatest value is obtained when organizations use the entire family of standards in an integrated manner. It is suggested that, beginning with ISO 9000:2000, organizations adopt ISO 9001:2000 to achieve a first level of performance. The practices described in ISO 9004:2000 may then be implemented to make the quality management system increasingly effective in achieving organizational goals. ISO 9001:2000 and ISO 9004:2000 have been formatted as a consistent pair of standards to facilitate their use. ISO maintains that using the standards in this way will help relate them to other management systems and many sector-specific requirements (such as ISO/TS/16949 in the automotive industry) and will assist companies in gaining recognition through national award programs.

For the Purchasing Department, ISO compliance generally means implementing a series of quality assurance procedures that cover:

- An evaluation process for the selection of qualified vendors
- A periodic review of supplier performance, along with remedial action for unsatisfactory performance
- Documentation of quality requirements in the purchase order
- Quality control procedures for incoming material
- Establishment of quality systems and monitoring at suppliers' plants
- Procedures for tracking supplier defects and resolving quality issues with them
- Implementation of supplier training programs
- Collaboration in establishing joint quality assurance programs

ISO 14000

ISO 14000 is a series of international standards on environmental management. It provides a framework for the development of an environmental management and evaluation system and the supporting audit program. The standard does not prescribe environmental performance targets but instead provide organizations with the tools to assess and control the environmental impact of their activities, products, or services. The standards currently address environmental management systems, environmental auditing, environmental labels and declarations, environmental performance evaluation, and life cycle assessment.

To learn more about this important set of standards, you might want to visit the ISO website at www.iso.org.

Summary

Managing quality at the supplier level is one of the key areas where Purchasing Departments can add value. This generally means working closely with your internal quality assurance team to ensure that your suppliers are fully measuring up to their contractual obligations.

Understanding quality management requires that you first have a clear definition of your organization's quality objectives and improvement programs. You can then use this information to develop and manage supplier certification and qualification programs as well as to monitor the day-to-day quality performance of suppliers through statistical processes and inspections. Some of the common methods you will be expected to work with include SPC, C_{pk}, Pareto charts, and benchmarking the performance of other organizations to determine best-in-class measures.

Ensuring the quality performance of your suppliers will include documenting and conveying your organization's standards and requirements as well as your participation in remediation activities such as corrective action processes, root cause analysis, and exercising a variety of other options available to supply management under the UCC.

You will also be required to understand various TQM processes (along with Kaizen and QFD), how they are structured, and how they are deployed in purchasing. This will mean developing a working knowledge of the principles and objectives of the predominant quality systems such as Six Sigma and ISO.

 For additional reading on topics related to this chapter, please see Appendix A.

Exam Essentials

Be able to define quality.   For purchasing, quality generally means the supplier's conformance to specifications.

Be able to identify management systems used to help control quality.   Commonly used systems such as supplier certification and acceptance testing supplement various inspection processes.

Understand how quality is measured.   Typically used measurement systems include SPC, C_{pk}, Pareto charts, and benchmarking.

Know how to enforce quality requirements.   Proper documentation and conveyance of standards and requirements is one way to enforce quality requirements. You will also use the corrective action process and root cause analysis to deal with discrepancies, and there are a number of options available to the buyer under the UCC.

Understand Total Quality Management.   The principles of TQM are founded on continuous improvement and universal participation in quality management. TQM also includes systems such as Kaizen and QFD.

Understand the principles of key quality systems.   Two key systems are being commonly employed today: Six Sigma and ISO. Six Sigma's basic process can be defined in the acronym DMAIC. ISO standards are based on the 9000 and new 14000 series that set forth compliance standards and activities.

Review Questions

1. Acceptance testing is most likely to be used for:
   A. Indirect material
   B. Inventoried material
   C. Capital equipment
   D. Services
   E. None of the above

2. Corrective action options include all of the following *except*:
   A. Renegotiation
   B. Reduction
   C. Rework
   D. Replacement
   E. Re-sourcing

3. TQM is primarily a process of:
   A. Inspection
   B. Continuous improvement
   C. Error reduction
   D. Conformance
   E. Compliance

4. Benchmarking of quality can be best used to:
   A. Document requirements
   B. Drive compliance
   C. Develop quality systems
   D. Identify performance gaps
   E. Compare quality systems

5. Six Sigma methodology includes all these activities *except*:
   A. Measuring process variables
   B. Determining system capability
   C. Analyzing data
   D. Controlling key variables
   E. Establishing inputs

6. The first level of ISO performance is:

    A. ISO 9004:2000

    B. ISO 9000:2000

    C. ISO 9001:2000

    D. ISO 9002:2000

    E. ISO 9000:2001

7. QFD is an adjunct of:

    A. Kaizen

    B. Continuous improvement

    C. Total Quality Management

    D. Root cause analysis

    E. Standardization

8. Root cause analysis does *not* employ:

    A. Data collection

    B. Follow-up

    C. Assessment

    D. Corrective action

    E. Benchmarking

9. If you were measuring the quality compliance of machine output, you would most likely use:

    A. C_{pk}

    B. TQM

    C. QFD

    D. Six Sigma

    E. SPC

10. Three standard deviations will account for what percentage of occurrences in a normal distribution?

    A. 99.7

    B. 99.9

    C. 95.0

    D. 68.0

    E. 92.5

Answers to Review Questions

1. C. Acceptance testing verifies performance and functionality of high value equipment. (It also verifies the efficacy of the first article of a direct material, but this was not one of the options.)

2. B. Reduction is not identified as a corrective action.

3. B. TQM is predicated on the fundamental principle of continuous improvement. The other criteria are subsets of this process.

4. D. Benchmarking can form the basis for a quality improvement program targeting those areas where quality gaps or deviations exist.

5. B. Determining system capability falls within the scope of C_{pk} analysis and is not a Six Sigma methodology.

6. C. ISO 9001:2000 is the first level of performance recommended by ISO.

7. C. Quality Functional Deployment (QFD) is another one of the many formats used by quality managers to assist with the process of TQM.

8. E. Benchmarking is an element of assessing performance. Root cause analysis is the process of determining the underlying cause of failure.

9. E. Statistical Process Control (SPC) measures the deviation from standard tolerance in fast moving environments.

10. A. Three sigma (three standard deviations) will encompass 97.5 percent of events in a normal distribution.

Chapter

9

Maintaining Internal Relations

THE C.P.M. EXAM SPECIFICATIONS COVERED IN THIS CHAPTER INCLUDE THE FOLLOWING:

- ✓ Conducting relationships with other departments in the organization
- ✓ Providing support and leadership to cross-functional teams
- ✓ Managing changes to the organization's supply management processes
- ✓ Developing and communicating supply management policies and providing training in procurement processes and methods

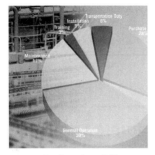

The Purchasing Department's organizational support role requires extensive coordination and collaboration with other internal departments. While some of these departments—for example, legal and finance—actually provide services to your purchasing team, all of them constitute the collective customer base that depend upon you to provide critical purchasing and supply management functions. You will be working collaboratively with many of these groups on cross-functional teams engaged in the development of a new product or service, for instance. You may also work with them in resolving quality issues in a manufacturing operation, or, even more likely, selecting a new supplier. Consequently, you will likely spend a major portion of your time working with them. For this reason, it is important that you understand other internal departments' corresponding roles in your organization and the common activities they perform in fulfilling their missions.

In this chapter, you will first examine the roles of the major organizational groups you are likely to encounter and how these roles interface with those of your department. We will then review the processes used to communicate with other departments and how you can best initiate and reinforce collaborative working relationships with each of them. And, finally, we'll examine how you can drive operational improvements within the Purchasing Department to better serve your internal customers.

Understanding Key Departmental Roles

During your career, you will quite possibly never encounter two enterprises with exactly the same organizational structure. However, in the section that follows we will try to describe the roles of the departments you will most commonly encounter so that you can gain a better understanding of how best to develop good working relationships with them. To provide some logical structure, you will find these grouped by their broader functional responsibilities: Administrative and support, production or service, sales and marketing, and engineering and design.

Figure 9.1 shows an organizational chart for a typical manufacturing organization. You might find this useful as a reference map as you go through this section.

Administrative and Support Functions

Administrative and support departments generally include those groups that provide the foundation for the smooth, day-to-day tactical operation of the organization as well as those that perform general management activities that serve the entire organization. Typically, within this subsection you will find the following.

FIGURE 9.1   Organizational chart

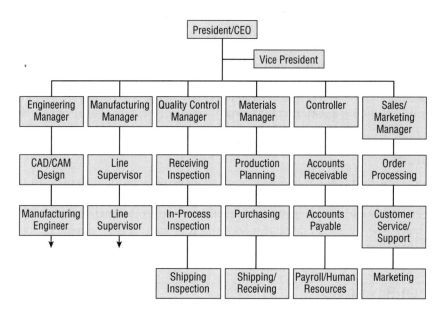

Senior Management

Senior management includes the organization's major executive functions such as the Chief Executive Officer (CEO) and President. In public corporations, it also applies to the Board of Directors, typically lead by a Chairperson.

Increasingly, purchasing departments have been gaining visibility at the senior management level as a result of the need for improved cost structures and the expanding complexity of managing the supply community for competitive advantage. As a result of this visibility, purchasing managers are finding that they must develop more finely tuned communication skills and the ability to deliver highly effective summary presentations. Generally speaking, you will find that senior management, as a result of the very nature of its role, has less time to spend on individual subjects than other organizational managers. To maintain credibility at this level, you will need to address your presentations to the competitive forces driving overall organizational mission and strategy.

Finance, Accounting, and Treasury

These three groups manage virtually all of the organization's monetary funds and provide the foundation for substantiating purchasing performance. They are often the audit compliance watchdogs of organizational spending, and they plan the cash flow that ensures your suppliers are paid in a timely manner. Establishing close communications and good working relationships with these groups will enhance your department's fiduciary performance by helping to ensure the effectiveness of decisions that create financial obligations.

Legal

Much of the Purchasing Department's activities are based on legal principles, and these principles are in continual flux, being modified often by actual decisions of the judiciary branches of state and federal governments. Consequently, you will find your organization's Legal Department to be an excellent support function for guidance on how specific legal technicalities can affect your business relationships with suppliers and how courts are currently interpreting statutory law. Through this guidance you will be able to provide more effective support to your internal customers by mitigating risks to the organization and ensuring decisions with potential legal implications are being made correctly.

Facilities

Facilities departments are responsible for maintaining the physical infrastructure of the workplace and planning for effective space utilization. To the extent that your needs for inventory storage will vary with changing economic conditions, close coordination with this group can be important. You will also find that this department provides a large amount of your transactional processing workload due to the wide variety of materials and services required to support the organization's physical facilities.

Human Resources

Human resources (HR) departments are generally responsible for recruiting new employees, as well as developing and managing personnel policies and employee benefits. Often, HR departments also support training as part of the employee development process, so you may find that your department's training needs can be coordinated and assisted through its resources. As a manager, you will find that HR offers support by providing up-to-date information on employee management affairs and regulations governing the workplace.

Information Technology

Your information technology (IT) group is generally responsible for all the computer and telecommunications requirements in the organization. It supports the organization's internal data and communications networks, ERP systems and can provide the integration services necessary to interface with multiple software platforms should you be working toward automating your supply base. In addition, the IT organization is a large user of purchasing services, so it is increasingly important that you are tuned in to planning for its future needs.

Logistics

Frequently an integral part of the supply management function, logistics services support the organization by handling finished goods distribution (in a manufacturing environment) and inbound freight. An effective logistics group can add significant value to purchasing activities by supporting the just-in-time processes that reduce inventory and by providing support for reduced costs associated with inbound shipments. The Purchasing Department can assist logistics operations by ensuring close adherence to shipping policy and using preferred carriers.

Production Functions

Production is a term widely used to refer to manufacturing, mining, or services that otherwise generate tangible goods or materials (such as baking and brewing). Production operations generally include the functions of manufacturing operations planning, quality assurance, and the maintenance of related equipment.

Manufacturing Operations

Purchasing supports manufacturing operations by ensuring it has delivered the proper supply of quality materials in the required quantity and at the right time. Failure to do so often results in unfortunate conditions where orders are unable to ship on time and the organization loses revenue. In extreme cases, the inability to ensure supply can lead to plant shutdowns, loss of customers and layoffs. For this reason, the Purchasing Department's responsibility to its manufacturing partners becomes very clear, and its management of the supply community is a mission-critical obligation.

Purchasing is also charged with the responsibility to reduce the costs of materials used in the manufacturing operation. This, too, is a mission-critical function since often an organization prices its end product relative to the costs of materials and labor. Improved supplier pricing can lead to a more competitive pricing strategy.

Planning

Planning is one of the keys to the successful operation of most manufacturing operations. Unless customer demand can be accurately forecasted, there is no guarantee that the available supply of materials will be sufficient to meet production objectives. In most operations, demand planning includes forecasting the mix of the various products customers might order, as well as the quantities that will be needed.

In some operations, the buying function is combined with the planning function in the form of a *buyer-planner* so there are times when the planning function actually falls in the Purchasing Department. In these situations, it is not unusual to find the Purchasing Department itself reporting to manufacturing management and becoming an integral part of the production environment.

Quality Assurance

Quality assurance is a production function tasked to ensure a given standard of quality. In manufacturing environments there are generally two groups engaged in quality assurance: an internal group monitoring manufacturing performance and a supplier-focused group monitoring the quality of incoming materials used in manufacturing. Considering the critical nature of these functions, purchasing departments are typically closely allied to quality management teams and often work collaboratively on cross-functional teams. As the role of outsourcing expands and organizations find themselves more closely tied to outside manufacturing sources, this function takes on an even greater importance. Today, the management of quality from subcontracting service organizations—whose products are often shipped directly to the customer and never seen at the plant site—is becoming an increasingly important issue, leading to the increased use of supplier quality engineers deployed directly to purchasing departments.

Manufacturing Maintenance

The Purchasing Department also closely supports manufacturing operations by ensuring that spare parts and tools are available so that maintenance activities can take place when needed. In machinery-intensive manufacturing operations, down time due to the loss of even one piece of equipment can severely limit production capacity. Ensuring the supply of spare parts and maintenance-related supplier services becomes as critical as the material that goes directly into manufacturing of the organization's products.

Sales and Marketing

Sales and marketing activities impact purchasing in a variety of ways: increased sales activities and merchandising campaigns generally create added demand that requires planning for additional flows of material and slower market demand requires greater agility in manufacturing to support the increased customer service required to gain business in a highly competitive environment.

The potential benefit from strong relationships between supplier management groups and the sales and marketing efforts of the organization are frequently overlooked. The supplier community represents a special source of potential sales for your own organization for rather obvious reasons: Purchasing your goods or services increases their sales. What could be simpler? Yet it might be surprising to learn that few organizations have programs to market to its own supply base.

WARNING

There is nothing illegal or unethical about selling to your suppliers as long as the sales are not directly related to your specific purchases. A so-called "tying contract," where a purchase of goods or services from the supplier is contingent upon a corresponding purchase from your organization, is usually illegal. However, there is nothing wrong with saying, "My organization prefers to purchase goods and services from its own customers."

Product/Business Development

Product managers and business development managers are generally charged with overseeing specific product lines within the enterprise and have broad responsibilities for developing new business opportunities. Consequently, the groups they manage often have important roles in the development of new products and end-of-life discontinuation of existing ones. As a source of information regarding the potential needs of the organization, these groups can provide the Purchasing Department with invaluable information that can be useful in formulating supply strategies and determining future directions for supplier partnerships.

Public Relations

The public image of your organization can significantly affect your relationships with suppliers. A strong, positive public image suggests that businesses associated with your organization will benefit beyond the direct profit they earn from their dealings with you, and they are more likely to offer concessions to gain your business. You can leverage this even further by ensuring that key executives of your suppliers are on the mailing list for press releases and other public relations materials...but be sure to send them only as long as the news continues to be favorable.

Advertising/Sales Collateral

Most of the advertising done by your organization will be placed with professional advertising agencies by staff members with marketing backgrounds and expertise, since vendor selection for this service can be highly subjective. Nevertheless, there can be significant opportunity for cost savings through the purchase of printed materials and promotional merchandise that should not be overlooked. Sourcing and supplier management can work very well when you stick to providing collaborative input on the business aspects of procurement and consider that aesthetic considerations may be the key driver in a successful marketing campaign.

Distribution

Distribution is one of the key physical aspects to sales management whose importance should be evident. Physical distribution processes—conveying goods or services to the customer—typically involve a host of disciplines such as warehousing, packaging, inventory management, security, transportation and *traffic*, information technology, and customer service, just to mention a few. Distribution is a critical strategic function in any organization that generates a strong demand for purchased services and will often require the Purchasing Department's assistance. You should work closely with this group to ensure that you have a clear understanding of its needs.

Similarly, distribution groups are in an excellent position to forecast incoming demand and sales trends, and so represent a primary source of planning information that can assist you in developing relevant supply strategies.

Engineering and Design Functions

Engineering and design functions are typically separated into those groups working on new products and technical research and development, and groups working with manufacturing operations and factory systems. Early involvement by the Purchasing Department in the new product introduction process can assist in aligning future strategies with sourcing needs and provide a smooth transition to new materials or suppliers. The Purchasing Department can often help accelerate the process by introducing potential suppliers to the organization's business requirements and taking the initial steps toward qualification.

Research and Development (R&D)

The research process focuses on the discovery of new technology and methods, while the development process seeks ways to exploit them through practical application. The Purchasing Department's ability to identify and develop new sources of supply can become a strategic resource to the organization when it is employed early in the design specification process.

New Product/Service Introduction

In conjunction with the R&D functions, the introduction of new products or services requires a great deal of planning by the Purchasing Department to ensure that new suppliers have been properly qualified and have the required capability to deliver. Early involvement by Purchasing is no longer just desirable; it has become a necessity to the organization to ensure a smooth product introduction ramp up from the development phase to actual marketing and distribution.

Developing Good Working Relationships

Throughout the procurement process, your effectiveness and your department's effectiveness will depend largely on the strength of your relationships with suppliers and your internal customers. For this reason, it is critical that you understand how to engage others proactively and how to establish the foundation for effective collaboration.

In this section, we will review the ways good communication skills can assist your efforts and how you might better assist your organization as a participant in a collaborative working environment.

Communicating within the Organization

Good communication skills are the essential cornerstone to building meaningful relationships with other internal departments. Unless your customers clearly understand your goals and objectives and how you work to achieve them, you run the risk of being held at arm's length and excluded from critical internal communication activities. Similarly, those in your department need to have a clear understanding of the activities of other groups you will provide services for in order to more effectively meet their needs. If the communication is not clear and timely, both groups run the risk of misunderstandings that can result in ineffective team performance. Keep in mind, improving total operational performance is your primary objective in developing effective communications. To do so, you will require the active participation of those with whom you interface.

Establishing Credibility and Trust

Your ability to execute to plan can be the key to establishing credibility and trust with other groups. Thus the need to accurately communicate your performance objectives and progress toward them frequently and appropriately becomes apparent. To the extent that you can do this prior to engaging in activities that affect other departments and solicit their input regarding your approach and how best to meet their needs, you will find that you are effectively establishing credibility and trust. You can do this best by aligning your activities to support the departmental goals of your internal customers.

Gaining visibility also assists your efforts in developing credibility and trust. The more your customers know about your value-adding activities, the more likely they are to engage you in future sourcing efforts. Far too often, the Purchasing Department is viewed as being stuck in administering meaningless details and transactional processes that seldom amount to any significant benefit to other departments. You can change this perception by creating frequent opportunities to "market" your strategic services and communicating success stories.

Using Appropriate Channels to Communicate

In this age of communication, there are virtually unlimited tools available to exchange information. In fact, there are so many avenues for information delivery, buyers often complain of information overload. To avoid inflicting numbing over-communication on your customers, you will want to select the most effective channels for gathering and disseminating information and use only those most appropriate to individual situations. Here are some of the more common methods:

Customer Surveys   The customer survey is one method commonly used for gathering information. Properly employed, the survey can focus input on specific issues and root out problems before they interfere with operations. The survey can also gather opinions and assess the perceptions customers have regarding departmental performance and effectiveness.

One-on-One Meetings   Individual meetings with your key customers can provide an opportunity to exchange information and ideas in a private setting. Personal conversations are often very productive simply because, by the nature of their privacy, they encourage collaboration and an open exchange of opinion. Although these meetings tend to be somewhat informal, it is always a good idea to prepare an agenda in advance so you and your customer can stay organized and both of you can come away with a sense of having accomplished a meaningful dialogue.

 **Real World Scenario**

Leveraging an Effective Survey

A national biotech company used several dozen travel agents in the 20 states where they had either a sales office or manufacturing operation. Because the company utilized so many travel agents, the level of service it experienced was relatively low, while the cost of service was high. Some of the travel agencies even proposed a consolidation, offering lower prices. To ensure that the company used the best travel services and agents, its Purchasing Department polled all end-users of travel services via a survey that the Purchasing Department developed and distributed. The results of the survey showed which of the many travel agency service providers met the expectations of the internal end users and which service providers did not. The survey input enabled the Purchasing Department to eliminate the nonperforming suppliers much more objectively because it was based on the input of the end-user customer. At the same time, additional business was moved to the service providers that met the expectations of the end user. The result: greater user satisfaction, improved supplier performance, and less purchasing management (and fewer travel agents).

Team Meetings   Held periodically, team meetings can be an excellent venue for communication. One of the greatest advantages is that you are able to pass along exactly the same information to all members of the team. You will also benefit from the interchange of ideas that typically occurs in a team environment, and you will find it an opportunity for gaining consensus in reaching decisions.

Newsletters and Websites   Newsletters and information posted on a Purchasing Department website, while certainly less personal than face-to-face meetings, can offer the advantage of reaching large numbers of readers with relatively minimal effort. When used regularly to convey relatively important information rather than minutia, these tools can provide a focal point for dispensing up-to-date information. Keep in mind, however, that typically these tools provide only one-way communication and are not often effective substitutes for the interaction that goes along with face-to-face interaction.

Gaining Early Involvement

Early involvement by the Purchasing Department in sourcing and new product introduction activities benefits the organization in several ways. Involving the Purchasing Department in the initial stages of supplier contact enables the organization to leverage cost reduction and supplier management efforts at a time when they can be best influenced. Then, as the buying organization gains a clearer understanding of the product needs and cost restraints, sourcing strategies and negotiating tactical plans can be more highly focused on achieving the customers' goals rather than simply reacting to compliance issues. With the purchasing team focusing on the business requirements, the technical team's time and energy is available to pursue optimal solutions.

From the supplier's perspective, early involvement by the Purchasing Department enables a smoother transition from the development phase to the operational working environment. When the purchasing manager explores terms and conditions early in the process, he can resolve potential contracting obstacles prior to their becoming "deal-breaking" roadblocks. By establishing solid relationships early, the purchasing manager also clears the way for more collaborative negotiations with suppliers since both parties will have a better understanding of one another's needs and a greater opportunity to produce mutually beneficial results.

Strategic leverage increases with early involvement in the procurement process. As suppliers gain certainty that their company will receive the order, the incentive for creative solutions tends to diminish. You might want to use the following table as a guide because it outlines the specific development stage (in the left column) and the areas readily influenced through the Purchasing Department's active role in the process at that stage (in the right column).

Stage	Areas of Influence
Product conception	Commodity strategy
	Alternative materials
	Supplier investment
	Comarketing development

Stage	Areas of Influence
Product Design	Sourcing strategy
	Total cost of ownership
	Quality requirements
	Partnerships and alliances
Product Engineering	Supplier qualification
	Make or buy decisions
	Value analysis
	Negotiation of cost-based pricing
Production Planning	Negotiation of availability
	Schedule creation
Introduction	Negotiation of volume-based pricing
	Negotiation of schedule allocations
	Schedule influence

Participating in Cross-functional Operations

A cross-functional team is composed of representatives from various segments of the organization with complementary skill sets and perspectives. In most organizations, the cross-functional team shares a common goal and its members are equally accountable for the team's results. Typically, projects related to strategic sourcing activities and the ongoing management of critical suppliers are where you will most likely participate and where your input can be most valuable. In many cases, you will even find yourself leading these teams, so it is important you understand the role you bring to the team and where you can be expected to add value.

In the section that follows, we will review the various roles and responsibilities of the Purchasing Department in cross-functional team participation and how you can be most effective in helping to build successful teams.

Supply Management Roles and Responsibilities

The Purchasing Department works with a number of typical operational and development teams where specific supply management expertise is useful. The most common of these teams include:

New Product Development   As we discussed earlier in the chapter (in the "Engineering and Design Functions" section), purchasing departments have an important role in new product development teams to provide sourcing and supplier management assistance.

Sourcing and New Supplier Development   Closely related to introducing new products is the development of new suppliers. Typically, purchasing departments will take a leading role in this business process, sourcing and helping to qualify potential new suppliers.

Cost Reduction   Specific products or service lines may require reduced cost to effectively compete with others in the marketplace. Cross-functional teams review all aspects of internal and supplier related costs with an objective of reducing the purchase price. Often, teams will adopt the value analysis methodology by looking at all the parts that are used in a particular product with the objective of reducing cost without impairing functionality.

Cycle Time Reduction   The cycle time for ordering and receiving purchased parts and service can often become the gating factor in delivering to the end customer. Organizations have come to realize that there are trade-offs of value to simply achieving the lowest possible price, and you will frequently find yourself discussing the need for cycle time reduction with your suppliers.

Budget   Input from the Purchasing Department on budget teams focuses on pricing trends and expected pricing in the future. Often, the Purchasing Department will be asked to forecast prices for areas of major commodity or category spending.

Capital Equipment   The purchasing group is often asked to participate in the selection of capital asset equipment as the business lead in negotiating price and delivery terms.

Information Technology   Purchasing departments take part in IT sourcing activities, both as a using group and as the buyer. As organizational computer and telecommunications systems become more fully integrated and more resources are dedicated to them, Purchasing spends increasingly more time working with this group.

Quality Assurance   Since the quality of your own product or service is often largely dependent upon the quality of purchased goods and services, the Purchasing Department will be asked to assume an important role in ensuring that specified quality requirements are met by suppliers.

Evaluating Teams

Under what conditions will a cross-functional team likely produce value? This, of course, is a topic for organizational design debate. However, there are circumstances that are generally recognized as favoring the use of a team and others that tend to reduce its benefits. From a procurement perspective, you should be able to distinguish those desired outcomes that will benefit from team involvement and those that will be hindered. Here are just a few aspects you should consider:

Speed   Overall, cross-functional teams tend to reduce the time it takes to reach objectives, especially in the product development process where ongoing coordination between functional elements can be critical. Speed is a critical factor in product and system development and cross-functional teams allow many parts of the development process to take place concurrently.

Degree of Change   Massive degrees of change generally require a great deal of communication, and teams can become excellent tools for introducing and communicating change throughout the organization. By jointly developing a plan for communication and through joint crafting of the messages, teams can help ensure that the rest of the organization is in sync with the overall objectives of the change.

Organizational Culture   To a large degree, organizational culture determines the effectiveness of team outcomes. In cultures where teams actually manage processes and have the decision making authority, team outputs are extremely effective. In cultures where tradition prevails, the teams may need to develop additional management buy-in for its recommendations, thus slowing the process considerably.

Decision Making   It has been shown that collectively teams make better decisions and produce more effective outcomes than any of their individual members, substantiating the adage that "two heads are better than one." However, teams can often take a lot more time debating issues prior to reaching a decision than an individual would take to reach a decision alone.

Leveraged Expertise   In a team environment, individual members gain the benefit of having subject matter experts to rely upon for technical information. This often reduces the time it takes to understand a specific problem. However, there is a down side: Frequently, individuals feel that the circumstances in their organizations are unique and substantially different from others in the industry. This thinking tends to restrict the options available to the team and often generates friction. Purchasing managers often refer to this as the NIH syndrome—Not Invented Here—to describe the reluctance of some to use new ideas.

Consensus Building   Consensus generally means that everyone on the team agrees to support an action or decision, even if some of them are not in full agreement. Consensus contrasts with voting where the majority rules. To the extent that teams are responsible for making strategic and operational decisions, consensus building has an important function because individual members of the team are required to provide public support for its decision. If the disagreement is strong, members will not be inclined to provide the needed effort and consensus will not be achieved.

Complacency   Teams, especially those of long standing, have a tendency toward entropy and can become complacent. Generally, one finds that goals are not updated and perhaps are no longer as valid as they were in the past. Under these circumstances, it is difficult for meaningful action to take place, and the individual members of the team become demotivated. This is one of the major pitfalls of the team process and seems to suggest that teams should be project oriented with a clearly established time for disbanding.

Developing Effective Teams

There is a tendency for teams to develop within a specific growth pattern, similar to that often referred to in organizational development literature as the four phases: "Forming, Storming, Norming, and Performing." Table 9.1 provides examples of these phases and what you might expect to encounter in each of them.

TABLE 9.1   Typical Stages of Team Development

Stage	Development Steps
Initial team organization	The team is chartered and formed. Team members learn about the project and one another.

TABLE 9.1 Typical Stages of Team Development *(continued)*

Stage	Development Steps
Defining needs and goals	The team establishes goals and objectives consistent with its assignment. The team develops a preliminary time line for completion.
Developing solutions and action plans	The team develops and refines potential solutions and builds consensus for one of the alternatives.
Achieving objectives	The team implements its plan, measures progress, adjusts actions to meet situation and celebrates success.

Team effectiveness depends upon establishing measurable goals early and developing a timeline with milestones for their achievement. These measurements work best if they parallel the team's expected deliverables. For example, if the team was established to develop cost savings you would want to identify and measure:

- Anticipated cost savings
- Method of measuring cost savings
- Timeline for producing cost savings
- Milestones
- Duration of the project or completion criteria

Reengineering Supply Management

As part of your duties, you will likely be called upon occasionally to lead or participate in formulating new procedures or revising existing ones. As organizational policy changes to meet changing economic or regulatory conditions, elements within the organization, such as supply management, also require realignment. Change also sometimes develops from newly available technology that offers greater efficiency or from new processes rolled out organizationally.

Dealing with change is a necessary skill that must be learned and continually employed as part of our professional lives. In purchasing departments, change has an even more profound effect on others, and you must also learn to continually consider how to assist internal customers as well as suppliers through these changes. This section reviews the scope of operations in most purchasing departments so that you can more clearly understand the functions that you will be responsible for improving. This section also discusses how change is best managed throughout the organization and supply base.

Understanding the Scope of Operations

When you consider the overall scope of purchasing and procurement operations, you can easily understand how it touches virtually every function within the organization. For the purpose of providing some reference points and as an aid to understanding how typical purchasing activities usually relate to one another, we've provided the following listing, which contains most of the common roles and responsibilities carried out in purchasing departments. Notice that they are grouped into three main categories: purchasing/procurement, materials management, and other supporting roles.

Purchasing/Procurement

The purchasing function manages the acquisition of goods and services, conducting a broad range of functional services that are used by all departments in the organization:

Commodity Expertise	Industry analysis
	Market analysis
	Commodity analysis
	Benchmarking
	Forecasting
Sourcing	Locating potential suppliers
	Supplier prequalification
	RFx preparation and response analysis
	Evaluation of supplier capabilities
	Competitive bidding
	Supplier selection leadership
Contracting	Contract formation
	Negotiation of terms and conditions
	Management and administration of contract compliance
	Termination
Supplier Development and Management	Conducting performance reviews
	Implementing continuous improvement programs

	Developing cost reductions
	Auditing
Risk Management	Risk assessment and evaluation
	Risk mitigation
	Ensuring supply
	Supplier ratings and approved supplier list
	Regulatory compliance
Licensing	Protection of intellectual property rights
	Licensing compliance
Quality Management	Supplier qualification
	Quality assessments
	Quality improvement programs
Transactional Processing	Issuing purchase orders
	Expediting supplier shipments
	Returned goods documentation
	ERP and systems implementation
	Procurement card management
	E-procurement solutions

Materials Management

The materials management function is responsible for the planning of supply requirements and the internal handling of purchased materials:

| **Logistics/Supply Chain Management** | Transportation and customs management |
| | Receiving |

Packaging

Physical distribution of finished goods

Internal movement of materials

Planning   Production planning and master scheduling

MRP management

Capacity planning

Forecasting

Just-in-time manufacturing

Inventory Management   Warehousing and stores operations

Part master maintenance

ABC inventory control

Economic ordering quantity analysis

Surplus Disposal   Hazardous materials handling

Scrap sales

End-of-life product sales

Surplus equipment sales

Other Supporting Roles

The Purchasing Department indirectly supports a variety of activities within the organization.
They include:

Project Management   New product introduction projects

Information technology and systems projects

Manufacturing/services improvement programs

Plant engineering and relocation projects

Policy and procedure revisions

Audit preparation

Value analysis

Finance and Budget   Cost center maintenance

Pricing forecasts for budgets

Spending analysis

Cost analysis

Accounts payable support

Return on Investment analysis

Managing the Change Process

Charles Darwin, the nineteenth century British evolutionist, is perhaps the preeminent student of change and one of the first to explore the way in which change affects our lives. "It is not the strongest species that survive," he wrote, "Nor the most intelligent, but the ones who are most responsive to change."

In order to improve organizational effectiveness, especially when responding to dynamic changes in the business environment, you must learn to master change. Despite its seeming randomness, change must be managed so that you can implement new methods. To a large extent, this means developing clear plans for structuring changes and communicating them to those within the organization who will be affected. People are generally resistant to change unless they fully understand it and even then only accept it with some trepidation. Unless you can manage change in measured increments, you run the risk of overwhelming them.

There are several factors that influence the effectiveness of change that you should take into consideration:

- The impetus for significant change needs to come from senior management or it gains little support.

- Your agenda for change must be shared by everyone, and you need to have a mutual vision of how the change will provide benefits to the entire organization.

- You need to have access to the resources—time, money, staff, and expertise—to implement the changes smoothly.

- Plan ahead, define each step, check before acting, and communicate so that there are no surprises; absorb feedback and make allowances to correct mistakes as required.

- Whenever possible, introduce change at the prototype level first, testing to see if it will work as expected and making any needed changes before going forward. Choose opportunities for learning rather than just attempting to prove the concept through a successful first test. Mistakes are opportunities for learning.

- It is important to deal with emerging issues as soon as possible so that dissatisfaction and frustration do not take root.

- Provide continual feedback to your team on progress—both success and failures.

- To the extent possible, avoid micro-management. Over-structuring finite details can be disenfranchising to team members and will only serve to slow the process by reducing initiative.

- Remember that if change moves too quickly, you may end up leaving a good many employees confused and in the dark as to what is expected of them. It is probably best to include in your plan a segment of time for feedback and questions as a way of ensuring you are moving ahead smoothly.

In your purchasing role, you will most likely encounter the need for change that results from new or redefined Purchasing Department roles and from changes in organization policy required by legislation such as that recently encountered through the Sarbanes-Oxley Act.

Redefining the Role of Purchasing   As transactional processing methods improve efficiency, fewer purchasing employees are being assigned to routine buyer duties. More and more, organizations are coming to rely on their purchasing departments to drive profitability improvement programs that translate to increased shareholder value and introducing innovation

Forming and Communicating Organizational Policy   Organizational policy needs to receive periodic reviews to ensure that they reflect up to date thinking. This is especially true for purchasing activities, which must adapt to continually changing legislation and regulatory requirements, as well as industry standards such as ISO. Ethical conduct has recently come under serious scrutiny in the business sector and many organizations—especially those publicly held—are struggling to revise policy to conform to new criteria. Recently, the Institute for Supply Management published a set of guidelines called "Principles of Social Responsibility" to provide guidance on what constitutes socially responsible conduct. (You can find an outline of the program at the Institute of Supply Management's webstite: www.ism.ws.) Since its intention is to include this criteria in supplier selection and qualification audits, this will likely result in a flurry of new internal policies to ensure compliance.

Purchasing Policy and Procedures Training

Internal organizational purchasing policy and procedures are often complex and not readily accessible, so they need to be supplemented with training and extended communication activities. Fostering a better understanding of the requirements and benefits of compliance with these policies will greatly assist you in carrying out the organization's purchasing strategy and objectives. Directing this task falls naturally in the hands of the purchasing manager.

Formulating Training Needs

Internal purchasing training requirements address two main areas, each with a somewhat distinct focus:

Purchasing Department Standard Operating Procedures (SOPs)   SOPs address the "how to" of purchasing, defining the specific tasks required to perform any given operation. Examples of typical purchasing procedures include how to qualify a supplier for inclusion on the approved supplier list or how to add a new supplier to the database. Training is typically required when new procedures are implemented and when existing procedures are revised. It is also important to have a structured training program to initiate new employees into the Purchasing Department to reduce the risk of costly mistakes.

Organizational Policy Regarding Purchasing   Most organizations have policies regarding who can purchase materials and services and who can approve purchases and their limit of authority. Policies also typically specify who can obligate the organization to contractual relationships in the course of business activities. In addition, many organizations specify codes of ethical conduct for dealing with suppliers and for maintaining internal confidentiality.

While much of this policy may be strictly common sense, it is, nevertheless, prudent to ensure compliance through some method of organized training.

Developing Training Materials

The format for training materials is generally determined by how the materials are intended to be used. Procedural and policy materials are often developed for classroom training or on-the-job training since this type of material often requires detailed explanation and coaching. Technical materials are often developed in manuals and used primarily for reference as needed. You will find that there are occasions when both systems will be useful.

Delivering the Training

How the training is delivered is often as important as the content of the training itself. Some training is best handled in a classroom environment, while other training can be delivered through *computer-based training (CBT)* or other methods of self-directed study. Sometimes it is more effective to develop combinations of training types such as instructor-led, web-based training (known as *blended learning*) or classroom training followed by on-the-job coaching.

It is widely accepted, however, that formal training should be provided only "as needed" to reinforce a specific skill requirement at the time of implementation. Skills are most effectively learned when they are introduced where there is some previous context on which to base their value. Thus the focus of training should be developmental rather than purely remedial and should be presented in that context.

Summary

Successful interaction with other departments within the organization should be a key element in the Purchasing Department's strategy. To accomplish this, you will need to develop a thorough understanding of the roles and duties of your internal customers and process partners. While no two organizations have exactly the same structure, most can be organized according to broad operational categories: administration, production (or service), sales and marketing, and engineering and design.

Your effectiveness within the organization will depend, to a large extent, on how well you can develop strong working relationships. Developing relationships with other departments (and employees) requires that you employ sound communication and trust building techniques. Using appropriate channels and tools effectively is also an important element in this process. By building trust you will be able to gain early involvement in the sourcing and contracting processes, which will further enable you to contribute effectively in your organizational role.

Purchasing departments typically participate in or lead cross-functional teams in most areas of the organizations, so you will be required to understand your role and responsibilities as a member of these teams. You will also need to know how these teams are formed, how the team process is carried out, and what the requirements are for effective team management. In order to improve operations and better meet organizational expectations, you should completely understand the scope of operations in the Purchasing Department and the major functions that go along with it. This will assist you in managing the change process, helping to formulate policy and procedures, and providing communication and training to your staff and other departments within the organization.

For additional reading on topics related to this chapter, please see Appendix A.

Exam Essentials

Be able to understand key departmental roles.   In the normal course of activities, you will interact with virtually all groups in the organization, so it is important that you understand their roles and responsibilities and where they fit within the overall structure of the organization.

Be able to develop good working relationships within the organization.   To a large extent, your success will depend upon others. You will need to develop strong communication skills and build trust with your internal customers and process partners so that you can effectively contribute to the organization's effectiveness.

Gain early involvement in sourcing and contracting processes.   Building trust and open communication channels with internal groups will assist you in gaining early involvement in the procurement process. Early involvement will enable you to more effectively coordinate and influence supply management activities.

Understand the roles of cross-functional teams.   Many organizations rely heavily on project management processes that employ cross-functional teams, so you will be required to know how to participate in, develop, lead, and evaluate team activities.

Know the Purchasing Department's scope of operations.   To be effective at managing and reengineering purchasing operations, you will need to understand the various duties of the department and how they are logically organized by function.

Be able to manage change.   Change is a common feature of today's organizations and you will need to understand how to manage and master it.

Lead training activities for purchasing policy and procedures.   As a purchasing manager, you will be required to formulate purchasing policy and procedures and be able to train others in the organization on how best to follow them.

Review Questions

1. Internal department that performs general management activities and provides the foundation for day-to-day operations:

    A. Senior Management

    B. Legal

    C. Administrative and support

    D. Facilities

    E. Finance, Accounting, and Treasury

2. Workplace department responsible for maintaining physical infrastructure and planning of space utilization:

    A. Human Resources

    B. Finance, Accounting, and Treasury

    C. Information Technology

    D. Facilities

    E. Logistics

3. Internal department responsible for computer and telecommunications requirements within the organization.

    A. Facilities

    B. Information Technology

    C. Human Resources

    D. Operations

    E. Senior Management

4. Production operations generally include all of the following functions *except*:

    A. Planning

    B. Equipment maintenance

    C. Facilities

    D. Making

    E. Quality assurance

5. What production function exists to monitor internal quality output or a supplier's manufacturing performance?

    A. Manufacturing maintenance

    B. Master scheduling

    C. Purchasing

    D. Planning

    E. Quality assurance

6. Improving total operational performance is your primary objective in developing effective:

    A. Operations

    B. Cross-functional teaming

    C. Supply management

    D. Communications

    E. Manufacturing operations

7. Name for a team composed of members from various departments within the organization with complementary skills sets and perspectives.

    A. Departmental

    B. Cross-functional

    C. Collaborative

    D. Distributive

    E. Diversity

8. Materials management's range of functional services includes all of the following *except*:

    A. Surplus disposal

    B. Planning

    C. Sourcing

    D. Inventory management

    E. Logistics

9. Term that addresses the "how to" of purchasing, defining the specific tasks required to perform any given operation.

    A. Organizational policy

    B. Mission statement

    C. Purchasing policy

    D. Standard Operating Procedures

    E. Desktop procedures

10. Term that outlines who can purchase materials and services and who can approve purchases and their limit of authority.

    A. Organizational policy

    B. Mission statement

    C. Purchasing policy

    D. Standard Operating Procedures

    E. Desktop procedures

Answers to Review Questions

1. C. General management activities fall into the category of administrative and support groups. The other groups have more specific functions.

2. D. The facilities group handles the physical infrastructure and workplace; the other groups manage areas outside of the scope of facilities.

3. B. Computer and telecommunications activities are assigned to the information technology group in most organizations where technically trained engineers and support staff are available to perform specific tasks.

4. C. Facilities is generally responsible for the physical plant. The other activities are typically included in production operations.

5. E. Quality is a fundamental element of manufacturing performance, typically managed by a quality assurance group. The other groups support different activities not directly related to monitoring performance.

6. D. The fundamental purpose for providing effective communications is to enhance organizational effectiveness.

7. B. Organizations generally employ cross-functional teams because they provide the complementary skills and perspectives required to accelerate reaching goals.

8. C. Sourcing is a function of purchasing.

9. D. SOPs address the steps required to perform a procedure; the others generally describe why the procedure is being performed.

10. C. Purchasing policy contains the elements of purchasing authority. The other policies and procedures are more general in nature and do not specifically address purchasing.

Chapter 10

Supplier Relationship Management

THE C.P.M. EXAM SPECIFICATIONS COVERED IN THIS CHAPTER INCLUDE THE FOLLOWING:

✓ Creating and managing productive supplier relationships through alliances and partnerships

✓ Coordinating supplier activities relating to pricing and available supply

✓ Meeting with current and potential suppliers' sales personnel

✓ Reviewing and answering supplier inquiries; handling protests and awarding appeals

✓ Formulating and managing a small/minority-owned supplier development program

✓ Representing your organization at meetings and events with all external groups

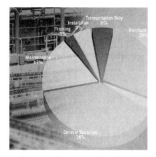

No progressive organization can operate in a vacuum. The purchasing manager is uniquely positioned to add strategic value to the organization by finding business opportunities to build strong relationships with other organizations in the supply chain, leveraging their innovation to seed fresh ideas and business processes. These supply relationships foster new learning that helps develop improved methods and generate new business opportunities.

In the multifaceted business climate of today, information gained from supply chain partners is often the key to competitive success. Consequently, managing supplier relationships is one of the most important functions performed by the Purchasing Department. It requires strategy, skill, and patience; it is a complex process that demands comprehensive attention in order to prove successful. And, most importantly, it has to be learned and practiced.

This chapter will review several key aspects to managing supplier relationships. To begin with, you will examine the steps you can take to develop the groundwork for more productive strategic supply relationships. Then you will review the more common day-to-day tactical activities of a Purchasing Department in its interface with the supplier community and how you can make these activities more meaningful. Finally, you will look at how you can effectively represent your organization through interaction with external supply groups.

Managing Productive Supplier Relationships

Productive supplier relationships do not just happen. As with any relationship of value, they demand effort and perseverance. In your role as purchasing manager, there are a number of disciplines you will have to master in order to better encourage strong supply relations. In this section, we'll review the more commonly used processes that enable and improve relations with your suppliers.

Creating Good Working Relations

You create good working relations with your suppliers through fair and consistent treatment, enhanced by the judicious use of communication tools and holding regular meetings. The benefits of building solid relationships can be enormous. When your working relationship is strong, suppliers are more likely to cooperate with you by moving up lead times when a product or service is needed immediately or by taking a return of product for your convenience.

A close, collaborative relationship also makes it easier to negotiate terms and prices with your suppliers and helps avoid disputes since your organization's business will be highly regarded.

The following sections outline some of the more common ways to enhance working relationships.

Meeting with Suppliers Regularly

You will want to arrange meetings with your key suppliers on a regular basis. Often these meetings will take the form of a formal supplier review or an executive conference. Such meetings provide the opportunity for the management of both organizations to get together to exchange technology or business development roadmaps so that strategic relationships can be better aligned and leveraged. At other times, you may want to meet less formally to review your immediate plans and ways that the supplier can provide support. Sometimes you may be able to help the supplier resolve an internal problem that your organization has already solved for itself.

While it is impossible to meet regularly with all of your suppliers, there are a number of other ways you can maintain regular contact:

Supplier Surveys   Periodic surveys of suppliers can provide information on how effective your organization has been in developing them as a resource. They can also help identify problem areas that are generating additional cost to your organization. Sometimes it is just good business practice to be open and listen to how suppliers view you as a customer.

Improvement Teams   Good working relationships with your suppliers provide an extra incentive for the suppliers to participate in cost reduction projects, regardless how critical their supplier role is to your organization. A good relationship can also provide incentive to work on multifunctional teams to help improve overall operations, keeping in mind that your best suppliers do not have a monopoly on good ideas. Inviting a talented supplier representative to participate in an improvement project, even if it does not directly relate to the product or service supplied, makes good business sense because it is another way to leverage the talent within your supply base.

Reciprocal Visits   You should visit the supplier's facility as often as possible. By putting a face to a name, you will be inviting the supplier's personnel to connect with your organization and create a common bond. Visits will also enable you to become more familiar with how the supplier's operation works so that you can better leverage its capabilities and strengths, as well as understand its limitations.

Holding a supplier open house—Supplier Day, as it is sometimes called—will introduce the supplier's team to your organization and enable them to see first hand how their products or services are employed. This can be an extremely powerful tool for personalizing your organization's needs, thus strengthening the bonds between you.

Improving Communication

Interorganizational communications are most effective when they are bidirectional and when they involve all levels of personnel. Effective communication can produce remarkable results. For example, forecasts of trends affecting your organization, even generalized ones, can reduce cycle time by preparing your suppliers to respond more rapidly to anticipated needs. To the extent that information such as this can be collaboratively shared, you will find that fill rates improve and that service levels rise. Information that provides a window into your operations can also be reassuring to supplier sales teams. Knowing which of your product lines are moving quickly, what products you intend to discontinue, and what new products you intend to introduce can be valuable intelligence to your supplier's sales organization, especially when it correlates with information from other sources.

You will also want to tap your suppliers as resources for trend information that will assist your internal customers by helping to determine the best time to place their orders. Sales departments often have better access to market information that can be a valuable asset when properly used.

There are a number of other ways your department can work with suppliers to better leverage information and improve communication. Here are just of few of the more common methods:

Website   Information about your company and your purchasing team can be posted on a public website. Some organizations actually establish a supplier section where information of special interest to suppliers—Invitations to Bid, for example—can be distributed. Visit the HP website at `http://h30173.www3.hp.com` to see a good model of one.

Focus Groups   The *focus group* is a useful method for gaining supplier feedback. Typically set in a somewhat structured environment led by a professional facilitator, and consisting of between 9 and 12 individuals, the group is brought together to examine a specific subject and share opinions. It can be a particularly effective way to test new ideas and gain feedback prior to implementation.

Newsletter   A newsletter can address the supply community specifically with information that will help them better understand what is happening inside your organization. Word processing software makes it relatively easy to publish a newsletter at your desk, and it can be quite effectively distributed at no cost through e-mail.

Reverse Marketing

Leenders and Blenkhorn's *Reverse Marketing; The New Buyer-Supplier Relationship* (The Free Press, 1988) identified the concept of *reverse marketing*. They pointed out that the traditional relationship where the seller takes the lead by seeking out the buyer is being replaced in many instances by one where the buyer actively searches for suppliers to fill a specific need. This practice occurs when there are few or no suppliers available and you have to employ some aggressive recruiting and persuasion to develop a source to meet your organization's needs. Reverse marketing generally sees the buyer making the offer, even to the point of suggesting the selling price.

Resolving Relations Issues

Reinforcing good business relationships with your supplier takes some measure of attention to detail and effort because there are numerous daily activities that, when not well performed, can lead to disputes and concerns. Normally, these issues are relatively minor and part of the normal course of business; however, when failure to perform routine supplier support activities becomes the rule rather than the exception, you run the risk of the supplier's performance levels diminishing.

While it is difficult to generalize the kinds of problems you may encounter, the next few sections discuss some of those that have been frequently mentioned in purchasing literature.

Paying Invoices on Time

Cash flow is important to every business enterprise, and the finance team at your supplier will continually monitor and rate your account on how timely the payments are made by your organization. Accounts that are continually past due present a problem. If you consider that money has a time value, the longer it takes to collect the payment, the lower will be the actual profit. As a result, late payments actually cut into the supplier's operating margin. While an occasional late payment can be overlooked, a pattern of late payments may require the supplier to raise its prices in compensation.

An associated issue related to late payments is the handling of invoices. It's extremely frustrating for the supplier's Accounts Receivable staff to find that one of the buyer's payments is overdue payment only to find that the buying organization has no record of ever receiving it. No matter how you look at it, this will require significant duplication of effort to correct. To reduce lost invoices, be sure suppliers have the correct address for submitting them to your organization and, if needed, have the suppliers include an individual's name or a mail stop in the address.

Organizations can maintain effective alignment with their suppliers by exchanging *aging* reports. The supplier's aging report shows when the invoice was submitted and how many days old it is, while the buyer's report shows when the invoice was received and when payment will be made based on the existing terms. In this way, each party can proactively identify problem payments before they get out of hand.

Maintaining Confidentiality

Any information given to you by the supplier should always be considered confidential and never disclosed to third parties outside your organization. Most of the time buyers and sellers exchange Confidentiality Agreements or Non-disclosure Agreements early in their relationship that require both to maintain certain levels of confidentiality. Regardless of the existence of such legal documents, it is of the utmost ethical importance that information given you in confidence never be shared with your suppliers' competitors.

Dealing Fairly and Equally with Suppliers

To maintain credibility requires that you treat all suppliers fairly and consistently, avoiding the perception that you favor one over the others. If your organization maintains a system of priorities based on the level of supplier qualification or certification, you will be obliged to follow it. However, you should continually encourage suppliers to work toward the preferred status, offering help and guidance as needed.

Many organizations develop close partnerships with some of their suppliers, including joint ventures and similar programs. Be sure to disclose this to suppliers who are new to doing business with you so that they do not waste effort in focusing on areas that will likely yield no results.

Trust is a key element in relations with your suppliers. One way to establish and continue to maintain trust is by always keeping your word.

Avoiding Illegal Situations

On the opposite end of the spectrum, there are many actions that may superficially appear to be solidifying relationships but that may bring up issues with restraint of trade. Providing preferred treatment to suppliers who also buy your products can be one of them. While it is legal and often preferable to buy from one's customers, trading purchase for purchase can be seen as a tying contract, which is illegal. So long as price, quality, delivery and the other fundamentals of supplier selection override decisions of personal preference, you will likely be viewed as exercising sound ethical judgment.

Certifying New Suppliers

Every organization has its own method for certifying suppliers. Some are general and based on conformance with specific qualifications, such as being ISO certified. Some require certification by a third party examiner. Others are more specific to the needs of your particular organization, such as ISO/TS 16949, which is an international quality management system standard for manufacturers of automotive parts. Perhaps you require a specific environmental policy or conformance to specific rules of social responsibility in order for your suppliers to reach certified status. You may find that some of these requirements are readily achievable, while others may be established only by your own organization. In this case, you may need to develop a program for communicating your requirements and assisting the supplier in achieving them.

Certification should not be confused with qualification. Supplier qualification is a process to determine if a particular supplier is capable of handling a specific job. Certification means that the supplier has met certain criteria and levels of performance—often determined through field audits—that enable it to be considered by your organization as an ongoing applicant for business.

Mentoring

Mentoring is a form of teaching and guidance that assists individuals and organizations to reach a certain level of performance. Mentoring is often an educational process where the mentor serves as a role model or teacher, providing opportunities for growth to less experienced organizations. It is based upon encouragement, constructive comments, openness, mutual trust, respect, and a willingness to learn and share.

An established organization will often assist a newly developing one through this kind of mentorship, but for the process to work well there has to be some mutual benefit. In some cases, the benefits can be an additional source of supply that makes an otherwise closely held industry more competitive. At other times, it can be the means to support small, minority businesses to ensure that they get a fair share of your business.

Developing Continuous Improvement

Continuous improvement as a quality concept was discussed in Chapter 8, "Managing Quality," in relation to the buyer's responsibility in managing suppliers. In this section, we look at it a bit further from the aspect of obtaining alignment with supplier activities.

Gaining Early Supplier Involvement

Early supplier involvement in new product design can beneficially influence both cost and cycle time by leveraging the supplier's process strengths and relying on the expertise of its staff to enable optimal solutions. Often, it makes sense to involve multiple tiers of suppliers so that you can assure alignment of processes within the immediate supply chain. This is best accomplished through cross-functional, multiorganizational teams that search out the methods and processes that best leverage all of their strengths.

Working Collaboratively

Supplier involvement in your organization's operations will generally focus on areas of mutual goals. Activities can range from the typical unilateral problem solving to participation in activities that reach far into your organization. The benefit of this close collaboration is that both organizations are able to leverage their individual strengths toward the development of a single process that divides the workload and responsibilities accordingly. Real gains, however, occur when technology and expertise pass freely among partners so that knowledge is shared as it is jointly developed, providing a competitive advantage to the entire supply chain. From this effort, products that are brought to the marketplace are likely to add more value and, because they are not easily copied, offer greater sustainability.

Forming Partnerships and Alliances

Partnerships and business alliances are generally formed to fill specific needs, such as the joint development of a new product or service that would fall outside the capabilities of each of the participants if they were to attempt to go forward alone. This need is generally defined through some specific market research or opportunity analysis, following a formal path of internal examinations and recommendations by management. Typically, a business case outlining the strategic benefits and potential threats is prepared prior to approval.

For the supplier's contribution, the alliance generally requires an additional investment in equipment or staff. The buyer's contribution usually comes in the form of an exclusive contract to buy certain volumes of specific items. When the alliance involves joint development, cross-organizational and cross-functional teams are generally formed, bringing the two organizations' strategic objectives into alignment.

It is typical for organizations engaged in partnerships or alliances to form contracts governing roles and responsibilities, as well as the accrual of benefits. Successful partnerships are based on the full involvement of each of the partners, so it is important to develop clear measurements for how effectively each partner is meeting its commitments.

Maintaining Partnerships and Alliances

To maintain the relationships, there must be continuing benefit to both parties. Successful long-term partnerships generally have high management visibility and support, so resources continue to be made available as long as there is a clear willingness by the working teams to continue to engage.

Strengthening Supplier Relations

There is no general rule for strengthening supplier relationships: many of the processes just outlined that are used to form the initial relationship can continue to strengthen it. However, please keep in mind that it is the Purchasing Department's responsibility—your responsibility—to develop and maintain valuable working relationships with suppliers.

One of the most important ingredients in strong relationships is trust. Trust is a characteristic and quality that typically develops when there is open and honest communication between parties and when both respect the behaviors of one another. Fundamental to this is keeping your word and honoring all of your commitments.

Implementing Small/Disadvantaged Business Programs

In order to have an effective corporate supplier diversity development program, both commitment and involvement from senior management is usually required. The major goal of developing a supplier diversity program is to provide all potential suppliers equal access to purchasing opportunities generated by your organization.

A written supplier diversity development policy formalizes the goals and objectives of the program. By formalizing the program with senior management support, you can generally ensure the dedication and support of the purchasing staff. In order to meet the formalization of the process, a comprehensive buyer training and accountability roadmap must be developed. This accountability roadmap must include tracking and reporting systems that show the results of awarding procurement business to small and disadvantaged suppliers. To ensure success, effective communication of the program objectives needs to be developed to internal customers, existing suppliers, and potential suppliers.

Minority Business, Defined

The National Minority Supplier Development Council defines a minority-owned business as: a for-profit enterprise, regardless of size, physically located in the United States or its trust territories, which is owned, operated, and controlled by minority group members. "Minority group members" are United States citizens who are Asian, African-American, Hispanic, or Native American. Ownership by minority individuals means the business is at least 51 percent owned by such individuals or, in the case of a publicly owned business, at least 51 percent of the stock is owned by one or more such individuals. Further, the management and daily operations are controlled by those minority group members. See www.nmsdcus.org for more information.

Locating Qualified Minority Suppliers

Effective identification and sourcing from minority suppliers is paramount to long term success. There are many minority supplier directories that can assist in this effort. Attendance in small business, minority, and woman-owned trade shows are also effective in identifying such suppliers. You can also network with various industry contacts to locate qualified minority suppliers within various commodities.

The following organizations and their corresponding URLs can assist in sourcing of minority suppliers:

Organization	URL
Diversity Information Resources, Inc.	www.DiversityInfoResources.com
DiversityBusiness.com	www.div2000.com
DiversityInc.com	www.diversityinc.com
Dynamic Small Business Search	http://dsbs.sba.gov/dsbs/dsp_dsbs.cfm
Industry Council for Small Business Development	www.icsbd.org
Minority Business Development Agency	www.mbda.gov
Minority Business Entrepreneur Magazine	www.mbemag.com
Minority Business News	www.mbemag.com/
National Minority Business Council Inc.	www.nmbc.org
National Minority Supplier Development Council	www.nmsdcus.org
Women's Business Enterprise National Council	www.wbenc.org

Developing and Managing Programs

Making small business and minority suppliers known within your organization is core in the development of any comprehensive procurement diversity program. Identifying the potential suppliers' capabilities is the domain of any procurement policy and supplier development strategy. To be truly effective, such information must be effectively communicated to the entire organization.

In order to determine if your supplier diversity development strategy is effective, a measurement and reporting system must be established to monitor results in a timely fashion. Many corporations use such reporting systems to establish various types of rewards and recognition programs for outstanding results for diversity suppliers and procurement commodity groups alike.

Pricing

The basics of supplier selection based on pricing have been initially discussed in Chapter 2, "Sourcing," Chapter 3, "Selecting Suppliers and Measuring Performance," and Chapter 6, "Managing Negotiations." In this section, however, we will round out those discussions by reviewing some of the factors that govern the actual pricing you will encounter.

Understanding Market Conditions

While strong relationships, as well as negotiation skills, play an important role in determining the prices your organization will be asked to pay for any particular product or service, *market conditions* at the time will also play a major role. Market conditions consist of a number of factors such as supply and demand, the overall economic climate, production capacity, competition, and numerous other elements that affect even the psychology of buyers and sellers. Because pricing is often a measure of your ability to manage the supply base, let's look more closely at some of the elements that affect your ability to control pricing from your suppliers.

Supply and Demand

You will recall in Chapter 6 we examined the role of market forces through supply and demand and stated that the imbalance of one in relation to the other directly affects pricing: "The ratio of supply to demand always affects prices. When supply is more plentiful than demand, suppliers must lower prices to make buying more attractive; when demand outstrips supply, buyers compete for the few available resources and prices rise." This is a fairly timeless concept.

However, there are times when an increase in pricing does not result in a corresponding decrease in demand. Automotive fuel is a paradigm example, with consumers purchasing the same amount regardless of the fluctuation in pricing. When this occurs we say that the price is "inelastic"; that is, it does not move in direct relationship to supply and demand.

Economic Factors

Economic conditions are generally what drive supply and demand. When the economy is strong, consumers tend to have ample cash to spend. This generally strains production capacity, creating shortages and raising prices. Conversely, when consumers have little cash to spend, capacity is plentiful and prices tend to spiral downward.

What causes these cycles? Good question! The best answer is that any given time, no one really knows. Economic cycles have been noted since the beginning of recorded time but, while theories abound, no agreement is readily available. In hindsight, however, you can always point to situational factors such as "the market was oversold" as causes for creating a downturn. Overall, though, upturns and downturns are naturally occurring phenomena that will always occur.

Industry Capacity

Within any given industry, capacity can be measured by the percentage of utilization of resources. As you approach 90 percent of utilization, overtime tends to rise and orders that were once profitable require increases in prices to sustain them. If you can adequately forecast these trends, you will likely be able to take very productive steps to take advantage of them.

Supplier Capacity

Individual supplier capacity can be constrained from time to time, as well, based on an influx of large orders or the unexpected loss of production capacity due to disaster. This may require you to move orders to a secondary source without the benefit of favorable pricing. Effective purchasing managers are always alert to the conditions affecting their most important suppliers and generally tend to avoid sole-sourcing situations for this very reason.

Available Labor

In unionized environments, conditions can change whenever a contract is under negotiations. Negotiation failure frequently results in strikes and work stoppages, followed by resultant shortages. Stockpiling in advance of a potential labor dispute can drive prices up even before the negotiation has concluded.

Cost-based Pricing Models

In addition to general market conditions, prices can be governed by supplier costs and *markup* strategies. Despite the fact that you may never have full access to the supplier's costs, there a number of profit models you can examine to get the full picture.

Standard Markup Model

Using a typical markup model, the supplier calculates the unit cost and then adds a percentage to cover overhead and profit. The overhead is generally composed of all the operating expenses for the organization and converted to a percentage of direct costs. For example, if an organization allocates 20 percent of its costs to direct materials and labor and 40 percent of its costs to overhead, the cost ratio of overhead costs to direct costs is 2:1 (40 / 20 = 2). This means that the supplier determines the price by adding an overhead and profit factor to its estimated product or service cost. Let's look at an example where the supplier's desired profit is 10 percent and the direct cost of the product is determined to be $1.80.

$$Selling\ Price = Total\ Cost + Profit$$
$$Total\ Cost = (Direct\ Cost + (Direct\ Cost \times Overhead))$$
$$(1.80 + (1.80 \times 2))$$
$$(1.80 + 3.6)$$
$$= 5.40$$
$$Selling\ Price = 5.40 + Profit\ (5.40 \times 10\%)$$
$$= 5.40 + .54$$
$$= 5.94$$

Specific Rate of Return Model

When the supplier expects to receive a specific rate of return for an investment, the calculation is based on the total cost of the investment plus the cost to produce the product or service. This figure is then multiplied by the rate of return desired to arrive at the selling price. As a simplified calculation it might look like this, given a 15 percent rate of return:

$$
\begin{aligned}
\text{Selling Price} &= \text{Average Cost} + \text{Desired Rate of Return (15\%)} \\
\text{Average Cost} &= \frac{\text{(Total Investment} + \text{Total Cost to Produce)}}{\text{Anticipated Sales Volume}} \\
&= \frac{\$150{,}000 + \$100{,}000}{100{,}000 \text{ Units}} \\
&= \$2.50 \text{ per unit} \\
\text{Selling Price} &= 2.50 + \text{Desired Rate of Return } (2.50 \times 15\%) \\
&= 2.50 + .375 \\
&= 2.875
\end{aligned}
$$

Price Analysis Methods

While there are many elaborate ways to analyze prices, in your day-to-day activities you will likely have little time for overly academic studies. From a practical point of view, the easiest and most productive method of analysis is to compare the prices being offered with some form of benchmark. In the next sections we discuss some of the more common tools.

Trend Analysis

Trend analysis employs statistic methodology to determine where prices are heading or how one price compares to another. Some of the more common statistical methods used in purchasing include linear regression analysis and exponential smoothing.

   Linear regression analysis calculates a mathematical formula for the best fitting straight line through a series of data points. By extending the calculation of this line to an event in the future, you can develop a forecast. The upper chart in Figure 10.1 shows the actual prices paid for purchases over a 26-week period. This data can then be used to calculate a trend line, which is shown as the dotted line in the lower chart. You can then use this trend line to forecast anticipated volumes, shown as the extension of the trend line in the lower chart.

   Exponential smoothing is an adjustment technique that takes the previous period's forecast and adjusts it up or down based on what actually occurred in that period. It accomplishes this by calculating a weighted average of the two values. As a historical projection, it allows the user to give more weight to most recent data.

Comparative Analysis

Comparative analysis can take a number of forms ranging from benchmarking industry standards to a side-by-side comparison of quoted prices. Table 10.1 shows an example of a price list analysis that compares the prices from three suppliers at different volume levels. As you can see, no single supplier has the best price throughout the volume range. How you make your selection will depend upon the volume you purchase and how well you can negotiate aggregated volumes over a period of time to obtain the highest discount.

FIGURE 10.1   Example of linear regression analysis

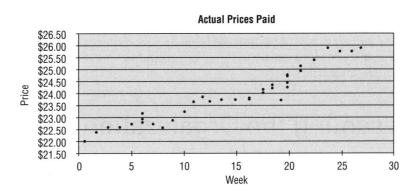

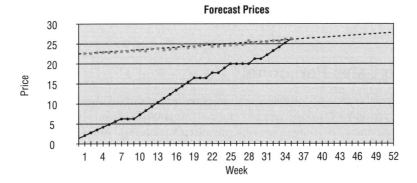

TABLE 10.1   Side by Side Comparison of Prices

Quantity	Supplier A	Supplier B	Supplier C
1,000	1.10	1.12	1.09
2,500	0.84	0.88	0.84
5,000	0.78	0.80	0.80
10,000	0.64	0.66	0.68
25,000	0.52	0.51	0.54
50,000	0.48	0.46	0.49

Product Analysis

Product analysis, or *functionality analysis* as it is sometimes called, examines products or services in terms of the functionality they provide, evaluating each element as a separate cost factor so that a comparative analysis of features can be made. This comparison helps determine the value and desirability of added functionality and can also help compare products considered to be as disparate as apples and oranges.

Representing the Organization

One of the key functions of the purchasing staff is managing the interface with suppliers and others outside the organization. This function requires an extremely tactful approach since in many ways your contacts are the public, and you must be certain the messages you give are in alignment with organizational policy. Close contact with your organization's public relations or communications teams will help ensure you are up to date on your current positioning and the correct message.

Meeting Sales Personnel

When effectively organized, meetings with sales personnel should always prove productive. While you have only the perspective of your own organization from which to gauge industry developments, your sales counterpart typically meets with several organizations during the normal course of business. Without compromising confidentiality, the sales representative can provide you with a host of ideas on how to improve operations.

As a result, it is important that you follow some specific protocol in dealing with sales personnel. To do so requires that you clearly understand the role of the sales professional.

The Role of the Sales Professional

Sales methods, of course, vary from organization to organization, industry to industry, and country to country. There are, however, a certain set of roles that are universal to virtually all those in sales. These roles generally include

- Researching and prospecting for potential customers
- Establishing rapport with a potential customer
- Identifying the customer's needs
- Matching the customer's needs with product offerings
- Presenting the offer, asking for the sale, overcoming objections
- Making the sale and closing
- Providing ongoing customer support

Keep in mind, however, that unlike the purchasing agent or buyer, the salesperson is rarely an agent of the organization and is therefore not empowered to commit the organization to contractual obligations. To do so generally requires an individual at the management level.

Sales training can be an extensive and detailed process, often quite mysterious to the buyer. For an excellent resource for learning more about selling techniques and the selling profession, go to: http://www.businessballs.com/salestraining.htm.

The Role of Purchasing

The Purchasing Department provides the initial interface with sales personnel and is responsible within the organization for responding to initial sales inquiries. In this role, the Purchasing Department must decide if there is any potential in the offering and if the salesperson has the ability to add value to the process. In addition, it is the Purchasing Department's function to work with the sales representative to further identify organizational needs that might fit and introduce the sales rep to others in the organization that may have an interest in the products or services being offered.

The purchasing team also has the opportunity through its interface with sales personnel to learn how others in the same marketplace may be conducting operations (without asking for confidential information) and can pass along this information to others in the form of intelligence.

It is also worth noting that Purchasing should be informed of any supplier visits paid directly to the user so that it can monitor information being disclosed. This helps ensure that other suppliers, should there be a competitive situation, gain access to the same information.

Extending Organizational Hospitality

Sales staff should be treated at all times with courtesy and respect and as valued representatives of their organizations. Here are some guidelines you might want to refer to when meeting with sales personnel:

- Meet promptly and courteously with sales representatives making scheduled calls.
- Offer as much hospitality as possible during your meeting.
- Provide equal opportunity for all representatives to present their products when you have a specific need.
- Maintain confidentiality at all times.
- Show concern for the representative's time and expense.
- When unable to provide the business being sought, explain the reasons as clearly as possible.

Handling Inquiries, Protests, and Complaints

The Purchasing Department handles numerous inquiries in the normal course of conducting business. Obviously, it is important that these be reviewed promptly and handled expeditiously as well as courteously. While many of these inquiries are simply prospecting efforts by sales personnel, many of them involve pending business and often require coordination with other departments in the organization.

When an inquiry refers to a current bid process or an open RFP, the buyer must be certain to respond accordingly to all participants as a measure of fairness and good business conduct. If the question materially affects the bidding, it may be necessary for the buyer to publish a formal addendum to the bid solicitation or the RFP addressing the issue.

From time to time, suppliers will want to protest an award decision or file a complaint regarding unfair treatment. Most organizations have well defined processes to handle this, including requirements for filing the objection in writing along with appropriate documentation. As part of an appeals process, some organizations provide for an escalation path to management or a standing committee for further review and action. In many cases, contracts or policy call for a formal dispute resolution process involving a neutral third party.

Regardless of the process used by your organization, it is important both that the suppliers understand the review process and that it be conducted expeditiously so as not to disrupt normal operations for either party.

Professional Conduct

Professional conduct is paramount to maintaining credibility with suppliers. Many organizations have a specific code of conduct, but if yours does not, consider using the one established by the Institute for Supply Management, shown next. You can also find ISM's Principles and Standards of Ethical Supply Management Conduct on the ISM website at: `http://www.ism.ws`.

Principles and Standards of Ethical Supply Management Conduct

LOYALTY TO YOUR ORGANIZATION

JUSTICE TO THOSE WITH WHOM YOU DEAL

FAITH IN YOUR PROFESSION

From these principles are derived the ISM standards of supply management conduct. (Global)

1. Avoid the intent and appearance of unethical or compromising practice in relationships, actions, and communications.

2. Demonstrate loyalty to the employer by diligently following the lawful instructions of the employer, using reasonable care and granted authority.

3. Avoid any personal business or professional activity that would create a conflict between personal interests and the interests of the employer.

4. Avoid soliciting or accepting money, loans, credits, or preferential discounts and the acceptance of gifts, entertainment, favors, or services from present or potential suppliers that might influence, or appear to influence, supply management decisions.

5. Handle confidential or proprietary information with due care and proper consideration of ethical and legal ramifications and governmental regulations.

6. Promote positive supplier relationships through courtesy and impartiality.

7. Avoid improper reciprocal agreements.

8. Know and obey the letter and spirit of laws applicable to supply management.

9. Encourage support for small, disadvantaged, and minority-owned businesses.

10. Acquire and maintain professional competence.

11. Conduct supply management activities in accordance with national and international laws, customs, and practices, your organization's policies, and these ethical principles and standards of conduct.

12. Enhance the stature of the supply management profession.

Approved January 2002

Participating in Meeting and External Events

From time to time, Purchasing Department staff will be required to represent the department or the organization in meetings and at outside events. For this reason, it is important that you understand how to conduct an effective meeting and how to prepare successful presentations.

Meetings

There are a few simple rules for conducting meetings that will help you make them more effective:

- Select the right participants based on the topic and input from others who might be interested in attending.
- Extend invitations in sufficient time to assure that everyone who wishes to attend will have ample time to make arrangements.
- Prepare an agenda and distribute it in advance of the meeting.
- Ensure that the meeting facilities are sufficient to accommodate the number invited and have the necessary supplies on hand.
- During the meeting, ensure that those who wish to participate in the discussion are provided with ample opportunity.
- Follow the agenda, including starting and ending on time.
- Maintain focus during the meeting.

- Periodically evaluate progress during the course of the meeting.
- Take and post notes as appropriate.
- Reach consensus or decision if and as planned.
- Following the meeting, publish notes and provide an opportunity for further input.

Presentation

Preparing and delivering an effective presentation is one of the most important skills you can develop and should not be difficult to achieve if you follow a few basic rules consistently. Many guides to effective presentations list the following as important considerations:

- Define the desired outcome of your presentation.
- Stay focused on your topic.
- Prepare your presentation with your specific audience in mind.
- Be in touch with your surroundings.
- Prepare carefully; use a script if needed.
- Organize material and present it in a logical sequence.
- Deal with one concept at a time.
- Leverage appropriate visual aids; be simple.
- Test regularly for clarity to be sure you are communicating with your audience.
- Deliver your material clearly.
- Define acronyms and unfamiliar terms.
- Maintain your audience's attention through eye contact.
- Encourage participation.
- Stay on schedule.

Ultimately, the most important consideration to bear in mind in meetings and presentations is to maintain your sincerity at all times. Most audiences feel uncomfortable around affectation.

Summary

In this chapter, we reviewed the requirements for managing productive supplier relations and how creating good working relationships requires a measure of effort. Meeting regularly with your suppliers, conducting surveys to garner input, and initiating reciprocal site visits are just a few of the ways to enhance relations. We also reviewed many of the tools available for improving communications with suppliers and how best to resolve ongoing relationship issues.

We then turned our attention to ways in which new suppliers could be certified and how to develop continuous improvement programs for existing suppliers. We looked at how early supplier involvement leads to better performance in procurement and the advantages of working collaboratively through supplier partnerships and alliances.

This chapter also covered the fundamentals of establishing and managing a supplier diversity program, including sourcing minority suppliers, as well as developing and managing programs.

As a key part of supplier relationship management, we examined how supplier pricing operates in response to market conditions and profit strategies. This included a look at pricing methods and analysis of pricing trend data.

We concluded the chapter with an examination of how the Purchasing Department represents the organization with suppliers, handling supplier inquiries and protests, and reviewing a standardized code of ethical conduct. And, finally, we reviewed how to conduct effective meetings and prepare presentations.

 For additional reading on topics related to this chapter, please see Appendix A.

Exam Essentials

Be able to create and foster effective supplier relationships. Meeting regularly with suppliers, conducting surveys to gain input, initiating improvement teams, and conducting supplier site visits are just a few of the ways to do this.

Develop methods for improved communication. Keeping suppliers informed also pays dividends through their continued involvement in your business. Websites, focus groups, and newsletters, along with reverse marketing, are some of the techniques available to you.

Be able to resolve relationship issues. Certain circumstances hamper good working relations, and the purchasing team must work to resolve them. These circumstances often include such issues as delayed payment, breach of confidentiality, and just plain fair dealing.

Understand supplier certification and how to mentor new suppliers. New suppliers are important to the organization as a means of infusing innovation. Typically, new suppliers require help and mentoring in order to achieve certification and better serve your organization.

Be able to develop continuous improvement and strengthen relationships. Gaining early supplier involvement and working collaboratively helps develop continuous improvement; forming partnerships and alliances typically cements those relationships.

Be able to implement a small/disadvantaged business program. Supplier diversity is key to corporate innovation. Recruiting and managing minority suppliers ensures that the entire community is represented in the organization's business dealings.

Understand conditions affecting supplier pricing. Market conditions as well as profitability formulas combine to influence supplier pricing methods. To obtain satisfactory pricing for the organization, the buyer must understand how these factors operate.

Be able to represent the organization. The Purchasing staff will be called upon frequently to represent the organization with external resources, especially sales professionals. To be effective in this role, you will need to know how and when to provide hospitality; how to handle inquiries, protests, and complaints; and how to follow a professional code of conduct. You will also be required to conduct effective meetings and deliver effective presentations.

Review Questions

1. Meeting with your suppliers on a regular basis can be done all of the following ways *except*:

    A. Improvement teams

    B. Supplier open house

    C. Cease and desist notices

    D. Supplier surveys

    E. Reciprocal visits

2. Which of the following is a useful environment for gaining supplier feedback?

    A. Surveys

    B. Supplier hotlines

    C. End user feedback

    D. A suggestion box

    E. Focus groups

3. Which term describes a buyer soliciting suppliers to fill a specific need?

    A. Supplier surveys

    B. Sourcing

    C. Reverse marketing

    D. Search engine

    E. Focus groups

4. Which term describes the condition where the supplier has met specific criteria and levels of performance?

    A. Qualification

    B. Service Level Agreement

    C. Acceptance test

    D. Incoming inspection

    E. Certification

5. Which term describes a for-profit enterprise, regardless of size, physically located in the United States, which is owned, operated, and controlled by minority group members?

    A. Diversity supplier

    B. Minority-owned business

    C. Disadvantaged supplier

    D. Small supplier

    E. Small business enterprise

6. Overall market conditions consist of the following factors *except*:

   A. Supply and demand

   B. Lead times

   C. Overall economic climate

   D. Competition

   E. Production capacity

7. Which term represents a supplier add-on to pricing as a percentage of total cost to cover overhead and profit?

   A. Selling price

   B. Direct cost

   C. Total cost

   D. Markup

   E. Service cost

8. A statistical methodology to determine where prices are heading is called:

   A. Statistic analysis

   B. Product analysis

   C. Trend analysis

   D. Gap analysis

   E. Comparative analysis

9. Professional purchasing principles and standards are usually outlined by a:

   A. Code of conduct

   B. Service level agreement

   C. Mission statement

   D. Supplier brochure

   E. Policy manual

10. Defining the desired outcome, focusing on the topic, and preparing for a specific audience are all ways to deliver effective:

   A. Scope of work

   B. Scorecards

   C. Presentations

   D. Service Level Agreements

   E. Specifications

Answers to Review Questions

1. C. Cease and desist notices are unrelated to supplier meetings.

2. E. Focus groups are events structured precisely to provide supplier feedback on specific topics.

3. C. Reverse marketing is a term coined to describe the buyer's solicitation of a supplier to fill a specific need when few or no suppliers exist.

4. E. Suppliers are certified when they have met certain levels of performance to warrant consideration for specific business.

5. B. The official term in the U.S. for this group is *minority-owned business*. The other terms, while they tend to describe a similar condition, are not the preferred reference.

6. B. Lead times do not directly refer to any specific market factor, whereas the other terms relate directly to economic factors.

7. D. Markup is the only term on this list that refers to an add-on.

8. C. Trend analysis works to forecast pricing trends. The other items in the list are forms of analysis that do not relate to forecasting.

9. A. A code of conduct outlines expectations for professional and ethical standards. The other items in this list do not specifically address purchasing principles.

10. C. These are the elements that describe the principles of an effective presentation. The other items in this list refer to other functions.

Providing
Added Value

Chapter 11

Making Sound Sourcing Decisions

THE C.P.M. EXAM SPECIFICATIONS COVERED IN THIS CHAPTER INCLUDE THE FOLLOWING:

- ✓ Performing a make or buy analysis
- ✓ Performing a make or lease analysis
- ✓ Formulating financial strategies

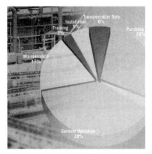

During the normal course of business, you will be required to assist in making many financial decisions related to the acquisition of goods and services for the organization. Many of these decisions will involve determining whether to acquire the goods and services from suppliers through direct purchase or if the organization can more efficiently provide them itself by using internal resources. In addition, determining whether to buy or lease is another typical business decision that must be made on an ongoing basis. These decisions are generally referred to as *make or buy* and *lease or buy* because they require a comparative analysis of those alternatives.

In addition, there are numerous other financial leveraging strategies that you will need to understand, such as how commodity markets operate and how the cost of money through interest rates is determined—factors that are most often driven by conditions in the marketplace. In this chapter, we will explore the processes for preparing for some of these key financial decisions and their importance to the modern organization.

Performing Make or Buy Analysis

Make or buy analysis, as its name implies, is the process that determines if the organization should produce a particular product or service in-house or if it should turn to a third party supplier and simply purchase it from them. Many companies in the semiconductor industry, for example, have increasingly turned to "fabless" operations, choosing to outsource the production of silicon die products, which requires large investments in sophisticated tools and equipment, to third parties who have already invested huge amounts of money in developing their state-of-the-art facilities. Today, approximately two-thirds of all semiconductor companies delegate manufacturing operations to outside foundries, focusing instead on what they consider to be their own core competencies, design and marketing strategies.

In the following section, we will examine the dynamics of make or buy analysis, looking at the process dynamics as well as the strategies behind them.

Make or Buy Dynamics

There are numerous opportunities for *outsourcing* the products your organization manufactures or the functions your organization performs internally by contracting them to third parties. Commonly targeted services include business functions such as information technology, facilities management, payroll management, logistics, and with more increasing frequency, procurement itself. It is also becoming increasingly common for manufacturing operations to outsource entire product-line assembly functions to firms specializing in material procurement, assembly, and testing. The benefits of outsourcing generally include reduced labor costs resulting from the transfer of operations to lower-paid workers, along with lower material prices due to the larger economies of scale with consolidated volumes purchased by third-party manufacturers. The offsetting disadvantages include loss of control and, sometimes, loss of scheduling flexibility.

Generally, make or buy decisions are conducted by a cross-functional team so that the benefit of all perspectives can be obtained and evaluated. Before deciding the viability of buying products or services currently handled internally, the team will need to look carefully at a number of factors and gather information from a number of sources.

Viability Study

The first step in a make or buy decision is determining if buying the product or outsourcing the service is viable. This depends largely on the existing supply base. You will likely find that this is actually a sourcing process involving finding suppliers capable of handling your organization's business. You will need to locate suppliers that have personnel with the proper skill set, as well as available equipment and facilities, to handle your needs. If you and your team are unable to locate viable suppliers, you are faced with either developing existing suppliers to handle your needs or continuing to do it in-house.

If the marketplace for your requirement has a limited number of suppliers, you will also want to analyze the risk involved. Are there viable back-up alternatives should the supplier you choose encounter difficulties? Do the physical logistics involved add significantly more costs and process complexity to your operations? How financially solvent are the potential providers—are they capable of making the financial investments required by developing technology?

You will also want to look into the resources required for managing the supplier. Will the supplier become a critical factor in producing your end product, requiring close audit tracking and frequent business reviews? Will the outsourcing engagement require engineering or quality staff to work closely with the supplier on a continuing basis? Will these support resources be available?

Requirements

The next step in the process is determining your organization's exact needs. This part of the process is very similar to the one we outlined in the section on developing requirements in Chapter 2, "Sourcing." You will need to develop a clear specification or statement of work (SOW), as well as an estimate of future requirements volume or frequency of service. This is necessary for two reasons: first, to establish a baseline for the current costs to your organization and second, to enable a relatively accurate quote from potential suppliers. Without either of these, you may not be able to determine accurately if there are financial advantages to buying.

Conducting Analysis

Having located viable sources and defined the exact requirements, the final step is actually conducting the analysis. To do this, you will first need to prepare an RFP or RFx to go out to the potential suppliers. Once the RFx is returned and analyzed, you will have enough data to do a comparative analysis between your current operating values—primarily cost— and those of the proposed outsourcing. As with any RFx comparison, you will want to analyze and compare the elements of quality, cost, technology, and service. Most importantly, you must be certain you are receiving equal or greater value from the supplier before making a final outsourcing decision.

The team's initial analysis will likely focus on those elements you consider tangible, such as cost, lead times, and scheduling flexibility. If, following this analysis, the team continues to find potential value in an outsourcing engagement, it should continue with the analysis and turn to a number of subjective criteria before making the actual decision.

In performing a basic analysis—with a new product, for example—cost and capacity may be the critical factors. In the analysis of cost, you will want to be sure to consider direct costs such as material, labor, and freight and indirect costs such as receiving, inspecting, and stocking, as well as scrap and the cost of resolving quality issues.

Subjective Make or Buy Analysis Factors

There are several intangible factors that should be considered by the team before coming to a final conclusion as to whether or not to actually go forward with the outsourcing engagement:

Strategy

In the long term, your team will want to determine how well the proposed outsourcing fits with the overall organizational strategy. Prior to making a recommendation, you will want to explore a number of questions such as these:

- Is the process or product a critical part of the organization's core competency? If so, your team must weigh the pros and cons of placing this in the hands of a third party supplier.

- Does learning from the development of this product or service drive learning in other business function areas? You will want to determine if this will weaken any existing technology development.

- Will your outsourced business provide adequate incentive to suppliers to continue participating? If there is not sufficient revenue from the outsourcing to continue to engage suppliers, you should consider the effect that future capacity constraints might place on the supplier.

- Can you actually reduce internal costs sufficiently enough to offset the acquisition costs? You need to analyze the true cost reduction to the organization as a result of outsourcing. Unless buying can produce reduced staffing by eliminating existing head count, the calculated savings may be "soft." You will also want to be certain that reduction in staffing in one area does not result in the need for increased staffing in another. For example, will outsourcing a manufacturing operation require additional quality and procurement personnel due to quality or delivery issues?

- To what extent will the organization be able to reverse its sourcing decision in the future, bringing back in-house the product or service if the supplier should fail? This is often a key strategic decision because the equipment and expertise needed to produce the outsourced item may require heavy investment to replace at some future date.

Risk

Although risk assessment is difficult or impossible to quantify, its evaluation is a critical part of any outsourcing determination. In the words of the famous Murphy: "Anything that can go wrong will go wrong." Therefore, when conducting any risk analysis, one should not hesitate to evaluate each and every one of the factors and assumptions made in the initial sourcing comparative analysis.

In performing risk analysis, you need to carefully balance the specific, expected benefits of the engagement with factors that you may not be able to control. For example, you will need to determine the effect of capacity constraints in the supply community hampering future production operations. Conversely, you will want to gauge the impact that a business downturn will have on your selected supplier. Will your supply needs continue to be met?

You will also want to analyze, where possible, the potential impact that changing technology may have on future requirements. With relatively low volumes, you may be unable to convince a supplier to invest in future research and technological development. This condition might favor keeping the product or service in-house. Similarly, with a new product or service about to be introduced to the market, your organization will want to determine if the resources that must be acquired to produce the product or service will result in an internal return on that investment. In these circumstances, turning to a supplier with existing capability may prove more effective.

WARNING   Some elements of risk cannot be tolerated at any level. Lack of SPC tools, for example, should immediately disqualify a potential supplier for technology-driven parts.

Quality Considerations

There is virtually no factual data to support the assumption that buying a product or service rather than making it will result in diminished quality. According to a recent survey, in fact, the majority of companies outsourcing found that work skill quality actually improved following the engagement, and 70 percent reported an increase in the quality of outsourced business processes.

As always, successful buying programs require a clear definition of quality and the definitive documentation of the business processes required for its support. Many organizations choose to outsource simply because they have little or no documented control of subordinate processes in the first place. Suppliers often have better process documentation in place and greater control of quality simply because the product or service is a core competency for them.

Support Capability

Support capability refers to the ability to develop advanced product technology. Supporting new product development in some areas is often a financial burden for the buying organization but a core competency for the supplier engaged in providing the service to a wide spectrum of customers. Suppliers are usually in a better position to absorb the costs of development simply because they can distribute it over a wider customer base.

Similarly, supporting business processes has become, for some organizations, a core competency due to their large customer base. Many have dedicated engineering staffs to work with customers during the product development cycle to ensure alignment between the design and the manufacturing process. Many are global and have multinational support. Most have sophisticated customer service systems capable of tracking customer orders and repair status on a 24x7 basis.

Outsourcing Business Processes

Today, outsourcing entire business processes, such as manufacturing assembly, information technology, or logistics is a common occurrence. While the process sometimes appears more complex and the resulting risk may be higher because of the broadened scope, it invariably follows a process similar to the make or buy analysis.

Outsourcing is defined as the transfer of a previously performed function from the organizational staff to a third party supplier. As we noted earlier in this chapter, many such functions within the organization have become subject to potential outsourcing. The prime drive appears to be lowered cost from the engagement, likely as a result of efficiencies the supplier is able to achieve by spreading the overhead across a larger group of users. However, many organizations are experiencing improved service as a result of the greater human resources available to the supplier in times of customer need.

The following sections discuss the make or buy process and some important elements you should consider when sourcing these services.

Needs Analysis

Needs analysis should be performed by a cross-functional team composed of subject matter experts and those familiar with the processes being used internally at the current time. Be sure to include stakeholders as well, so that all user groups are represented.

Your team must define the requirements in terms of an SOW, just as it would with any other service. At a minimum you will want to have:

- A detailed description of the work to be performed
- Costs of the present operation, by function
- Required service levels—how you intend to measure performance
- Critical risks in the engagement

Decision-Making Process

From these elements, your team should be able to incorporate its needs into an RFP and submit it to qualified or qualifiable suppliers. Be certain to include your typical contract terms for this type of engagement so you can determine quickly if suppliers are not willing to accept your existing business and legal terms. You should also be able to construct an assessment criteria matrix to objectively rate the suppliers' responses to your RFP once received.

Based on the initial responses (or noticeable lack of response), your team will need to decide if the potential exists to actually conduct the proposed outsourcing. You'll base this on the nature of the responses and the costs being proposed. If it appears to be feasible, proceed to the supplier selection process; if not, consider revising the SOW or dropping the outsourcing project.

Supplier Selection

Many organizations use a pre-established selection criteria based on comparative rating methodologies that rates suppliers on the basis of proposed cost, service levels, technology capability, quality, and the level of ongoing investment in the process you are outsourcing. We reviewed this in Chapter 3, "Selecting Suppliers and Measuring Performance," and you may want to refer back to it for further details.

Performing Lease or Buy Analysis

Leasing is an alternative to buying that's used primarily when acquiring capital equipment. In many respects, leasing can be considered similar to renting.

Lease or buy analysis is the process of comparing the overall costs associated with leasing compared to owning a particular asset. Depending on the cost of capital for a given organization, the lease may provide significant advantages. Lease payments are typically expensed rather than capitalized so they can be related directly to the accounting period in which they occur. While it is common for an equipment lease to require a long term contract, there is usually little or no down payment needed. Table 11.1 is a comparison between the two options.

TABLE 11.1 Benefits of Buying vs. Benefits of Leasing

Benefits of Buying	Benefits of Leasing
No fees for early termination	Little or no cash to obtain the equipment
Can be sold at any time	Payments are considered expenses and may provide tax advantages
Total costs are usually lower over time	Several disposal options at end of lease
Use of the equipment can extend far after it is paid for	Does not affect bank line of credit
	Little fear of obsolescence

Leasing Features

A lease agreement grants the *lessee* possession of equipment or property for a stated period of time and at an agreed upon rate of payment. The lessee is not the owner of the asset but commonly bears all responsibility for maintaining it in good working order. At the end of the lease, the lessee may have the option of purchasing the equipment at a *fair market value* or for a previously agreed upon amount if such a clause is included in the contract.

Lease Types

There are several common types of leases that you should become familiar with:

Finance Lease   A *finance lease* is a financing device whereby a lessee can acquire an asset for most of its useful life. Generally, a finance lease is noncancelable during the term of the lease. Leases of this type are generally net to the lessor so the lessee is responsible for maintenance, taxes, and insurance.

Full Payout Lease   A *full payout lease* is a lease in which the actual cash payments will return the lessor the full equipment cost plus a satisfactory return over the lease term.

Leveraged Lease   A *leveraged lease* is a lease in which the lessor borrows a portion of the purchase price of the leased equipment from institutional investors. In a typical transaction, 20 to 40 percent of the purchase price is provided by one or more investors who become owners and lessors of the equipment. The balance of the purchase price is borrowed from banks or other sources of capital.

Net Lease   In a *net lease*, the fees are payable net to the lessor; that is, the lessee pays all out-of-pocket expenses such as taxes, insurance, and maintenance. The lease, therefore, only addresses the equipment itself. All costs in connection with the use of the equipment (usually hard to predict) are to be paid by the lessee over and above the agreed rental payments. Most finance leases are net leases.

Operating Lease   An *operating lease* is a short-term lease whereby a user can acquire an asset for a fraction of the useful life of the asset. The lessor may provide services in connection with the lease, such as maintenance, insurance, and payment of personal property taxes. From a strict accounting standpoint, the specific requirements of FASB 13 (discussed later in the chapter) must be met for a lease to be qualified as an operating lease.

Lessors

Lessors are persons or entities who own the property being leased (for example, real estate or equipment), which a lessee receives use and possession of in exchange for a payment of fees. Lessors typically include banks, manufacturers of equipment, third party owners, and capital funding organizations.

Decision-Making Factors

As with any decision, leasing raises a number of considerations, both favorable and unfavorable. The next sections discuss some of those you should usually consider.

Advantages of Leasing

Some of the advantages to leasing include

Better Cash Flow   Leasing gives you access to the asset with minimal up-front payments and spreads the cost over time. You can pay for the asset with the income it generates while minimizing the drain on your working capital.

No Debt   An operating lease preserves your credit options and does not influence your credit limit because it is generally classified as expense, not debt.

Maximum Financial Leverage   Your lease can often finance everything related to the purchase and installation of the asset and may free up cash flow to pay for items such as training.

Cash Flow Management   Lease payments are usually constant, making cash management more predictable.

Tax Advantage   Operating lease payments are generally tax deductible just like depreciation charges but are made with pre-tax money. Cash purchases, in contrast, are made with after-tax money.

Flexible Time Frames   Leasing contracts can be structured to fit your requirements. You can use an asset as long as you need it without owning it forever.

Protection Against Obsolescence   Depending on your end-of-lease option, you can return the asset to the lessor.

Disadvantages of Leasing

Some of the disadvantages to leasing are

More Expensive   A finance lease is usually more expensive than an outright cash purchase because the payments include finance charges. However, leasing may cost less than other forms of financing.

Additional Guarantees Required   Depending on the credit rating of your company, the lessor might require additional guarantees. These may be provided by officers of your organization or your bank and could affect your organization's credit rating or financial standing with bankers reviewing debt-to-asset ratios.

Fixed Term   It may be impossible, or very costly, to terminate a leasing contract early.

Locked Interest Rates   Interest rates are usually fixed throughout the lease, which may prove a disadvantage in times of falling interest rates.

Cost Factors

Any lease analysis must consider typical total cost of ownership factors such as acquisition cost, operating costs, and maintenance and disposal. Acquisition costs typically include the down payment (if required), taxes, shipping costs, installation, and financing or loan fees. Operating costs typically include any enhancements to the original equipment, consumables, and energy/fuel consumption. Maintenance factors include preventative maintenance, spare parts, and down time. Disposal costs include reconditioning costs, facility removal costs, shipping, early lease termination fees, and "fair market value" salvage value.

   Here are some of the more subtle cost factors that you will need to take into account in any complete analysis:

Return of Asset Reconditioning   If you choose to return the asset at the end of your lease, the condition to which it must be reconditioned and the place where it must be returned are important cost factors to consider.

Notice Period   If your lease includes an automatic option to renew, take note of any time periods in which you must give notice in case you do not want to renew the contract. Some leasing companies will automatically renew the contract if you fail to give notice.

Purchase Rights When returning the asset at the end of your lease, a predetermined fixed price offers more options than the fair market value, which theoretically is always available to you.

Maintenance Responsibility Clarify which service and maintenance programs are included in the lease. If you are responsible for service and maintenance, make sure it is in line with the manufacturer's recommendations.

Budget Considerations

Organizations needing to balance the need for new technology with budget constraints find that leasing helps stretch budget dollars with monthly payments that are often lower than purchase installments. With a lease, organizational cash remains untouched and available for other profitable uses. In addition, leasing often expands financial resources without affecting established credit lines.

Many companies realize significant tax benefits from leasing their technology. Monthly lease payments are generally tax deductible and can be treated as a business expense. Conventional bank financing typically requires a minimum balance. With leasing, there is no minimum balance or down payment required.

24. FASB 13

The Financial Accounting Standards Board (FASB) established standards of financial accounting and reporting for leases by lessees and lessors for transactions and revisions entered into on or after January 1, 1977. For lessees, a lease is a financing transaction called a capital lease if it meets any one of four specified criteria; if not, it is an operating lease. Capital leases are treated as the acquisition of assets and the incurrence of obligations by the lessee. Operating leases are treated as current operating expenses.

For lessors, a financing transaction lease is classified as a sales type, direct financing, or leveraged lease. To be a sales type, direct financing, or leveraged lease, the lease must meet one of the same criteria used for lessees to classify a lease as a capital lease, in addition to two criteria dealing with future uncertainties.

Leveraged leases also have to meet further criteria. These types of leases are recorded as investments under different specifications for each type of lease. Leases not meeting the criteria are considered operating leases and are accounted for like rental property.

Formulating Financial Strategies

The Purchasing Department is in one of the best positions in the organization to influence and improve the bottom line by leveraging relationships and information from the supply community. But to do so, the manager must understand existing processes and strategies within the organization so that, for example, a cost saving in one operating area does not resurface as financial burden in another.

In this section, let's examine some of the finance-based avenues and tools available to you to better perform your job.

Organizational Considerations

The type of organization you are employed by will have a large influence on the nature of its financial strategies and will require different approaches from the Purchasing Department. Consider some of the various ways organizations might respond to similar situations depending upon their sectors and organizational structures.

Commercial

Commercial enterprises can be divided into two sectors:

Public Corporation   Public corporations, businesses whose stock is publicly owned and traded on one of the many stock exchanges, owe a measure of fiduciary due diligence to their many stockholders. In addition to its efforts to reduce cost, the Purchasing Department must follow standard operating procedures so that the public can rely on the management's ability to produce profit. The department is always under audit scrutiny and must ensure that procedures are followed at all times.

Privately Owned Enterprises   Businesses that are privately held are free to develop financial strategies within the constraints of their mission and the direction provided by the owners. The Purchasing Department's responsibility, however, remains the same: provide value for the organization.

Nonprofit

Nonprofit organizations include schools, churches, charities, and other organizations working for the benefit of the community. Obviously, with nonprofit organizations, the "profit" motive is largely absent. Nevertheless, these organizations want to stretch their operating budgets as far as possible in order to better fulfill their mission, and the Purchasing Department can serve the mission by enabling a fixed budget to be leveraged that much further.

Government

Government purchasing requirements are possibly the most stringent and certainly the most complex in regard to process and procedure compliance. Purchasing departments in these environments must conform to a host of complex and sometimes obscure regulations originally designed to ensure that the public is protected while receiving the most value for its tax dollar and that suppliers are treated fairly and equally. This has, unfortunately, made the purchasing process more cumbersome than most would like it to be, and it's certainly more difficult for the purchaser to achieve outstanding results. To many, conformance to the prescribed process and completion of proper documentation have become more important considerations than desirable results. While improvements in the system to make them more strategically responsive to financial objectives are taking place all of the time, it is by nature a slow process and we (the authors) have unbridled admiration for those who manage to consistently produce outstanding results despite the often formidable obstacles and roadblocks.

Procurement Structure

How the procurement organization is structured and where it resides in the organization can definitely affect its performance and fit with the organization's overall financial and operational strategies. An astute purchasing manager will make every possible effort to ensure that those in the organization developing the strategic goals will understand how the current structure of the purchasing group both supports and hinders those goals.

While there are infinite variations of Purchasing Department structure, the next sections list some of the standard types you are likely to encounter.

Centralized

A centralized Purchasing Department exists when it is the sole authorized agency to purchase goods and service for the organization. This group supports the entire organization, regardless of location or the nature of operations. The advantage of this structure is that it supports compliance with organizational policy, and it can better leverage the supplier community through combined volumes. The downside is that it is extremely difficult to find expertise capable of servicing a product or diverse organization.

Lead/Divisional

In a a lead/divisional Purchasing Department, the purchasing groups are distributed across the organization to support local user groups, and each purchasing group places its own purchase orders. However, the group with the greatest expertise in a specific area is responsible for negotiating prices and contracts for the entire organization.

Cooperative

Centralized buying services, known unofficially as cooperatives or *buying consortiums*, have become relatively popular recently. They are able to save money by combining the volumes of several customers and making one purchase. Several of these have become successful and quite well known.

WARNING   Consortiums need to have a common basis for organization in order to comply with antitrust regulations when receiving preferential pricing. One important requirement is that the organizations participating in the buying have a significant similarity, such as being part of the same industry or being engaged in a similar nonprofit mission. Be sure to check with your legal counsel before proceeding with forming a consortium.

Monetary Considerations

Related to the development of financial strategies are a number of elements that will affect how and when purchases are made. Here we'll look at some of the more common areas where purchasing and financial influences overlap.

Depreciation

It is generally recognized that equipment and certain other assets purchased by an organization have a finite useful life, at the end of which they will theoretically no longer be of any salvage value. *Depreciation* is the process of allowing for and recording this decline in value over a specified period of time. If, for example, a copier cost $100,000 and has a recognized useful life of five years, then each year it would depreciate by another $20,000.

This has two important considerations: first, since depreciation is an expense for tax reporting purposes, it represents a *liability* on the organization's books. Second, the "book" value or asset value also declines at this rate, reducing the organization's book value on the *balance sheet* and, potentially, the possible resale or salvage value.

This needs to be taken into consideration when preparing Return on Investment (ROI) analysis and when calculating costs for a make or buy/lease or buy decision.

Bond and Currency Markets

Purchasers involved in foreign trade understand that currencies fluctuate frequently, rising or declining in value against the U.S. dollar or other base currency. If you are purchasing in foreign currencies, you need to know how this can affect the future price of your purchase at the time of contracting. If your base currency—let's use U.S. dollars for this example—declines relative to the purchase currency, you will need more dollars to pay the invoice. If the opposite is the case, the supplier may receive less than expected in terms of global market value.

To maintain the stability of your transaction (and to some extent, the profitability of your purchase), you can often use a process called hedging. Hedging is a strategy designed to reduce the risk of fluctuations in forward-looking contracts requiring payment in a foreign currency. Your organization's actions will depend on how it forecasts currency changes: If it expects the foreign currency to decline in value relative to the dollar, it will place aside the dollars needed for payment, purchasing the foreign currency when it appears to be at its lowest point. On the other hand, if the currency is expected to increase in relation to the U.S. dollar, it might prove wise to purchase the foreign currency as soon as the contract is signed.

WARNING   Currency hedging is best left to experts because of its inherent financial risk. To date, no one has figured out how to predict the future value of any currency very far in the future. Most organizations rely on their treasury group to handle this or use an outside broker who is an expert in the currency under consideration.

Commodity Markets

To constitute a *commodity*, products must be relatively standardized, undifferentiated, and capable of being traded in a formalized market environment, such as an exchange. In the past, typical commodities have been related to metals, lumber, agricultural products, chemicals, and fuels. They are typically traded on open exchanges where the price fluctuates according to supply and demand. In these open exchanges, it is possible to purchase a number of so-called "instruments" that can reduce risk of future fluctuations, including the purchase of contracts for future delivery at a designated date and at the price specified in the contract, regardless of the actual market price at the time of purchase. Contracts can be created and sold even for product not yet physically owned by the seller. Once created, these contracts can then be bought and sold as desired.

These financial instruments all have one aspect in common: risk. As you know, it is impossible to forecast where prices are heading from one period to the next. Expert advice, sound forecasts of demand, and lots of diligent scrutiny are the minimum requirements for success in mastering commodity markets.

Interest Rates

Interest rates can have a significant impact on purchasing decisions, especially those related to timing. As interest rates rise, companies pay more to the lenders for additional capital, thus raising their costs and their selling prices. For the same reason, buyers are under increased pressure to reduce inventory and the price of equipment purchased.

Payment Terms

Payment terms refer to the agreement between buyer and seller regarding the timing and method of payment for goods and services supplied. Payment terms are closely related to interest rates because in many senses they represent a loan to the buyer by the seller for the period between receiving the product or service and the time that it takes for the payment to actually reach the sellers' coffers.

Payment terms for purchases generally follow a standard format, indicating the number of days in which the payment is due and any discounts that can be taken for payment at some specific, earlier date. For example:

Net 45   Means that payment in full is due in 45 days.

Net 10th prox   Means that payment in full is due on the tenth day of the following month.

2 percent 10/Net 30   Means that payments received within 10 days of the invoice date will receive a 2 percent discount and the balance is payable in full in 30 days.

Some organizations maintain the policy that payment is due from receipt of the invoice rather than its date since this is easier to verify. Most sellers invoice upon shipment, so this does not seem unfair, especially in a situation where the product being shipped takes weeks to arrive.

Buyer Financing

There are always situations where suppliers require advance payment, either to ensure that the contract can be started or to provide financing for equipment and materials in quantities not affordable at the supplier's current level of operation. Sometimes organizations advance loans to suppliers or provide equipment already owned in order to help them along. This practice has its pros and cons. Nonetheless, organizations must ensure fairness to other suppliers and conformance to applicable laws and regulations.

Cash Flow

The term *cash flow* is often used rather vaguely. Operating cash flow is the cash generated by the business after changes in working capital; net cash flow is the amount of money left after expenses at any particular time period. It may not be a good time to make large purchases when cash flow is at a low point because funds may need to be borrowed to cover the bill. Timing purchases to coincide with cash inputs can prove an effective tool in adding to the bottom line.

Legal Aspects

While most of the legal aspects affecting purchasing have been outlined in Chapter 4, "Administering Contracts," as a manager you should be reminded of the importance of tracking legal developments so that you are in full compliance with the law. Sarbanes-Oxley, for example, which requires reporting commencing in November 2004, is likely to have a major impact on purchasing and compliance reporting requirements for publicly held U.S. companies.

Tax Laws

While you will not have direct responsibility for taxes, you will need to know some basic principles under which tax laws operate so that you can take them into account when making certain purchasing decisions. For example, in many states, purchases for products being resold (or that go into products being resold) do not require the payment of sales tax. In many areas, taxes on inventory are assessed just as they would be for real property. Software downloaded via the Internet is usually exempt from sales tax (considered a service rather than a product), while the same software purchased in a box will be subject to tax.

 Use tax is a tax levied on goods that are bought outside the taxing authority's jurisdiction and then brought into the jurisdiction. This tax is designed to discourage the purchase of products that are not subject to a sales tax.

Regulations

As noted, most of the regulations governing purchasing operations relate to commonly used processes. These include regulations governing antitrust, intellectual property, environmental health and safety (including hazardous materials), international trade, and the Uniform Commercial Code. You will likely be required to track changes to these regulations as the compliance source for your organization.

Summary

One of the Purchasing Department's most frequently used analytical tools is the make or buy analysis. This comparative analysis enables you to determine whether or not outsourcing a product or service or manufacturing or performing it in-house is the most advantageous path for your organization. There are a number of dynamics that must be considered, including specific analysis of needs and requirements, technical viability, risk, quality, and service capability. There is also the ever-important aspect of price to consider.

Similar to considerations you must take to determine whether to outsource a product or service is the process of determining whether to lease or buy. Leasing has a number of additional considerations that should be taken into account, including the impact on cash flow, tax liability, cost factors, budget considerations, and regulatory requirements. There are various lease types to consider and they differ from one another significantly, each providing its own advantages and disadvantages.

There are also a number of financial tools you will be required to understand and use as part of developing strategies. Divided into two aspects—organizational and monetary considerations—these cover organizational and procurement structures and common financial factors such as depreciation, payment terms, interest rates, bond and commodity markets, financing, and cash flow.

 For additional reading on topics related to this chapter, please see Appendix A.

Exam Essentials

Be able to conduct a make or buy analysis.   You should understand and be able to compare the variables that must be examined as part of the make or buy decision process, including supplier viability, risks, quality, and service considerations.

Be able to conduct lease or buy analysis.   You should recognize the financial implications of the various leasing options and be able to compare their advantages and disadvantages to direct purchase.

Understand the requirements of FASB 13.   The financial accounting requirements set forth by FASB 13 govern the tax implications of various lease types you will encounter.

Recognize the various organizational structures and their impact on financial strategies. Each organizational type, commercial, nonprofit, and governmental, requires different financial strategies. In addition, Purchasing Departments have specific structures that impact how they operate and what specific strategies should be developed for them.

Understand basic monetary factors.   You should be familiar with how certain factors affect purchasing decisions, including depreciation, bond and currency markets, commodity markets, interest rates, payment terms, buyer financing, and cash flow.

Be able to identify tax laws and regulations that impact financial strategy.   You will be required to know what items of purchase are taxable and where general regulations governing the Purchasing Department's financial role can be found.

Review Questions

1. Process that determines if the organization should produce a product or service in-house or purchase it from a supplier.
   - **A.** Viability study
   - **B.** Standardization
   - **C.** Lease or buy analysis
   - **D.** Risk assessment
   - **E.** Make or buy analysis

2. The first step in the make or buy decision process that determines if buying the product or outsourcing the service is feasible.
   - **A.** Viability study
   - **B.** Standardization
   - **C.** Lease or buy analysis
   - **D.** Risk assessment
   - **E.** Make or buy

3. Performed by a cross-functional team composed of subject-matter experts and those familiar with the processes being used internally at the current time.
   - **A.** Viability study
   - **B.** Needs analysis
   - **C.** Lease or buy analysis
   - **D.** Risk assessment
   - **E.** Make or buy

4. Process of comparing the total costs associated with leasing compared to owning a given asset.
   - **A.** Finance lease
   - **B.** Leveraged lease
   - **C.** Lease or buy
   - **D.** Operating lease
   - **E.** Net lease

5. Financing device whereby a lessee can acquire use of an asset for most of its useful life.
   - **A.** Finance lease
   - **B.** Leveraged lease
   - **C.** Full payout lease
   - **D.** Operating lease
   - **E.** Net lease

6. Not considered a long-term debt or liability, it does not appear as debt on your financial statement.

    A. Finance lease

    B. Leveraged lease

    C. Full payout lease

    D. Operating lease

    E. Net lease

7. Type of Purchasing Department that performs all activities related to the purchase of goods and services for the organization.

    A. Lead/divisional

    B. Consortium

    C. Corporate

    D. Cooperative

    E. Centralized

8. Process of allowing for and recording the write-off of an asset's value over a specified period of time.

    A. Salvage value

    B. Depreciation

    C. Residual value

    D. Net value

    E. Scrap value

9. Financial strategy designed to reduce the risk of fluctuations in forward-looking contracts requiring payment in a foreign currency.

    A. Currency float

    B. Commodity markets

    C. Insurance

    D. Hedging

    E. Foreign trade

10. Markets for products that are standardized, undifferentiated, and capable of being traded in a formalized exchange environment.

    A. Spot

    B. Futures

    C. Commodity

    D. Instruments

    E. Stock

Answers to Review Questions

1. E. The title for this process is make or buy. The other items listed are typically elements of the analysis.

2. A. The viability study examines the supply base to ensure that there are suppliers capable of handling this business.

3. B. The needs analysis determines the requirements for the product or service being considered for outsourcing and requires input from those who are responsible for them.

4. C. Lease or buy analysis compares the various financial advantages and disadvantages of leasing or buying based on total costs. The other options are lease types rather than a comparison.

5. A. The finance lease allows the lessee to use an asset and then turn it in at the end of its predetermined life.

6. D. An operating lease is similar to a rental and can be turned back at any time in compliance with other terms and conditions so it is not considered a debt or liability.

7. E. The centralized Purchasing Department is the only one of these options where all purchasing for the organization would be conducted.

8. B. Accounting rules recognize that equipment loses its value over a period of time and its value should be removed from the asset ledger accordingly. This is called depreciation.

9. D. Hedging is the process of purchasing or banking currency in anticipation of future fluctuations.

10. C. Products that are so described are commodities and are frequently traded on exchanges called commodity markets.

Chapter 12

Managing Material and Supply Operations

THE C.P.M. EXAM SPECIFICATIONS COVERED IN THIS CHAPTER INCLUDE THE FOLLOWING:

- ✓ Establishing inventory strategies and reviewing inventory and stocking levels with internal departments
- ✓ Resolving inventory discrepancies
- ✓ Effectively managing the storage of materials
- ✓ Disposing of surplus equipment, materials, and scrap

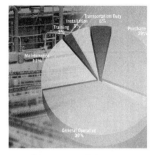

Controlling the flow, storage, and stocking levels of materials is another of the key functions of supply management. Organizations, particularly those engaged in manufacturing operations, consider material management a core competency because production processes and materials go hand in hand. The effective flow of materials can, and often does, significantly affect the overall productivity—and thus the costs—of the manufacturer.

Because, in many instances, there is a great deal of capital invested in stored inventory, how the inventory is controlled and managed can also affect the organization's profitability. When profit is viewed as a return on the investment, it becomes clear that maximizing that return will depend largely on how rapidly existing inventory can be consumed and converted back into cash. Obviously, if all other conditions are equal, the organization with the smallest ratio of inventory to sales is the organization that will likely be the most profitable.

In this chapter, we will examine the various methods of controlling inventory so that it can be used as a valuable resource to support operations rather than as a black hole for cash. These controls include strategies and methods for ordering and stocking materials, as well as effective processes for disposing of inventory that is no longer needed.

Inventory Control and Management Systems

Organizations that own and manage inventory are constantly seeking ways to reduce the size of that inventory in order to reduce the amount of nonproductive funds that are thus tied up. As you know, inventory generally doesn't do anything except consume valuable space and require a lot of cycle counting. For organizations that require inventory for perhaps justifiable reasons, such as using it as a buffer for unreliable supply or large swings in demand, the challenge comes with managing it so that as little as possible is needed. From this effort, a number of systems have been developed for determining when to order inventory and automating the management process. We'll describe some of these systems in this section.

Types of Inventory

Inventory is generally classified according to its functional type and, if used in manufacturing, its current state of production. Thus it is typical for material to be classified as *raw material*

(RM), *work-in-process (WIP)*, or *finished goods (FG)*. Raw material, in turn, can be classified as *direct material* (that is, material that goes directly into the product being manufactured) or *indirect material* (material that supports manufacturing operations but does not ship out with the final product). In addition, there are inventories of materials you maintain that are not directly related to any production functions, such as MRO (Maintenance, Repair and Operations) supplies and marketing support materials.

Before we look at how these inventories are managed, it might be useful to define their various natures. Let's start with raw materials.

Raw Material Classifications

Raw materials, as the title implies, are materials in their basic state as they have been received and to which no manufacturing operations have been performed. They are in the first stage of the transformation process to the final manufactured product.

There are two major categories of raw materials: direct material and indirect material.

Direct Material   Direct material is the primary classification for raw materials in manufacturing operations. It is only the material that, after manufacturing processes are applied, ships out to a distributor or the final customer. If, for example, you manufacture hammers, then steel would be your primary direct material.

The level of inventory for direct material is considered one of the manufacturing organization's key financial indicators. To demonstrate effective management of inventory, organizations use the term *turns* referring to the number of times the current inventory of direct materials will be sold during a period (usually a year). In simplest form, inventory turnover are calculated as the number of times the inventory is sold during the period or as the ratio of inventory to sales. Inventory turnover is also calculated as the cost of goods sold divided by the average level of inventory on hand.

Indirect Material   Indirect material is the class of materials in the manufacturing process that does not actually ship to the customer as part of the final product. For example, the gas used to heat the furnaces that melt the steel in the manufacture of hammers is an indirect material. Similarly, the water that cools the metal is also an indirect material.

Work-in-Process

Work-in-process (WIP) describes manufactured goods that have not yet been completed. However, in order to be considered work, some labor other than handling and storage must have been directly applied. Components and assemblies are the typical types of WIP in most manufacturing operations.

Finished Goods

Finished goods are those products that have completed the manufacturing production process and for which all necessary labor operations have been completed. Depending on the industry, finished goods are usually packaged and ready for shipment.

Nonproduction Related Materials

Nonproduction related materials are those not used in manufacturing at all, but rather that support the administrative operations of the organizations. MRO items such as light bulbs, copy paper, maintenance, construction and janitorial supplies are a few examples. Nonproduction materials may also include inventories of promotional materials such as advertising flyers and catalogs. Many of them are managed by the same inventory management methods used in manufacturing so that their levels can remain as low as possible.

Capital goods are also a form of large expenditure assets tracked by the organization as though it were inventory. Capital goods are assets purchased for long-term use, such as machinery and other equipment that *depreciate* or lose value over a predetermined period of time.

The Role of Inventory

Inventory has a specific role in manufacturing entities, and inventories are maintained by these organizations for a number of specific reasons:

- Inventory protects the organization from the uncertainties of supply and ensures that material is readily available when it is needed. Inventory buffers are most common in operations where demand and lead times vary considerably and are hard to predict.

- Inventory is often held in anticipation of a seasonal demand or other specific increase in demand or for a particular customer order. It can also be the result of canceled sales orders.

- Some situations result in inventory being created by the minimum quantity of orders required by a supplier or as a result of ordering larger amounts to receive special price breaks.

- Extra large WIP inventories are often created through long production cycle times.

Regardless of the specific reason for maintaining the inventory in the first place, inventory must be closely controlled and monitored since it absorbs a great deal of the organization's available working capital. For a review of inventory management, let's turn to a look at the systems typically used to keep inventory to a minimum.

Systems for Managing Inventory

Inventory management systems are tools used to control inventory so that materials are on hand when needed while at the same time minimizing the financial liability to the organization. Fundamental to these tools are the various ordering strategies you ultimately employ and the automated systems that support these tools.

Ordering Strategies

An inventory ordering strategy is basically a method for determining the quantity of materials to be ordered and the timing for delivery of that order. There are several common methodologies in use that you should be familiar with that we will discuss in this section.

Order Point Reordering

The *order point* method of inventory replenishment establishes a predetermined minimum level of inventory that, when reached, will trigger a reorder. The calculation subtracts incoming orders from the stock on hand to determine when the reorder point has been reached. This method may require the calculation of a *safety stock*, typically based on the anticipated amount that will be used during the lead time it takes to replenish the stock. The actual formula is:

On Hand Inventory – Incoming Orders – Safety Stock (if used) = Reorder Point

Fixed Order Quantity

The *fixed order quantity* rule (sometimes called FOQ) states that the quantity ordered is the same fixed amount each time an order is required to cover a potential shortage, regardless of how much is actually needed to cover that shortage. Table 12.1 shows the incoming demand for a number of given weeks and the effect of this demand on the available balance of inventory at the end of each week. From the information in the bottom row, you can see that, based on a lead time of two weeks and a fixed order quantity of 200 parts (a number determined, perhaps, by the minimum order the supplier requires)—you will need to place an order in Week 3 to cover a planned deficit of 135 parts in Week 7 and in Week 5 to cover a planned deficit of 35 parts. Notice that while the shortages are different quantities, the amount ordered is always the same. Week 8 shows a question mark in the quantity to order because you do not have demand figures to cover the two-week lead time.

TABLE 12.1   Fixed Quantity Order Method

Week #	1	2	3	4	5	6	7	8
Demand	150	0	70	0	175	0	90	60
Net Balance	110	110	40	40	(135)	65	(35)	(135)
Planned Receipts	0	0	0	0	200	0	200	0
On Hand End of Week	110	110	40	40	65	65	165	30
Quantity to Order	0	0	200	0	200		0	?

Periodic Order Quantity

The *periodic order quantity* rule (sometimes called POQ) requires that the quantity ordered be enough to cover requirements for a fixed number of periods. Table 12.2 shows the same demand as Table 12.1, and you can see that orders are placed in the same intervals (every two weeks), but the orders are placed in the amount needed to cover the shortage during the two-week period following receipt. Notice that in Week 5 150 parts need to be ordered to cover the cumulative demand for Weeks 7 and 8 (90 + 60). Since you are ordering every two weeks exactly, your next scheduled order in Week 7 shows a question mark because you don't know what the demand will be in Week 9, at the end of the two-week lead time.

TABLE 12.2   Periodic Order Quantity Method

Week #	1	2	3	4	5	6	7	8
Demand	150	0	70	0	175	0	90	60
Net Balance	110	110	40	40	(135)	0	(90)	60
Planned Receipts	0	0	0	0	135	0	150	0
On Hand End of Week	110	110	40	40	0	0	60	0
Quantity to Order	0	0	135	0	150	0	?	0

Lot for Lot

As the title implies, with a *lot for lot (L4L or LFL)* system, you order exactly what is needed for a given period. With respect to the quantity, you always order exactly enough to avoid a stock outage while ordering as little as possible. With respect to timing, you always order in time to ensure that no outages occur. Using the same figures used for Table 12.2, you can see that the only change is that the order originally placed in Week 5 for 150 parts is split into two orders one week apart, for 90 and 60 parts, respectively.

TABLE 12.3   Lot for Lot Ordering Method

Week #	1	2	3	4	5	6	7	8
Demand	150	0	70	0	175	0	90	60
Net Balance	110	110	40	40	(135)	0	(90)	60
Planned Receipts	0	0	0	0	135	0	150	0
On Hand End of Week	110	110	40	40	0	0	60	0
Quantity to Order	0	0	135	0	90	60	?	0

Economic Order Quantity

Economic order quantity (EOQ) is another inventory ordering model that attempts to minimize total inventory cost by answering the following two questions.

- How much should I order?
- How often should I place each order?

This model assumes that the demand faced by the firm is linear, that is, the rate of demand is constant or at least nearly constant. It also assumes that the purchase price of the product is not dependent on the quantity ordered at any given time but determined between purchaser and supplier in advance based upon the anticipated number of units to meet the demand over the coming period, typically annually.

The goal of the EOQ formula is to minimize total inventory cost. Inventory costs are assumed to be made up of total holding costs and ordering costs. Holding costs include the cost of financing the inventory along with the cost of physically storing and managing the inventory. These costs are usually expressed as a percentage of the value of the inventory. Ordering costs include the costs associated with actually placing the order. These include a labor cost as well as a material and overhead cost.

The basic economic order quantity formula is calculated as the square root of twice the annual usage times the ordering cost, divided by the carrying cost per unit. It's shown the following formula:

$$EOQ = \sqrt{\frac{2(\text{Annual usage in units})(\text{Order cost})}{(\text{Carrying cost per unit})}}$$

As an example, say that the usage for a particular part is 15,000 per year. Let's also assume that the organization orders the parts three times per year and that the average cost of placing an order is $129. Thus, the numerator in this calculation would appear as:

$2 \times (15000 \times 129) = 3{,}870{,}000$

Carrying cost, the denominator in the formula, consists of the cost of storage and handling plus the theoretical cost of interest for the value of the inventory should it be financed. Calculating the carrying cost is a bit more difficult. Let's take some shortcuts in establishing the interest cost by assuming the average daily inventory volume is 7,500 parts, and each part costs $1.10. This means that there is an average daily value of $8,250 on hand ($7500 \times 1.10 = 8250$). If interest rates were 5 percent per year, the interest for one day would be approximately $1.13 per day ($(.05/365) \times 8250 = 1.13$). Calculating the annual interest cost per unit is as follows:

Average Interest Cost/Unit = $(1.13 \times 365) / 7500 = \$0.055$

Continuing the calculation requires a determination of the storage and handling costs. Let's assume that 7,500 parts (the average daily inventory) uses 50 square feet of storage at a monthly cost of $0.45 per square foot or $22.50 per month. If you multiply this by 12 months and then divide by the average number of parts stored, you can calculate the average storage costs per unit:

Average Storage Cost/Unit = $(22.50 \times 12) / 7500 = \$0.036$

The remaining calculation requires an estimate of the handling costs per unit. Let's assume that the handling costs are simply the cost of cycle counting. If you cycle count four times each year (once per quarter) and it takes 10 minutes (.1667 hour) at an average labor cost of $18 per hour, the cost would be calculated as follows:

Handling Cost/Unit = $((18 \times .1667) \times 4) / 7500 = \$.002$

You now have the denominator for the formula:

Carrying Cost = Interest Cost + Storage Cost + Handling Cost

= (.055 + .036 + .002) = $0.093/Unit

Using these numbers to complete the formula:

Square Root of (3,870,000/.093)

= 6,451 parts per order

Using this formula, you would then order parts approximately twice per year at an interval of 157 days. To calculate this, you divide the parts per order by the annual requirements and then multiply 365 by that fraction:

Days to Reorder = 365 × (6451/15000) = 156.95

Using EOQ effectively requires strict adherence to a number of requirements:

- Demand is known with certainty
- Demand is relatively constant over time
- No shortages are allowed
- Lead time for the receipt of orders remains constant
- The order quantity is received all at once

If you are lacking any one of these criteria, use caution because your calculation will probably have a wide margin of error.

Automated Processes

Managing inventory through automated processes has become fairly common as a result of the widespread use of ERP systems. Most organizations maintain computerized *perpetual inventories* that automatically add incoming receipts to the quantity on hand and then subtract issues from that amount to provide an up to the minute tally of the inventory on hand. In addition to using automated systems, many organizations today also rely on their suppliers to manage and keep track of inventories that are held on consignment. Ultimately, this may prove to be the most effective way of managing inventory because, among other factors, it enables the supplier to integrate usage in its customer's facility with its own planning strategy. (Supplier Managed Inventory is discussed later in this section.)

MRP and MRPII

As we discussed earlier in Chapter 7, "Using Computer-based Systems," Material Requirements Planning (MRP) and Manufacturing Resource Planning (MRPII) are computerized, time-based priority planning techniques that calculate material requirements and schedule supply to meet changing demand across all products lines. MRP, the initially developed system, was created in the U.S. and Canada during the 1960s. MRP takes into consideration customer orders and planning forecasts to determine inventory requirements. MRPII is essentially MRP but with some additional features. Typically, an MRPII package includes elements such as cost information, management reports, and the ability to model situations through "what-if" analysis. It may also include *capacity requirements planning,* a tool that determines the loading at a work station or throughout the entire factory so that capacity constraints can be reflected in the planning process).

MRPII stands for Manufacturing Resource Planning, signifying a concentration on the planning of all manufacturing resources, rather than limiting planning to just the material requirements. The "II" designation is used to distinguish this form from its MRP predecessor.

When relevant data has been gathered regarding the status of parts, assemblies, and resources, the lead time of every component can be determined based upon a variety of manufacturing conditions. As soon as an incoming customer order is received, the backlog for the manufacturing organization and the delivery time for product can be calculated. An MRP system can call attention to constraints such as overloaded production centers, the effect of incoming orders, changes in capacity, shortages, delays in manufacturing, and delays by suppliers so that effective action can be taken to reduce them in a timely fashion.

From a systemic perspective, MRP relies on two basic types of information to calculate requirements:

Structural Information   Structural information is information about the organization's items (parts or components) and how each of the different items is related to one another. It includes important ordering information for each item such as lead time, lot (or batch) size, and where the item is obtained from (for example, whether it's purchased or manufactured in-house). The key point about structural information is that it changes relatively infrequently.

Tactical Information   Tactical information is information about the current state of manufacturing; for example, sales orders (real and forecast) pending, the master production schedule, on-hand inventory levels, and unfilled purchase orders. Obviously, the key point about this information is that it changes frequently.

Demand Concepts

In purchasing, *demand* generally means the actual or projected usage of the items you are monitoring. The concept of demand is very closely related to the MRP process and is an integral aspect of inventory management. For this reason, demand is typically classified in terms of the conditions that generate it. Thus, there are two basic types of demand:

Independent Demand   *Independent demand* is any demand for a product or service that is generated externally, usually by customer orders. It is difficult to predict and quantify.

Dependent Demand   A dependent demand is dependent in quantity, quality, and timing on its related independent demand, usually in the form of an incoming customer order or aggregation of orders. The materials needed to fulfill such incoming orders are by nature dependent upon that order in the first place. An independent order for a computer from an assembly facility, for example, creates a dependent demand for a motherboard and a certain set of other specific subassembly components. MRP and MRPII systems are primarily dedicated to tracking these dependencies and calculating dependent demand patterns as a primary function in inventory control.

In most MRP systems, the dependent demand generated by "exploding" the BOMs for incoming orders does not assume an infinite capacity for capacity-constrained resources (such as machines and people). Therefore, specific methods are required to schedule capacity-constrained resources. This scheduling process usually generates a manufacturing plan, and it is the responsibility of the Purchasing Department or materials control group to ensure that the materials are available as required by the plan.

Just-in-Time Inventory Management

Meeting the requirements of a manufacturing plan and at the same time allowing for maximum flexibility and last-minute changes due to customer orders changes requires a truly flexible demand management system. Just-in-time (JIT) inventory management processes (also known as lean or stockless manufacturing) were developed for just this reason.

JIT and MRP are two distinctly different systems for controlling production. While MRP is based on meeting predicted demand during a period of time, JIT is based on actual usage. Just-in-time (JIT) is a means of market pull inventory management conducted in an environment of continuing improvement. Use of just-in-time methods results in considerably reduced inventory and enhanced customer response time. However, to be successful it requires a systemic and highly cooperative approach to inventory receipt, throughput, and delivery.

Although JIT was developed for production environments, the process can be extended to all business environments. The basic concept is to receive what is needed just in time for it to be used. This, in effect, places the responsibility on the supplier to get what is needed to where it is needed, just before it is needed.

JIT is also a management philosophy that works to eliminate sources of manufacturing waste by producing the proverbial "right part in the right place at the right time." In theory, waste results from any activity that adds cost without adding value, such as moving and storing. JIT is thus designed to improve profits and Return on Investment by reducing inventory levels (increasing the inventory turnover rate), improving product quality, reducing production and delivery lead times, and reducing other costs (such as those associated with machine setup and equipment breakdown).

Supplier Managed Inventory

The concept of Supplier Managed Inventory (SMI) or Vendor Managed Inventory (VMI), whichever you prefer to call it, is a logical progression from ideas that generated JIT inventory management in the first place. The goal of both is to build enough flexibility into the manufacturing system (or the supply chain itself) so that customer demand can be met in as short a time frame as possible. In today's business environment, the consumer wants immediate gratification and will likely turn to another product if the one chosen is not available relatively instantly.

Supplier Managed Inventory places the responsibility on the supplier to meet incoming customer demand (or rapidly changing forecasts). Often working from the manufacturer's MRP outputs, the supplier assesses incoming demand and plans operations accordingly to ensure that material is available for production exactly when it is needed. Although in most SMI applications the supplier is responsible for managing the inventory, the buying organization pays for it when received as it would if it had ordered the material directly. Consequently, there must exist a very close partnership built upon mutual trust in order for the management of materials to be confidently turned over to the supplier. In these situations, however, the materials management group (or purchasing department) must closely monitor activities, working with the supplier on a continuous improvement process.

The ultimate extension of SMI is consignment inventory. Managed in essentially the same way as SMI, the major difference is that the supplier owns the inventory until it is actually withdrawn from stock for production. To be considered true consignment, the stock must be located at the buyer's facility and owned by the supplier with no contingencies for automatic purchase of obsolescent stock.

Inventory Economics

Since manufacturing organizations often have a great deal of capital resources tied up in inventory, minimizing inventory can result in better overall financial performance. However, there should always be a balance maintained between inefficient use of inventory and the needs of meeting market demand. In general, you will want to consider how to maximize the return on the organization's investment in inventory. In this evaluation, you may want to consider that Return on Investment (ROI) is a ratio that measures how much over how long. So you can conceivably improve the performance of inventory investment both by reducing the overall size of the inventory, and therefore its value, and by shortening the length of time your organization owns it, and thereby its rate of return.

Inventory Turnover

One typical measure of the efficient use of inventory is its *turnover* ratio. Inventory turnover measures the speed that inventory is used relative to sales. It's typically calculated by dividing annual sales by average inventory, using the average inventory over an accounting period rather than just an ending-inventory value. Inventory turnover can also be calculated by dividing the total annual value of all inventory used (or issued) by the amount of inventory currently on hand:

Annual Inventory Used / On-hand Inventory = Turnover

For example, if the annual inventory used was $100 million and the current inventory is valued at $10 million, the turnover rate would be 10 times annually. Low turnover is an indication that inventory is too high for the accompanying level of sales.

Lead Time Considerations

As noted earlier in this chapter, inventory can be used to buffer stock outages caused by suppliers and to support variable customer demand. Strategically, the consideration of when to carry inventory and how much should be held can be rationalized according to the service levels the organization is attempting to achieve. Service levels can be measured in terms of the frequency of stock outages and the seriousness of the effects of the outages, such as production stoppages or order cancellations. For the most part, these effects can be financially evaluated and related to the cost of carrying various levels of inventory, with strategic decisions made according to the degree of support desired.

Physical Management and Inventory Accounting

In order to effectively manage inventory, it must be properly maintained, reported, and carried on the business records. Automated systems rely on a virtual accuracy of 100 percent in order to properly maintain minimal amounts of inventory. In a JIT environment, even the smallest discrepancy can result in a planning or financial disaster. In this section, we'll review some of the methods and tools available to maintain accurate records and account for discrepancies.

Controlling Inventory

Inventory control refers to the activities and methods used by organizations to receive, track, maintain, and issue materials. It also includes the management of inventory from a financial standpoint to ensure that it is accurately accounted for and valued. This process involves the actual physical storage, handling, and issuance of materials, as well as the record keeping that goes along with it.

Stores

Organizations that maintain substantial amounts of inventory usually manage it by keeping it in specific locations. These stocking locations are usually referred to as *stores*. The general function of the stores operation is to physically manage and issue parts and supplies to internal groups as they are needed. There are two broad systems for managing stores:

Open Stores   When the value of inventory or the need for security is relatively low, or when access to it is required quite frequently, materials may be stored in open locations that are accessible directly by production staff, known as *open stores*. Record keeping is typically loose, relying primarily on physical cycle counting to reconcile on-hand inventory levels.

Closed Stores   Conversely, when inventory must be tightly controlled because of its value, scarcity, or potential safety issues, it is generally maintained in a limited access stockroom, called *closed stores*. Here, receipts and issues are closely recorded and often require authorized signatures or approvals before inventory release.

Storage and Retrieval Systems

Within the storage facility, and regardless of its type, material is physically stored using various systems for stocking and retrieval:

Specified Locations   In some storage schemes, designated bins or storage shelves are allocated for the same specific items of inventory. This enables rapid retrieval when goods are uncontrolled because the staff becomes familiar with where materials are actually located and can find them quite easily.

Random Access Locations   In automated storage and retrieval systems, inventory locations are stored on a computer system. When inventory is received, it is automatically allocated the first open space designated on the computer system and physically placed in that location. When it is needed, the material is found by using the computer system to report its exact location.

Automated Storage and Retrieval Systems   Automated storage and retrieval systems rely on computerized mechanical systems—often robotic—to store and retrieve material with little human intervention. Parts are delivered to specified locations either on demand or in accordance with a manufacturing schedule.

Record Systems

Today, most inventory record keeping systems are automated. However, depending on the system used for controlling inventory—open or closed stores, for example—inventory records are updated on *periodic* or *perpetual* basis.

Periodic updating requires that physical counts are taken at designated intervals and used to update the records of quantities on hand. This system is most commonly used for small parts such as nails or screws or liquids that are difficult to account for precisely.

Perpetual inventory is used when precise and up-to-date accounting is required. This system records exact receipts and issues as they occur so that the on-hand inventory is precise.

Cycle Counting

Cycle counting, physically counting inventory on a scheduled basis to ensure its accuracy, is used to update inventory records when usage varies imprecisely or is nonstandard (as may be the case with commodities, liquids, and fasteners) and when inventory accuracy is critical. It is also commonly employed when auditing or verifying the actual value of the inventory at a specific time.

The timing for cycle counting often follows a specific schedule based on the value of the inventory as segmented according to the typical Pareto Principle of *ABC analysis*, where the most valuable materials are counted most frequently: A items may be counted monthly, B items quarterly, and C items annually. Cycle counts are also taken more frequently for parts that are used more frequently since there may be a higher risk of inaccuracy.

Reconciling Discrepancies

The difference between the recorded inventory and the actual inventory found on hand when it is physically counted requires some form of reconciliation. Most commonly, the recorded inventory is adjusted to reflect the actual inventory counted during the cycle count. However, you should always keep in mind that such variation has financial implications and how it is accounted for financially depends upon the organization's policy. Low value errors associated with high volumes of transactions are common and typically tolerated. Generally, such losses are absorbed by an overhead variance account. However, loss of valuable inventory through damage or theft can become a serious financial issue if it becomes commonplace, so you will want to ensure that proper safeguards are in place so that it does not become a serious issue. Judicious use of closed stores for inventory security may circumvent such problems.

Disposition Surplus Assets

Most organizations, at one time or another, generate surplus materials, scrap, or obsolete equipment that may have value to others outside the organization. Surplus materials and equipment can be generated in a number of ways:

- Scrap or waste generated by manufacturing operations

- Excess purchases

- Obsolete material and supplies

- Discontinued finished products

- Decommissioned equipment

Converting these nonproductive assets to cash or, at the very least, minimizing the cost of their disposal, can certainly add financial value to the organization. Nevertheless, it is surprising to learn that many organizations have no process or system at all for effectively handling these assets.

One of Our Authors (Fred Sollish's) First Visit to Corporate Storage

As a newly appointed purchasing manager, Fred was assigned the task of supervising the revamping of his organization's 5,000 square foot storage facility. He was told it was used mostly for retired records. Although it sounded simple, he was immediately challenged: on his first visit, Fred was unable to open the door because it was apparently blocked by something inside. With some help, he was able to raise the rollup receiving door and was presented with a startling scene: equipment and surplus materials were randomly piled everywhere, from floor to ceiling, covering every available square foot of the facility. It was impossible to enter without climbing upon or over something.

Fred hired a disposal firm who inventoried the usable equipment and placed it in an already scheduled auction for a similar firm. The company recovered close to $900,000. What's more, with all the equipment and surplus removed, they found that the records occupied a very small portion of the warehouse. The company sent them to a records storage facility and turned in the lease on the warehouse, saving another $2,200 per month.

Disposal Strategies

The Purchasing Department is a natural resource for surplus disposal since it has continuing contact with both internal users and suppliers. With knowledge of the needs of internal users, Purchasing has an opportunity to find secondary uses for surplus within the organization. Purchasing may also have specialized knowledge about where the material or equipment was purchased from initially and may have access to reselling channels through them. There are two main concerns you'll have as a purchasing manager when it comes to disposal of materials: the first are your legal obligations, and the second is the disposal of hazardous materials. Let's discuss these in more detail.

Legal Aspects

Before beginning any disposal operations, you should first acquaint yourself with any key legal aspects that might be associated with the specific items you are proposing to dispose of, such as transfer of legal title, liabilities, and implied warranties. You will also want to be certain that you prepare the appropriate sales "as is" documents. Since legal requirements can be as varied as the materials and equipment you are giving up for disposal, it is imperative to get the proper legal counsel prior to going forward.

Hazardous Materials Disposal

Hazardous materials must be disposed of in accordance with applicable laws and regulations. In the United States, the U.S. Environmental Protection Agency (EPA) defines the nature of specific hazardous materials and prescribes the methods for their disposal. The U.S. Department of Transportation (DOT) prescribes the method for transporting hazardous materials and their required documentation. There are also numerous state and local regulations governing the disposal of hazardous waste. New York State, for example, has enacted a series of regulations that is intended to supplement those of the federal government. (For more information, visit `www.dec.state.ny.us/website/dshm/regs/370parts.htm`.)

Other Environmental Considerations

ISO 14000 is a group of environmental management standards developed by the International Organization for Standardization in 1996. It is designed to provide an internationally accepted framework for environmental management, measurement, evaluation, and auditing, to provide organizations with the tools needed to assess and control the environmental impact of their activities. In addition to environmental management systems, the standards address environmental auditing, environmental labels and declarations, environmental performance evaluation, and life-cycle assessments.

In Europe, the *WEEE (Waste Electrical and Electronic Equipment)* regulation, which was designed to tackle the issue of surplus TV and computer equipment recycling, requires the original equipment manufacturer to take back all surplus for disposal. With an effective date of August 2005, this regulation will require manufacturers and importers to recycle a large variety of equipment from customers ranging from mobile phones to tea kettles. Further, businesses are expected to provide for the recycling of existing electrical and electronic equipment that will become waste in the future.

The Basel Convention, an international agreement on the control of cross-boundary movements of hazardous wastes and their disposal was adopted in 1989 by a United Nations–sponsored conference of 116 nations held in Basel, Switzerland. It restricts trade in hazardous waste, some nonhazardous wastes, solid wastes, and incinerator ash.

The *Kyoto Protocol* (`http://unfccc.int/resource/docs/convkp/kpeng.html`), also known as the *Kyoto Agreement*, is a United Nations–sponsored agreement to prevent global warming signed by 38 developed countries. At a summit held in 1997, those signing the treaty agreed to reduce their emission of *greenhouse gases* by the year 2012. Greenhouse gases are gases such as carbon dioxide (CO_2), water vapor, methane (CH_4), nitrous oxide (NO_2), and other trace gases that trap heat in the atmospheres and produce a greenhouse effect that causes an increase in global temperatures. However, by 2002, several countries, including the U.S. and Japan, had all but reneged on their promises. The use of public areas for landfill has also come under tighter regulation all around the globe by local governments, and many of these local governments have enacted regulations supplementing those issued by their respective governments. By focusing on landfills, environmental movements have addressed two major issues: first, there is an urgent need to develop more sustainable resources through recycling, and one way to drive recycling is through limitations on the amount of solid waste allowed in landfills. Second, the gases emitted by landfills are considered a source of global warming.

Disposal Methods

Depending upon their nature and the legal and environmental considerations governing them, surplus materials and equipment can be disposed of in a variety of ways. To be truly effective, however, the process requires proper planning, organization, and assessment. Not surprisingly, the market demand for surplus materials and equipment follows a similar pattern as its newly manufactured counterparts. It would be wise for you to understand the nature of the marketplace so that you can make informed decisions on the value and salability of your organization's surplus.

The methods for asset disposal are fairly common and are listed below. The challenge lies in matching the material with its optimum method of disposal, which will of course depend on the nature of the materials and the needs of your organization. Following are some of the disposal methods you may utilize as a purchasing manager:

Return   One of the easiest alternatives is to return excess material or equipment to its original manufacturer. Often this also provides the best value since the supplier can offer a credit on future sales that can be timed to the actual revenue generated by your organization. Keep in mind, however, that if you are a small buyer of these items, you will not likely have a great deal of leverage to compel the supplier to accept the return.

Re-use   Another excellent method of disposal is to transfer the materials or equipment internally to another department that can use it. This not only avoids the expense of disposal, it may also save money by avoiding the direct purchase of similar materials.

Sale   Sale of excess assets provides an excellent way to generate cash. However, keep in mind that your sale of this material will likely compete with the sale of new products and may be discouraged by your supplier. Also keep in mind that it might be costly to find potential buyers and to make the sale.

One alternative is to consign the material to a third party reseller who already has channels for moving this. You will likely have to pay a large percentage of the revenue, but using a third party might provide the path of least resistance for you.

You may also want to explore surplus auctions. These are conducted both live and online. Be cautious, however, of the effort involved not only in selling but in collecting the funds.

Trade-in   Trading in old equipment for credit toward the purchase of similar new equipment may also prove effective, if the need to purchase new equipment actually exists. Even when the value of the surplus is low, this may be an easy way for the supplier to offer you a discount and may save you the trouble of actually having to go through the physical disposal process yourself.

Donation   Depending on the material or equipment, donating it to a charitable operation may provide excellent community relations and may also offer a tax deduction (if your organization is otherwise profitable). Donating surplus materials and usable equipment fulfills a social responsibility, as well.

Don't count on your ability to give the surplus away to charity. Many charities are inundated with such donations and have little ability to use or accept them.

Cannibalization   If you have no use for the entire surplus product (or equipment), you might want to consider tearing it down for usable spare parts. While this is not a preferred use for excess assets, it may prove more profitable than having to put it in a landfill or sell it for scrap.

Scrap   Again, depending upon the exact nature of the surplus, scrap dealers may have a use for it and may be willing to purchase it and pick it up if the price is right. You can expect, at best, to realize a few pennies on the initial dollar your organization has spent for its initial purchase. However, as previously noted, regulations such as WEEE may soon spawn new recycling industries that of necessity find increasing value in scrap materials.

Summary

Managing and controlling inventory, often one of the major assets of the organization, is another key area where the Purchasing Department can add value. To accomplish this effectively requires an understanding of the various reasons for keeping inventory, such as safety stock and economic ordering methods, as well as being familiar with the specific classifications of inventory such as direct and indirect materials, work-in-process, and finished goods. The purchasing manager must also be able to implement and utilize various common systems for managing inventory levels and reordering stock. These systems are often automated and include MRP and MRPII, along with various demand-based strategies such as just-in-time and Supplier Managed Inventory.

In this chapter, you also looked at various methods for managing and controlling inventory, including stores, storage and retrieval systems, and records systems. In this role, the purchasing manager will also need to know how to maintain accurate inventory counts and reconcile discrepancies that may occur.

As a central focus for managing the disposal of surplus and obsolete assets, the purchasing team is frequently responsible for determining the most valuable method of disposal for the organization.

For additional reading on topics related to this chapter, please see Appendix A.

Exam Essentials

Understand the various uses of inventory.   Inventory is held by most organizations as a safety factor to buffer various unknown conditions that can affect the source of supply

Be able to distinguish the various types of inventory and their uses.   Know the definition of raw materials and their classifications, as well as work-in-process, finished goods, and nonproduction-related materials.

Understand the various systems for calculating reorder quantities.   There are a number of ordering strategies you should be familiar with, including order point, fixed order, periodic order, lot for lot, and economic order quantity methods.

Be able to identify various types of automated replenishing methods.   Automated reordering and inventory control systems within larger systems such as MRP and MRPII assist with the efficient management of key resources such as inventory.

Understand the economics of inventory stocking and replenishment.   Inventory turnover and lead time considerations should be used to develop an economic approach to maintaining inventories.

Be able to identify various methods and tools for controlling physical inventory.   Using stores, storage retrieval, and specialized record systems for inventory are part of the management tools available for controlling inventory.

Be able to identify methods for maintaining accurate inventory records.   Perpetual inventory systems and periodic inventory systems (cycle counting) are some of the ways to ensure the accuracy of inventory records.

Be able to identify types of surplus assets and how best to dispose of them.   Many organizations turn to the Purchasing Department to manage and dispose of surplus inventory. Commonly employed methods of disposal include return, re-use, sale, donation, and scrap.

Review Questions

1. The primary classification for raw materials used in manufacturing the product.

    A. Work-in-process

    B. Finished goods

    C. Indirect material

    D. Direct material

    E. Maintenance, Repair, and Operations

2. Class of materials used in the manufacturing process but which does not ship to customer as part of the final product.

    A. Work-in-process

    B. Finished goods

    C. Indirect materials

    D. Direct materials

    E. Maintenance, Repair, and Operating

3. Term that describes manufactured goods that have not yet been produced.

    A. Work-in-process

    B. Finished goods

    C. Indirect materials

    D. Direct materials

    E. Maintenance, Repair, and Operating

4. Method of inventory replenishment where a reorder is triggered at a predetermined minimum level of inventory stock.

    A. Fixed order quantity

    B. Safety stock

    C. Lot for lot

    D. Order point

    E. Periodic order quantity

5. An inventory replenishment method that requires that the order is the same amount each time:

    A. Periodic order quantity

    B. Order point

    C. Fixed order quantity

    D. Lot for lot

    E. Safety stock

6. Material planning system that includes cost information, management reports, and model situations through "what-if" analysis.

   A. MRP

   B. EOQ

   C. ERP

   D. MRPII

   E. JIT

7. Inventory system that builds flexibility into the manufacturing system to meet customer demand in as short a time frame as possible:

   A. Just-in-time

   B. MRPII

   C. MRP

   D. EOQ

   E. Supplier Managed Inventory

8. Periodically ensures inventory accuracy.

   A. Perpetual inventory

   B. Cycle count

   C. Inventory control

   D. Open stores

   E. ABC analysis

9. Inventory turnover is a calculation of the rate in which:

   A. Inventory is reconciled

   B. Parts become obsolete

   C. Sales generate purchase orders

   D. Inventory is depleted

   E. Ending inventory differs from beginning inventory

10. The Purchasing Department is in the best position to dispose of surplus assets because:

   A. Its staff understands internal customer needs.

   B. Its staff understands available disposal options.

   C. Its staff understands conditions in the marketplace.

   D. Its staff understands supplier requirements.

   E. All of the above.

Answers to Review Questions

1. D. Direct material is the only classification of raw materials used to manufacture product. Brass used in the manufacture of brass castings is an example of a direct material.

2. C. Indirect materials are materials that support the manufacturing operation but do not go into the finished product. Mold release used in the manufacture of injection molded plastics is an example of indirect material.

3. A. Work-in-process is the class of materials between raw materials and finished goods and applies to any unfinished product that has had labor operations performed.

4. D. In an order point inventory reorder system, when a specific level of stocked inventory is reached, either through customer demand or forecast, an order is automatically generated.

5. C. A fixed order quantity system requires the same amount be ordered each time, regardless of the variation in ordering intervals.

6. D. MRPII expands on MRP by providing modeling analysis and overall cost data.

7. E. When inventory is managed by the supplier, turnaround time is much faster because orders do not have to be placed.

8. B. Cycle counting periodically takes a physical inventory count and uses the results to reconcile inventory records.

9. D. The calculation of inventory turnover is made by dividing annual sales by the average amount of inventory on hand.

10. E. Since the Purchasing Department interacts with and becomes familiar with all of these elements in the normal course of business, it is in the best position to make decisions regarding the disposal of surplus assets.

Chapter

13

Adding Value to the Organization

THE C.P.M. EXAM SPECIFICATIONS COVERED IN THIS CHAPTER INCLUDE THE FOLLOWING:

✓ Standardizing purchased materials

✓ Improving purchasing-related processes

✓ Controlling and reducing cost

✓ Supporting new product introduction

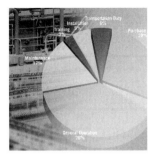

As you have already learned, the Purchasing Department is in a unique position to add value to the organization as the key interface between internal consumers of goods and services and the corresponding supplier community. In this role, the buyer has the opportunity to exert considerable influence on reducing costs and significantly adding to the organization's profit and loss statement's bottom line. This can be particularly effective when applying methods that aid in the *standardization* of materials and provide a proactive supply sourcing approach to the *new product introduction (NPI)* process. You will likely find that the major drivers in these efforts will be initiatives to improve the efficiency of supply management processes and to effectively control the costs of purchased goods and services.

In this chapter, we will examine ways that you can effectively improve purchasing operations and save money for the organization by standardizing materials and developing other cost-reduction activities. We will also examine how these elements can be combined in the new product introduction process.

Standardizing Purchased Materials

Material standardization refers to the process of finding ways to use as few purchased items as possible to perform as many functions as possible. Let's explore the many avenues available to the Purchasing Department to formulate material standardization programs.

Standardization Considerations

There are a number of factors to consider when looking at material standardization. First of all, materials *standards* can refer to common specifications for designed and engineered materials used within a single organization, an industry, or even an international body of nations. Secondly, standards can apply to materials to enable them to share the same functional specifications. Having the same specifications allows materials to be interchangeable from one environment to another as substitutes. And finally, standardization can apply to methods for producing and distributing materials. Standardized methods ensure uniform operations, processes, procedures and therefore, results, throughout the supply base. As an example, imagine the cost and potential unreliability of air travel if every airport in the world performed take-off and landing operations using a different air traffic control system.

Benefits of Standardization

There are many obvious benefits to standardization. They reduce or eliminate one-time processes that produce variability and add cost, and they allow organizations to understand the true cost associated with producing a particular product or providing a service.

Standardized parts reduce the level of inventory since fewer items must be stocked. When parts are standardized across an industry, they tend to become readily available "off-the-shelf" commodity items and therefore require lower levels of stock to support. Standardization also reduces the cost of parts by enabling organizations to purchase a consolidated assortment of parts in greater quantities. This, in turn, can reduce administrative and handling costs since fewer items need to be ordered, received, inspected, stocked, and distributed.

Standardized parts also enable interchangeability and interoperation from one environment to another, regardless of where it is produced, thus reducing engineering and design costs across the supply chain. This also tends to reduce prices as a result of greater competition in the marketplace.

Standardization tends to improve quality through uniform processes and specifications that can be easily understood and measured with most quality systems.

Standardization Development Processes

The Purchasing Department can take the lead in developing a standardization program in the organization simply because it places the purchase orders and therefore has greater access to the organization's overall buying history. While there are many ways to develop a standardization program, most programs share a degree of similarity in their operational process steps.

Here are some common steps you should consider when developing and implementing a standardization program:

1. Establish team involvement.

    Cross-function participation helps ensure that all appropriate parties are represented during the development phase, saving the time that would be needed to later obtain their buy-in. Typically, a standardization team will consist of members from purchasing, manufacturing, engineering, quality, and finance. Depending on the project, it may also require a member from sales. Organizations often have a semipermanent standing team for this particular purpose.

2. Establish team objectives.

    Determine what outcomes the team would like to have in place at the conclusion of the standardization process. These will likely include goals related to part reduction, inventory reduction, improved pricing through part consolidation, or reduced errors in shipped products.

3. Gather information.

    Determine what conditions actually exist currently—how many parts are being used to do similar tasks, for example.

4. Outline a plan.

    Develop a proposal and timeline for accomplishing the objectives that the sponsoring team can use to gain team member and management support.

5. Develop standards.

   Define and document the industry or commodity standards that will be followed going forward.

6. Implement the plan.

   Roll out the plan to the using groups accompanied by specific instructions for meeting plan objectives. Part of this process includes developing an awareness of the program to gain as much support as possible.

7. Measure results and provide continuous feedback.

   Periodic surveys can be used to provide information on the efficacy of the program.

Common Areas for Standardization

There are likely endless areas for standardization in the typical organization. However, you should first consider parts that are used in relatively high volumes since the opportunity for cost savings will be greatest there. These are often parts that are incidental to the design and function, such as common fasteners, and there will be little resistance to their standardization. Parts that are relatively low in individual value but are frequently ordered, and thus have higher administrative costs to manage, are also prime candidates for consolidation.

You should also consider the standardization process when specifying new equipment. Standardized equipment helps drive standardization throughout the manufacturing process, from maintaining spare parts inventory to training new employees in the equipment's operation.

Potential Issues

Standards require continuous review and updating, especially when they apply to the organization's direct operations. If they are proprietary standards, applicable only to your organization, someone will need to ensure that changes are conveyed to your suppliers in a timely manner. Whenever new standards are established, there should be a procedure for maintenance that clearly outlines roles and responsibilities for keeping them aligned with present needs and changes in technology.

In the case of externally developed standards, a specific monitoring procedure and system should be in place to ensure that changes made by the originating entity are conveyed to users within your organization. Without this contact, your organization risks the possibility of not remaining aligned with its customers and suppliers.

Standards Organizations

Standards are developed by a wide variety of organizations, both locally and internationally, within or across industries and geographical boundaries. As you will see in this section, standards are also developed by both independent and government sponsored organizations. What generally unifies various interests to develop standards is their common need for *interoperability*. In computer science, for example, interoperability refers to the ability to exchange and use information across platforms and networks. Without interoperability, computer systems would be unable to communicate with one another and would thus have little value.

Individual Organizations

Each individual organization has its own areas where standards might apply, but there are a number of common areas where standards most often apply.

Materials   For an individual organization, specifications define the standard dimensions, utility, and useful life of purchased parts and supplies to ensure that they consistently meet its needs.

Equipment   Performance, functions, and productivity requirements define the standards in an organization for purchased equipment, along with useful life and, occasionally, physical characteristics and dimensions.

Processes and Procedures   Standards for processes and procedures ensure uniform operating environments and repeatable results for various operations that are similar throughout the organization.

Independent Standards Associations and Functions

There are numerous organizations—mostly nonprofit and serving a specific community—that identify the need for standards and develop them for common use. Some of the most commonly recognized include ANSI, SAE, and ASTM.

ANSI   The *American National Standards Institute (ANSI)* is the administering and coordinating body for voluntary standards in the United States, although it remains a nonprofit, private organization by charter. It is responsible for approving standards in a number of areas, including those that apply to computers. Originally founded in 1918 as the American Engineering Standards Committee (AESC), its first approved standard was for pipe threads. In 1928, it was reorganized and renamed the American Standards Association (ASA), and it adopted its current name in 1969. ANSI currently provides a forum for over 270 ANSI-accredited standards developers representing over 200 distinct organizations in the private and public sectors. The organizations work together to develop the American National Standards (ANS). For more information, visit www.ansi.org.

SAE   The *Society of Automotive Engineers (SAE)* is an organization that establishes voluntary standards for mobility products, automotive and aerospace components, vehicles, and systems. Founded in the early 1900s, today it represents nearly 85,000 members in 97 countries. Visit www.sae.org for more information.

ASTM   *ASTM International*, formerly the *American Society for Testing and Materials (ASTM)*, was also formed in the early 1900s, initially to address issues in the railroad industry. Today, its stated purpose is to work toward consensus for "stakeholders involved in issues ranging from safety in recreational aviation to fiber optic cable installations in underground utilities to homeland security." The organization currently represents over 30,000 members. For more information, visit www.astm.org.

U.S. Government Standards Organizations

While there are numerous U.S. standards organizations, the *National Institute of Standards and Technology (NIST)*, formerly the *National Bureau of Standards (NBS)* is the central government supported agency for standards. Founded in 1901, NIST is a nonregulatory federal agency within the U.S. Commerce Department's Technology Administration. NIST's mission is "to develop and promote measurement, standards, and technology to enhance productivity, facilitate trade, and improve the quality of life." NIST maintains and promotes *open measurement standards* to facilitate commerce, including the maintenance of the official U.S. time. For more information, visit `http://nist.time.gov`.

NIST also manages the Baldrige National Quality Program under The Malcolm Baldrige National Quality Improvement Act of 1987.

International Standards Organizations

There are also many international standards organizations. Some are independent, while others are sponsored by the United Nations. The most commonly known are the International Organization for Standardization, Underwriters Laboratories Inc., and the Institute of Electrical and Electronics Engineers.

International Organization for Standardization (ISO)   This organization was formed to consolidate widely dispersed methods of approaching quality standards. As we discussed in Chapter 8, "Managing Quality," its stated goal is to facilitate a means of coordinating, developing, and unifying industrial and technical quality standards (`www.iso.org`).

Underwriters Laboratories Inc. (UL)   This organization is a private not-for-profit institution that was established by the insurance industry to test and rate devices, materials, and systems, especially electrical and electronic products, for safety. Items that pass specific tests can include a UL certificate on the product (`www.ul.com`).

Institute of Electrical and Electronics Engineers, Inc. (IEEE)   This nonprofit, technical professional association has more than 360,000 members in over 175 countries. IEEE is the leading authority in technical areas ranging from computer engineering, biomedical technology, and telecommunications. IEEE has 900 active standards with hundreds under constant development (`www.ieee.org`).

Improving Purchasing-related Processes

Because an organization's procurement process itself is so highly dynamic and changes often as new technologies are put in place or markets evolve, it is an area rich with potential for cost-reducing improvements. While standardization is one way to improve purchasing performance, there are many others. As a purchasing manager, you will responsible for developing a mindset in your group that seeks out and embraces *continuous improvement*, responding pro-actively to changing needs and conditions. Continuous improvement is the ongoing improvement of processes, methods, and products that takes place over a period of time through incremental, progressive steps.

To effectively implement a continuous improvement program in your group, you will first need to identify where opportunities for improvement exist and then establish goals. You'll likely find that one of the most productive areas for improvement lies in streamlining your purchasing processes themselves. Systematic analysis of the processes used should produce clear documentation of each of the steps in the process being reviewed so that you have a clear picture of existing conditions. You will then want to know how their effectiveness compares to other organizations. This will likely require a bit of benchmarking (as we described in Chapter 8.

The mechanics of implementing a continuous improvement process requires following these basic steps:

1. Form an improvement team.

   As noted in the previous section "Standardization Development Process," cross-functional participation helps ensure that all appropriate parties are represented during the development phase, saving the time needed to obtain their buy-in later.

2. Initiate a *gap analysis* study.

   Gap analysis identifies the difference between the existing process and a best practice. For example, if there is a lag in your receiving process of two working days before an incoming receipt is logged into the system (and thus available for use in production), and you find that best practices indicate it should take no longer than two hours, you have measured a gap of approximately 14 hours (assuming an eight-hour workday). It is usually helpful to document each of the steps in the process, along with their associated times, by using a *flowchart*—a step-by-step diagram—so that you can be relatively certain that all process activities are accounted for.

3. Develop a plan.

   A continuous improvement plan will be directed toward achieving the team's objective by reducing or eliminating the identified gap over a period of time or with repeated effort. The plan might include such elements as changes to the workflow, elimination of unnecessary steps, or reduction in waiting time. The redesigned process can be documented with a written narrative outlining the new process, along with a new process flowchart. The implementation may also require a project timeline to use for tracking progress. Part of the plan development process will also likely include getting buy-in for the program from management and affected users, so this should be documented as well.

4. Implement the plan.

   Assign roles and responsibilities to team members and begin executing the redesigned process. Track progress against the established timeline.

5. Measure results.

   Using the same methods employed during the gap analysis, measure the resulting improvement following implementation. If the results are not as anticipated, it may be necessary to audit the implementation process to determine if it was carried out according to plan. You may also have to review the initial analysis and plan to determine if some element was missed.

6. Repeat the process.

   Remember, continuous improvement requires incremental steps so the process analysis will be ongoing.

Measuring Performance Improvement

As the adage goes, what gets measured gets done. Accordingly, one of the key elements in continuous improvement is the measuring process. Meaningful metrics—those clearly linked to the improvement objectives—can tell you how effectively the improvement is going. Keep in mind, you are concerned with measuring business results and process improvements that directly impact your organization's bottom line. Simply measuring the degree of compliance to a given set of procedures adds little value. It is even possible to follow procedures precisely without producing added value. It is important to also determine the rate of progress being made so that you can estimate the resources required to complete the project. When the rate of improvement diminishes, it may signal the proper time for reengineering the process and repeating the continuous improvement steps.

Controlling and Reducing Cost

No organization can survive for long without employing a method for cost control. While much of the impetus for containing costs generates from the user groups or finance group within the organization, the Purchasing Department, because of its unique role as the custodian of supplier relationships, generally takes the lead in such projects.

While there are numerous methodologies for containing or reducing cost, those that appear to be the most effective share a systematic approach that tries to look at all aspects of the cost of acquiring the product or service. Far too often, purchasing managers reduce the purchase order price they pay for a product or service just to find that in doing so they have increased some other area of expenses. Only by examining the full cost structure of an acquisition can purchasing managers implement a truly effective cost containment or reduction program.

In this section, we'll explore some of the considerations you will need to evaluate when implementing cost reduction programs as well as some of the methods typically used in purchasing operations to manage these programs.

Cost Reduction Considerations

Cost reduction must be carefully distinguished from a related process, *cost avoidance*. Cost reduction activities can be regarded as the proactive steps taken to actually lower the costs of the products and services you are currently purchasing from their present levels, while cost avoidance refers to analytical measures used to prevent their increase in the future. As an adjunct to cost avoidance, purchasing managers frequently include the process of *cost containment* (mentioned in the preceding section), which applies most often to a more systematic, project-oriented approach to both cost reduction and cost avoidance at the same time.

Keep in mind, however, that "cost" means more than just the price you pay for the product or service. It also means all of the combined expenses associated with the acquisition, such as the total cost of ownership to the organization over the entire period of time that it's in use, as well as the administrative cost associated with its acquisition and disposal. (We covered this consideration in the section "Total Cost of Ownership" in Chapter 1, "Procurement for Best Business Practices.")

Organization of Effort

Cost reduction efforts can be linked as a supplement to a number of other ongoing programs, such as parts or methods standardization projects or a supplier consolidation project. The benefit of this approach is that you can immediately leverage the synergy of combining efforts within an existing framework and being able to providing additional value through a closely related project. For example, combining a part standardization program with a supplier consolidation effort can result in more benefits than either one alone, but would not require many additional resources since the teams could be composed of the same members.

From another perspective, you may also want to consider working with ongoing engineering efforts or work simplification projects within user departments as a way of developing additional synergy that doesn't require a great deal of dedicated resources. These teams are likely already in place, and it will just be a matter of linking up with them.

One important point you might also want to keep in mind is that cost reduction efforts can be accelerated with strong senior management sponsorship and team member participation. When the need to reduce cost in a particular area is driven from senior management, it seems to receive more attention and thus, a higher priority for team accomplishment. Resources are often more readily available. Similarly, forming a cross-functional team, just as you did in your negotiation efforts, can provide technical resources that can ensure that you are not trading off lower prices for additional internal costs down the road.

Quality Concerns

In the effort to reduce cost, it is important to be certain that lower prices are not simply a trade-off for reduced or compromised quality for a product or service. Your goal as a buyer is to continually obtain increased value for the buying organization. You will find that your internal users are very sensitive to the potential for reduced quality and service, so you may have a difficult time convincing them of the value in your proposed program unless they can see clear evidence that the cost reduction will not adversely affect their own functional operations.

To ensure that there is a proper balance between cost reduction and quality requirements, you will need to be able to understand the quality issues in your organization and effectively communicate them to your suppliers. This often requires a close working relationship with the quality control group. In fact, many organizations, recognizing this need, have embedded quality control into the purchasing group in the form of a *Supplier Quality Engineering (SQE)* group. To a large extent, it is this group's responsibility to work with suppliers to achieve the optimal balance of cost and quality and to continually monitor supplier production output performance as a method of assuring that this cost and quality balance is not compromised. In this role, they often represent the Purchasing Department objectives to both internal users and suppliers.

Cost Control and Reduction Opportunities

Finding opportunities for cost reduction is not always as straightforward as it may sound. If your organization is like most, the low-hanging branches have already been cleared of their fruit. You are going to have to stretch a bit to find rewarding opportunities. Let's turn our attention now to some of the areas you might want to investigate.

Areas for Cost Review

Using the concept of ABC analysis (as we discussed in Chapter 12, "Managing Material and Supply Operations," when looking at inventory management), you are likely to find that a major portion of your organization's spending (the 80 percent or "A" category) falls within the scope of perhaps 20 percent of the products and services you buy. This is a good starting point, because if you can control costs of the major portion of the organization's purchases, you will certainly be successful. Consider too, that even a minor cost reduction in a costly product or service is likely to produce greater results than a significant reduction in a seldom-used one.

As you probably know, the Pareto Principle (or 80/20 rule) gets bandied about quite a bit. Do not take it literally; it is used today in its less scientific context simply as an expression of the disproportion of certain types of categorization.

It may also be appropriate to look into the detail of unit costs (cost per unit produced) or total costs (including overhead) within the organization in descending order of their variance from budget objectives. Costs that are higher than your budgeted costs may indicate opportunities to reduce costs in the short term. In general, the larger the cost overrun, the more scope there should be for savings. Costs that are higher than your *standard cost*—the engineering estimate on which your selling price may be predicated—usually indicate opportunities to reduce costs in the longer term. It is also considerably more important to review costs during the initial phases of the product life cycle for much the same reason: the longer the product is in use, the greater will be the accumulated savings.

In a manufacturing organization, the emphasis is generally on savings for direct materials since direct material costs have a greater accounting impact on the ultimate selling price of the product. However, savings can often be generated in much the same way for areas of overhead, such as MRO or facilities services.

Internal Approaches to Cost Reduction

As discussed in Chapter 11, "Making Sound Sourcing Decisions," the structure of the buying organization can have considerable impact on the cost of purchased products and services. Centralized buying, lead divisional buying, and cooperative purchasing all have benefits and counter-balancing drawbacks. However, in any given situation, changing the method of procurement from centralized consolidation to locally purchased can have an impact on the cost of a specific product or service and should be routinely analyzed.

A *commodity council*, or commodity team, is perhaps one of the best avenues for determining cost reduction strategies. Commodity councils are generally composed of members from various user departments across the organization and are empowered to develop procurement sourcing policy related to the specific commodity. This ensures a uniform approach to cost reduction with centralized decision making throughout the organization. As the name implies, commodity councils focus primarily on materials rather than services, so there may be a somewhat limited application of this process in any given organization. However, as of this writing, similar concepts are being adopted as spending increases in the services areas.

An analysis of spending data provided by the U.S. Census Bureau for 1997 indicated that spending for services was approaching 22 percent in the United States.

External Approaches to Cost Reduction

Aside from typical negotiations, there are several ways to work with suppliers to help reduce costs, which we will discuss in this section.

Long-term contracts   Generally, extending the length of an agreement to purchase specific quantities can result in price reductions and other concessions from the supplier who's anxious to book forward-looking business.

Consolidating purchases   Providing the supplier with greater volumes by consolidating purchases across the organization or reducing the number of suppliers for a wider range of products or services can result in lower prices.

Consortia and Pool Buying   Consolidating purchases between organizations can also result in lower prices and additional concessions. Interorganizational purchasing consortia, however, must meet specific legal requirements regarding competition and trade restraint. As a result, buying consortia have not been as successful in the private sector as they have been in the non-profit and governmental sector.

Target Cost and Target Price   These are concepts that rely on the cumulative effects of new technology and on production *learning curves* to help plan future pricing reductions as a result of the supplier's internal cost reductions. They may also be based on the projected dynamics of market conditions such as supply and demand, which are a bit riskier to try to predict.

Collaboration and Joint Ventures   Teaming up with suppliers to jointly develop new products or processes can be a way of sharing the cost (and the resulting benefits) to reduce overall costs in the supply chain.

Value Analysis

Value analysis is a systematic process used in the design or redesign of products and services that is based on providing all the necessary functions at the most economic cost within the required level of quality and performance. The process employs techniques that identify all of the required functions and characteristics of an item and establishes values for each of them, arriving at the lowest overall cost within the scope of its required performance. Value analysis, therefore, links cost and function.

Developed at the General Electric Company during World War II, two employees, Lawrence Miles and Harry Erlicher, are credited with creating value analysis, which almost immediately became a critical part of manufacturing. Because of the war, there were always shortages of materials and component parts. By utilizing value analysis, Miles and Erlicher continually looked for acceptable substitutes for items that were in scarce supply. They found that these substitutions frequently reduced costs or improved the product, or both. What originated from critical necessity turned into a systematic process that they named value analysis.

Looking at it another way, value analysis is a tool for analyzing the value of any specific element's function in relation to its cost, eliminating those elements that add cost without adding corresponding value. For example, it may be possible to eliminate certain expensive housing materials for a machine by improving the shipping container at a lower cost.

Supporting New Product Introduction

Today's business model relies on the fact that with shorter and shorter product life cycles, the organization that is first to market a new concept generally maintains the lead in both revenue and profit throughout the product's sales life. As a result, decisions that rely on processes such as make or buy analysis or value analysis must be accelerated and started early in the design process.

The Purchasing Department supports the organization's design and new product introduction (NPI) process primarily through its sourcing activities. The task here is to find suppliers that can support the requirements generated by new products or services or, if none are available, to work with existing suppliers to develop new capabilities. In this role, the purchasing manager acts as a consultant to the design and engineering teams by leveraging the appropriate sources of knowledge and information within the supplier community, often recommending one solution over another as a result of experience with the supply base.

Early Supplier Involvement (ESI) is a process in which manufacturers collaborate with suppliers at the beginning stages of the product development process, often as early as the concept phase. This process works to leverage the specialized domain expertise of the supplier and help accelerate the development of specifications so that the product can reach the market more quickly.

During the NPI phase, the purchasing manager often works in the role of liaison between the internal design team and the supplier's engineering group to develop a collaborative approach to new product development. Because of the high cost of developing new products or new technologies and the speed at which they are required to reach the market, collaboration within the entire supply chain is of paramount importance. This is where the potential for adding strategic value is at its greatest. Sourcing potential partners for joint ventures or collaborative development is just coming into its own as the concept of outsourcing gains currency. In fact, outsourcing engineering and design functions has become increasingly more attractive because suppliers have the domain expertise as their core competency.

Summary

Material standardization is the process of reducing the number of parts being used by the organization to make the products it markets. There are many benefits to standardization, including cost reduction through consolidated purchasing volumes and lower inventories. Standardization also enhances quality by concentrating focus since there are fewer items to control. Implementing a standardization program relies on a cross-function team and generally follows a project team methodology.

🌐 Real World Scenario

Too Many Engineers?

One now-defunct multibillion dollar company in the high tech manufacturing sector required more than 3,000 engineers to keep up with its new product development. The development cycle for a new product in this field, including its design and engineering, was about 10 months. The corresponding product's life cycle, however, was only three months. Technology was moving so quickly and the competition was so keen that platforms were going obsolete almost as they were introduced.

As a result of the high tech boom and the employment opportunities it generated, the average longevity of an engineer in this company was about two years. But it took close to a year to fully train an engineer in the company's processes. Wasn't this a formula that could have predicted the company's ensuing demise?

In addition to relying on internal standardization efforts, there are numerous official and quasi-official organizations that develop and publish standards that can be used in many organizations and often across industries and geographical boundaries. These range from independent standards organizations such as ANSI, SAE, and ASTM International to government standards organizations such as NIST and ISO.

Continuous improvement methods also apply to improving purchasing-related processes There are specific steps involved in this process that include the use of gap analysis and flow-charting, as well as the use of appropriate measurements to assess progress.

Controlling and reducing costs is another key function of the Purchasing Department. Purchasing managers need to know the difference between cost reduction and cost avoidance and understand the major areas where cost reduction efforts might be most appropriate. There are internal and external approaches to cost reduction to be considered, as well. Internal cost approaches deal primarily with the strategy for organizing purchasing decisions, while external approaches focus on ways to tactically address the marketplace to leverage buying power. Value analysis is another important method of developing cost reductions by examining each individual part in a product to determine if it can be eliminated or if a less costly part or material can be substituted.

Finally, the Purchasing Department's support for new product introduction, including early supplier involvement and the increasing collaborative use of suppliers, is vital to the development process.

For additional reading on topics related to this chapter, please see Appendix A.

Exam Essentials

Be able to describe the material standardization process. Material standardization requires input from internal users, and it is likely best handled in a cross-functional team environment. You will also need to know what common areas exist for standardization throughout the organization.

Be able to identify the benefits of standardization. These include cost reduction, reduced inventory, interchangeability that reduces design and engineering cost, and better focus on quality.

Be able to identify major standards organizations and their functional roles. You should be able to identify organizations such as ANSI, SAE, ASTM, NIST, ISO, and UL.

Understand how to support the improvement of purchasing related processes. This includes the concepts of implementing a continuous improvement process and managing performance improvement.

Understand how the Purchasing Department helps control and reduce costs. You will need to be able to distinguish between cost reduction and cost control, as well as cost containment. You will need to know how to organize a cost reduction program and what areas to review to find opportunities.

Be able to identify the elements of value analysis. Value analysis is a tool for analyzing the cost/benefit relationship of various functional elements in purchased products or services.

Understand how the Purchasing Department supports new product introduction. The Purchasing Department works as an intermediary between suppliers and internal designers/ engineers to develop a collaborative approach to reduced turn-around time in sourcing and product development.

Review Questions

1. The process of finding ways to use as few purchased items as possible to perform as many functions as possible.
   A. Continuous improvement
   B. Performance improvement
   C. Value analysis
   D. Material standardization
   E. ABC analysis

2. All of the following are benefits of standardization *except*:
   A. Allows organizations to understand true costs
   B. Reduces the level of inventory
   C. Increases administrative and handling costs
   D. Improves quality with uniform processes and specifications
   E. Reduces or eliminates one-time processes

3. All of the following are steps taken when developing a standardization program *except*:
   A. Establishing team involvement and objectives
   B. Measuring results
   C. Gathering information
   D. Outlining a plan
   E. Excluding the participation of the Sales Department

4. Standards most commonly apply to all of the following *except*:
   A. Materials
   B. Processes
   C. Professional services
   D. Equipment
   E. Procedures

5. The standards organization tasked with the official maintenance of U.S. time.
   A. American National Standards Institute
   B. National Institute of Standards and Technology
   C. Underwriters Laboratories Inc.
   D. Institute of Electrical and Electronics Engineers, Inc.
   E. ASTM International

6. The standards organization that manages the Baldrige National Quality Program.

    A. American National Standards Institute

    B. National Institute of Standards and Technology

    C. Underwriters Laboratories Inc.

    D. Institute of Electrical and Electronics Engineers, Inc.

    E. ASTM International

7. The key element in continuous improvement is to:

    A. Form an improvement team

    B. Initiate a gap analysis study

    C. Measure the process

    D. Implement the plan

    E. Develop a plan

8. The systematic, project-oriented approach to both cost reduction and cost avoidance at the same time.

    A. Cost containment

    B. Cost reduction

    C. Cost avoidance

    D. Cost analysis

    E. Cost of ownership

9. The systematic process used in the design of products with the required level of quality and performance at the most economic cost.

    A. Continuous improvement

    B. Performance improvement

    C. Value analysis

    D. Material standardization

    E. ABC analysis

10. All of the following are approaches to cost reduction *except*:

    A. Long-term contracts

    B. Consolidating purchases

    C. Consortia and pool buying

    D. Standard cost trend analysis

    E. Collaboration and joint ventures

Answers to Review Questions

1. D. Material standardization adds value by consolidating the parts used in a manufacturing organization so that greater volumes of the remaining parts can be leveraged for cost reduction. Fewer parts require less inventory.

2. C. Standardization actually reduces administrative and handling costs since there are fewer parts to order, receive, inspect, stock, and distribute.

3. E. The Sales Department often has a particular stake in product reduction, especially as it makes the product more competitive in the marketplace and generates price reductions for its customers. Sales staff can also be valuable partners in helping to benchmark the processes used by your competitors.

4. C. By their nature, professional services are exceptionally diversified.

5. B. NIST, along with the U.S. Naval Observatory, maintains the standard time in the United States.

6. B. NIST also manages one of the most prestigious awards for corporate quality, the Malcolm Baldrige National Quality Award, presented annually by the President of the United States.

7. C. While all of these processes are important considerations of continuous improvement, measuring the process to determine further actions is the most critical element.

8. A. Cost containment combines the processes of planned cost reduction (its primary objective) and cost avoidance over a future period of time.

9. C. Value analysis is one of the key tools used to analyze the cost/benefits of a particular part or solution.

10. D. Cost trend analysis is an analytic tool and does not work as a measure that reduces cost.

Chapter

14

Strategic Procurement Planning

THE C.P.M. EXAM SPECIFICATIONS COVERED IN THIS CHAPTER INCLUDE THE FOLLOWING:

- ✓ Developing demand- and forecast-based procurement strategies
- ✓ Implementing procurement strategies
- ✓ Forecasting requirements
- ✓ Coordinating forecasted requirements with suppliers
- ✓ Performing market analysis
- ✓ Forecasting market trends

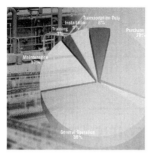

Sound procurement planning is the cornerstone of effective supply management. By its nature, planning is focused on the future, so developing effective plans enables the purchaser to proactively address and eliminate potential supply constraints that may arise in future activities. Also in this regard, good planning requires a thorough understanding of the particular market for the goods and services being purchased and where that marketplace is heading. With this knowledge, the purchaser can develop procurement strategies to meet evolving business conditions as needed. These important concepts are the focus of this chapter.

Developing Demand- and Forecast-Based Purchasing Strategies

The situation for the organization can be this critical: forecast accurately to meet changing market conditions or perish. The dilemma is that as the pace of business accelerates, the reaction time available to adjust to changing market conditions diminishes dramatically. Your organization needs to get the product or service to its customers in the right time frame and at a viable market price. Keeping pace with changing marketplace conditions is the only way that organizations can continue to maintain their competitive positions. If your organization is unable to fulfill your customer's needs, you can be assured that another organization will.

Accordingly, procurement strategy, also dynamically linked to changes in the market, requires continual reassessment. Effective practice relies heavily on the ability to employ forecasts of future demand and link them to strategic planning. Minor shifts in buying patterns or new technology, for example, can send significant ripples—sometimes even major waves—through the entire supply chain. As demand parameters change, the purchasing manager needs to be certain that they are identified and that the organization's supply base is prepared to respond quickly.

Demand-based strategies develop from actual customer orders, whereas *forecast-based* strategies are estimates (or, in some cases, best guesses) of customer demand during a future period.

To understand these concepts, let's begin with an analysis of various procurement strategies and how they are commonly implemented. We can then turn our attention to recognizing how these strategies can be supported through market analysis and forecasting.

Defining Purchasing Strategies

In one sense, a purchasing strategy can be looked at as the method you and your team choose to employ to buy specific goods or services. Since many goods and services share the same or similar characteristics, it is probably not surprising that these strategies tend to coagulate into several common approaches, which we will discuss in this section.

Purchasing for Current Requirements *Requirements* in a purchasing context refers to the amount of any particular material or service you may expect to buy within a given time frame. Current requirements can be loosely characterized as those needed within a three week to three month time frame. While they can, of course, be demand-based or forecast-based depending upon the nature of your organization's marketplace sector, you will generally find that the more distant the timeline horizon, the greater the likelihood that you will rely on forecasts.

Organizations that rely on forecast-based planning generally require some form of assurance that the purchase will actually occur before committing their inventory and a specific amount of their production capacity. For example, if you are collaboratively scheduling the next 13 weeks' requirements with your supplier, you may have to commit to a guaranteed purchase for the amount you are predicting you will need in the next five weeks, 75 percent of what your are predicting in the following five weeks, and perhaps 50 percent of what you indicate in the remaining three weeks. Thus, your forecast might look something like that shown in Table 14.1.

TABLE 14.1 Illustration of Forecasted Requirements Guarantee

Week	1	2	3	4	5	6	7	8	9	10	11	12	13
Guarantee	100%					75%					50%		
Part # and Quantity													
69782, Board	65	65	65	60	60	60	50	50	50	50	60	60	60
17962, Assembly	20	20	20	18	18	18	15	15	15	15	18	18	18

Spot Buying *Spot buying* (or short-term buying on a hand-to-mouth basis) is a strategy in which minimum amounts are purchased as needed, sometimes even on a daily basis. This approach is often taken when demand is generated at the last minute, when the product is perishable, or when prices are declining and the buyer hopes to benefit in the immediate short term as prices continue to fall. This approach can also be taken to protect cash flow when the organization is cash restricted.

Volume Purchasing Agreement (VPA)   The *Volume Purchasing Agreement (VPA)* is used for larger purchases that will take place on an ongoing basis. The VPA generally sets forth the pricing for specific goods or services over a designated period of time and is based on some agreed volume during a specific time period horizon. However, it is not usually an actual purchase order or commitment to purchase; it simply fixes prices for a given period of time.

Forward Purchasing   Occasionally, the concern for projected market shortages or price increases gives rise to the practice of buying in advance of actual demand or forecasted needs. This process, often referred to as *forward buying*, is generally used to ensure supply at a fixed price when prices are trending upward or market conditions indicate there may be potential shortages in supply.

Speculative Purchasing   There are occasionally opportunities to profit from buying in larger quantities than your organization requires and reselling the amount in excess of your needs at a profit. This practice generally occurs when the quantity purchased substantially reduces the price paid *and* there is a readily available market for the excess.

Product Life Cycle Purchasing   When a collaborative relationship with the supplier exists, or when both buyer and supplier are jointly developing a product, it may prove advantageous to develop a contract for the life of the product. This reduces the financial risk of product development to the supplier and provides an incentive to go forward with expenses that may be needed for product development. The practice also ensures there will be an ongoing source of supply at stable pricing for the buyer.

Just-in-Time (JIT) Purchasing   Just-in-time (JIT) is a management philosophy that strives to eliminate waste sources—resulting from any activity that adds cost without adding value, such as moving and storing inventory—by producing and delivering the right part in the right place at the right time. JIT (also known as lean production or stockless production) works to improve profits and return on investment by reducing inventory levels (increasing the inventory turnover rate), improving product quality, reducing production and delivery lead times, and reducing other costs (such as those associated with machine setup and equipment breakdown).

JIT is a means of enabling market demand to drive inventory management and is typically embedded within an environment of Six Sigma continuous improvement. However, to be successful it requires a systematic and highly cooperative approach to inventory planning, receipt, throughput, and delivery that focuses on smaller lot sizes delivered more frequently.

Although JIT was developed for production environments, there seems to be no reason the concept cannot be extended to all business environments. The basic concept is to receive what is needed just in time for it to be used. This places the responsibility on the supplier to get what is needed to where it is needed, just before the time it is needed.

Commodity Purchasing   *Commodities* are generally products that have uniform natures and are traded in an open marketplace, usually an exchange. They include many raw materials and natural resources such as aluminum and copper, as well as common agricultural products like grains and livestock.

On a *commodity exchange*, prices move in relation to projected supply and demand, often in a highly speculative manner. They are traded using financial instruments such as *futures options* (a contract for a specified product and amount to be delivered at some future date), so rarely does any physical exchange take place until the actual time of delivery called for in the contract. In commodities trading on an exchange, a *spot price* is the price of a product available for immediate delivery.

Some examples of popular commodity exchanges include:

> Chicago Board of Trade
>
> New York Mercantile Exchange
>
> London International Financial Futures
>
> International Petroleum Exchange
>
> Fukuoka Futures Exchange (Japan)

A comprehensive listing of worldwide commodity exchanges can be found at the Rutgers University Library: www.libraries.rutgers.edu/rul/rr_gateway/research_guides/busi/stocks.shtml#A.

Supplier Managed Systems   In Supplier Managed Inventory (SMI), the supplier is responsible for maintaining the proper level of inventory (often at the buyer's site) based on an agreed upon formula of minimum and maximum levels. In an SMI system, the buying organization typically sends a periodic report of current inventory levels and incoming demand (or forecasts) and the supplier then ships the correct amount to maintain the agreed upon level of stock.

Consignment   Suppliers are sometimes required to maintain inventory that they continue to own and manage at the buyer's site. In a true *consignment* environment, the buyer does not pay for this material until it is actually sold or used in its application. Consignment inventory, despite the fact that it is not billed to the buying organization until it is used, is nevertheless inventory and does not eliminate the wasteful nature of maintaining unsold stock.

Implementing Procurement Strategies

Once a procurement strategy is established, the purchaser should develop an appropriately related technique for its implementation. While there are endless numbers of purchasing situations that may arise, some of the most common techniques for dealing with them are outlined in the following sections.

Contracting

Contracting is one of the most widely used methods for implementing any particular buying strategy, especially when the purchasing volume tied to a strategy is of significant value to the organization and when the objective of the strategy is to reduce risk. In this section, we cover some common contracting techniques.

Long-Term (and Multi-Year) Contracting

Extended contracting periods—beyond the typical yearly renewal contract—are used when there is a need to develop partnerships as an inducement for suppliers to invest in initial startup production costs or when internal processes such as implementing a JIT program require close collaboration between the two organizations. These contracts often cover a range of requirements (such as servicing training and spare parts, in the case of capital equipment) as a means of reducing the supply base and providing more value to the supplier.

Contracts of this nature are usually established following a time-consuming, detailed sourcing and selection process, so the buying organization also has a stake in maintaining a long-term relationship to avoid having to repeat the sourcing process. Consequently, these contracts typically include provisions for comprehensive performance criteria, accompanied by a continuous improvement and review program. They may also contain provisions for price escalation (or de-escalation) based on predetermined levels of fluctuation in materials or labor—for changes over five percent, for example—as a way of sharing the risk of uncertain pricing structures in a dynamic market. These adjustments are often based on changes in a specific published price index or the rate of exchange between the monetary currencies used by the two parties.

Life of Product Contracting

As we pointed out earlier, it is often advantageous for the contracting parties to develop agreements that cover the entire life cycle of the product being sold to offset the risk of the supplier's initial investment and startup costs and to provide a longer basis to amortize its costs. When the cost of new technology, for example, is relatively high, it can provide restraints to effective marketing if the development cost must be recovered in a shorter time frame, such as one year.

Future Contracts (and Options)

A contract for future delivery—similar to the commodities futures contracts traded on public exchanges—can gain a supplier's commitment for production capacity when demand is random but nevertheless critical. Similarly, it can also fix prices during periods of uncertain supply and demand.

Options—the rights to buy something at a set price for a specified period of time—are also used when constraints to finalizing a purchase exist. This can occur, for example, when a sale is likely but the customer has not fully committed to a particular configuration. Usually an option such as this is purchased for a fee that is either applied to the purchase should it be completed or given back should the project be cancelled.

Contracting for Capacity

When overall volume can be estimated but the *product mix* required from a specific supplier cannot be determined, the best solution to ensure supply might be to contract for a portion of the supplier's production capacity in exchange for a firm commitment for volume. The volume may not actually be needed, but by reserving this production capacity in advance, you can reduce the risk of losing potential future sales due to lack of production capacity, or you can increase the chances of gaining last minute business from unanticipated demand.

Spot Buying

Spot buying, as described in the "Defining Purchasing Strategies" section, refers to the practice of purchasing a product on the open market for immediate delivery at the current cash price. Traditionally, spot markets exist primarily for those commodities traded on the futures markets, but in today's practice the term might refer to any purchase made without a contract or blanket order, as might be the case with on-time purchases, or it can refer to purchases made to meet unplanned demand.

Because of the immediacy of its requirement, spot buying rarely allows the buyer time for competitive bidding. For products or services not normally available for purchase through an exchange, the purchase goes to a supplier that is already doing business with the organization and has capacity to meet the volume. If there are no such suppliers available, the next preferable option would be some form of competitive bid, usually taken in the form of quotations. Again, depending on the immediacy of the need, this will likely be possible only in the case of off-the-shelf items.

Dollar Averaging

When short-term pricing fluctuates to the extent that it is difficult to determine your organization's basis for selling prices, it is common practice to use the averaged price of the commodity purchased for the recent period. Table 14.2 shows how this can help stabilize the calculations used for cost purposes. Note the average Price differs from the individual prices paid at each purchase.

TABLE 14.2　Example of Dollar Averaging

Date	Quantity	Price/Unit	Total Price	Average Price
Mar 7	210	$8.22	$1,726.20	
Apr 22	160	$11.70	$1,872.00	
Jun 3	450	$7.94	$3,573.00	
TOTAL	820		$7,171.20	$8.75

Hedging

Hedging, in its purest form, is the practice of offsetting the current contracted price by taking the opposite position in the futures market. This enables the organization to protect against any adverse price changes. Let's say, for example, a U.S. organization signs a contract to purchase some capital equipment for €12 million with delivery and payment due in 90 days. Because of potential fluctuations in the Euro, the currency in which the payment is to be made, the organization immediately enters into a financial contract to buy the €12 million at the current exchange rate of $1.28 per Euro in 90 days when the payment is due. It also purchases an option to sell the same amount of currency at the same time and at the same rate. In this way, whatever direction, up or down, the currency exchange rate moves, your organization will pay no more than the current market value.

Decision Tree Techniques

Decision tree analysis is a support tool to help review alternative strategies in a standard format and represents the decision making process in a graphical format. Decisions that can be made sequentially are shown as branches of a tree, beginning with the initial point of decision and extending to the probable final outcome. Each branch represents a separate set of decisions and probable outcomes.

In procurement, the decision tree is useful in the planning process as a means of evaluating the risk and benefit relationships between possible courses of sourcing action. By assigning a value to both the successful outcome of a particular course of action and its failure and linking it with the probability of an outcome, an expected value can be calculated.

In the example shown in Figure 14.1, a decision tree is employed to determine allocations between four suppliers. For each supplier, a probability factor of a purchase being required at a specific level of demand is estimated. The quoted price is then multiplied by this factor to calculate a probable price outcome. Capacity is calculated at that level of demand for the period during which the requirement exists. Choices based on projected price and capacity can then be made. In this example, demand for 1 million units could go only to Supplier #1, the only supplier with that level of capacity; demand for 750,000 and 500,000 units could go to Supplier #4, who has the best probable delivery price with available capacity.

FIGURE 14.1   Example of a decision tree analysis

Sourcing Decision Tree

Supplier Decision	Probability (P) of Demand	Production Demand (units)	Outcome (Price per Unit)	Production Capacity
Supplier #1	P = .20	1,000,000	$45.75	Yes
	P = .40	750,000	$55.25	Yes
	P = .30	500,000	$75.00	Yes
Supplier #2	P = .20	1,000,000	$42.50	No
	P = .40	750,000	$46.20	No
	P = .30	500,000	$54.25	Yes
Supplier #3	P = .20	1,000,000	$38.65	No
	P = .40	750,000	$44.50	Yes
	P = .30	500,000	$49.25	Yes
Supplier #4	P = .20	1,000,000	$36.85	No
	P = .40	750,000	$42.35	Yes
	P = .30	500,000	$47.85	Yes

Supply Chain Management

The supply chain is generally referred to as consisting of all organizations involved in the creation of a specific product or service, its distribution to the final consumer, and its retirement and disposal. In broad terms, you can divide the supply chain into two segments: supply management and distribution management. Supply management is concerned primarily with creating the product or service, whereas distribution management focuses on sales, delivery, and customer service.

Supply chain management strategies will vary widely, depending on the industry or market segment to which it is applied, and it would be impossible to formulate a one-size-fits-all supply solution. However, it is safe to say that virtually all strategies will involve the collaboration and integration of multiple organizations as a means to strengthen the group's position in relation to competing supply chains. In some cases this might involve consortium buying (where not legally prohibited) or perhaps even sharing manufacturing production facilities or distribution channels. The key ingredient appears to be leveraging the synergy between trading partners.

Planning Procurement Requirements

Regardless of the strategies or methods developed to secure materials and services, most future-focused procurement activities rely heavily on sound and effective forecasting and planning. Operationally, the forecast enables the buyer to determine the timing required for the actual purchase and provides the supplier with the tools needed to better support the buying organization. Based upon internally generated information relating to demand and externally generated information relating to supply, the buyer is able to effectively manage and ensure supply.

In this section we will examine the nature of forecasting and demand planning, as well as the methods available to coordinate planning with your suppliers.

Forecasting and Demand Planning

As noted earlier in this chapter, demand planning is based upon incoming customer orders, while forecasting is based on estimates of future requirements. The distinction between them is primarily their planning horizon. The key to either of these processes, however, is to accurately define and predict future requirements so that the availability of supply can be ensured.

Short-Term Planning

The challenge of short-term planning is to provide sufficient detail and granularity so that orders for materials can be placed with the suppliers to meet the demand of actual customer requirements. The goal of the short-term plan is to optimize inventory while meeting 100 percent of customer demand in a timely manner. This is usually accomplished by prioritizing incoming customer orders and grouping them according to production capacity. Generally, short-term planning and coordination with the supplier is handled by the organization's operational units—the production control or manufacturing planning sections, for example—since contracts with suppliers have most likely already been put in place by the Purchasing Department for commonly used materials.

Forecasting

Planning for the longer term requires that purchasing managers develop processes to accurately predict future requirements so that potential supply contingencies or constraints can be met proactively. While opinion-based forecasts are helpful and occasionally used to establish reliable future trends (when expert information is available), the forecasts most common in purchasing are fact-based and derived from historical usage data. These are used because they can be mathematically extrapolated to establish future needs. Purchasing also uses standard industrial predictors that rely on *change indexes* such as the *Consumer Price Index (CPI)* or ISM's *Report on Business* to help define business trends.

Forecasting Specific Elements

Forecasting supports strategy by providing reasonably accurate predictions for information that can assist the organization's planners to meet future demand in a manner that both ensures supply and develops a competitive advantage. While the precise nature of the information will vary from situation to situation, there are a number of key elements that are typically of special interest to the forecasting processes, and we will discuss them here.

Pricing Trends   Supply and demand are the primary drivers of pricing, so it is important to gain an understanding of their future interaction in your marketplace. You also need to have information available regarding the length and severity of pricing movements so that you can better time purchases and contracts for most-favorable pricing. Keep in mind, however, that there are numerous other factors that may drive pricing that are difficult to predict, such as natural disasters or wars.

Capacity and Material Availability   Capacity constraints and the availability of materials can be closely related to economic trends. Examining long-term supply and demand in its relation to future investment in capital and new technology can provide invaluable insights to planning supply operations. In times of severe capacity restrictions, production output allocations from suppliers can be critical to continued operations, so it is important to identify areas where potential constraints may require strong supply partnerships and solid contractual relations.

Changing Technology   The introduction of new technology and its timing has serious implications for purchasing. For example, in the semiconductor industry, the shift from 200mm wafers to 300mm wafers impacts all aspects of procurement, from capital equipment to raw materials to auxiliary professional services. Detailed insight into the timing of such technology changes is important for planning inventory reductions to minimize financial loss as a result of the changeover and to limit contractual obligations. It is also important simply from a workload balancing perspective because there will be an obvious spike in purchasing activity as a result of most technology conversions.

Forecasting Processes

In order to effectively develop appropriate forecasting processes, the purchasing manager will have to put in place a number of elements:

- Establish forecast metrics. Define those measures that will drive desired planning results, such as planning horizons, scheduling interval buckets, and levels of detail that will be required by others in the supply chain to support your operations.

- Develop and implement collaborative processes with customers so that a continuous stream of *actionable* market information is available as the basis of the forecasts and forecast revisions.

- Create a feedback mechanism so that customers can be made aware of potential supply constraints and pricing changes.

- Acquire systems tools that will prioritize incoming demand and optimize supply operations.

- Determine internal accountability and periodic timing requirements for forecast generation.

Coordinating Forecasted Requirements with Suppliers

Coordinating the information obtained through forecasting activities with your suppliers is equally as important as generating the forecasts themselves. Working collaboratively with your suppliers often means involving them early in the development and distribution of actionable information. Early Supplier Involvement (ESI) is a process that enables suppliers to participate in the early stages of product development and production planning so that they can better support your organization through their domain expertise. ESI also has the added potential of reducing turnaround time for new product introduction by leveraging the added expertise of the supplier's technical resources.

Supplier Involvement

ESI is an effective collaborative process that adds value in many ways. In supply planning, it enables the supplier to ensure ongoing materials and services consistent with actual customer requirements. It also enables the supplier to better plan the utilization of its resources—especially important if you are a key customer—to help control and reduce manufacturing costs.

Implementing collaborative planning and replenishment processes enables the supply chain to more effectively respond to rapid changes in demand and to improve allocation activities by anticipating the conditions that create peaks and valleys in requirements. Early supplier involvement also provides time to identify potential constraints and select possible alternatives. By encouraging the development of these collaborative processes you will help ensure the continued balance of supply and demand.

Some of the specific areas on which you will likely want to focus your efforts at developing collaboration to improve procurement processes are discussed next.

Manufacturing Processes and Planning   By working closely with your supplier's team, you have the opportunity to increase its responsiveness to changes in demand by helping to shorten the production planning cycle. Shorter planning cycles generally result in leaner operations through less buildup of inventory and reduced inventory obsolescence. This, in turn, leads to reduced costs to the buyer.

Effective manufacturing and fulfillment planning always involves the optimization of plant and asset utilization and is especially effective when the buying organization's staff understands the supplier's potential constraints. *Constraint-based planning* between collaborative partners is certain to better serve the consumer by ensuring the orderly allocation of resources and providing a mechanism to avoid supply shortages.

Capital Requirements   Forecasts of needed equipment—replacements or new acquisitions—can be useful to suppliers in the same way as material requirements. By engaging suppliers early, special requirements can often be included in new equipment being designed without the need for additional engineering cost. Similarly, early involvement helps ensure that production capacity and engineering staff are available to work on your projects when they are needed.

Cost Requirements   Early involvement of key suppliers can be critical to controlling and reducing costs. As the design process evolves in your organization, the supplier can provide assessments regarding the cost of various alternatives. Often this intervention will prevent decisions that lead to costly mistakes and avoidable lapses in judgment. In a competitive environment, this input can often provide a critical advantage to new product introduction.

Technology Requirements   Collaboration and early supplier involvement often results in the added capability of leveraging the expertise of the supplier to identify trends that might materially affect the products or services your organization is marketing. Obviously, you would not encourage investment in tooling or equipment that might become obsolete prior to its Return on Investment (ROI). On the other hand, you would want to encourage your organization to prepare for changes in materials and processes being driven by technology that your supplier may have special access to and can pass along to your organization.

Product Design   Suppliers often have design expertise in areas that can supplement what is available in your own organization. Knowing what works and what doesn't work in a specific feature can add great value in designing new products, especially in areas where the supplier's expertise is superior to your own. Leveraging this expertise often develops from close collaboration and interaction between the two organizations' design and engineering teams. To the extent that it is possible for you to encourage and facilitate this level of collaboration, you can help provide further competitive advantage for your organization.

Quality Requirements   Improved quality at a reduced cost often comes with the early involvement of suppliers in the development of specifications. Here you must assume that the supplier has unique knowledge of the processes and methods being used to fulfill your requirements. By bringing suppliers into the specification development process early, you can frequently assist them in preparing to meet special quality requirements and industry quality standards.

Lead-Time Requirements   It is important to sufficiently plan for supplier capacity and lead-time requirements. In doing so, you should involve your internal customers in the process to ensure early supplier response. This can often make a significant difference in supplier performance because it allows sufficient time for the supplier to increase capacity to meet your needs in a timely and orderly fashion. Insufficient supplier capacity can often lead to an unreliable source of supply and loss of consumer confidence.

Disclosure

Prior to engaging a supplier in any activity that allows access to your organization's confidential information, you must be certain that its staff has the capability of protecting it from unwanted access. Similarly, in order to earn the trust and confidence of your suppliers, you will want to ensure the protection of its information as well. You will not want to shake that confidence by disclosing proprietary information about one supplier to another.

Confidentiality   Confidential information can take a surprisingly broad scope, so you must be vigilant with the information you disclose. It will certainly include the obvious, such as pricing and intellectual property; it may also include other information that appears to be less sensitive but nevertheless should not be disclosed, such as final positions in bidding events, software systems in use, organizational structure, staffing, and anything related to future business planning.

Legal Aspects   Typically, organizations use instruments such as a Non-disclosure Agreement (NDA) to ensure the maintenance of confidential information between it and its customers and suppliers. In developing such a document, it is important to fully define what it covers and how the information being disclosed may be used. Since this can be associated with extensive legal and liability issues, it is not a good idea to simply execute a standard form for each and every situation. Many companies with extensive intellectual property will require specific legal review by experts prior to executing such documents.

Developing Market Analysis

Market analysis is a discipline that examines all of the key economic and technological aspects within an industry or industry segment and systematically gathers data that can help predict future trends in that market. It is an important element in procurement planning because it produces information on the composition and growth of the marketplace—suppliers as well as buyers— that can form the foundation of an organization's competitive business strategy. This information can help you determine future pricing trends and what capacity will be available to fill your needs. It can also provide insight into potential new sources of supply.

While market analysis can be as much of an art as a science, requiring advanced skill and learning, there are some basic principles you can employ to answer the fundamental questions posed in procurement planning. We will explore these in the following section.

Developing Market Awareness and Early Involvement

The Purchasing Department is in a unique position to gather information from the marketplace through its role as the key interface in the supplier relationship. Data available from suppliers often provides the most current perspectives on market trends and technological advances, giving the Purchasing Department an opportunity to funnel this information to other groups within the organization that can use it to further their competitive business advantage. In some organizations, the Purchasing Department may be called upon to facilitate supplier involvement in major activities, providing expert input on product viability and sourcing strategies.

New Product Introduction

Getting early participation in new product development activities from your suppliers can significantly reduce the cycle time required to bring a new product to market and help to avoid major difficulties with design and production failures down the road. The Purchasing

Department can also leverage the resources of the supply community by proactively seeking input from suppliers regarding possible issues with new products, such as those related to product applications, manufacturing strategies, quality, and pricing. It is important that activities involving suppliers take place as early in the research and development stage as possible to fully leverage its expertise before making any significant commitments to design.

The Purchasing Department can add value to the new product development process in a number of other ways as well, including providing advice on the cost impact of various substitution alternatives being considered, negotiating prices with suppliers to meet initial targeted budget requirements, laying the groundwork for future sourcing activities, and coordinating the development of material specifications. By using market driven data, the Purchasing Department can help provide the foundation for design decisions with material choices, determining if adequate supplies will be available in the future and what, if any, capital investments may be required to produce the product. By analyzing the nature of competition within the industry, the purchaser can also advise the organization where opportunities for joint design and development partnerships might be found.

Source Development

Market analysis can assist you with the identification of key marketplace suppliers for the products or services you may need in the future. Taking a proactive approach by investigating possible sources in advance of actual requirements will enable you to provide wider competition, which will drive more favorable terms when the time comes for an actual purchase. Identifying secondary (or backup) sources also reduces the risk inherent in selecting a new supplier; without early involvement you will likely not have adequate time to do so when you must make the actual purchase.

Technology Impact

Getting information on the latest developments in technology for the products you buy can become quite challenging, given the time constraints of today. Here, early involvement often includes attending trade shows and working with suppliers who are on the leading edge of technological developments in the industry. You can also subscribe to leading trade journals, many of which are available online, that can deliver periodic summaries of recent developments in technology. Professional associations and industry trade organizations often offer similar information and can provide up-to-date studies and surveys to help you understand the direction and challenges of the industry you are analyzing.

Market Capacity

The ability of the market to absorb the volume of your organization's future purchases should not be taken for granted. You should always be alert to market conditions when you are anticipating significant purchasing volumes or when prices could rise significantly as a result of production capacity constraints. An early understanding of the major factors that drive market price will help you to develop offsetting strategies and negotiate in advance the most favorable terms possible.

Collecting and Distributing Data

Sources for information are abundant. Depending upon your objectives, you should therefore restrict your data collection to stay aligned with your objectives. Are you looking for economic information such as pricing trends and capacity, or are you interested in gaining a better understanding of the individual suppliers in the industry? If you are looking for industry or economic data, you may want to consult secondary sources such as government published data; if you are interested in company-based information, you may want to go to the primary sources such as the companies themselves. A company's website is an excellent place to gather public information about a potential supplier and the marketplace it operates in.

Government Data   There are a number of excellent government sources for industry specific data available in the U.S. Here are a few of those widely used:

- U.S. Department of Labor, Bureau of Labor Statistics, provides data on employment and employment trends: `http://stats.bls.gov/`.

- U.S. Census Bureau, Economic Census, profiles the U.S. economy every five years: `www.census.gov/`.

- U.S. Securities and Exchange Commission, EDGAR Database, provides information for public companies based on real-time filings and other company information: `www.sec.gov/edgar/searchedgar/webusers.htm`.

- U.S. Department of Commerce, STAT-USA, provides U.S. import and export statistics including the National Trade Data Bank (NTDB), as well as access to Country Commercial Guides and Market Research reports: `www.stat-usa.gov/`.

- U.S. International Trade Administration, Trade Stats, provides trade data and statistics: `www.ita.doc.gov/`.

Commercial Databases   There are also a number of excellent commercial databases available that can provide market information:

- Dun and Bradstreet provides financial information, business ratings, and company profiles on public and privately held companies: `www.dnb.com/us/`.

- Hoover's Online provides business information on publicly held companies: `www.hoovers.com/free/`.

- Wall Street Journal, Tech Library, offers a compendium of white papers and free market analysis: `http://techlibrary.wallstreetandtech.com/data/rlist?t=busofit_10_30_10`.

- ThomasNet is a comprehensive resource for industrial information: `www.thomasnet.com`.

Publications and Government Reports   Several well-known publications and government reports are also available to provide detailed information on business and economic trends. Those more commonly used include:

- ISM's *Report on Business* (Manufacturing and Nonmanufacturing) measures the change in activity levels through polling selected companies and industries and is the basis for the

Purchasing Manager's Index (PMI), a highly regarded leading economic indicator: www.ism.ws.

- *Survey of Current Business*, published by the U.S. Department of Commerce, Bureau of Economic Analysis, provides up-to-date analysis of economic conditions: www.bea.doc.gov/ bea/pubs.htm.

- *Federal Reserve Bulletin* contains articles and reports that analyze economic developments: www.federalreserve.gov/pubs/bulletin/default.htm.

- The U.S. Government Printing Office (GPO) hosts a website with links to useful economic publications from all three government branches, including the *Economic Report of the President* and the *Statistical Abstract of the U.S.*: www.gpoaccess.gov/ index.html.

- Industry publications are widely distributed to buyers in their particular areas of interest and are usually free. CMP Media, for example, publishes several online and paper journals (www.cmp.com/), as does Reed Business Information (www.pubservice.com/ CH.htm).

Internal Communication

Once you have gathered relevant information, the challenge will be to distribute it to others in your organization. While the way you handle this will vary depending on the nature of your organization, it is wise to consider that information should be sent only to those interested in receiving it to avoid adding to the information overload problem.

Try posting market and up-to-date supplier information on a dedicated website (or portal) on your organization's intranet server. If properly sorted, this will enable users to access only the data they need. It will also provide the added benefit of giving you statistics on the number of times specific information is accessed so that you can better determine what the users deem valuable.

Forecasting Market Trends

Forecasts of future market conditions provide the purchasing manager with information on pricing and potential risk factors. This information is needed to develop effective strategic plans, so it is important that the data be gathered and analyzed in a timely and methodical fashion to avoid errors and incorrect conclusions.

Forecasting Processes and Methods

Depending upon your specific requirements, short-term forecasts (one year or less) can be used for tactical planning, while long-term forecasts can be used to develop strategic plans. There are numerous methods available for use in forecasting, and we'll discuss some of the more common methods here.

Correlation Analysis   *Correlation analysis* measures the degree to which changes in one variable are associated with changes in another. Its measure, the correlation coefficient, describes the degree of association (or co-variance) with –1, indicating a perfect negative correlation; through 0, meaning no correlation; to +1, a perfect positive correlation.

Regression Analysis   *Regression analysis* is a statistical technique that determines, for predictive purposes, the degree of correlation of one variable (the dependent variable) with one or more independent variables. This determines if a strong or weak cause and effect relationship exists between two elements.

Trend Analysis   Similar to regression analysis, trend analysis seeks to determine variations in the rate of change so that predictions regarding future conditions (such as product demand) can be extrapolated.

Time Series Analysis   *Time series analysis* is the analysis of a sequence of measurements made at specified time intervals, usually taken from the organization's historical records. Time is usually the dominating dimension of the data, and the measure is usually used to predict trends that may contain cyclical variations.

Measures of Central Tendency   Measures of central tendency are likely the most common statistics available. They describe the grouping of values in a data set around some common value—the median, arithmetic mean, or geometric mean.

Measures of Dispersion   *Measures of dispersion* (or measures of variability) describe how two sets of numbers differ from one another. They include measures such as range (the difference between the largest number and the smallest), variance (the square of the sum of individual variations from the mean, divided by the number of values in the group), and the standard deviation (the square root of the variance).

Delphi Method   When no verifiable statistical data exists, forecasters often turn to the *Delphi method*, a procedure for developing opinion-based forecasts. The process consists of a series of repeated interrogations of selected individuals. After a set of responses is analyzed, and its recommendations incorporated into a revised interrogation, it is resubmitted to the group for reconsideration, with encouragement to change the revised version if appropriate until a final composite can be obtained, when no further changes are made.

Economic Considerations

Rarely do economic events take place in isolation. There are often complex marketplace interactions between related segments and a general economic environment operating as a support backdrop. These blend to create a specific context in which factors and events can be analyzed. Applying the proper context to the information being analyzed places it in the correct perspective so that accurate conclusions can be drawn and appropriate courses of action established. In order to establish the appropriate context for data review, you should consider the overall business picture of the industry and how it relates to general market and *macro economic* trends. In doing so, you can better select the thrust of your analytical efforts, leading to your business and supply plan.

In any free-market economy (such as the U.S.'s), price and production levels are established by open market factors such as supply and demand. On the other hand, in a centrally controlled economy (such as China's), prices can be determined by policies and regulatory administrators; that is, they can be "legislated" without regard to fundamental economic factors. While there are crossovers—for example, government-regulated commodities in the U.S. such as pharmaceuticals that exhibit both open market and centralized influences—purchasers generally agree that market factors are the driving forces behind most pricing structures. For this reason, you must pay especially close attention to what you expect conditions to be like in the future.

Industry and Market Economics

Products and markets that respond to supply and demand exhibit a degree of price elasticity. Elasticity refers to the relative change in demand for a product or service as a response to a change in price or, conversely, the relative change in price in response to a change in demand. When there is little or no response, price or demand is considered inelastic. Similarly, if price elasticity is low, a large movement in price will produce only a small change in demand. Markedly elastic prices are often referred to as volatile and require the most attention since they present the greatest risk.

Keep in mind that there is also a principle of equilibrium at work in the supply and demand equation. In the longer term, supply and demand move to match one another and develop a balance so that prices remain fairly stable, but there are other factors to consider, too. Obviously, as the amount of money available to a purchaser changes, the demand curve also changes. The *law of diminishing marginal utility* indicates that additional satisfaction (or utility) decreases as additional units of a product are consumed. This is perhaps the point at which a product line might begin moving into the end-of-life phase, and this helps redirect available purchase funds to more recently introduced products that may have greater utility to the buying organization.

There is also another key economic factor to consider: business organizations seek to maximize profit. When prices drop below actual cost, there is little incentive to continue to produce; however, when profit becomes excessive, competition for the lucrative market increases. For this reason, economists agree that in the long run the supply curve of any particular commodity will tend to reflect the actual cost to produce the good or service. Ideally, the market stabilizes at the point where the marginal cost (the additional cost of the last unit produced) equals marginal revenue (the additional revenue produced by the last unit sold). Competitive markets are thus most likely to exist where the price buyers are willing to pay at a level that will at least balance the costs to the supplier.

Perfect competition may never exist, and most suppliers usually operate in an environment of limited or *imperfect competition*. This environment is characterized by the existence of some competitors whose products can provide relative distinction from one another and suppliers having some degree of control over marketplace pricing.

Global Trends

The global economy is characterized by continual change, with some countries or geographical regions holding advantages only in specific commodities. For example, natural resources such as petroleum or timber are common in one area, while low-priced labor is common in another. Countries that have higher efficiency or greater resources in a particular area will always hold a competitive advantage over others, unless somehow restricted by laws or other governmental actions. In some areas, government subsidies or tariffs help local producers of a particular product to compete with outsiders where they would not likely have an advantage. When production exceeds local demand in such situations, products are often *dumped* in other countries, that is, exported at below cost.

Business Cycles

Economic conditions tend to move in cyclical fashion, creating what are known as business cycles. While these cycles are by no means regularly timed, as in the case of *seasonal cycles*, they do have certain common characteristics of *expansion* (an increase in *gross domestic product [GDP]*) followed by *contraction* (a decrease in GDP), with specific economic turning points and troughs in between.

Economic Terms and Indicators

Forecasting business cycles is not an exact science, but there are certain economic indicators—such as housing starts, stock prices, or ISM's *Report on Business*—that can be used for short-term prediction of a changing economic phase. The purchasing manager can use these indicators to determine the direction of market conditions and develop appropriate procurement strategies.

Economic Indicators

Economic indicators are usually statistical signals of changes in an economy's trend. In the U.S., the Bureau of Economic Analysis of the Department of Commerce groups these indicators by their timing relationship to the general economy. There are three primary indicators:

- *Leading indicators* are those that forecast changes in the economy before they occur. They include elements such as the money supply, stock prices, commodity prices (raw materials and agricultural products), new unemployment claims, new building permits, new orders for consumer goods, new orders for investments goods, and unfilled orders.

- *Coincident indicators* are economic elements that measure changes in the economy as they occur, providing information related to the present condition of the economy. Personal income and the unemployment rate are examples.

- *Lagging (trailing) indicators* are market indicators that follow general trends in the economy, often continuing either an upward trend after the peak of the economy is signaled by other economic indicators, or a downward trend after a rise is signaled. Examples include business expenditures for new plants and equipment, consumers' installment credit, short-term business loans, and the overall value of manufacturing and trade inventories.

Economic Price Indexes

A *price index* is a statistical tool that compares prices from one period (usually a base period) to the next in specific areas of the economy. Numerous indices of this kind exist, but the more commonly used ones in the U.S. include:

- The *Consumer Price Index (CPI)*, published by the U.S. Bureau of Labor Statistics, is one of the most widely cited examples of a price index. It measures the cost of a representative "market basket" of typically purchased consumer goods that changes in composition very slowly. As a measure of the change in the cost of living, it has become commonly used as an indicator of the degree of *inflation* in the economy. There are two official CPIs, the CPI-U and the CPI-W. The CPI-U is an index of consumer prices based on the typical market basket of goods and services consumed by all urban consumers during a base period. The CPI-W is an index of consumer prices based on the typical market basket of goods and services consumed by urban wage earners and clerical workers during a base period.

- The *Producer Price Index (PPI)* is a group of indexes (also published by the Bureau of Labor Statistics) that measures the average change over time in wholesale selling prices received by domestic producers of goods and services. The index is reported by commodity, industry sector, and stage of processing and is separated into finished goods (those that will not experience any further change), intermediate goods (those that have had some processing but are not finished), and raw materials (those in their original, unprocessed state).

- The *Implicit Price Deflator* (or GDP deflator) is an index-based ratio that measures inflation by converting output in current prices into a constant-dollar GDP, showing how much of the change relative to the base year's GDP (1992) can be attributed to changes in price levels.

The rate of change in an index can be used to assess changes in direction of the overall economy. An index is calculated from a base period (or year) that is assigned a value of 100. Subsequent calculations are made as a percentage of change from that base period. For example, if the price of a market basket of goods during the base period is valued at $1,195.00 (which equals 100) and in the second year it is valued at $1,254, it has increased by 5 percent. This puts the index for year two at 105.

Interest Rates

Interest rates are the charges assessed by a lender for borrowing money. They are usually expressed as a percentage of the loan over a period of time. Fixed rates are calculated on the basis of a specific periodic rate that remains unchanged and are the same amount for each period, while variable rates vary according to changes in a specified index and can vary from period to period. The rates themselves, however, are based on factors such as the borrower's credit risk rating and the relative level of supply and demand for money.

Employment Levels

Employment levels are most commonly measured in terms of the rate of unemployment. You should also consider the size of the labor force overall and the number of new jobs created in any given period. These measures help shape public policy. In times of recession with accompanying high unemployment, government subsidized programs may be used to stimulate employment, which in turn results in an increase in overall economic spending.

Gross Domestic Product (GDP)

GDP is the total market value of all the goods and services produced domestically during a given period. GDP equals total consumer spending on final products, business investment, and government spending and investment, plus the value of exports, minus the value of imports. In the United States, it is calculated by the Department of Commerce each quarter and is considered the key measure of economic output. You measure expansion and contraction in terms of GDP.

Money Supply

Money supply refers to the amount of money in circulation. There are two main measures: *M1* measures the funds readily available for spending, that is, currency and liquid bank and investment accounts. *M2* is M1 plus relatively accessible savings, such as small time deposits held for the most part by households. When the money supply figure is up, it is an inflationary factor and therefore, generates concern that the Federal Reserve will tighten money growth by allowing short-term interest rates to rise. A rise in interest rates often leads to less spending, and a cooling off of the economy usually takes place.

Exchange Rates

Rate of exchange refers to the value of one country's currency in relation to another. Fluctuations in these rates are of considerable concern to buyers engaged in international purchasing because of the potential for price erosion as the value of one currency declines in relation to the other. Currency rates are typically established by the central banks in response to market conditions. Countries generally seek a level of exchange that is low enough to encourage other countries to purchase their products (because their currency has greater purchasing power) while at the same time not so low that it produces a low rate of return and discourages foreign investment.

Balance of Trade/Balance of Payments

Simply defined, the *balance of trade* is the difference between a country's imports and its exports from the rest of the world for any given period. It is an element of the larger *balance of payments*, which reflects additional nontangible flows such as capital investment, dividends, debt payments, and interest payments. A deficit in payments means the country is paying out more than it receives. This has been the case in the United States for more than the past 50 years.

Inflation/Deflation

In its simplest terms, inflation is the measurement of the rate of increase in the general level of prices in an economy, producing a decline in purchasing power of the currency. Inflation most commonly occurs when overall economic demand exceeds the supply of goods and services, driving prices upward. This can be the result of a rise in the money supply increasing at a rate that exceeds the rise in output. It can also result from a steep decline in supply or an increase in demand when industrial capacity is full. Inflation has been relatively stable in the U.S. economy at about 2.5 percent during the past decade.

Deflation is the opposite of inflation and is typically characterized by an actual decline in the general level of prices in the economy and a resulting increase in purchasing power. In the U.S., the last major period of deflation occurred during the Depression of the 1930s.

Capacity Utilization

The Federal Reserve Board calculates and reports the output of factories, industries, and the entire economy in terms of their *capacity utilization*. When factories are operating above 85 percent of capacity, industrial output is considered to be at full capacity. As the rate approaches 90 percent it is assumed to be inflationary, while at a figure close to 70 percent it is considered recessionary.

Government Policies

Most governments attempt to influence the overall conditions in their economy to help ensure the welfare of its citizens and to influence public objectives. Depending, of course, on the specific circumstances, common objectives might include reducing unemployment, increasing the rate of economic development, managing inflation or deflation, providing higher rates of return for foreign investment, and maintaining price stability. We'll discuss the most widely used government policies in this section.

Monetary Policy

Monetary policy controls economic activity by regulating the amount of money available to the public. In the U.S., monetary policy is governed by the *Federal Reserve System* through its Board of Governors. An "easy" monetary policy leads to faster money growth and initially lower short-term interest rates in an attempt to increase overall demand, but it may also lead to a higher rate of inflation. A "tight" monetary policy restricts money growth and higher interest rates in the near term in an attempt to reduce inflationary pressure by reducing overall demand. During periods of recession, lower interest rates and higher money growth can help stimulate the economy. During periods of declining unemployment and increasing inflation, the Federal Reserve usually emphasizes monetary restraint by raising interest rates and slowing the growth of money.

Fiscal Policy: Taxes

Because of their relative size, most governments can influence economic activity through their fiscal policy, both by supporting public spending as a stimulant or by raising taxes to cool off the economy. Conversely, corporate and consumer tax cuts have a tendency to stimulate economic activity by placing more spending power in the hands of consumers and corporations. Public policy can also be used to create benefits such as investment tax credits that will, in turn, stimulate further economic activity.

Budgets and Deficits

Government budgets and budget deficits affect economic conditions, influence the money supply, and affect monetary policy. A country's need for borrowed funds due to deficits will usually affect overall interest rates and create competition with private industry for expansion funds. This can certainly slow economic growth.

National Income

Government reports provide a great source of information that the purchasing manager can use to better understand broad trends that affect overall business conditions in the economy. These trends, in turn, can help you develop estimates for how individual industries may perform.

National Income is an important indicator of the resources available for spending, and its growth or contraction can signal major turning points in economic cycles. It is defined as the sum of the incomes of all the individuals in the country in the form of wages, interest, rents, dividends, and profits. It is calculated prior to any deductions for income taxes.

Figure 14.2 shows how the key economic measures in an economy (the U.S. in this case) relate to one another. Working from the bottom up, you can see that National Income is a derivative of *personal income* and rolls up to *Net National Product (NNP)*, *Gross National Product (GNP)* and, finally, Gross Domestic Product (GDP).

FIGURE 14.2   Relation of gross domestic product, gross national product, net national product, national income, and personal income (billions of dollars)

Line		2003
1	**Gross domestic product**	**11,004.0**
2	Plus: Income receipts from the rest of the world	329.0
3	Less: Income payments from the rest of the world	273.9
4	**Equals: Gross national product**	**11,059.2**
5	Less: Consumption of fixed capital	1,353.9
6	Private	1,135.9
7	Domestic business	942.6
8	Captial consumption allowances	1,225.6
9	Less: Capital consumption adjustment	283.0
10	Households and institutions	193.3
11	Government	218.1
12	General government	183.6
13	Government enterprises	34.5
14	**Equals: Net national product**	**9,705.2**
15	**Less: Statistical discrepancy**	**25.6**
16	**Equals: National income**	**9,679.6**
17	Less: Corporate profits with inventory valuation and capital consumption adjustments	1,021.1
18	Taxes on production and imports less subsidies[1]	751.3
19	Contributions for government social insurance	773.2
20	Net interest and miscellaneous payments on assets	543.0
21	Business current transfer payments (net)	77.7
22	Current surplus of government enterprises[1]	9.5
23	Wage accruals less disbursements	0.0
24	Plus: Personal income receipts on assets	1,322.7
25	Personal current transfer receipts	1,335.4
26	**Equals: Personal income**	**9,161.8**
	Addenda:	
27	Gross domestic income	10,978.5
28	Gross national income	11.033.6
29	Gross national factor income[2]	10,195.1
30	Net domestic product	9,650.1
31	Net domestic income	9,624.5
32	Net national factor income[3]	8,841.1

Source: U.S. Department of Commerce, Bureau of Economic Analysis

Politics

Economic conditions are closely related to the political climate in virtually all economies and, depending on the specific area of the world, can be characterized as stable or unstable. Obviously for the purchaser, risk increases dramatically during periods of political instability due to its effect on government services. In turn, this can significantly impact the availability of material, labor, and capital resources and can lead to escalating prices or unreliable supply. It is important, therefore, that the purchasing manager pay particularly close attention to conditions in countries where the organization is purchasing strategic materials or conducting outsourced manufacturing.

Import and Export Considerations

Market trends are also influenced by conditions affecting international trade, but because these conditions are typically governed by political considerations, they can be difficult to forecast.

Some of the key areas to consider from this perspective include free trade, trade deficit and surplus, and countertrade.

Free Trade   *Free trade* means the flow of goods and services across national borders without restrictions or tariffs. This rarely exists because most countries adopt some form of protectionist stance in order to favor internal resources. Despite this, however, there have been numerous attempts to reduce trade barriers in some international circles and limited success on a regional basis. For example, in 1993, the United States, Canada, and Mexico entered into a trilateral free trade agreement, the North American Free Trade Agreement (NAFTA), designed to encourage trade between the partners as a means of providing long-term economic benefit to the region.

Trade Deficit and Surplus   A *trade deficit* is created when a country's imports exceed its exports. It is considered to be a good measure of a country's economic condition because it is a calculation of the investment flows between other countries, as well as the balance of goods and services exchange. It is likely that the U.S. trade deficit—which reached its historical high of more than $500 billion in 2003—is the result of a net inflow of capital to the United States from the rest of the world because domestic investment has not kept pace with the opportunities. This is largely reflected in the lowered value of the U.S. dollar in relation to other currencies as a result of investors' fears that the trade and budget deficits will create higher investment risk.

Countertrade   *Countertrade* is a form of barter where goods are exchanged for financial credits that can be used only to buy other goods from the originating country or the trading partner. Countertrade also refers to reciprocal and compensatory trade agreements, whereby the seller assists the buyer in reducing the amount of net cost of the purchase through some form of compensatory financing or bartering. This form of business was favored by developing nations with abundant resources but limited liquid capital but has fallen into disfavor to a large extent in more recent time because of the burdensome administration associated with governing it and the often slow rate of receiving compensation.

Ongoing Monitoring of Data

Forecasts require frequent updating simply because economic conditions are continually changing. New technology, government policies, natural disasters, and a variety of related issues cause market-specific directions to alter in ways that often significantly affect the organization's planning horizon. Some of the more significant areas you will want to monitor to ensure your forecasts are updated are discussed next.

Financial Markets   Financial markets that include stock exchanges, commodity exchanges, and money markets worldwide reflect the climate of business in their particular marketplace segments. They should be monitored for changes that may impact your procurement and economic forecasts. Money supply also affects economic conditions, influencing interest rates and the level of new investment. These, in turn, can have a significant impact on market pricing and the pace of new product development investment.

Labor Markets   The stability of labor conditions is critical to the long-range planning of organizations that purchase goods or services from labor intensive sources. Obviously, increases in labor costs can have a direct impact on pricing, but you should also be concerned with the potential for strikes and work slowdowns resulting from organized labor movements or political unrest. While such events are difficult to forecast, they should nevertheless be monitored to validate the continued availability of supply at your projected levels of production and pricing requirements.

Capacity and Lead Times   Material shortages, plant shutdowns, financial crises, and adverse natural conditions can all directly impact delivery schedules and lead times. Spikes in demand can also strain production capacity and result in extended lead times. As you know, supply constraints usually lead to price increases and can significantly disrupt your planning assumptions. They should be continually monitored for trend changes.

Political Climate   Although it would be impossible for you to become an expert in the politics of each nation your organization does business with, it is important that you remain sensitive to major changes in governmental policies that might affect the items you purchase. Despite the relatively stable political systems in many countries, including the U.S., changes in government can bring changes in fiscal policy. Policy shifts can alter economic conditions, favoring certain industries over others, changing tariffs and quotas, adding or removing taxes, and altering the investment and monetary policies prevailing in the country. Consequently, it is important that you include these factors in any continuing risk assessments you perform for critical suppliers. They should be closely monitored for changes and addressed in your planning forecasts.

Technology   Shifts in technology are typically accompanied by shifts in economic conditions. Sometimes these shifts are global, such as in the telecommunications industry, and sometimes they are localized to the development of entirely new products to meet evolving technical standards. New technologies often give rise to new centers of innovative excellence and attention shifts from one geographical region to another.

Technology also affects the methods of production and delivery for the goods and service you buy. Improved productivity as a result of automation is certainly one clear trend in many industries, and it can have a profound effect on output and prices. By leveraging this process, many organizations plan for declining prices by setting clear production learning curve goals with their suppliers to deliver built-in price reductions.

To the extent that changes in technology can affect the products and services your organization markets, it is important that you monitor their potential impact on a regular basis and account for them as alternate scenarios in your planning forecasts.

Environmental Conditions   Changes in environmental conditions such as weather and natural disasters are difficult, if not impossible, to predict, and you will not be expected to do so. However, once such an event occurs you must react quickly, assessing its impact on the goods and services you plan to purchase. Forecasts of the availability of supply and pricing trends should be evaluated in terms of their effect on your business and communicated to those in your organization who are most critically affected.

As part of their risk mitigation plans, most organizations look to their suppliers to have in place documented disaster recovery plans and backup sources of production.

Summary

As you already know, developing effective procurement strategies is one of the most critical purchasing manager responsibilities. Effective strategies reduce risk by ensuring continued supplies of favorably priced materials and services when they are needed. In this chapter, we examined the elements of various strategies and how they are best implemented and monitored. We also reviewed the most common methods for developing planning forecasts and coordinating them with suppliers, leveraging information gained from market analysis.

Demand- and forecast-based purchasing strategies determine the method and timing of your purchases. Commonly used strategies include spot buying, purchasing for current requirements only, JIT, long-term contracts, forward purchasing, product life cycle purchasing, and commodity-based procurement. They also include strategies involving close supplier collaboration such as supplier managed inventory and consignment methods. Implementing these strategies involves a number of specialized techniques such as hedging, speculative buying, dollar averaging, decision tree analysis, and supply chain management. Demand- and forecast-based planning also requires employing processes to estimate future demand requirements including developing metrics, establishing collaboration with customers and suppliers for timely feedback, and creating internal accountability for timely forecast generation.

Market analysis examines economic and technology trends that might impact the organization's supply management planning. In areas such as new product introduction, market analysis assists with source development and pricing strategies. Typically, information is garnered from government and commercial databases, as well as publications and government reports as a basis for analysis. You can apply a number of techniques to develop your projections, such as correlation analysis, regression analysis, trend analysis, time series analysis, measures of central tendency and dispersion, and the Delphi method. You should also examine current and projected economic conditions for the markets you are analyzing using specific economic indicators, price indexes, and government policies to assist your projections. Be sure to monitor these elements continually to ensure that your strategies address changing marketplace conditions.

For additional reading on topics related to this chapter, please see Appendix A.

Exam Essentials

Be able to identify common demand- and forecast-based strategies.   Common strategies include spot buying, purchasing for current requirements only, JIT purchasing, long-term contracts, forward purchasing, product life cycle purchasing, and commodity-based procurement. They also include strategies involving close supplier collaboration, such as supplier managed inventory and consignment.

Understand how to implement demand- and forecast-based strategies.   Demand- and forecast-based strategies are implemented through long-term contracting, life of product contracting, contracting for capacity, and future contracts. Other techniques include spot buying, dollar averaging, hedging, and supply chain management.

Be able to develop supplier involvement in supply planning.   Collaborative planning and replenishment strategies require early supplier involvement. Areas for specific consideration include coordinating manufacturing and fulfillment plans, developing capital requirements, and new product introduction. These activities address product design as well as cost, technology, quality, and lead-time requirements.

Be able to develop market analysis to project future trends.   Market analysis helps project future trends and relies on specific sources of information such as data gathered from government and commercial databases, as well as publications and government reports.

Understand how to employ forecasting techniques.   Forecasting typically focuses on the projection of pricing trends, future capacity, material availability, and changes in technology. Common analysis tools include correlation analysis, regression analysis, trend analysis, time series analysis, measures of central tendency and dispersion, and the Delphi method.

Be able to use economic indicators to assist in forecasting.   Common economic indicators are grouped according to their timing relationship to the economy and include criteria such as money supply, stock prices, price indexes, and business investment. Also used are interest rates, employment levels, GDP, trade balances, exchange rates, and economic price indexes such as the CPI and PPI to project future trends.

Understand how government policy affects future planning.   Governments influence future economic conditions through monetary policy, taxes, spending, and political decisions that affect tariffs and trade policy.

Review Questions

1. The type of buying that ensures supply at a fixed price.
   A. Just-in-time buying
   B. Forecast-based buying
   C. Speculative buying
   D. Spot buying
   E. Forward buying

2. Spot buying is considered:
   A. Demand-based
   B. Forecast-based
   C. Best guess
   D. Hand-to-mouth
   E. Occasional

3. The practice that offsets the risk in a contracted price by taking the opposite position in the futures market.
   A. Spot buying
   B. Forecast-based
   C. Hedging
   D. Speculative
   E. Dollar averaging

4. The planning process that evaluates risk and the benefit of relationships between possible courses of sourcing action.
   A. Decision tree
   B. Contracting
   C. Procurement strategy
   D. Product life cycle
   E. Hedging

5. The term that describes providing projected information to assist supply planners meet future demand.
   A. Demand planning
   B. Contracting
   C. Product life cycle
   D. Forecasting
   E. Decision tree

6. A key method of coordinating forecasted requirements with suppliers.

    A. Demand planning

    B. Early supplier involvement

    C. Product life cycle

    D. Decision tree

    E. Contracting

7. Type of document that ensures confidential information exchanged between buyer and supplier is protected.

    A. Long-term contract

    B. Future contract

    C. Non-disclosure Agreement

    D. Life of Product contract

    E. Options contract

8. The total market value produced in an economy is known as:

    A. Net National Product

    B. Money supply

    C. Balance of Payments

    D. Gross Domestic Product

    E. National Income

9. A statistic to determine if a strong or weak cause and effect relationship exists between two elements.

    A. Correlation analysis

    B. Trend analysis

    C. Regression analysis

    D. Time series analysis

    E. Measure of dispersion

10. One of the most widely cited indexes published by the Bureau of Labor Statistics.

    A. Consumer Price Index

    B. Producer Price Index

    C. GDP deflator

    D. Rate of Change Index

    E. Dow Jones Industrial Averages

Answers to Review Questions

1. E. When prices are moving upward or there is an anticipated shortage of supply, placing binding orders in advance of actual requirements, known as forward buying, ensures supply at the current price.

2. D. Spot buying is based only on the needs at the current moment and not on future demand, thus it is termed "hand-to-mouth."

3. C. Hedging is a technique generally used to reduce the risk of currency fluctuations in the contracted price by purchasing the opposite position in the futures market. In this way, losses in the declining currency are offset by gains in the futures and vice versa.

4. A. A decision tree enables the forecaster to project the value of specific courses of action based on their estimated risk by arithmetically calculating the outcomes of potential choices.

5. D. A forecast is an estimate of future conditions, such as supply and demand, that helps plan strategies.

6. B. Early supplier involvement develops a collaborative approach with suppliers, enabling them to integrate your forecasts into their own planning to better ensure that they are able to meet your requirements.

7. C. The Non-disclosure Agreement requires that both parties maintain the confidentiality of disclosed information. It protects intellectual property and strategic plans from competitors.

8. D. GDP is the measure of all goods and services produced in an economy during a given period. It represents total consumer spending on final products, business investment, and government spending and investment, plus the value of exports, minus the value of imports.

9. A. As typically defined, correlation is a number between +1 and -1 that reflects the degree to which two variables have a linear relationship. The purpose of correlation analysis is to measure the strength of the relationship between two variables. A high positive correlation indicates a strong cause and effect relationship between two measures, while a strong negative correlation indicates none whatsoever.

10. A. The Consumer Price Index (CPI) measures the cost of a representative market basket of typically purchased consumer goods that changes in composition very slowly. As a measure of the change in the cost of living, it has become a common indicator of the degree of inflation in the economy.

Leading the Procurement Organization

Chapter 15

Managing the Procurement Organization

THE C.P.M. EXAM SPECIFICATIONS COVERED IN THIS CHAPTER INCLUDE THE FOLLOWING:

- ✓ Planning procurement strategy and objectives
- ✓ Developing departmental goals and plans
- ✓ Formulating operational policies and procedures
- ✓ Preparing departmental reports
- ✓ Responding to audits
- ✓ Evaluating Purchasing Department performance
- ✓ Administering departmental budgets
- ✓ Working with operational forms

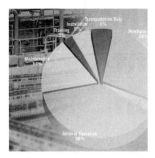

The internal operation of the Purchasing Department achieves focus through the development of procurement strategies and objectives. These are wide-ranging strategies and objectives created primarily to ensure that the department is in alignment with, and can support, the goals of its internal customers as well as the overall goals of the organization. To ensure alignment and, consequently, to effectively implement strategy, requires that you formulate specific and measurable goals for achieving the objectives of your strategy and establish a detailed plan so that your implementation can stay on track. These activities should also align with your operational policies and procedures so that they can be clearly and effectively put into practice.

The Purchasing Department must continually inform its internal customers and the organization's senior management of the department's contributions and progress toward goal completion, so it is important that you understand what activities are relevant to their needs and how best to report on the status of these activities. Reporting typically requires the close management of large amounts of data. This data, along with the ongoing documentation of key activities, helps your group prepare timely reports as they are needed. It also helps when it is necessary to respond to financial or quality audits and when you are required to prepare corrective action reports to ensure compliance.

In addition to these activities, you will also find it necessary to develop and manage the departmental budget. You will be required to continually measure the department's performance in relation to the budget and in relation to several other key areas of metrics we will discuss in this chapter. These measures will not only determine your effectiveness as a manager, they will also point out areas for needed improvement so that you can incorporate continuous improvement processes in your operational activities.

Planning Procurement Strategies and Objectives

Strategic planning is the process of defining the organization's long-term objectives and identifying the best methods to reach them. It is a disciplined technique of developing fundamental decisions and actions that will guide an organization's activities and provide structure for each of its individual functions. Effective strategic planning requires gathering a wide range of relevant information, exploring various alternative courses of action, and attempting to assess the future implications of current decisions. For successful implementation, strategic plans require clear communication and the ability to absorb divergent values and interests for the common organizational good.

We will explore these concepts in further detail in the following section.

Supporting the Organization

Purchasing supports the organization primarily through the acquisition process and the department's management of the supplier community. To carry out these functions effectively, the department management needs to clearly understand the organization's strategy and plans so that it can develop a complementary supply strategy.

Aligning with Organizational Strategy

In general terms, Purchasing will typically support its organization through activities focused on sourcing, cost reduction, developing supplier alliances, finding sources for collaboration in new technology development, financial audit compliance, and implementing process improvements. When these activities are performed exceptionally well, they can provide the organization with a clear competitive advantage. Sourcing strategy can be leveraged to ensure supply in times of strong demand. Cost reduction activities that examine the benefits of long-term contracts and collaborative product development with suppliers can add savings directly to the bottom line and create a significant competitive edge. Effectively implemented strategies in areas that are consumer focused (such as price and technology), clearly aid the organization's ability to increase market share and revenue. Simplifying or eliminating tactical procurement processes and reducing parts and the number of suppliers, as well as employing a process improvement approach to all activities, adds even more value to the procurement process.

Can these activities lead the organization's efforts to implement its strategic vision? You bet—especially when they are executed superbly.

Strategic Planning Methods

Planning should begin with an assessment of the organization's current and future supply needs. This usually requires gathering a detailed knowledge of your overall spending trends—by industry, supplier, customer or function, and transactional volume—as well as the priorities of your customers. You will generally want to focus your external efforts in areas that account for significant spending or encompass high risk while directing your internal efforts to processes and constraints, workload, and customer satisfaction. This information will assist you in narrowing the scope to areas where you will be able to add maximum value.

Once you have identified potential areas for added value, you will want to determine the objectives and metrics that will produce a successful outcome and the resources that may be required to achieve it. It serves little purpose to develop unachievable objectives or objectives outside the practical reach of available or potentially available resources.

Organizations often use a process known as *SWOT analysis* to assist them in developing strategic plans. SWOT is an acronym for strengths, weaknesses, opportunities, and threats.

Strengths Internal resources such as key personnel, supplier partnerships, distribution channels, patents, branding, funding, low cost profiles, and any other competitive differentiators.

Weaknesses Internal shortcomings that can open the door to competitions including poor cash flow, high cost structure and, in general, the absence of any of the strengths just listed.

Opportunities External factors that can provide additional revenue, profit, and growth. Opportunities are found in new markets, new products, and the development of new technologies.

Threats   External factors that can work to the detriment of the organization, such as rising interest rates that affect funding, a declining customer base, increased competition, international trade barriers, and new regulations.

Contingency Planning

Contingency plans are usually associated with a specific project or situation and set out a series of actions to take in case of unanticipated circumstances that threaten to produce a negative outcome. Contingency planning addresses both strategic and tactical elements of the organization's operations. In routine procurement operations, for example, a commonly employed contingency plan provides for alternative sourcing in the event that a primary source is unable to meet its commitments.

Since developing contingency plans can become a time-wasting activity—there's little payback because you won't use the plan unless something goes wrong—the strategic aspect lies in the development of risk analysis and risk mitigation criteria so that contingency plans are restricted to high risk, high impact areas only.

Refer to the decision tree model covered in Chapter 14, "Strategic Procurement Planning" for what-if scenarios.

Typically, risk mitigation strategies involve developing alternative sources of supply or production capacity, holding safety inventory, forming partnerships and joint ventures, and closely monitoring market conditions for important trend signals.

Decision Making

As part of the strategic planning process, you will want to make or coordinate a number of decisions relating to the overall plan. You will need to determine individual or team responsibilities for specific actions that will evolve from the plan, what resources are available and where others will come from; timeframes for completing actions, metrics, and reporting; and who has authority to approve the plan or deviate from the plan.

Planning Horizons

Strategic plans have traditional horizons, with timeframes for short-term plans in the range of one to two years and long-term planning covering three to ten years. This contrasts with tactical or operational planning, which covers periods from 30 days to one year.

Supply Management Strategies

Supply planning and supply management strategies evolve primarily from the long-term needs of the organization as it responds to external factors. These strategies often focus on how best to manage suppliers and the various elements in the supply base and how to formulate a consistent approach to managing inventories. In developing supply management strategies, you should evaluate a number of specific conditions at various levels, including:

- Capacity, technology, market dispersion, and business trends affecting the industry
- Materials, complexity, and supply issues affecting the commodity
- Purchasing trends, supply base flexibility, and the level of standardization affecting the buying organization

You should then look at the strategies you may want to use in developing your supply base. These could include, for example:

- Supplier consolidation
- Requirements consolidation
- Contracts
- Alliances and partnerships
- Competitive bidding
- Supplier development
- Supplier Managed Inventory (SMI)
- Consignment
- Negotiations

One methodology for developing strategies from these elements is to link your approach to individual suppliers with the supply conditions observed in the industry, the commodity, or your organization. One method of analyzing this is through a supply positioning matrix such as the one discussed next.

Supply Positioning Strategies

Supply positioning analysis is a commonly used tool for taking the key areas of spending by cost and associated risk, dividing them into categories and formulating an approach to each of them. While there are many ways to look at purchases within the context of this approach, as shown in Figure 15.1, there are four common categories of spending: Strategic, Tactical, Commodity, and Incidental. The matrix also shows typical items each category contains and a brief synopsis of the kind of strategy that might be employed.

Let's define low risk items as those commonly capable of being substituted, such as off-the-shelf items like copy paper or interchangeable parts and tools such as capacitors or screwdrivers and pliers. High risk items are those in limited supply, those with critical quality or technology features, or those requiring high levels of customization. From a cost perspective, high cost categories are goods and services that account for a certain percentage of spending (for example, above five percent), whereas low cost categories fall below that level.

The Strategic category represents the highest cost, highest risk items, such as capital equipment, customized direct materials, and operational software (to cite a few examples). The strategy can be characterized as requiring the organization to closely manage the supply chain by actions such as forming alliances and partnerships with suppliers, developing long-term contracts, and managing the products and services through teams and with cross-functional input.

FIGURE 15.1   Supply positioning analysis matrix

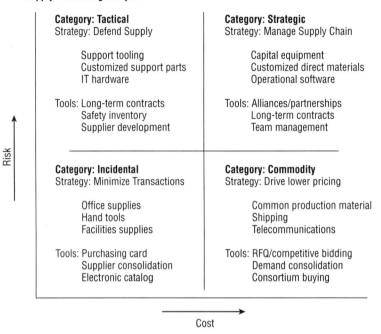

The Commodity category represents goods and services that, in aggregate, account for large amounts of spending but because of their interchangeable, off-the-shelf nature represent low risk. This category includes items such as common production material, freight and product shipping, and telecommunications. The tools commonly used for this category include, for example, competitive bidding, consolidation of demand, and consortium buying.

For the Tactical category, composed of elements such as support tooling, customized support parts, and IT hardware, the primary strategy is to ensure (or defend) supply using long-term contracts and safety inventory and developing supplier capabilities (as well as alternative suppliers).

The Incidental category represents low-cost, low-risk items such as office supplies, hand tools, and facilities supplies that can be purchased virtually anywhere. The strategy here might be to minimize the transactions associated with such purchases, removing the workload and associated overhead costs from the Purchasing Department. This might be accomplished by using purchasing cards or electronic catalogs or by supplier consolidation or complete outsourcing.

Keep in mind that no single strategy can be applied universally to all situations and under all circumstances, so a strategy that is effectively employed in a particular procurement segment may be ineffective in another.

Commodity Strategies

Categorizing purchases by their respective commodities often helps to develop a uniform strategy to manage multiple products that have closely related commodity attributes. This can enable the Purchasing Department to employ an individual with specific expertise in the commodity (also known as a subject matter expert [SME]) who can focus primarily on managing a strategy for that specific group of suppliers. The added value of this approach is that the organization's management is given the opportunity to recognize the discipline required to establish specific commodity excellence in the procurement operation.

Developing Departmental Goals and Objectives

How the Purchasing Department intends to support organizational procurement needs (and its goals) is often expressed in the form of a mission or charter statement. This statement, to a large extent, reflects the approach the Purchasing Department takes in helping to meet organizational objectives and is fundamentally reflected in its choice of goals cited.

In this section, we'll look at how the department's mission or charter is typically defined and how it is used to formulate procurement goals and objectives.

Defining the Department's Mission

The department's mission is generally expressed as an adjunct to a vision statement and is often written in the present tense to indicate a condition of being. The vision statement serves as the guiding principle for answering questions such as, "How are we different from other organizations?" or "What value do we add?" The department's mission statement then flows from its vision and guides the development of its goals and objectives.

In the following simplified examples, observe how the mission statement evolves from the organization's vision and how it applies that vision:

Vision: Our organization focuses on supporting organizational strategies that maximize value to our customers.

Mission: Our organization's mission is to obtain the greatest value in the acquisition of goods and services while ensuring the integrity and accountability of our processes.

Formulating Goals and Objectives

To carry the progression further, the department's specific objectives are linked to its mission statement, ensuring that the purpose and intent of the vision is translated into action. The Purchasing Department's objective can then be expressed in terms of general activity statements. Following are some examples of possible objectives.

Objectives

- Reduce the overall cost of purchases by selecting the most qualified suppliers.
- Achieve maximum value in each acquisition.
- Support corporate directives to provide accountability.
- Minimize risk by ensuring alternative sources of supply for critical items.
- Hire and train staff to develop a world-class procurement practice.
- Actively promote strong supplier relationships.
- Encourage the use of small, minority owned, and disadvantaged businesses.

Objectives can be translated into quantifiable and measurable goals as part of an annual plan. The preceding objectives might appear as specific goals, as listed next.

Goals

- Reduce the average unit cost of direct materials by 6 percent.
- Develop a consignment program for spare parts that will eliminate 90 percent of current inventory.
- Report all take or pay purchases.
- Develop secondary sources for all "A" category supplies.
- Establish a training program to qualify 10 members of the staff as Certified Purchasing Managers.
- Hold quarterly business reviews with all key suppliers on the approved supplier list.
- Increase the use of small, minority owned, and disadvantaged businesses by 50 percent.

Keys to Successful Planning

Several aspects related to the development of objectives and goals must be considered to ensure successful outcomes. Some of those commonly noted include measurability, priority, and alignment.

Measurability   Metrics need to be established so that the value of each goal to the organization can be clearly shown. By quantifying goals, you will be more able to demonstrate your department's effectiveness and measure the effectiveness of individual team members. Remember the adage, "What gets measured gets done." Notice how the goals in the preceding section were developed with built-in measures that are quantified.

Priority   Competing priorities can defeat accomplishment; that is, they can interfere with one another to the extent that none are completely successful. Therefore, it is critical that you establish priorities for the goals based on their potential impact for the organization, with goals that produce the most value receiving the greatest organizational resources.

Alignment   It is important that the process for developing the Purchasing Department's goals considers integration with the organization's overall goals. The importance of aligning with the goals and objectives of other departments is obvious, and you will want to avoid the appearance of "pulling the cart" in the wrong direction. This means that the priorities established by the organization should also be reflected in the priorities established by your department.

WARNING When establishing goals, it is also important to consider potential conflict between them. Conflicting goals can lead to counterproductive internal competition for available resources. This is an excellent way to ensure that nothing gets accomplished.

Formulating Operational Policies and Procedures

Operational policies and procedures are developed within the organization to ensure that standard methods are employed across the enterprise to accomplish goals and objectives. By using standard methods, communicating policies and procedures becomes much easier, and better control of the organization's resources is achieved. This helps safeguard the effectiveness of the organization's efforts to achieve success.

In this section, we will review the elements of formulating operational policies and procedures and how they are structured effectively.

Management Control

Management control is a mechanism used by the organization to achieve stated goals and objectives. Controls can be categorized according to the timing of their occurrence.

Pre-operational Controls   These controls are established in advance of the specific operational activity. They include organizational policies, standard operating procedures (SOPs), strategic plans, budgets, and a variety of operational and contingency plans. *Pre-operational controls* govern the tactical manner in which activities are intended to be conducted.

Operational Controls   *Operational control* mechanisms are intended to manage activities as they occur. Typically, they will include quality and inventory control, status reports, *Environmental Health and Safety (EHS)* monitoring, and security.

Post-operational Controls   Audits are the most common *post-operational control* mechanism. Designed to measure how activities were actually conducted, they provide a variance feedback mechanism to assist in root cause analysis and foster continuous improvement. Post-operational controls also include performance reports and periodic reviews of processes and are used for providing input to management to help determine areas for further process improvement.

Workload Distribution

The structure and distribution of purchasing workload and responsibilities, while varying from organization to organization, typically responds to the nature of the working environment. You will find one type of structure prevalent in large manufacturing organizations and another in small to midsized service organizations and still others in governmental organizations of various sizes.

Commonly used organizational work structures fall into a number of categories, as listed next.

Rotational   A rotational method generally assigns work to buyers on a random basis to provide active cross-training and achieve greater commodity and domain expertise across the staff. Its goal is typically to provide workload flexibility within the buying organization.

User Department   Buyers are often assigned to specific departments within the organization to focus commodity expertise in servicing a specific set of customer needs. While this often requires redundant skills development within the Purchasing Department, the method can be key to proactive servicing of internal customers such as sales and marketing.

Supplier   Duties are sometimes divided by suppliers to enhance supplier management and overall control objectives.

Commodity or Category   Commonly used in larger manufacturing environments, this workload division focuses individual responsibilities according to commodity, industry, or category of goods and services (such as capital equipment or Maintenance Repair and Operations [MRO]). The intended result is to leverage commodity and domain expertise in specific areas to gain efficient use of talent.

Type   Work can often be divided by the nature of the purchasing process itself, with contracts going to a specific group, inventory items to another, and incidental purchases to still another.

Transactional Volume   In some environments, the tactical transaction workload created by purchase orders and inventory account adjustments becomes an issue. To maintain departmental efficiency, work is assigned to balance individual workloads and thereby reduce cycle time.

Workload Tracking

Most organizations today rely on computerized systems such as Enterprise Resource Planning (ERP) to determine the electronic routing of requisitions to specific buyers, the status of individual orders, cycle times, and buyer transactional productivity. While in the past requisition approval was recorded on paper forms and PO activity was recorded on individual buyers' logs, today the level of tracking sophistication in computerized applications generally dispenses with the need to manually record and monitor these activities.

Organizational Structure

When purchasing departments span multiple geographical sites or divisions, questions regarding the degree to which control should be centralized generally arise. While each organization views its issues separately, there are a number of considerations that may be taken into account universally.

Centralized versus Decentralized

In the centralized organization, all major purchasing is controlled from one central location. In the decentralized organization, the major purchasing decisions are made at the divisional or business unit level. Many hybrid versions are also common, where responsibilities are shared to one extent or another or where broad policy is developed centrally but implemented locally.

In general, centralized procurement is more commonly used when the need for control is stringent or when the purchased products or services are used by many groups within the organization. Conversely, decentralized purchasing occurs most often when divisions are engaged in dissimilar operations and purchase widely divergent goods and services. Each method has advantages in specific situations. The advantages of centralization include the following.

Pricing   Leverages larger volumes for price improvements.

Expertise   Volume enables the development of specialized areas of commodity and domain expertise.

Operational Cost   Greater purchasing efficiencies can be gained through automation in a centralized operation. There is also less likelihood that tactical tasks such as reporting and filing will be duplicated.

Supplier Consolidation   Fewer suppliers are required when purchasing from central locations and when purchases from several locations can be consolidated.

Terms   In addition to lower prices, centralized purchasing can leverage increased volumes to gain more-advantageous terms and conditions such as consignment inventory, freight discounts, or supplier payment terms.

The advantages of decentralization include the following.

Timing   Purchases can be better timed when made closer to the source of the requirement.

Communication   Improved contact with the internal customer generally results in improved support and responsiveness.

Control   Local management of the procurement generally improves control and supplier performance.

Ownership   Local procurement results in greater buyer ownership of problems and issues.

Reengineering

Reengineering is the broad process of examining and altering an existing business process and reconstituting it in an improved form. In purchasing, reengineering efforts generally focus on automating the requisitioning system and ordering process as a means of improving responsiveness and reducing ordering-cycle time. As a result, there are significant reductions in inventory levels and greater support for just-in-time operations.

Process mapping is employed to reduce total cycle time by tracking and recording each step in the ordering process. This provides a detailed analysis of each step in the work flow and systems, defining the relationships between each of their elements. Once mapped, the opportunities to eliminate tasks that add no value or waste time become apparent. Mapping also reveals steps that are currently sequential but that can often be performed in parallel, thus further reducing cycle time.

Reengineering also allows more detailed analysis of spending patterns which, in turn, enables greater supplier consolidation and reduced pricing. It has also led to a more disciplined approach to continuous process improvement, eliminating activities that do not add value.

Preparing Departmental Reports

Reports are an essential means of communication in most organizations. In a variety of formats—written, oral, or a combination as in a PowerPoint presentation—reports inform management of the department's progress toward its goals and the status of current tactical and strategic activities. The reporting process is also an important tool that can call attention to the department's contributions to the overall objectives of the organization. Significant achievements, especially those that can be measured and that add value to the organization's bottom line, can be a powerful tool for obtaining resources when they are needed, so it is important that you communicate your department's success with management. You can view this communication not so much as a matter of tooting your own horn as sharing the added value of the purchasing organization.

Identifying Relevant Activities

Most often, activities that are relevant to reporting are those closely linked to the department's current goals and objectives. While these, of course, vary from organization to organization, there are several areas that are of common interest.

Spending and Savings

Negotiated savings and cost avoidance are key areas of interest to most senior managers, especially to the extent that they apply to their own operating budgets. Your report structure should always acknowledge this fact by highlighting both accomplishments and areas that have not been as productive as planned.

As you report spending and savings, you will want to keep in mind some of the following points:

- Metrics are vital. Be certain your numbers are meaningful, timely, and correct.

- The Finance Department is generally charged with the responsibility for reporting budget performance. Coordinate your spending reports with its staff as a means of substantiating your numbers.

- Savings are usually generated by a cross-functional team's effort and, not just your department's.

- In most cases, the savings belong to your internal customer through the budgeting process. Allow your customer the option of reporting it first.

- Distinguish between actual savings and cost avoidance. The former may affect budget performance while the latter may not.

- Easing of specifications that result in savings should be credited to the group doing the specification review.
- Consider savings from internal productivity improvements as *soft dollars* that typically do not impact the bottom line unless there is some accompanying reduction in head count.

To provide additional perspective, consider grouping your savings and spending reports according to the category of spending: Strategic, Commodity, Tactical, or Incidental. You might also want to highlight more-specific areas of savings such as indirect or MRO, direct materials, capital equipment, or inventoried materials or services. Be careful to keep your audience in mind and provide detail according to individual needs and interests. Chances are, for example, that the Chief Financial Officer will already know the extent of the savings and may have only a casual interest in how it was accomplished.

Acquisition Plans

As part of reporting on future activities, you should consider highlighting significant planned acquisitions and noting their current status. Specifically, cover any important concerns you might have regarding constraints or challenges that may affect the outcome of major acquisitions.

Supplier Relationships

Continuous improvement is the hallmark of a successfully managed supply base. Key measures for reporting include quality performance, delivery performance (cycle time), service levels, and cost. These should be reported graphically, showing relevant trends for easy comprehension. Figure 15.2 provides an example of a trend analysis chart for the quality performance of a supplier.

FIGURE 15.2 Quality performance trend chart

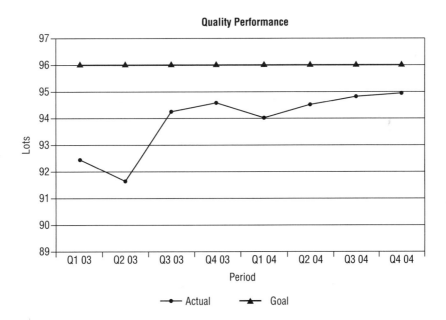

In addition to statistical data, you will want to present information from the supply community that will impact the performance of internal users, such as planned technology releases, mergers and acquisitions, change of key personnel, and benchmarks of your competition. This information is often not readily available to internal customers when they have little contact with the supplier.

Selecting and Managing Data

In selecting information to report, you must also consider how you will gather data and manage the systems that provide it. While there are no specific criteria available to define a set of measures universally and no best way to measure performance, you should consider some basic criteria for selecting data:

- Make it easily accessible—you won't want to invest huge amounts of time gathering basic information.

- It should be well-maintained so that you can be confident it is accurate and up-to-date.

- It should be used by others in the organization to avoid lengthy discussions on its meaning.

- Make sure you can quantify value by using metrics to describe performance.

- Benchmark with other similar organizations to select goals and provide performance comparisons between your organization and others in the same sector.

- It should relate to goals and objectives—show how performance supports the organization's goals.

- You should highlight key accomplishments to avoid overwhelming the audience with minutia.

Methods of Presentation

Having excellent material available is of little value unless you can present it properly. From this perspective, there are two considerations: the method you will use to convey the information and the type and level of detail of the information you will present. The guiding principle to selecting both is to understand your audience and know where their interests lie.

Presentation Formats

Presentations can be written or oral or a combination of both. Following are some of the basic principles you should keep in mind when preparing them.

Written Presentations   Written presentations can take many forms—statistical reports, PowerPoint presentations, charts, graphs, e-mail, memos, or formal letters. Your choice depends upon organizational preference and the nature of your audience. Some points to keep in mind while preparing a written presentation include the following:

- The written document must be well organized. This will likely depend upon the material being presented. An executive summary is a common way to present summarized information about a specific subject or project. (See the sidebar "Elements of an Executive

Summary" for more details.) Ideally, the summary provides a brief synopsis in a structured format that guides a reader to the major elements of review.

- The written document should be clear and easy to understand. Simplicity can be accomplished by limiting the subject matter to one or two key points and by introducing these at the beginning of the presentation. Everything that follows should readily tie back in to the introductory points. Obviously, you will want to avoid the use of unfamiliar technical terms or acronyms—or at least define them as they are introduced.

- Written documents may contain large amounts of technical information, as in the case of a statement of work used in an RFP. In such documents, it may be advisable to include a glossary of terms or a definitions section so that your readers will have a common reference point.

Elements of an Executive Summary

There are some basic elements that should be included in every written summary so that you can ensure the majority of the reader's questions will be addressed:

Background

Briefly describe the history related to this project or contract and explain what led to the determination of its need or why it is under consideration at this time.

Known Risks and Threats

Outline specific elements that require special care or attention.

Prior Experience

Reference other similar projects or contracts, how they were handled, and their current status or outcome.

Key Facts

List key facts describing the current situation. Possible questions you may want to answer:

What is generating the need?

What is the scope/spend of the project?

Who is involved and what are their roles?

Who are the suppliers and what are their market positions?

Are there competing proposals?

Who are the internal customers and what are their issues?

What are the critical dates? Milestones?

Opportunities

Describe the program's objectives and outline what might be accomplished by the successful completion of the contract or project. Some examples include:

Cost savings

Improved quality

Greater capacity

Strategic competitive advantage

Better service or customer satisfaction

Faster time to market

Ensured supply

Alternative Courses of Action

Alternative courses of action outline the different options available to achieve the objectives. For example:

Develop new source of supply

Competitive bidding event

Revisit specifications to reduce cost

Under each potential alternative, list the following:

Known risks

Pros and cons

Cost estimates

Recommendation

Submit the alternative you believe provides the greatest opportunity to achieve the objective. Briefly describe why this alternative is best. For example:

"The first option outlined has a greater possibility of success because it leverages the competitive marketplace to provide the lowest possible price for the existing statement of work."

Anticipated Outcome

In a brief narrative, describe the results your recommendation will achieve. For example:

"This project will result in savings of approximately $240,000 against the budget. It will help mitigate our risk by combining several existing purchase orders into a single contract."

Threats and Potential Negative Outcomes

Outline potential conditions or events that could negatively impact your desired results. For example:

> A change in market conditions
>
> Schedule slippage
>
> Material shortages
>
> Unproven technology
>
> Quality issues

Defense

Describe what steps can be taken to minimize these threats and reduce the risk of potential negative impacts. For example:

> Dual sourcing
>
> Penalty clause in contract
>
> Liquidated damages

Oral Presentations   Oral presentations can be extremely demanding since you must deal with the presentation format and your manner of presenting, as well as the material itself. However, there are a number of methods you can use to help make the presentation successful:

- Begin the presentation by stating your objectives. Are you asking for approval of a project proposal? Are you conducting a review or briefing to update those in attendance?

- Build your presentation by clearly linking your purpose with organizational goals and objectives. State the objective you are addressing and the solution you propose. Demonstrate the efficacy of your proposed solution with solid reasoning.

- Thoroughly understand your material. Questions will arise during any presentation and you must be prepared to answer them. Avoid getting flustered if you can't answer; simply offer to follow up later with the information requested.

- Thoroughly understand your audience and how the information you are presenting might be received. How much do they know about your subject?

- If you are presenting new ideas or concepts, clearly establish the background without being overly detailed. Try to relate the new ideas to specific problems faced by the organization.

- Pay attention to your appearance and demeanor. Dress appropriately and deliver your presentation with confidence, avoiding poor posture and mumbled speech. If you are uncomfortable speaking in public, consider taking a class or joining an organization such as Toastmasters that will provide experience and feedback. Above all, demonstrate your enthusiasm for the topic.

- Use appropriate and easy-to-understand language and avoid the use of acronyms. Be concrete and deliver solid facts. Tie accomplishments to backup data without over-reliance on unimportant details. Use the present tense and include action verbs as much as possible.

- When presenting PowerPoint or other graphical information, be sure to keep your slides simple and uncluttered. One rule of thumb suggests no more than five bullets on each slide, but even two can be excessive if they are totally unrelated to one another. Similarly, do not try to cram graphs and charts together in a way that could confuse your audience. It might be best to limit each slide to one main point and to use more slides if you are in doubt. Try to supplement the slides with additional data and commentary. Reading slides verbatim is a sure way to put your audience to sleep.

Responding to Audits

An audit is usually an independent review and examination of records and activities to assess the adequacy of Purchasing Department controls. It determines if purchases have been properly authorized and if awards to suppliers have been made correctly and fairly. Audits also seek to verify that procedures are being followed correctly and that organizational policy is being observed in the acquisition of goods and services. Some audits look at the performance of the Purchasing Department in relation to others in the industry—for example, are prices being paid for common goods in line with what would normally be expected—as well as the performance of its staff. Audits are conducted by financial organizations, government agencies, and international quality certification bodies (such as the ISO).

Audits are best prepared for in advance by routinely following established processes and procedures (not at the last minute when the auditors are in the lobby). In all cases, the purchasing manager is responsible to ensure compliance from the purchasing staff.

Validating Current Processes

Planning for the audit requires specific knowledge of the standard used in the process being audited and how that process will be evaluated. Aside from the specific focus of the audit—financial, quality, or process control—most audits are geared to determining how well existing activities conform to written documentation established by the organization and legal requirements established by legislation and regulatory agencies.

Depending on their general purpose, audits are conducted by internal or external resources.

- An *internal audit* is an appraisal activity within the organization using internal staff that is used to verify the reliability of accounting records, determine the proper expenditure of funds and the safeguarding of company assets, and determine whether management's policies are being carried out.

- An *external audit* is an appraisal conducted by a third party, usually for the same purposes as internal audits. In the case of a financial audit, the third party may be the organization's accounting firm; in the case of ISO 9000:2000, QS-9000, ISO/TS 16949, there are specially trained and designated auditors for hire. Recent legislation such as Sarbanes-Oxley will likely create additional audit requirements.

Some of the more common processes that will be observed include:

- Proper authorization and approval processes for contracts, purchases, and payments
- Documentation of competitive bids and awards
- Effective monitoring of supplier selection and performance
- Planning and forecasting activities
- Inventory management
- Adherence to proper receiving and inspection processes
- Effective selection of transportation methods
- Audit trails for invoices
- Internal customer satisfaction
- Tax coding of POs
- Proper training of the purchasing staff

Audits themselves generally progress according to a recognized routine. There is typically an initial meeting between the auditors and the managers in the department to review the process. The auditor will expect that a specific process owner will be assigned to the audit team to collect documentation as it is requested and to find the correct staff member to answer specific process questions. Following the audit, there is usually a closing meeting during which some of the preliminary findings may be disclosed and dates established for area(s) cited for corrective action. This is followed some time later by an official audit finding report to the organization's management.

Responding to Corrective Actions

In its final report, the auditors will point out areas where significant deficiencies exist and other areas where improvements may be needed. When auditors find instances of significant nonconformance to processes, typically a corrective action request (CAR) will be issued. The CAR will require a response that outlines what actions are being taken to immediately contain the nonconformance and what actions will be taken to ensure that it will not reoccur. Generally, these issues have previously been discussed in the closing meeting with the auditors, so you will likely be prepared to take action immediately.

At the basic level, corrective actions should resolve the immediate problem and prevent the problem from reoccurring within the organization. The process should also define the individuals responsible for the actions, and the timetable for completion. Typically, the corrective action process includes the following steps:

1. Identify the problem.
2. Investigate to identify the root cause.
3. Define the solution.
4. Implement the solution.

5. Document the solution.

6. Communicate the solution.

7. Evaluate the effectiveness of the solution.

Conflict Resolution

Audits often uncover internal conflicts that have gone unnoticed by management but that can seriously hamper the organization's tactical performance. They may develop from a failure to clearly assign responsibility for performing a specific function when one party feels that another party should be doing the job or one group feels another group has not provided sufficient information to ensure the process completes properly. Regardless of the circumstances, as a manager, you will be responsible for resolving such conflicts.

There is no widely established method for resolving conflicts, but certainly whatever process you establish will require a fact-finding initiative and an opportunity for each individual involved to be heard. Once the facts and points of view are established, a logical approach can be proposed in order to obtain buy-in from all of those concerned. If this process doesn't produce results, it may be possible to benchmark how other organizations handle similar issues and from that analysis draw a course of action.

Having established an initial resolution, you will want to follow up at regular intervals to ensure that it is working as intended. Make corrections as though the process were one of continuous improvement.

Evaluating Purchasing Department Performance

Effective performance requires continuous evaluation and improvement to ensure that the department is meeting organizational objectives and expectations. While many objectives are formalized by departmental goals, new expectations will arise as conditions change. As a result, you will need to develop relevant assessments of your department's performance in terms of how well you are achieving established goals *and* how well you are able to respond to evolving situations.

Purpose of the Performance Evaluation

Evaluating purchasing performance on a regular basis serves to assess the department's effectiveness. It helps determine if the department is contributing as planned to the goals and objectives of the organization and to validate that it is on track to reach its own planned objectives. It also evaluates the manager's performance in leading the department and deploying its talent.

Regular performance evaluation also identifies areas for improvement and provides a framework for continuous improvement activities.

Performing the Evaluation

While there does not appear to be a standard method for evaluating the Purchasing Department's performance specifically, the following several actions are important elements that apply to most organizations in general.

Analyze Objectives   As an initial point of departure, the department's key objectives need to be clearly identified so that functional activities can be specifically tied back to them. Activities and accomplishments can thus be evaluated in terms of how well they serve the department's primary objectives. For example, if the organization's stated goal is performance quality and technical leadership, the Purchasing Department needs to find and measure suppliers who lead their commodity peers in high quality and advanced technology.

Determine Adequacy of Metrics   How well do the measures chosen for the department's goals actually demonstrate its performance? Naturally, measures must reflect the true performance of the department in relation to its goals and in relation to the goals of the organization. For example, reporting cost savings alone does not demonstrate added value when the organization is committed to technological leadership.

Validate Evaluation Criteria   As part of the evaluation, the criteria you are using should be vetted for its applicability to the department's goals. The next section describes this in more detail.

Evaluation and Appraisal Criteria

The primary criterion for evaluating any department's performance is the degree to which that department adds value to the organization. Looking at it another way, this can mean determining how effective your group is in relation to the assets being deployed—staff, training, systems, and support—and how effective it *could* be in comparison to similar operations elsewhere.

   The following sections discuss some of the key factors that are likely to be addressed in performance measures.

Cost Reduction and Cost Containment

Cost reduction and cost containment are measures of overall savings and include the following:

- Savings due to negotiated contracts or purchasing initiatives
- Value of additional benefits that are negotiated, such as longer payment terms, extended warranties, or consignment inventory
- Cost reductions due to competitive bidding or use of alternative products
- Savings developed from improved supplier quality and lower loss rates
- Savings as a contribution to the bottom line

Supplier Performance

Supplier performance measures supplier support by assessing the following:

- Quality improvement and performance relative to goals
- On-time delivery performance

- Responsiveness to service requests
- Flexibility to accommodate late scheduling
- Favorable return policy
- Overall reliability

Supplier Development

Supplier development measures how effectively the supply community is leveraged by looking at the following:

- Formation of supplier alliances for competitive advantage
- Identification of new sources for key goods and services
- Supplier consolidation
- Increased use of small, minority, and women-owned or disadvantaged businesses

Internal Procurement Systems and Processes

Internal procurement systems and processes measure the efficiency of the Purchasing Department by determining:

- The volume of procurement transactions conducted electronically
- The volume of procurement transactions conducted through other transaction methods such as the purchasing card
- The volume of transactions conducted through aggregated contracts
- The reduction in transaction and inventory management costs

Internal Customer Satisfaction

Internal customer satisfaction is usually determined through customer surveys that measure the following:

- Degree of satisfaction with service levels and response times
- Level of satisfaction with purchasing processes
- Perceived value of purchased goods and services for the money spent
- Perceived degree of effectiveness of procurement decision-making and authority lines
- Overall satisfaction with purchasing systems and processes

Benchmarking Performance

Taken in isolation, there is no way to substantiate the adequacy of any department's goals. To better assess the validity of your goals (and their accompanying metrics) you should consider developing benchmarks with other organizations in your industry. Benchmarking is the process of comparing the performance of other organizations with that of your own. It is often accomplished using data from industry organizations or by engaging consultants to gather the information independently.

Administering Departmental Budgets

In most cases, purchasing managers are held responsible for the fiscal budgets of their departments. A budget is simply a financial plan outlining anticipated expenditures for a specified period of time, typically one fiscal or calendar year. It is detailed by the nature of the expenditure—salaries, office supplies, subscriptions, and so on—usually broken down by an accounting *cost code*.

The Purchasing Department is also often held responsible for the part of the budgets affecting other departments that it may manage, such as inventory, direct material, and some outside services such as travel services. These expenditures, while perhaps not directly charged to the Purchasing Department, will be included in its goals and objectives and in evaluations of its performance.

Budget Functions

Budgets serve a number of specific functions. Let's look briefly at just a few of them:

- A budget creates a financial baseline that can be used to measure actual results as a way of evaluating performance.

- It forces an organization to carefully consider the expected resources that will be required to meet the business plan goals.

- It keeps managers informed and fosters improved coordination within the organization.

- It can be used to reflect priorities for the organization and convert them into the appropriate resources required to achieve those priorities.

- It can be used to preapprove specific spending and monitor certain types of spending (such as capital equipment) that are not aggregated into operational departments or sections.

- As an operational tool, budgets can highlight potential funding allocation problems in sufficient time to take corrective actions.

Budgeting Processes

Budgeting processes vary a great deal from one organization to another, but there are a number of common elements that will likely be found in all of them. Budgets in some organizations are developed from the top down; that is, funding is allocated to each department or section based on anticipated revenue and a pre-established formula for dividing up funding allocation. In other organizations, budgets are developed from the bottom up; that is, the budget is initially established at the departmental level and then reviewed, adjusted, and approved by senior management.

General Budget Types

There are numerous types of budgets commonly used by organizations. However, in general, these can be described in terms of two major categories: operating budgets and capital expenditure budgets.

Operating Budgets   *Operating budgets* present the financial plan for each cost center during the budget period and reflect day-to-day operating activities involving both revenues and expenses. In the case of the Purchasing Department, revenues are not applicable so only expenses will be listed, although at some point a relationship between cost savings or cost avoidance (or volumes) and operational activities can be used for evaluation.

Capital Expenditures Budgets   *Capital Expenditures* budgets present plans for the acquisition (or disposal) of major fixed capital assets. Typically, the Purchasing Department will be concerned with equipment rather than real estate or other financial holdings.

Other Budget Types

As adjuncts to these general categories, budgets can also be developed for a number of other purposes:

- *Cash flow budgets* are used for determining the availability of cash so that the timing of major expenditures can be coordinated.

- *Project budgets* track expenditures by specific project so that profit (or loss) can be attributed to a particular contract. These are commonly used in construction or in the military contracting areas.

- *Zero-based budgets* do not rely on prior years' expenditures or budgets; instead they start fresh from a zero base. As a result, each item must be justified separately, usually in terms of the organization's current goals. Zero-based budgets are often tied to a bottom-up budgeting approach so that they are generated at the operational level.

- *Flexible budgets* are based on a set of revenue and expense projections at various volume levels. The cost allowances for each expense item are thus able to vary as income or production varies.

- *Open-to-buy budgets* are used primarily in retail operations to control inventory restocking. Funds are allocated to each budgeting period and released based on a planned investment schedule.

Budgets versus Forecasts

Budgets invariably change. They are commonly derailed for a number of reasons; for example, often customer demand changes or technology becomes obsolete and needs to be replaced. Sometimes unexpected changes in the economy or the global political situation cause prices to rise or fall.

It is virtually impossible to accurately predict the future, regardless of what systems, tools, or models are employed. For this reason, many organizations also develop forecasts throughout the budget execution period. The purpose of a forecast is to continually update the expected results for the period based upon the latest information available. Forecasts then get tied back to an adjusted budget and a new profit/loss expectation is established. This is why publicly traded companies (and the analysts that follow them) so often focus on quarterly results—they are based on updated forecasts and are therefore more accurate.

Working with Operational Forms

Forms are used extensively within the purchasing function, and they will often play a key role in the processes and systems that you use. Traditionally, forms were designed to be completed by hand, but they are increasingly being automated, and it is just a matter of time before paper is no longer used at all. However, you must continue to be prepared to design, use, file, and store a great variety of forms as part of routine operations. It is perhaps symbolic that your very life both begins with a form—the birth certificate—and ends with a form—the death certificate.

Functional Purpose of Forms

The use of forms helps standardize information and provide a framework for communication. Forms function as records of activities or the status of a set of conditions, such as inventory reconciliations, and so generally demand a uniform approach. This uniformity aids in reducing the time it takes to report routine actions and provides a basis for summarizing data that can be used in consolidated reports. Forms also serve as written documentation for audit trails and are often used as legal records.

Commonly Used Forms

Purchasing organizations employ a number of processes that are documented through the use of forms. Varying in design from organization to organization, they apply, nevertheless, to a fairly standard set of functions. Listed here are those you might find commonly assigned to your department (in either paper or electronic formats).

Purchase Requisition (PR) or Material Requisition (MR)   A purchase requisition (PR) or *material requisition (MR)* is completed by the user to request materials and services ordered from suppliers through the Purchasing Department. It is also traditionally used to document approval authority by recording the signatures of those authorizing the purchase.

Purchase Order (PO)   A contract used to convey requirements and authorization to the supplier. POs usually contain a standard set of terms and conditions, as well as a description of the goods or services and quantity ordered, the price paid, and how and when the goods or services should be shipped or completed.

Receiver or Receiving Form   A *receiver form* is used to document the receipt of goods and notify users of their receipt. Receiving documents are typically submitted with the shipment (as a *packing slip* and/or *bill of lading*) and include information directly from the original purchase order. Receiving documents may be used to record the condition of the shipment when it arrives. Receiving documents are also used as part of the traditional three-way match to authorize invoice payment.

Inspection Documents   Used by the Quality Control Department (when it exists) to record the quality of the material being received and to note any nonconformity or rejection. These documents supplement the receiving document in most cases when they are used.

Traveling Requisitions   *Traveling requisitions* contain standard information (such as descriptions and part numbers) and are used to request repetitive purchases or the release of production materials under a blanket order from the supplier. They are also used to request material from storeroom stock.

Change Orders   Similar to purchase requisitions but used only for changes to (or cancellations of) existing orders.

Return Authorization (RA) or Material Return Form   A *return authorization (RA)* is used to document the required return of materials to the supplier. Typically, a supplier will issue an RA number that is recorded internally as the supplier's authorization to ship back the product.

Check Request   A *check request* is a form used by many organizations to request payment by the Accounting Department to a supplier when no purchase order exists.

Contracts   Often exist in standardized format but vary widely in their nature and use from organization to organization. The Non-disclosure Agreement (NDA) is one of the more frequently used contract forms in most environments.

Designing and Managing Forms

Despite the fact that forms are increasingly becoming automated as elements in computerized systems, you'll still find the need to design the occasional form to customize it to your organization's needs. For those instances, here is a set of guidelines for a well-designed form you may want to consider:

- Decide what information you want to capture.

- Lay out the form so that it can be completed in logical order and it is easy for the user to fill out.

- Ensure that instructions are written in clear, precise language.

- Use white space as much as possible to balance the look and feel of the form.

- Use as few methods as possible for collecting the information. For example, try not to mix check boxes with other information you want circled.

- Clearly define the data fields to encourage correctly formatted information.

- Allow enough space in the data fields to properly complete the form without running outside the field.

- Choose a font style that is easy to use and that can be later scanned for Optical Character Recognition (OCR). Courier, Arial, and Times Roman are the more commonly used fonts.

Forms should be numbered and titled. Keep them consistent with your organization's policy and indicate if they are subject to any specific record retention program.

Summary

The Purchasing Department establishes its strategic plans in alignment with those of the organization as a means of providing maximum support. Planning usually begins with an assessment of the organization's needs and an analysis of where value can be added. SWOT analysis can be used as a tool to aid this process. In selecting strategies, the purchasing manager reviews specific conditions related to capacity, market conditions, business trends, and numerous other factors affecting the materials and services being purchased. Supply positioning analysis is one method of developing strategy.

Similarly, departmental goals are developed in alignment with organizational goals so that they can provide maximum support. Goals and objectives are formulated in alignment with the department's vision and mission statement. When planning goals, the purchasing manager should ensure that they are measurable and attainable.

The purchasing manager also leads the department in formulating operational policies and procedures. These are designed as a means of developing management control to help ensure the attainment of its goals. They are often translated into organizational structure and workload distribution as methods of control that assist in securing positive outcomes. As a part of standard procedure in most organizations, periodic reports are essential to monitoring departmental progress. Identifying relevant reports and determining the most appropriate format for presenting them thus becomes essential. Typically, reports on cost savings and supplier relationships are fundamental to the purchasing function.

Responding to internal and external audits as a means of validating current processes is another purchasing manager responsibility. Integral to this is handling corrective actions in a systematic manner. Similarly, evaluating Purchasing Department performance is a way of determining the department's effectiveness in managing cost and supplier performance and validating the efficacy of internal systems and processes. Customer satisfaction is always a key factor in this evaluation.

The purchasing manager is also responsible for managing the department's budget effectively. To do this, you will need to understand the budget function and its purpose, as well as the various elements of the budgeting process.

We also reviewed the elements of working with operational forms, including their function and design. There are several common forms that are relevant to purchasing activities and the purchasing manager is generally their owner.

For additional reading on topics related to this chapter, please see Appendix A.

Exam Essentials

Be able to plan procurement strategy and objectives. Purchasing Department strategies and objectives require alignment with those of the organization to provide maximum support.

Be able to develop departmental goals and plans. Department goals and plans to achieve them require alignment with those of the organization as well as alignment with the department's vision and mission statement.

Be able to formulate operational policies and procedures. Policies and procedures provide the framework for the department's effective operation.

Be able to prepare departmental reports. Preparing and presenting reports is integral to the purchasing manager's activities. Reports update management on the department's progress toward its goals and indicate how well the operation is being controlled.

Be able to prepare for and respond to audits. Audits are an essential means of validating the effectiveness of the department and its compliance with good business practices.

Know how to evaluate Purchasing Department performance. Evaluating the department's performance is another means of management control to ensure that the department is performing within the range of expectations.

Be able to formulate and administer departmental budgets. As a financial plan that reflects the allocation of resources available in the organization, the budget is a carefully formulated tool for effective management. It provides the basis for measuring performance and a means to discover issues early.

Know how to design and work with operational forms. Paper forms are rapidly giving way to computerized forms. Nevertheless, the purchasing manager will be called upon to design effective forms to meet specific requirements and will be required to follow good design processes.

Review Questions

1. The process of defining an organization's long-term objectives and identifying the best methods to reach them.

    A. Contingency planning

    B. Positioning strategies

    C. Successful planning

    D. Strategic planning

    E. Decision making

2. The process used to help the organization develop strategic plans.

    A. Decision making

    B. Successful planning

    C. SWOT analysis

    D. Positioning strategies

    E. Contingency planning

3. Sets out a series of actions that are triggered by unanticipated circumstances.

    A. Decision making

    B. Successful planning

    C. SWOT analysis

    D. Positioning strategies

    E. Contingency planning

4. Tool used for categorizing areas of spending by cost and associated risk.

    A. Decision making

    B. Successful planning

    C. SWOT analysis

    D. Supply positioning strategies

    E. Contingency planning

5. Spending category that accounts for large amounts dollars but represents low risk.

    A. Strategic

    B. Tactical

    C. Commodity

    D. Direct

    E. Incidental

6. Serves as the guiding principle for the purchasing organization.

    A. Mission statement

    B. Goals and objectives

    C. Operational policies

    D. Operational controls

    E. Vision statement

7. Established so that the value to the organization of each purchasing goal can be clearly measured.

    A. Planning horizon

    B. Metrics

    C. Contingency planning

    D. Positioning strategies

    E. SWOT analysis

8. Governs the tactical manner in which operational activities are intended to be conducted.

    A. Operational control

    B. SWOT analysis

    C. Metrics

    D. Pre-operational controls

    E. Post-operational control

9. Broad process of examining and altering an existing business process and reconstituting it in an improved form.

    A. Process mapping

    B. Operational control

    C. Reengineering

    D. Contingency plan

    E. Commodity management

10. Briefly describes the history of a project or contract, explaining what led to the determination of its need and why it is under consideration at the present time.

    A. Acquisition plan

    B. Operational control

    C. Executive summary

    D. Scorecard

    E. Commodity review

Answers to Review Questions

1. D. Strategic planning aligns the organization's mission with its goals and objectives.

2. C. SWOT analysis reviews the organization's internal strengths and weaknesses and links them to external opportunities and threats.

3. E. Contingency plans are implemented when the initial plan appears to be failing.

4. D. Supply positioning develops strategies associated with the degree of risk and amount spending in a particular category.

5. C. Commodities are generally purchased in large quantities for use as direct materials. Because they are typically off-the-shelf items, they present low risk.

6. E. The vision statement fosters the development of the mission statement from which the goals and objectives are specified.

7. B. "If it's worth doing, it's worth measuring." This adage drives the establishment of each goal and the development of its metrics.

8. D. Controls for tactical activities are established in advance of the specific operational activity. They include organizational policies, tandard operating procedures (SOPs), strategic plans, budgets, and a variety of operational and contingency plans.

9. C. Reengineering efforts in purchasing have generally focused on automating the requisitioning system and ordering processes as a means of improving responsiveness and reducing ordering-cycle time.

10. C. The executive summary is used to orient managers to a specific project, providing details in a specific framework so that reviews can be accomplished quickly.

Chapter 16

Managing Human Resources

THE C.P.M. EXAM SPECIFICATIONS COVERED IN THIS CHAPTER INCLUDE THE FOLLOWING:

- ✓ Leading the supply management team
- ✓ Recruiting, hiring, promoting, and terminating employees
- ✓ Training for professional competence
- ✓ Appraising job performance
- ✓ Handling employee performance issues
- ✓ Preventing workplace discrimination and harassment

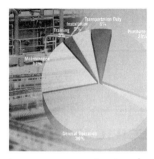

In addition to supply management responsibilities, the purchasing manager has the responsibility of leading and managing the Purchasing Department's staff. This role includes a number of important organizational responsibilities such as recruiting and hiring new team members to replace or complement existing team members and strengthen the entire purchasing group. It also includes training the staff for new or improved skills and in new methods that enhance the department's competency level.

Managing the department also involves appraising job performance on a regular basis and providing employees with feedback and coaching that helps improve their performance. Feedback is relevant in the assessment of both positive and negative performance: it involves recognizing and rewarding outstanding contributions and promoting employees when merited. It similarly includes correcting performance issues and taking disciplinary action when required.

In leading the department, it is also the purchasing manager's responsibility to ensure compliance with internal and external audit requirements, applicable statutory workplace regulations, and policies regarding environment, health, and safety. Compliance also means preventing workplace discrimination and sexual harassment.

In this, the final chapter of this book, we'll cover the important aspects of managing personnel and leading the supply management team in an effective and rewarding manner.

Leading the Supply Management Team

While leadership is a very difficult characteristic to define, it is generally recognized as the ability to influence others in a way that guides and directs their activities toward some specific goal(s). Implied in this concept is that leadership combines the efforts of many individuals into a team that performs operations in a manner the leader determines as most effective. Teamwork also involves the ability of a group of individuals to work together toward a common mission or vision and so, to this extent, leadership incorporates the ability to direct individual accomplishments toward organizational objectives.

Nothing in the concept of leadership, however, implies control. Management, on the other hand, specifically requires the exercise of control. That is essentially the difference between leading and managing. Management is a function that requires an individual—the manager or supervisor—to control resources and processes within a specific span of responsibility. As an administrator, the manager's function encompasses providing technical and administrative direction to individuals to ensure the accomplishment of specific organizational goals. The traditional responsibilities of a manager thus include functions such as planning, organizing, directing, and controlling work within a given area of authority.

Understanding Management Theory

In the course of collective human endeavors, a variety of theories have developed to describe how best to manage and motivate individuals and teams engaged in work activities. Many of these focus on the key aspects of leadership, while others focus on the planning and administrative roles of management. Let's review some of the more commonly referenced theories.

Bureaucracy

Max Weber (1864–1920), one of the pioneers of modern sociology, observed that *bureaucracy* was the most rational structure for the newly emerging large organization. Bureaucratic management theory provides guidelines in the form of policy and procedures, clearly defined hierarchy, and a systematic division of labor. The basic elements of this structure have been in existence since humans began forming into goal-directed groups:

- Organizations operate on the basis of rules and regulations.

- Behavior is governed by these formal rules.

- Authority is delegated through an organizational hierarchy.

- Uniform operations and continuity are maintained despite changes in personnel.

- Authority is based on position rather than on an individual.

- Authority is limited by the scope of the position.

- Tasks are allocated according to some logical method.

- Division of labor is based on functional specialties.

- Promotion is based on demonstrated competence and merit.

- Officers have limited discretion.

- Employment is based on tenure.

Scientific Management and Operational Theory

Historically, much of today's management theory begins with Frederick Taylor (1856–1915), considered the father of scientific management. Taylor theorized that management failed to provide the correct motivational incentives to its workers. He took the approach that work should be broken down into its individual components and that workers should focus on the core components of their tasks and receive compensation based on their ability to perform these tasks. From Taylor's bottom-up approach developed the practice of work specialization designed to increase worker productivity by removing the planning and discretionary control from job duties. This, in turn, gave rise to the assembly line and, eventually, the *time-in-motion work standardization* method. This also led to the centralization of the planning and control functions in the hands of managers, allowing for the additional specialization of the management function.

Administrative Management

At about the same time as scientific management gained popularity, *administrative theory* was also introduced. Its key proponent, Henri Fayol (1841–1925), opted to view management in broad administrative terms, looking at organizational structure from the top down, in contrast to Taylor's bottom-up approach. Advocates viewed the employee as secondary to the job to the and developed guidelines to formalize organizational structures and internal relationships. This theory emphasized the manager and the functions of management, developing the concept of the manager's five functions:

1. Planning
2. Organizing
3. Commanding
4. Coordinating
5. Controlling

Behavioral or Human Relations Theories

Behavioral or human relations management originated in the 1920s and placed the emphasis on the human aspects of organizations. This approach gained influence as a result of the Hawthorne Studies that demonstrated that people tend to perform better when they know they are being studied (or, in effect, considered important).

The Hawthorne Effect

During the period from 1927 to 1932, a team of Harvard Business School researchers conducted a series of experiments at the Hawthorne Plant of Western Electric in Cicero, Illinois. The most notable of these were the illumination experiments that intended to determine the effect of better lighting on workers' productivity. The surprising results were that both the experimental group (those receiving improved lighting) and the control group (those with the original lighting) achieved higher productivity rates during the period. The landmark conclusion was that the improvement was based on the attention the workers were given and not the improved lighting. There was no causal relationship between productivity and working conditions; it was the attitude of the workers that determined their productivity.

Adherents thus emphasized motivation and leadership as the key drivers of worker incentive. The human relations school held that much of employees' creativity and competencies remain untapped by employers due to inadequate recognition systems. Employees, they held, want meaningful assignments where they can participate in decision making and can contribute to the organization's overall well-being.

System Theory

By definition, a system is a combination of related parts organized into a complex whole. The *systems theory of management*, therefore, views the organization as an interrelated, interdependent group of elements that functions as a single entity. An open system—one that interacts with its environment—consists of external inputs such as customer requirements, materials, and personnel and outputs such as final products that are put back into the environment. External feedback from the environment then completes the loop. Included in the systems view are functional subsystems such as manufacturing, finance, and supply management.

The systems approach holds that a synergy develops from these interdependent functional elements that create a greater whole than the theoretical sum of its parts. The combined and synchronized activities of the system are held to create more value than the individual parts could achieve independently.

Contingency Theory

Contingency theory allows that management and decision making styles should flow from the particular situation based on the best possible analysis at the time. In a highly creative environment, for example, the framework of a collaborative style might be most appropriate, whereas in a military environment the style would be autocratic. To be effective, however, the manager's actions must clearly communicate expectations to subordinates.

Chaos Theory

Chaos theory recognizes that events can rarely be completely controlled in an organization and to survive, its systems must adapt and evolve. Organizational systems, by their very nature, tend toward increasing complexity. As this occurs, the systems become unstable and more effort is required to maintain their complexity. As systems expend more energy, they seek more structure to maintain stability. This trend continues until the system divides, combines with another system, or completely disintegrates.

Principles of Organizational Management

In addition to the broad concepts of organizational theory, you might also want to consider a number of common principles that define how the actual management structure operates and how work is distributed. The following are some of the more commonly referenced of these principles.

Scalar Principle   The *Scalar Principle* describes an essentially hierarchical system of work distribution, where authority and accountability move directly from the highest levels in the organization to the lowest level of competency.

Unity or Chain of Command Principle   The *Chain of Command Principle* suggests that each individual report to only one supervisor or manager. Responsibility and accountability are therefore clearly defined, and work can be effectively delegated. This concept commonly also includes the Scalar Principle.

Line-Staff Principle   The *Line-Staff Principle* distinguishes production (or operational) functions from support functions.

Span of Control Principle   The *Span of Control Principle* describes the number of subordinates that reports to a specific manager. There are no particular metrics indicating what this number should be, but the general principle appears to specify that individuals should have no more subordinates than they can effectively supervise. Of course, this number depends upon the situation and the individual's ability.

Exception Management Principle The *Exception Management Principle* suggests that routine duties are handled by subordinates and that the manager respond only to issues outside the normal course of events.

Departmentalization Principle The *Departmentalization Principle* maintains that similar activities should be grouped within the same administrative section. Activities can be related by similarities in process, product lines, location, or purpose.

Management by Objective Management by Objective (MBO) is a widely used method of goal setting in which performance objectives are agreed upon by subordinates and managers. In this process, periodic reviews of progress toward objectives take place and rewards are allocated on the basis of this progress. Other important considerations of MBO include:

- Objectives are properly identified and defined.

- Organizational goals and objectives flow from the top down.

- Goals and objectives are realistic and achievable, as well as challenging.

- Plans for goal achievement are detailed and milestones identified.

- Measurements and time tables are well-defined and agreed upon in advance.

- Performance monitoring and feedback systems are in place.

The Flat Organization The *Flat Organization* attempts to reduce the levels of management hierarchy in the organizational structure. It is a decentralized approach to management that encourages high employee involvement in decisions. The purpose of this structure is to create independent small businesses or enterprises that can rapidly respond to customers' needs or changes in the business environment. In this organizational structure, managers tend to have a more personal relationship with their employees.

Management Styles

Management styles vary widely and often depend significantly upon the individual and the organization's personality. Indeed, very few managers exhibit consistent and predictable managerial behavior all the time. Nevertheless, there appear to be some general patterns that can be used as a source of categorization. In his book *The Human Side of Enterprise*, Douglas McGregor defined ways that managers typically view subordinates as *Theory X* and *Theory Y*.

Traditional or Manager-Controlled The traditional view of managerial direction and control is termed Theory X. Its central tenets are as follows:

- Most employees dislike work and will avoid it whenever possible.

- Because of the inherent dislike of work, most people must be controlled and threatened with punishment to get them to demonstrate adequate effort toward the achievement of organizational objectives.

- The average person prefers to be directed and has no desire for responsibility and relatively little ambition.

- Employees are motivated mainly by money.

The organization and manager following the traditional approach rely primarily on control tactics such as using procedures and techniques for directing employees, measuring compliance, and administering rewards and punishment.

Employee-Focused   McGregor's Theory Y holds the view that organizational goals and individual goals can be mutually compatible. Theory Y managers believe that employees are capable of hard work and have cooperative, positive attitudes. In practice this means:

- Physical and mental work efforts are no different than play or rest.

- Commitment is directly related to the reward associated with the achievement of a goal.

- The average person learns to accept and even seek responsibility.

- Individuals have the ability to exercise a relatively high degree of imagination and creativity in the workplace.

- Creativity, imagination, and ingenuity are not limited to the exceptional few; rather, they are widely distributed in the general population.

- Under typical conditions, the average person's intellectual potential is only partially utilized.

The organization and manager following this approach tend to create an environment in which the employee's goals and the organization's goals can be achieved together. Overall, the style in this environment is participative, collaborative, and nurturing.

Group Dynamics

People learn social skills from one another when they begin socializing as children. As adults, most people work in a group environment. In this context, the term "group dynamics" refers to the observation that an individual's behavior tends to differ in relation to current connections to a particular group. Urges to belong to a particular group may result in different behaviors, and the influence of a group may override an individual's natural tendencies and actions.

Organizational development theory recognizes that groups go through four main phases:

1. Forming: Individuals are introduced to one another.

2. Storming: Competition between the interests of members emerges.

3. Norming: Team members learn to work together.

4. Performing: The team produces results and meets objectives.

Work groups also tend to follow formal and informal organization patterns. The formal work group is generally the officially sanctioned team or department, functioning within the scope of a specific task or responsibility. The informal work group is usually a subset of the formal group that develops around special interests or social needs.

Managing Change

An additional consideration closely related to group dynamics is the *management of change*. Change, of course, is an important part of the organizational process and it has to be managed so that employees embrace new processes positively. Creating successful change often depends on your ability to implement a number of key processes:

- Initiating the change as early as possible

- Developing strong and effective executive sponsorship

- Reducing employee resistance (at all levels, including management)

- Providing aligned communications, with the same message delivered across all organizational boundaries

- Eliminating fear of the unknown or of losing control

- Avoiding work overload during change implementation

Recruiting, Hiring, Promoting, and Terminating Employees

As a manager, few aspects of your career will carry more importance than your ability to facilitate the work of others. Regardless of the management style or methodology you might use, the results you produce through the direction of others will be the true measure of your effectiveness. In this section, we'll examine some of the fundamental tasks inherent in this managerial process.

Recruiting and Hiring Staff

Managers are generally responsible for selecting and hiring competent individual professionals for their team. Working with the Human Resources representative in your organization, you may use a variety of methods to recruit candidates when a position is open in your department, including newspaper ads, solicitations through professional organizations, and your own personal network. Depending upon the experience level and specificity of the position, you may be recruiting from regional, national, or international labor markets.

Specifying Position Requirements

To begin the recruitment process, you will be required to specify the scope of the job duties and the level of skill required. In general, you will want to develop these specifications carefully so that you and your recruiter can select only the most qualified people applying for the position.

Creating a job analysis essentially involves describing a list of duties or work that must be performed by the individual being hired. This often means beginning with a basic categorization of the job level, such as manager, buyer, senior buyer, and so on. This title can then be cross-referenced to standard job descriptions for your industry or geographical region, which can be obtained through your HR Department, as a means of ensuring that you have captured sufficient detail.

In preparing the job description, keep in mind not only your present requirements but also possible future needs. You will also want to include a description of the typical decisions that the individual will be making in the normal course of work, as well as levels and types of communications necessary and any specific supervisory responsibilities. It is a good idea to rank the importance of each of the functions and the frequency or percentage of the job that it will encompass once you get the list compiled.

A typical job description will most likely include:

- Position title
- A description of each major duty function
- The relative importance of the job function
- The approximate time spent performing each duty function
- The expected performance level of each functional duty
- The level (or amount) of supervision required
- Educational requirements
- Competencies (such as facility with specific software programs)
- Professional certifications desired or required
- Amount of time spent traveling
- Citizenship requirements
- Expected working hours

Determining the Required Level of Skills

Following the preparation of the job description, you will want to list the knowledge, skills, and abilities it takes to perform each of the most important tasks of the job, as well. Include in this list specific industry or product knowledge, level of negotiation responsibility, acquisition amounts, supplier development and management abilities, analytical skills, project management expertise, presentation and communication skills, and specific computer-based knowledge.

This information can help form the basis for determining the education, accreditation, and experience qualifications. Consider expected outcomes, level of negotiation responsibility, and criticality of performing appropriately when applying the knowledge or skill or using a given skill set ability. Determine the degree of experience, training, and education needed to gain this knowledge, skill, or ability. The highest level of performance in any of the critical tasks should determine the minimum level of experience you will require.

Evaluating Previous Experience

How do you determine if the individual meets your basic requirements? Most commonly, candidates' resumes are reviewed, and those that are most promising are selected for a telephone interview to screen for skills and experience and to determine personal compatibility. The top two or three candidates are then interviewed in person by you and key internal customers, along with other interested managers and HR. (See the next section for more detail on the interviewing process.)

Following the interview, you will likely require some form of written documentation such as a college transcript to verify education. Your HR department can perform most of these routine checks to ensure veracity. However, to evaluate years of experience and level of experience, *you* should always conduct a reference check. It is a good idea to prepare for this process ahead of time. Know exactly what you need to find out before you start the process. Be sure to get the permission of the candidate before conducting a reference check so you do not jeopardize the individual's current employment. Speak with several previous managers who actually reviewed the individual's work performance. You can ask questions regarding the level of performance and how the individual was ranked in relations to peers. However, be aware that some organizations have specific policies regarding disclosure and you may not always get the information you request.

Interviewing

The interview, like other selection processes, should be structured to measure important knowledge, skills, and abilities. A *structured interview* process is designed to assess past behaviors and accomplishments. Focus your questions on some well-defined, important areas of knowledge, which will be needed to perform the key job duties.

- Ask candidates to indicate how they perform specific duties that require the knowledge you want to assess.

- Ask all candidates the same questions.

- Probe each candidate's answers with further questions structured to find out the individual's level of knowledge and ability.

- Select a few questions that can be covered in detail rather than many questions that produce inconclusive results.

- Consider asking candidates about their experience with one or two projects they worked on that are closely associated with the work you will assign.

It is usually a good idea to ask each of the interviewers to cover specific areas (such as communication skills or analytical ability) so that you can put together a more complete picture at the end of the process. A rating sheet is often helpful so that you can standardize the feedback and use it to help make a final decision.

Making the Selection

In the final selection process you should be certain to follow organizational hiring policies and procedures. These are typically established to ensure fairness and meet regulatory obligations.

From your evaluation, select the candidate whose abilities are most closely associated with solving your department and organization's problems or challenges. Evaluate skills that complement and balance those in the present work group team and are most likely to be needed in the future. It is often recommended that you list the strengths and weaknesses as discovered in the selection process and to consider each as objectively as possible. Remember to base your evaluation on the needs of the job and always refer back to your original job specification.

Promoting Employees

Promoting existing employees can be a motivational tool of encouragement to the team and can serve as an example of the results of improved effort. But it can also have its downside. As a manager, you should asses the pros and cons of promoting from within for each particular situation and then consider them in relation to the overall goals of the organization, as well as the needs of the individual employees.

Pros

In addition to their motivational aspects, internal promotions can also improve retention rates since employees are encouraged to feel that the organization provides future value to their careers. Higher retention rates in turn mean lower hiring and training costs for the department and the organization. Promoting from within can also provide a somewhat greater depth of experience for the position since the internal candidate is already familiar with other areas of the organization and knows its history.

Cons

Promoting from within does not necessarily reduce the hiring process since it invariably creates another opening. One promotion can often lead to a cascade of promotions creating several sets of training requirements in the department that can seriously affect productivity. Promoting internal candidates can also affect the budget because typically external candidates will have less seniority and therefore earn less for the same work. External hiring promotes new ideas and new ways of looking at problems; conversely, internal promotions tend to produce inbreeding using the same methods and processes as those currently in place.

Training for Professional Competence

Training is the key to individual job performance improvement. In the working environment, training generally consists of expanding knowledge, developing and improving skill sets, and providing opportunities for professional development. Training is also used when new processes or procedures are introduced into the workplace.

This section outlines some of the more important characteristics that the manager must keep in mind when analyzing training needs and implementing related programs.

Determining Training Requirements

It is advisable to begin your assessment of training needs by starting with an analysis of any anticipated organizational changes and developments to determine which skills will be needed in the future and to what degree. A side-by-side comparison of these needs with current skill levels can help you estimate training requirements and accompanying budgets. Analysis should also identify the elements of current or future tasks to be done so that you can identify broad requirements. Performing a gap analysis between future requirements and current skills sets is often helpful. Typically, you will be required to do this on an annual or quarterly basis.

In addition, training requirements are often developed through a personal needs analysis. This involves an assessment of each individual's developmental requirements and interests and an agreed plan for accomplishment. Clear and measurable objectives should be developed before training begins and after you have identified the employees' training needs. You might consider developing goals and objectives for specific training by using the tools of collaborative planning and jointly determining an acceptable level of overall performance.

Having clearly defined objectives will enable you and the employee to evaluate when (and if) the objectives have been reached. For a training objective to be effective, it should identify as precisely as possible what the employees will do to demonstrate that the objective has been reached. Using specific, action-oriented language, training objectives should describe the desired knowledge, practice, or skill and its observable behavior. Objectives should also describe the important conditions under which the individual will demonstrate competence and define what constitutes acceptable performance. Objectives are most effective when worded in sufficient detail so that others can recognize when the desired knowledge or behavior is exhibited.

Employing Training Methods

For training to be effective, employees should be convinced that it is important to them. To ensure this, explain the goals of the training and provide training that is clearly relevant to the individual's work environment. Training should be simple but, at the same time, carefully thorough.

Commonly employed training methods include:

- On-the-job training (OJT), where individuals learn from actually performing job duties
- Job rotation, where individuals are cross-trained to enhance department's staffing flexibility
- Instructor-led classroom training, for a more formal approach to learning new skills and the reinforcement of the learning developed from peer groups
- Lecture, demonstration, and hands-on training—the "see/do" approach—to enable a combination of instruction and OJT in a controlled environment
- Computer-based training (or online distance learning), for self-paced learning using a multimedia approach that reinforces written instruction with audio and visual aids
- Blended learning, a combination of instructor-led and self-paced training that provides the benefits of both systems
- Self-study, through reading and other individualized learning tools

Physical training environments often include training on the job; at a corporate training center or conference facility, community college or university site, hotel meeting room; or at workshops, seminars, and professional conferences. Materials can include handouts, posters, operations manuals, magazine articles, slides and photographs, films, instructional manuals, books, outlines, and diagrams.

Periodic evaluation of the training is a key element in developing a successful and effective training program. Training should be reevaluated whenever new processes or techniques are introduced into the workplace. As the manager, you should evaluate the training to ensure that it continues to be effective and to determine if any further training is needed given current circumstances. Evaluations should consider the complexity of the job for which the training is conducted since more complex tasks may require more frequent training. Evaluation of the training's effectiveness should be conducted periodically—at least annually—for ongoing training.

It is also a good idea to involve employees in the training evaluation. Feedback from each class will help ensure that future groups gain the benefit of those preceding them. You will specifically want to measure how effectively the objectives of the training are being reached.

Conducting the Training

The manager or training instructor should combine domain expertise and the ability to effectively transfer knowledge to those being instructed. Some of the typical steps in the training cycle include:

- Providing an oral and written overview of the training objective
- Illustrating the material with examples of the task
- Enabling employees to apply the training on the job
- Monitoring employees' progress and offering additional coaching
- Evaluating employees' success rate and adjusting the training as required
- Retraining where improvement is needed
- Reviewing training objectives
- Employing methods to continually evaluate training effectiveness during future job performance

Trainers sometimes use a simple principle: "Tell the students what they are about to learn, teach the material, and then reinforce the lesson by summarizing what the students just learned."

Encouraging Professional Development

Professional development generally refers to the ongoing process of improving personal skill sets, knowledge, and abilities in order to improve job performance and, ostensibly, further one's career.

Professional development usually takes the form of advanced education and formal training. This is encouraged by many organizations that reimburse their employees for such expenses if they demonstrate a relation to their jobs. In addition, professional certification as a *Certified Purchasing Manager (C.P.M.)* through the Institute for Supply Management (ISM) or similar certifications offered by other professional groups should be formally encouraged.

Other purchasing and supply management–related certifications include:

- Certified Federal Contracts Manager (CFCM), Certified Commercial Contracts Manager (CCCM), and Certified Professional Contracts Manager (CPCM), offered by the National Contract Management Association (NCMA), www.ncmahq.org.

- Certified Public Purchasing Officer (CPPO) and Certified Professional Public Buyer (CPPB), administered by the National Institute for Governmental Purchasing (NIGP), www.nigp.org.

- Certified in Production and Inventory Management (CPIM), Certified Fellow in Production and Inventory Management (CFPIM), and Certified in Integrated Resource Management (CIRM), designations awarded by APICS (the Association for Operations Management, formerly just APICS), www.apics.org.

Appraising Job Performance

Job *performance appraisal* and employee evaluations are processes that take place—formally and informally—in the organization on a daily and an annual basis. In fact, the continuing evaluation of individual work performance is a method of control, tying ongoing performance to rewards or corrective actions. However, in most organizations the performance appraisal process is a formal, structured system that compares employee performance to established standards and agreed upon goals. The manager's assessment of the employee's job performance is presented to the employees being appraised through one of several traditional methods of formal reviews.

Developing Appraisal Factors

Performance appraisals should include objective criteria for measuring employee performance and ratings that summarize how well the employee is doing against stated objectives. Successful appraisal methods have clearly defined and explicitly communicated standards or expectations of employee performance on the job.

Selecting Performance Appraisal Methods

While it is important that an organization (and department) maintains a uniform method of approach to ensure fairness, appraisals can be structured in a number of different ways. Some of the more commonly used methods are discussed next.

Traditional Form-Based Approach   Goals are listed on a standardized review document and performance is evaluated by the manager on a sliding numerical scale. Scores are then calculated arithmetically according to a predetermined weighting method.

Graphic Rating Scale System   In a similar process to the form-based approach, the *graphic rating scale* is a set of performance factors such as job knowledge, work quality, and cooperation that the reviewing manager uses to rate employee performance on an incremental scale.

Written Narrative Appraisal   This assesses an employee's strengths, weaknesses, past performance, and potential, along with recommendations for improvement.

Comparative Standards or Multi-person Comparison   Rather than an absolute method of the traditional form-based approach, the *comparative standards* or *multi-person comparison* is a relative system that compares one employee's job performance with that of others in the same function or at the same level of compensation.

Individual Rank Ordering System   The *individual rank ordering system* requires the reviewing manager to list employees from highest to lowest in performance rating.

Group Rank Ordering System   The *group rank ordering system* requires the reviewing manager to place employees into a particular classification such as the top 25 percent or the bottom 25 percent. This forces a ranking according to group levels.

Paired Comparison Method   In the *paired comparison method*, the reviewing manager compares each employee with every other employee in the group and rates each as either the superior or weaker of the pair. After all comparisons are made, each employee is assigned a summary or ranking based on the number of superior scores received.

Critical Incidents Review Process   During the *critical incidents review process*, the manager reviews specific or key performance factors that separate effective from ineffective performance.

Behaviorally Anchored Rating Scales (BARS)   The *behaviorally anchored rating scales (BARS)* system combines elements from the critical incident and graphic rating scale approaches. The manager thus evaluates employees according to items on a numerical scale.

Management by Objective (MBO)   This method evaluates how well an employee has accomplished goals agreed upon at the beginning of the reviewing period. It also attempts to align objectives with quantitative performance measures such as cost savings or completed contracts.

360 Degree Feedback Process   The *360 degree feedback process* provides a comprehensive perspective of employee performance by utilizing feedback from the full circle of people with whom the employee interacts: supervisors, subordinates, and coworkers. It is effective for career coaching and identifying strengths and weaknesses.

Forming Appraisal Judgments

Appraisal judgments can be either objective or subjective, that is, quantitative or qualitative. Objective factors are observable and measurable results that can be readily documented. They include such factors as errors and missed deadlines. Subjective factors, on the other hand, are simply opinions. They can be difficult or impossible to quantify and often open the door to charges of bias. Examples of subjective factors include such elements as personality traits, dependability, initiative, and perseverance. To remain objective, managers should double-check ratings to be sure they don't favor one employee or make unsupported judgments. Supported judgments will have documented incidents of employee performance to illustrate the ratings.

   The halo effect is a rating error that occurs when the evaluator tends to base overall judgments or evaluations on selected pieces of information rather than on all available relevant information. This usually occurs as the result of specific knowledge of an employee's performance on one favorable or unfavorable incident that affects the ratings on all others. The halo effect can be reduced by rating and comparing all employees' performance on a single factor before going on to another factor.

Leveraging Performance Appraisals

Performance appraisals can be employed in a number of important management functions, both evaluative and developmental. In addition to assessing the progress of the employee's efforts toward reaching objectives and providing the framework in which to develop improvements, the appraisal process often helps determine future compensation. Typically, organizations budget annual salary increases based upon merit, and it is the manager's job to divide the dollar amount set aside for the department equitably among the staff. As such, it is an important tool in providing recognition and reward that fosters individual motivation and talent retention.

The appraisal also can be a tool to recommend individuals for promotion. A strong record of documented achievements can provide the basis for evaluating an employee for future assignments. On the other hand, inadequate performance can also be documented, and the review process can be used to develop ways in which to improve. In both of these cases, the review becomes part of the employee's official record and can help guide the employee's future managers in setting goals in a way that provides objective continuity.

Conducting the Review

Because the review can be critical to an employee's career, it is important that you conduct the appraisal conference in a consistent and professional manner. While techniques for conducting the review vary widely from organization to organization, there are a number of elements you should consider.

Communicate   Begin your meeting with a summary of your evaluation, touching upon the major accomplishments during the period, as well as areas of potential improvement.

Develop Consensus   Ask for input and listen to the employee's comments, being certain to take notes and acknowledge your understanding. Resolve any significant differences of opinion using as many examples as you can.

Gain Acceptance   While full agreement may not be possible, it is important that the employee accepts the rating.

Review Areas for Improvement   Go over specific areas for improvement and the reasons it is needed. Cover how these might work into future goals.

Agree   Develop targets to consider in the next period and gain the employee's commitment to them. Determine what you can do to help. Consider setting a date to discuss goals and objectives for the next period.

Handling Employee Performance Issues

The manager's goal is to continually improve employee performance. However, you should also be able to identify situations and behavior patterns that may require immediate corrective action and understand what steps should be taken to resolve them.

Identifying Problems and Performance Issues

Managers need to be able to recognize early signs that an employee may be heading for difficulties. These commonly include:

- Sudden change of behavior
- Poor attendance
- Negative attitude
- Stress
- Reduced productivity
- Carelessness
- Irritability
- Insubordination
- Signs of fatigue
- Missed deadlines
- Difficulty following instructions

In addition, there are some situations that may call for additional intervention by security or Human Resources, such as signs of substance abuse, theft, sexual harassment, threats of physical violence, and ethical or legal violations.

Implementing Corrective Action

Corrective action generally takes one of two forms: counseling or formal discipline. Because of potential legal implications, most organizations have established specific policies and procedures for conducting such activities, and you should be sure you understand them before engaging in corrective action. Here are some general processes you might want to cover.

Counseling

Counseling is a behavioral control technique that you can use to help resolve performance problems. It is often a process where the manager assists an employee through purposeful conversation in a collaborative and understanding atmosphere. It has as a goal the clarification of issues and guidance in resolving them. As a counselor, the manager seeks to assist the employee by discussing the problems that are preventing adequate job performance with the specific intent of resolving them.

Effective counseling requires active listening and reflection. Listening is reassuring and helps the employee feel more valued. During the counseling session, the employee should be encouraged to talk and actively explore ways to better understand the particular performance issues. By providing support, the manager will help the individual focus on the underlying causes of the performance issue and examine a corrective course of action that might provide effective resolution.

Counseling techniques cover a fairly broad range from directive to nondirective and are usually dependent upon the specific situation. *Nondirective counseling* simply summarizes what has been said. Using the nondirective approach you might say, "You feel stressed because you have not had enough team support in conducting the project." *Directive counseling*, on the other hand, provides direct advice. Using the directive approach you could say, "I want you to assign a specific responsibility to each team member." *Interactive counseling* is a combination of both nondirective and directive techniques.

Following are some of the steps you should consider when the situation calls for counseling.

Identify the Problem Behavior   Let the employee know that work performance has faltered. Explain in very specific terms what the issues appear to be and what needs to be done so the employee can perform to the organization's performance expectations.

Ask for Comments   Let the employee describe what might be causing the unacceptable behavior. Listen and protect confidentiality.

Help Develop a Solution   Emphasize positive and affirmative actions. Allow the employee the time to demonstrate positive improvement and reinforce any visible efforts.

Gain Commitment   Seek ways to establish the employee's course of action and direct special attention to correcting the problem.

Follow Up   Continue to monitor the situation, even after it has been seemingly resolved. Consider providing additional skills training, if appropriate, as a way of ensuring that the problem does not resurface.

Disciplining

Discipline is a form of corrective action and behavioral control taken when an employee is unable to correct performance issues. Effective discipline helps eliminate misconduct and inappropriate behavior such as rules violations or an unwillingness to meet established performance criteria.

Discipline processes generally involve progressive escalation from a verbal reprimand through termination. Two of the steps to consider for disciplinary actions prior to termination are a written reprimand and suspension.

Written Reprimand

Following the procedure just outlined for the counseling process (when appropriate) and after documenting the verbal warnings, the manager may escalate the process by issuing a formal letter of reprimand. The letter should outline previous informal efforts and the current problem. It should also state the required actions to be taken by the individual to correct the problem.

Since this procedure may have further legal implications, it is important that organizational policy and procedures are followed precisely. Prior to issuing the letter, it's wise to consider involving your HR and Legal Departments.

Suspension

In a formal letter, summarize the prior progressive discipline and the current problem. Specify the timeframe for suspension. Identify further discipline and possible termination as a potential consequence for not meeting and maintaining standards for improvement outlined in the previous warning letters.

As with the written reprimand, this serious action should involve your HR Department.

Terminating Employees

Termination may be necessary when disciplinary measures are not successful in improving performance. It is usually a very difficult and somewhat emotional process that requires both structure and sensitivity. In general, since most employment is based on mutual consent, both the employee and the organization have the right to terminate employment at will, with or without cause, at any time. However, it is extremely important that you follow proper procedure to legally protect your organization from actions for *wrongful termination.*

Once the decision to terminate an employee has been made, you should schedule the formal action as soon as possible. Identify and contact your internal resources such as HR and Legal for assistance and advice on moving through the process in conformance to legal practice and organizational policy. Some of the typical steps you will take are listed here.

Prepare a Summary and Termination Letter　Clearly cite the reasons for the termination. List any actions that have preceded termination. In addition to performance issues, reasons for the termination might include a reorganization, new technology, or change in strategic direction.

Establish a Security Procedure　Prepare for the individual to collect personal effects from the organization's property. Personal effects can also be forwarded later, after a qualified security person has had the opportunity to evaluate their contents. If the individual has access to confidential material, take whatever precautions are possible to ensure their safekeeping. For example, change computer passwords and secure documents.

Determine the Time and Location　Establish a specific time for the action, keeping disruption to other team members at a minimum. Have ready whatever documents need to be signed and the individual's final paycheck prepared.

Plan Official Announcements　Establish who needs to be informed of the departure, both internally and externally, and what form the announcement should take.

An outline of the steps in a termination plan might look something like this:

1. Communicate the decision to the individual.
2. Explain the reasons for the decision and events leading up to it.
3. Explain severance terms in the case of a layoff.
4. If appropriate, offer the option to resign.
5. Review outplacement assistance, if applicable.
6. Review procedures for references.
7. Make arrangements to gather personal belongings.
8. Collect company property and security badges.
9. Obtain signatures on required documents.
10. Ensure that the individual exits the premises.

Preventing Workplace Discrimination and Harassment

What constitutes discrimination in the workplace? The precise definition of discrimination in the workplace and what is illegal discrimination varies somewhat from state to state. However, discrimination can be defined as treating one person unfairly over another according to factors unrelated to their ability or potential, such as age, race, disability, sex, sexual orientation, religion, or national origin.

There are numerous laws and regulations that attempt to eliminate unfair discrimination, and many organizations have established policies and procedures to align with them. In this section, we'll outline some of the regulations you are most likely to encounter.

Administering Equal Opportunity Processes

While it would be hard for you as a manager to be completely up-to-date on all the specifics of existing laws, it is nevertheless your responsibility to ensure that discrimination and harassment are never present in your workplace. To accomplish this, you will need to be familiar with some of the key laws and regulations and how they operate to provide equal opportunity for all employees.

Laws and Regulations

The U.S. *Equal Employment Opportunity Commission (EEOC)* (www.eeoc.gov) is charged with the enforcement of the body of federal laws governing equal employment opportunity.

The key federal laws prohibiting job discrimination are discussed next.

Title VII of the Civil Rights Act of 1964, 1972, 1991   Prohibits employment discrimination based on race, color, religion, sex, or national origin. It also allows for employers to use a Bona Fide Occupational Qualification (BFOQ) to establish employment requirements where a need legitimately exists. (For example, an advertising director can require a female model for a bathing suit ad.)

Equal Pay Act of 1963 (EPA)   Protects men and women who perform substantially equal work in the same establishment from sex-based wage discrimination.

Age Discrimination in Employment Act of 1967, 1978,1986 (ADEA)   Protects individuals who are 40 years of age or older.

Title I and Title V of the Americans with Disabilities Act of 1990 (ADA)   Prohibit employment discrimination against qualified individuals with disabilities in the private sector and in state and local governments.

Sections 501 and 505 of the Rehabilitation Act of 1973   Prohibit discrimination against qualified individuals with disabilities who work in the federal government.

Civil Rights Act of 1991   Provides, among other things, monetary damages in cases of intentional employment discrimination.

In general, the presence of a specific set of conditions can confirm the existence of illegal discrimination. Unfair treatment does not necessarily equal unlawful discrimination. Treating a person differently from others violates Equal Employment Opportunity (EEO) laws only when the treatment is based on the presence of a protected characteristic rather than on job performance or even on something as arbitrary as an employee's personality. Keep in mind, however, that discrimination claims can be highly subjective when reviewed by an arbitrator or a jury.

To avoid discrimination, you do not have to extend preferential treatment to any employee. The law requires only that you extend the same employment opportunities and enforce the same policies for all employees.

Affirmative Action

Affirmative action became law with the passage of the Equal Employment Opportunity Act of 1972, whereby employers, labor unions, employment agencies, and labor management apprenticeship programs must actively seek to increase the employment opportunities for protected groups such as racial minorities and the disabled. Although Title VII of the Civil Rights Act of 1964 outlawed future discriminations in employment practices, it did nothing to redress already existing imbalances. The 1972 law, later strengthened by Executive Order 11246, required employers to draw up a detailed written plan for equalizing economic salaries, training programs, fringe benefits, and other conditions of employment. These plans included numerical goals and timetables for achieving such changes.

In recent decisions, however, the U.S. Supreme Court has significantly reduced the scope of federal affirmative action programs requiring that such actions serve a compelling interest and be narrowly defined. In 1994, the Fourth U.S. Circuit Court of Appeals rejected a University of Maryland scholarship program restricted to African-American students. In 2004, the Fifth Circuit rejected an admissions procedure at the University of Texas Law School that divided applicants into two groups—first, blacks and Mexican-Americans, and second, all others—and then applied different admissions quotas to each group. The court held that the law school's interest in diversity did not constitute a compelling state interest and that the school could not take race into account in any form in its admissions process. The Supreme Court let both decisions stand without further review. While as a matter of law other states are not absolutely debarred from continuing race-restricted scholarships or preferential admissions policies, the consensus is that these programs are unlikely to survive the all but certain legal challenges they will face.

Some areas of affirmative action are still being enforced, though. Title 5, Section 503 of the Rehabilitation Act does require that affirmative action be taken in employment of persons with disabilities by federal contractors.

Americans with Disability Act (ADA)

The EEOC provides an outline of the basic principles of the Americans with Disability Act. We will discuss those principles next.

The ADA prohibits discrimination on the basis of disability in all employment practices. It is necessary to understand several important ADA definitions to know who is protected by the law and what constitutes illegal discrimination.

Individual with a Disability

An individual with a disability under the ADA is a person who has a physical or mental impairment that substantially limits one or more major life activities, has a record of such an impairment, or is regarded as having such an impairment. Major life activities are activities that an average person can perform with little or no difficulty such as walking, breathing, seeing, hearing, speaking, learning, and working.

Qualified Individual with a Disability

A qualified employee or applicant with a disability is someone who satisfies skill, experience, education, and other job-related requirements of the position held or desired, and who, with or without reasonable accommodation, can perform the essential functions of that position.

Reasonable Accommodation

Reasonable accommodation may include, but is not limited to, making existing employee facilities readily accessible to and usable by persons with disabilities; job restructuring; modification of work schedules; providing additional unpaid leave; reassignment to a vacant position; acquiring or modifying equipment or devices; adjusting or modifying examinations, training materials, or policies; and providing qualified readers or interpreters. Reasonable accommodation may be necessary to apply for a job, to perform job functions, or to enjoy the benefits and privileges of employment that are enjoyed by people without disabilities. An employer is not required to lower production standards to make an accommodation. An employer generally is not obligated to provide personal use items such as eyeglasses or hearing aids.

Undue Hardship

An employer is required to make a reasonable accommodation to a qualified individual with a disability unless doing so would impose an undue hardship on the operation of the employer's business. Undue hardship means an action that involves significant difficulty or expense when considered in relation to factors such as a business's size, financial resources, and the nature and structure of its operation.

Prohibited Inquiries and Examinations

Before making an offer of employment, an employer may not ask job applicants about the existence, nature, or severity of a disability. Applicants may be asked about their ability to perform job functions. A job offer may be conditioned on the results of a medical examination, but only if the examination is required for all entering employees in the same job category. Medical examinations of employees must be job-related and consistent with business necessity.

Drug and Alcohol Use

Employees and applicants currently engaging in the illegal use of drugs are not protected by the ADA when an employer acts on the basis of such use. Tests for illegal use of drugs are not considered medical examinations and, therefore, are not subject to the ADA's restrictions on medical examinations. Employers may hold individuals who are illegally using drugs and individuals with alcoholism to the same standards of performance as other employees.

Eliminating Sexual Harassment

Sexual harassment in employment is any kind of sexual behavior that is unwelcome and/or inappropriate for the workplace. The EEOC has defined sexual harassment as "unwelcome sexual advances, requests for sexual favors, and other verbal or physical conduct of a sexual nature...when...submission to or rejection of such conduct is used as the basis for employment decisions...or such conduct has the purpose or effect of...creating an intimidating, hostile, or offensive working environment."

Sexual harassment is also defined as unwelcome sexual advances or conduct. Sexual harassment can include verbal harassment (derogatory comments or dirty jokes), visual harassment (sexually explicit posters, cartoons, or drawings), physical harassment, and outright sexual advances or confrontation with sexual demands. Sexual harassment also includes animosity that is gender-based and a sexually charged work environment. In the workplace, sexual harassment can come from the owner, supervisor, manager, lead person, foreperson, coworker, and/or customer.

In a series of major decisions in 1998, the United States Supreme Court clarified and broadened the law. In a unanimous decision in March 1998, the Court ruled that when the workplace is permeated with discriminatory intimidation, ridicule, and insult that is sufficiently severe or pervasive to alter the conditions of the victim's employment and create an abusive working environment, Title VII is violated.

To prevent sexual harassment, organizations typically develop a written policy concerning sexual harassment that clearly states that it is not only against the law, but against company policy, and will not be tolerated. Organizations also create an effective complaint or grievance procedure for employees who feel they have been victims of sexual harassment. The procedure should make it easy and comfortable for an employee to file a complaint, especially if the harasser is a direct supervisor. The procedure should also be such that a solution to the problem can be arrived at quickly and effectively.

As a manager, you should ensure that your staff is aware of the organization's policy and that they value treatment of others in a professional manner.

Summary

The examination requirement for Module 4 includes a significant number of questions related to "current issues." These issues are reviewed in *Articles for C.P.M. Exam Preparation* published by ISM and are not presented in our review. You may wish to purchase the latest version directly from ISM by going to its website: www.ism.ws

Managing the Purchasing Department requires specific knowledge and skills focused on leadership and team management. Various systems of management and management theory have been applied in contemporary organizations, including bureaucracy, scientific management, administrative management, behavioral and human relations theory, systems theory, contingency theory, and chaos theory. Invariably, no one management concept applies to all situations.

Similarly, a number of common principles have been identified to define how management structures operate and how work is distributed. These principles include the Scalar, Unity or Chain of Command, Line-Staff, Span of Control, Exception Management, Departmentalization, Management by Objective (MBO) and Flat Organization principles. In conjunction, management styles take the form of traditional or manager-controlled and its counterpart, employee focused (Theory X and Theory Y).

Recruiting, hiring, training, promoting, and terminating staff is another set of the key responsibilities of the manager. Recruiting and hiring require the ability to specify job requirements and skill levels and to evaluate the experience of candidates for employment. Managers are also required to conduct interviews with candidates and to make the final hiring decision.

During the course of employment, virtually all employees will require some degree of training, depending on changes within the organization and the organization's environment. This means the manager will need to understand the methods commonly used in the training process and how to employ them. The manager should also be aware of professional development opportunities and encourage staff participation.

Another key responsibility of the manager is developing and conducting the job performance appraisal in a manner that reinforces continuous improvement. Managers will also be required to identify and resolve problems and performance issues, taking appropriate corrective and disciplinary action up to and including termination of employment.

As the management representative for the department, the purchasing manager is also responsible for ensuring that applicable laws and organizational policies regarding workplace discrimination and sexual harassment are uniformly enforced. To perform effectively, the manager should be familiar with Federal Equal Employment Opportunity legislation and what constitutes sexual harassment so that all employees value the fair treatment of others.

For additional reading on topics related to this chapter, please see Appendix A.

Exam Essentials

Be able to lead the supply management team.   Purchasing managers should understand the nature of leadership and management and how various theories and styles can be applied.

Be able to recruit, hire, promote, and terminate employees.   The purchasing manager is responsible for the development of job analysis and descriptions, as well as the processes related to recruiting, hiring, promoting, or terminating employees.

Know how to train for professional competence.   The purchasing manager should understand the methods commonly used in the training process and how to employ them.

Be able to appraise job performance.   A key responsibility of any manager is developing and conducting the job performance appraisal in a manner that helps reinforce continuous improvement and organizational goals.

Be able to handle employee performance issues.   You should be able to identify and provide corrective actions that resolve problems and performance issues, taking appropriate corrective and disciplinary action up to and including termination of employment.

Understand workplace discrimination and harassment and know how to prevent it.   The purchasing manager is responsible for ensuring that applicable laws and policies regarding workplace discrimination and sexual harassment are uniformly enforced.

Review Questions

1. Management theory that provides guidelines in the form of policy and procedures, clearly defined hierarchy, and a systematic division of labor.

   A. Scientific management

   B. Behavioral or human relations

   C. System theory

   D. Bureaucracy

   E. Administrative management

2. Management theory approach holding that work should be broken down into its individual components.

   A. Scientific management

   B. Behavioral or human relations

   C. System theory

   D. Bureaucracy

   E. Administrative management

3. Principle system of hierarchical work distribution.

   A. Chain of Command

   B. Exception Management

   C. Span of Control

   D. Scalar

   E. Line-Staff

4. View that organizational goals and individual goals can be mutually compatible.

   A. Theory Y

   B. Management by Objective

   C. The Hawthorne Effect

   D. Human Relations Theories

   E. Theory X

5. A part or piece of the hiring process used to assess individual experience.

   A. Job analysis

   B. Corrective action

   C. Résumé

   D. Interview

   E. Reference

6. Type of training where individuals learn through actual performance.

   A. Job rotation

   B. Professional development

   C. Self-study

   D. On-the-job training

   E. Blended learning

7. Refers to the ongoing process of improving one's personal skill sets, knowledge, and abilities.

   A. Job rotation

   B. Professional development

   C. Self-study

   D. On-the-job training

   E. Blended learning

8. The incremental system used by the reviewing manager to rate employee performance.

   A. Critical incidents review

   B. Group rank ordering system

   C. Paired comparison

   D. Graphic rating scale

   E. Multi-person comparison

9. Process where the manager helps an employee correct performance issues in a collaborative and understanding atmosphere.

   A. Corrective action

   B. Written reprimand

   C. Counseling

   D. Termination

   E. Disciplining

10. Treating a person differently from others during the hiring process violates:

   A. The Civil Rights Act

   B. The Americans with Disability Act

   C. Sexual harassment laws

   D. Affirmative Action

   E. Equal Employment Opportunity

Answers to Review Questions

1. D. Original proponents of the organizational system now called bureaucracy (such as the noted sociologist Max Weber) believed it provided the most rational structure for organizations.

2. A. First formulated by Frederick Taylor, the scientific management principle took the approach that work can be most efficiently performed if it is specialized, that is, divided according to specific task.

3. D. The Scalar Principle describes an essentially hierarchical system of work distribution where authority and accountability move directly from the highest levels in the organization to the lowest level of competency.

4. A. Theory Y contrasts with Theory X, which offers the traditional view that strong managerial control is required because work is generally disliked by employees. Theory Y holds that employees find work satisfying and rewarding, and therefore are capable of having positive attitudes.

5. E. To evaluate years of experience and level of experience, *you* should always conduct a reference check by contacting the candidate's previous employers.

6. D. One of the most common forms of training, OJT allows the employee to actually perform the job function under supervision as a means of accelerating learning.

7. B. Professional development usually takes the form of advanced education and formal training. It is typically directed to improving job performance to further one's career.

8. D. The graphic rating scale system is a set of performance factors such as job knowledge, work quality, and cooperation that the reviewing manager uses to rate employee performance on an incremental scale.

9. C. Counseling is a behavioral control technique that can help resolve performance problems. Its goal is the clarification of issues and guidance in resolving them, which can best be accomplished in a collaborative atmosphere.

10. A. Title VII of the Civil Rights Act of 1964 prohibits employment discrimination based on race, color, religion, sex, or national origin. It is enforced on the federal level by the U.S. Equal Employment Opportunity Commission (EEOC).

Appendix A

Bibliography

Chapter 1

Cavinato, Joseph, et al. *The Purchasing Handbook: A Guide for the Purchasing and Supply Professional.* 6th ed. New York: McGraw-Hill, 2000.

Leenders, Michiel, et al. *Purchasing & Supply Management.* 12th ed. New York: McGraw-Hill, 2002

Burt, David, et al. *World Class Supply Management: The Key to Supply Chain Management.* 7th ed. New York: McGraw-Hill, 2003

Ostring, Pirkko. *Profit-Focused Supplier Management: How to Identify Risks and Recognize Opportunities.* New York: AMACOM, 2004

Chapter 2

Leenders, Michiel, et al. *Purchasing & Supply Management.* 12th ed. New York: McGraw-Hill, 2002

Burt, David, et al. *World Class Supply Management: The Key to Supply Chain Management.* 7th ed. New York: McGraw-Hill, 2003

Ostring, Pirkko. *Profit-Focused Supplier Management: How to Identify Risks and Recognize Opportunities.* New York: AMACOM, 2004

Chapter 3

Leenders, Michiel, et al. *Purchasing & Supply Management.* 12th ed. New York: McGraw-Hill, 2002

Burt, David, et al. *World Class Supply Management: The Key to Supply Chain Management.* 7th ed. New York: McGraw-Hill, 2003

Ostring, Pirkko. *Profit-Focused Supplier Management: How to Identify Risks and Recognize Opportunities.* New York: AMACOM, 2004

Chapter 4

Cavinato, Joseph, et al. *The Purchasing Handbook: A Guide for the Purchasing and Supply Professional.* 6th ed. New York: McGraw-Hill, 2000.

Leenders, Michiel, et al. *Purchasing & Supply Management.* 12th ed. New York: McGraw-Hill, 2002

Burt, David, et al. *World Class Supply Management: The Key to Supply Chain Management.* 7th ed. New York: McGraw-Hill, 2003

Chapter 5

Cavinato, Joseph, et al. *The Purchasing Handbook: A Guide for the Purchasing and Supply Professional.* 6th ed. New York: McGraw-Hill, 2000.

Burt, David, et al. World Class Supply Management: The Key to Supply Chain Management. 7th ed. New York: McGraw-Hill, 2003

Christopher, Martin. Logistics and Supply Chain Management: Strategies for Reducing Cost and Improving Service. 2nd ed. London: Financial Times, 1998

Chapter 6

Cavinato, Joseph, et al. *The Purchasing Handbook: A Guide for the Purchasing and Supply Professional.* 6th ed. New York: McGraw-Hill, 2000.

Stark, Peter, et al. *The Only Negotiating Guide You'll Ever Need: 101 Ways to Win Every Time in Any Situation.* Broadway Books, 2003.

Brett, Jeanne. *Negotiating Globally: How to Negotiate Deals, Resolve Disputes, and Make Decisions Across Cultural Boundaries.* New York: Jossey Bass, 2001

Chapter 7

Leenders, Michiel, et al. *Purchasing & Supply Management.* 12th ed. New York: McGraw-Hill, 2002

Burt, David, et al. *World Class Supply Management: The Key to Supply Chain Management.* 7th ed. New York: McGraw-Hill, 2003

Arnold, Tony, et al. *Introduction to Materials Management.* 5th ed. Columbus: Prentice Hall, 2004

Nelson, Dave, et al. *The Purchasing Machine: How the Top Ten Companies Use Best Practices to Manage Their Supply Chains.* New York: Free Press, 2001

Simchi-Levi, David, et al. *Managing the Supply Chain: The Definitive Guide for the Business Professional.* New York: McGraw-Hill, 2004

Walker, William. *Supply Chain Architecture: A Blueprint for Networking the Flow of Material, Information, and Cash.* Boca Raton: CRC Press, 2005

Chapter 8

Cavinato, Joseph, et al. *The Purchasing Handbook: A Guide for the Purchasing and Supply Professional.* 6th ed. New York: McGraw-Hill, 2000.

Burt, David, et al. *World Class Supply Management: The Key to Supply Chain Management.* 7th ed. New York: McGraw-Hill, 2003

Leenders, Michiel, et al. *Purchasing & Supply Management.* 12th ed. New York: McGraw-Hill, 2002

Chapter 9

Leenders, Michiel, et al. *Purchasing & Supply Management.* 12th ed. New York: McGraw-Hill, 2002

Burt, David, et al. *World Class Supply Management: The Key to Supply Chain Management.* 7th ed. New York: McGraw-Hill, 2003

Greenhalgh, Leonard. *Managing Strategic Relationships: The Key to Business Success.* New York: Free Press, 2001

Chapter 10

Cavinato, Joseph, et al. *The Purchasing Handbook: A Guide for the Purchasing and Supply Professional.* 6th ed. New York: McGraw-Hill, 2000.

Christopher, Martin. *Logistics and Supply Chain Management: Strategies for Reducing Cost and Improving Service.* 2nd ed. London: Financial Times, 1998

Neef, Dale. *The Supply Chain Imperative: How to Ensure Ethical Behavior in Your Global Suppliers.* New York: AMACOM, 2004

Nelson, Dave, et al. *The Purchasing Machine: How the Top Ten Companies Use Best Practices to Manage Their Supply Chains.* New York: Free Press, 2001

Simchi-Levi, David, et al. *Managing the Supply Chain: The Definitive Guide for the Business Professional.* New York: McGraw-Hill, 2004

Chapter 11

Leenders, Michiel, et al. *Purchasing & Supply Management.* 12th ed. New York: McGraw-Hill, 2002

Burt, David, et al. World Class Supply Management: *The Key to Supply Chain Management.* 7th ed. New York: McGraw-Hill, 2003

Nevitt, Peter, et al. *Equipment Leasing.* 4th ed. New Hope: Frank J, Fabozzi Assoc., 2000

Mayer, David. *Business Leasing for Dummies.* New York: Hungry Minds, Inc., 2001

Brown, Douglas, et al. *The Black Book of Outsourcing: How to Manage the Changes, Challenges, and Opportunities.* New York: John Wiley & Sons, 2005

Chapter 12

Leenders, Michiel, et al. *Purchasing & Supply Management.* 12th ed. New York: McGraw-Hill, 2002

Arnold, Tony, et al. *Introduction to Materials Management.* 5th ed. Columbus: Prentice Hall, 2004

Simchi-Levi, David, et al. *Managing the Supply Chain: The Definitive Guide for the Business Professional.* New York: McGraw-Hill, 2004

Chapter 13

Leenders, Michiel, et al. *Purchasing & Supply Management.* 12th ed. New York: McGraw-Hill, 2002

Burt, David, et al. *World Class Supply Management: The Key to Supply Chain Management.* 7th ed. New York: McGraw-Hill, 2003

Nelson, Dave, et al. *The Purchasing Machine: How the Top Ten Companies Use Best Practices to Manage Their Supply Chains.* New York: Free Press, 2001

Chapter 14

Leenders, Michiel, et al. *Purchasing & Supply Management.* 12th ed. New York: McGraw-Hill, 2002

Walker, William. *Supply Chain Architecture: A Blueprint for Networking the Flow of Material, Information, and Cash.* Boca Raton: CRC Press, 2005

Boone, Tonya, et al. *New Directions in Supply-Chain Management: Technology, Strategy, and Implementation.* New York: AMACOM, 2002

Chapter 15

Cavinato, Joseph, et al. *The Purchasing Handbook: A Guide for the Purchasing and Supply Professional.* 6th ed. New York: McGraw-Hill, 2000.

Burt, David, et al. *World Class Supply Management: The Key to Supply Chain Management.* 7th ed. New York: McGraw-Hill, 2003

Nelson, Dave, et al. *The Purchasing Machine: How the Top Ten Companies Use Best Practices to Manage Their Supply Chains.* New York: Free Press, 2001

Chapter 16

Cavinato, Joseph, et al. *The Purchasing Handbook: A Guide for the Purchasing and Supply Professional.* 6th ed. New York: McGraw-Hill, 2000.

Leenders, Michiel, et al. *Purchasing & Supply Management.* 12th ed. New York: McGraw-Hill, 2002

Dessler, Gary. *Human Resource Management.* 10th ed. Upper Saddle River: Prentice Hall, 2004.

Glossary

10-K reports   A report filed by public companies with the U.S. Securities and Exchange Commission (SEC) that includes income statement, balance sheet, cash flow statement, and related footnotes for the year, together with management's discussion and analysis of these results.

360-degree feedback   Provides a view of employee performance by utilizing input from the circle of people with whom the employee interacts: supervisors, subordinates, peers, and supplier representatives.

A

ABC analysis   A method of classifying purchased items for control purposes, usually by value or importance, with Category A being the highest.

Acceptable Quality Level (AQL)   The largest quantity of defects in a particular sample size that can determine that the lot is acceptable.

acceptance   An express or implied act that accepts an obligation, offer, or contract and all of its legal consequences.

acceptance testing   Testing performed to determine whether a product meets the requirements specified in the contract or by the user and whether or not to accept it.

accounts payable (AP)   Money an organization owes to vendors for products and services purchased on credit. Also refers to the internal department that processes such payments.

accounts receivable (AR)   Money owed by customers to an organization for products or services provided on credit. Also refers to the internal department that processes such payments.

actionable   Providing a basis for action. Example: "After analyzing the quotation, we recommend these four actionable steps." Also used in legal terminology to mean providing cause for legal action.

Activity Based Costing (ABC)   A method used for cost allocation that breaks down overhead costs into specific activities or cost centers (cost drivers) in order to more accurately distribute the costs in product costing.

actual authority   The authority an agent or representative is granted to bind its principal to an agreement or to act on its behalf.

actual damages   The amount of compensation awarded for damages to an injured party for losses incurred as a result of the actions or omissions of another party.

ad hoc   Latin term meaning "for this purpose; for a specific purpose." An ad hoc committee, for example, is created with a unique and specific purpose or task, as it is needed.

ad valorem   Latin term meaning "according to value." A method of taxation using the value of the item being taxed to determine the amount of the tax. Taxes can be either ad valorem or specific: a tax of $8.00 per $100.00 of value is ad valorem, whereas a tax of $8.00 per shipment (irrespective of value) is specific.

administrative management   Planning, organizing, and overseeing administrative tasks of documentation, such as typing and records keeping

administrative theory   Views management in broad administrative terms, looking at organizational structure from the top down. This theory emphasizes the manager and the functions of management, developing the concept of the manager's five functions: Planning, Organizing, Commanding, Coordinating, and Controlling.

Advanced Encryption Standard (AES)   The standard name for the Rijndael (Rain-doll) algorithm used as a decision-support tool in planning, scheduling, and employing computer-based optimization.

Affirmative Action   A policy that addressed the employer's underutilization of individuals from certain protected classes where discrimination in employment was recognized; the policy included the steps that had to be taken to improve these individuals' representation in the employer's workforce.

Age Discrimination in Employment Act   Enacted in 1967, this act is intended to prohibit failure to hire, discharge, or in any way limit or adversely affect an employee's status due to age.

agent   A representative who has been granted the power to act on behalf of another, binding that other to an agreement or decision.

aging   The separation of invoices, orders, inventory, and production lots into time buckets based on due dates, receipt dates, expiration dates, or other factors in order to focus attention on past due and most urgent items.

agreement   An understanding between two or more parties, either oral or written, which forms a binding promise.

allocations   The actual demand created by sales orders or production orders against a specific item. Also indicates suppliers' apportionment of production capacity to individual customers.

American National Standards Institute (ANSI)   A private, nonprofit, quasi-governmental organization that administers, regulates, issues, and coordinates the U.S. voluntary standardization and conformity assessment system for the manufacturing industry.

American Production & Inventory Control Society (APICS)   The former name of a professional organization established for certification and continuing education in the areas of production and inventory control. Its new name is APICS, the Association for Operations Management.

American Society for Quality (ASQ)   A professional organization established for the continuing advancement of quality improvement through learning and knowledge exchange to improve business results. Formerly known as ASQC.

American Society for Testing and Materials (ASTM)   An organization that develops and publishes global technical standards for materials, products, systems, and services established by technical experts who represent producers, users, consumers, government, and academia from over 100 countries. Known today as ASTM International.

Americans with Disabilities Act (ADA)   Legislation that prohibits employment discrimination against qualified individuals with disabilities in job application procedures, hiring, firing, advancement, compensation, job training, and other terms, conditions, and privileges of employment.

ANSI X12   A uniform set of rules for the interchange of business documents and transactions for commercial Electronic Data Interchange (EDI) transactions defined by the American National Standards Institute (ANSI).

anticipatory breach   Occurs when one party to a contract, prior to time of performance, informs the other party of their intent not to perform according to the terms of an agreement.

anticipatory repudiation   After a statement of anticipatory breach (see above), the aggrieved party is entitled to damages and, depending upon the nature of the nonperformance, may also be discharged from performing its remaining obligations under the contract.

apparent authority   A perceived, obvious, or understood authority as demonstrated by a third party or agent whose actions appear to have the authority to bind a principal.

Application Programming Interface (API)   A set of coded routines that a computer or Enterprise Resource Program application uses to request and carry out lower-level services performed by a computer's operating system. Often used to either augment functionality or link one application to another.

Application Service Provider (ASP)   An online supplier of outsourced or hosting services for computer applications, that allows companies to rent instead of buy applications and services such as auctions, exchanges, and catalog aggregation.

application software   A computer software program designed to perform a specific task. Examples include word processing, spreadsheets, and database management systems.

approved supplier list (ASL)   A list of suppliers that has been approved by the buying organization as a qualified source for the parts or services required.

arbitration   A process to settle a legal dispute between two or more parties by referring them to an impartial third party (arbitrator) acting as a judge. The parties agree in advance to abide by the decision of the arbitrator.

assemble to order (ATO)   An operation where manufactured products are booked into stock to await final completion upon receipt of a customer's order.

assignment   The act of transferring the right to sell or purchase from the primary seller or buyer to another party.

ASTM International   An organization that develops and publishes global technical standards for materials, products, systems, and services established by technical experts who represent producers, users, consumers, government, and academia from over 100 countries. Formerly known as the American Society for Testing and Materials (ASTM).

auction   A method of offering and selling products to the highest or lowest bidder, depending on the type of auction employed.

audit   The professional examination of an organization's processes and documentation performed by internal or external resources.

audit trail   The record of chronological activities sufficient to enable the reconstruction and review of events surrounding an operation from inception to final results.

authentication   A process to confirm the identity of a person or to verify the integrity of specific information.

B

back order   Any past due, unfilled portion of an order due to insufficient stock or supplier stock outages.

balance of payments   An accounting of the money value of transactions between one nation and the rest of the world over a specific time period.

balance of trade   The difference in monetary value of a nation's imports and exports.

bank guarantee   An agreement given by a bank on behalf of a customer to pay the seller a sum of money if the buyer cannot or will not pay.

bar code   A printed arrangement of bars and spaces on a label or stamped or embossed onto an item or container for identification of products and quantity. A bar code is designed so it can be read by electronic scanner.

bargain   An agreement between parties fixing the obligations of each.

Basel Convention   An international convention adopted at a United Nations conference in 1989 restricting trade in hazardous waste, some nonhazardous wastes, solid wastes, and incinerator ash.

Behaviorally Anchored Rating Scales (BARS)   A method of performance evaluation based on statements (behavioral anchors) about job behavior and worker activity that is under the control of the employee being rated. These statements are attached to scales in order to rate performance as good, fair, or poor.

benchmark   A structured approach for identifying the best practices from other organizations in industry and government and comparing and adapting them to the organization's operations.

Best Alternative to a Negotiated Agreement (BATNA)   A term coined by Roger Fisher and William Ury in their 1981 book *Getting to Yes: Negotiating Without Giving In*. The BATNA "is the only standard which can protect you both from accepting terms that are too unfavorable and from rejecting terms it would be in your interest to accept."

best practices   The processes, practices, and systems identified in public and private organizations that performed exceptionally well and are widely recognized as improving an organization's performance and efficiency in specific areas.

best-in-class performance   A benchmarking term that identifies organizations, processes, or products that outperform all others in their category.

bilateral contract   An agreement in which the parties exchange promises for each to do something in the future. Also known as a reciprocal contract.

bill of lading (BOL)   A document issued by a freight carrier that establishes the terms of a contract between a shipper and a transportation company under which freight is to be moved between specified points for a specified charge. It serves as a receipt for the goods to be delivered to a designated person. A BOL also describes the conditions under which the goods are accepted by the carrier and details that nature and quantity of the goods.

Bill of Materials (BOM)   A descriptive and quantitative list of materials, parts, and components required to produce an item.

bits   The binary digits a computer uses to represent all data, comprising of solely 0s and 1s. See also *bytes*.

blanket purchase order   A purchasing tool that allows for a firm commitment to buy a specific quantity of goods and/or services provided by a supplier over a specified period of time and at a specified price.

blended learning   A training curriculum that combines multiple types of media, including face-to-face classroom-based training with self-paced e-learning.

brand name   A name or symbol that identifies a seller's goods or services and differentiates them from those of competitors.

breach of contract   A failure to perform as agreed to within the contract.

break-even point   The point in operations at which there is neither a profit nor loss and the volume of revenues exactly equals total expenses.

bribe   An illegal payment to an individual in exchange for an action to which the person or organization offering the bribe is not otherwise entitled.

budget   A plan or estimate of expected income and/or expense for a period of time. Also, a sum of money allocated for a specific purpose.

burden   Overhead expenses distributed over an appropriate direct labor and/or material cost base.

bureaucracy   A form of organization with many layers of management, procedures, rules, and regulations.

business plan   The written strategic plan that details a proposed or existing venture, describing the current status, vision, expected needs, defined markets, future opportunities, and projected results of the business for several years into the future.

business process   The execution of a series of activities undertaken in pursuit of a specific objective, leading to the achievement of an expected business outcome.

Business Process Reengineering (BPR)   The analysis and redesign of workflow and operations within and between enterprises.

business unit   A specific segment of a business organization organized to market specific products or services and responsible for its own revenues and expenses.

business-to-business (B2B)   Transactions conducted primarily between two businesses.

business-to-consumer (B2C)   Transactions conducted between a business enterprise and end users.

Buy American Act   The major domestic preference statute governing procurement by the federal government. It is primarily concerned with the protection of domestic labor.

buyer-planner   A job function responsible for both the planning of requirements and procurement for manufacturing operations.

buying consortium   A group of several organizations combining requirements for purchased goods or services in order to obtain more favorable pricing.

bytes   A sequence of eight bits put together to create a single computer alphabetical or numerical character. See also *bits*.

C

capability index   A ratio that measures both the centering and the variability of a process in relation to specification limits.

capacity requirements planning (CRP)   A process for determining and balancing the amount of machine and labor resources required to meet production commitments.

capacity utilization   A term used by the Federal Reserve to describe the output of factories, industries, and the entire economy in relation to its total capacity. A change in the rate indicates a change in the direction of economic activity. At a higher percentage rate (70–90 percent), industrial output indicates full capacity and an expanding economy and is inflationary. The term is also applied to individual organizations.

capital expenditures budgets   Capital expenditures budgets present plans for the acquisition (or disposal) of major fixed capital assets.

capital goods   Manufactured products that are used to produce other goods such as buildings, tools, machinery, and other equipment.

Carriage and Insurance Paid To (CIP)   The international shipping designation indicating that the exporter is responsible for the cost of freight up to the point where the goods are delivered to a specified destination, including the cost of insurance against loss or damage during transit. It is the exporter's responsibility to clear the goods for export.

carrying costs   Costs incurred through acquiring, transporting, holding, and issuing inventories. The largest element of inventory carrying cost is inventory. Inventory carrying costs also include direct labor costs; facility costs, including building and material handling equipment; variable costs such as electricity, taxes, and insurance; and inventory tracking costs such as computer and operator time.

cash discounts   Reduction of invoice price awarded for prompt payment. Also, the offer of a lower price for cash payment versus credit.

cash flow   An accounting showing how much of the cash generated by the business remains after both expenses (including interest) and principal repayment on financing are paid at a given time.

cash flow budgets   Budgets for determining the availability of cash so that the timing of major expenditures can be coordinated.

cash on delivery (COD)   A term of sale where a buyer pays the carrier the price of goods (and possibly the delivery/freight charges) before they are released. In shipping COD, the seller assumes the risk of the purchaser refusing to accept goods.

Center for Advanced Purchasing Studies (CAPS)   A research forum for supply management conducted jointly by the Institute for Supply Management and Arizona State University College of Business.

central processing unit (CPU)   The main processing chip of a computer that interprets and executes the actual computing tasks.

centralized computer system   A computer system located at one central point, servicing multiple locations. Typically, users are networked to a single mainframe computer and their individual workstations consist of terminals without independent processing units or storage.

centralized procurement   A procurement system in which decision making, flow of data or goods and services, or the beginning of activities is initiated at the same central point and disseminated to remote points in the chain or organization.

Certificate Authority (CA)   An issuer of security certificates verifying the authenticity of processed data used in Single Socket Layers (SSL) connections over the Internet.

Certificate of Origin (COO)   A document required by certain foreign countries for tariff purposes certifying and identifying the country of origin of specified goods.

Certified Purchasing Manager (C.P.M.)   A professional designation and certification granted by the Institute for Supply Management (ISM) to individuals who have met established criteria and successfully passed all modules of the C.P.M. exam. It is designed for experienced supply managers and focuses on managerial and leadership skills plus a variety of specialized functions designed to enhance the value of the profession.

certified supplier   A supplier that does not furnish direct materials and is therefore not included on the Approved Supplier List (ASL) but who has met a particular set of requirements established by the organization. This designation might apply to a supplier removing hazardous waste or a specially licensed consultants, as well as companies supplying certain types of telecommunications or network hardware.

Chain of Command Principle   An organizational system in which each individual reports to only one supervisor or manager so that responsibility and accountability are clearly defined and work can be effectively delegated.

change index   An economic indicator that measures the change over a period of time in the value of specific items. A change index is typified by the Consumer Price Index (CPI).

change management   Activities involved in defining and instilling new values, attitudes, norms, and behaviors within an organization that support new ways of doing work and overcome resistance to change. Change management includes building consensus among customers and stakeholders on specific changes designed to better meet their needs, and planning, testing, and implementing all aspects of the transition from one organizational structure or business process to another.

change order   A written order signed by the buyer or contracting officer authorizing a change in the work or an adjustment in the contract sum or time spent.

chaos theory   A theory of complex and unpredictable dynamics in systems that exhibit discontinuous change. In management, chaos theory recognizes that events can rarely be completely controlled in an organization and, to survive, its systems must adapt and evolve.

Chart of Accounts   The listing of individual account files in the General Ledger that provides a means for collecting, classifying, and reporting on financial transactions. Each account contains a description, account type (asset, liability, capital, income, expense, or subledger), and active status.

Check Request   A form used by many organizations to request payment by the Accounting Department to a supplier when no purchase order exists.

Chief Procurement Officer (CPO)   The senior individual responsible for the entire organization's procurement processes.

Choice of Law   A clause that indicates what venue of law will apply in the event of a dispute.

Civil Rights Act   Legislation that furthers constitutional guarantees, with particular emphasis on preventing employment discrimination based on race, gender, sex, religion, disability, or age.

client/server   A computer network configuration in which application processing is split between the "client," typically a desktop computing device, and a program "served" by another networked computing device, typically a mainframe computer.

closed orders   Orders are closed when the ordered quantity and invoiced quantity match and fulfill the total obligations of the purchase.

closed stores   Inventory maintained in a storage facility under continuous, active control and with access limited to authorized personnel only.

Code of Federal Regulations (CFR)   Compilation of all U.S. Federal regulations published by the Office of the Federal Register, National Archives and Records Service of the General Services Administration. The CFR is divided into numbered titles, primarily by federal agency.

coincident indicators   An economic indicator that varies directly with and at the same time as the related economic trend, thereby providing information about the current state of the economy.

collaboration   The process of two or more persons or organizations working together to achieve a common goal.

Collaborative Planning, Forecasting, and Replenishment (CPFR)   The sharing of forecast and related business information among business partners in the supply chain to enable automatic product replenishment.

commercial law   A body of case law and rules applied to commercial transactions.

Commercial Lease Agreements   A written agreement outlining the terms and conditions governing the lease of commercial property and equipment.

commodities   An article of commerce in a specific category of goods where each item is undifferentiated from the other.

commodity council   A cross-functional organization team tasked with oversight of the acquisition and use of specific commodities.

commodity exchange   An established marketplace where commodities are bought and sold for future delivery and prices are established according to supply and demand.

commodity management   The system of procurement management in which groups of similar products and services are assigned to specific individuals in order to leverage sourcing expertise and reduce costs and risks.

communication device   Equipment with or without related software capable of sending and/or receiving data or voice input and output.

comparative analysis   The process of examining the similarities and differences of two or more products to determine which one to purchase.

comparative standards   A relative system that compares an employee's job performance with that of others in the same function or at the same grade level of compensation.

competent   An individual who is duly qualified and possesses the requisite natural or legal qualifications to enter into a contract.

Compound Annual Growth Rate (CAGR)   The year-to-year growth rate applied to an investment or other aspect of value using a base amount.

compound duties   A form of import tax imposed on imported merchandise that incorporates features of both ad valorem and specific duties. This tax can be assessed based on a percentage of value as well as on the net weight or number of pieces.

Computer Aided Manufacturing (CAM)   A computer application used to design and control the manufacture of products in an automated factory.

computer-based training (CBT)   A generic term for training or instruction by a learner to acquire knowledge or skills via a computer program, sometimes referred to as distance learning. It can deliver lessons, provide practice and work simulations, test learners, and manage training administration.

Confidentiality Agreement   An agreement between two parties to maintain the confidentiality of information received from the other party. Typically, this information should be clearly identified as proprietary and/or confidential, and a time limit must be specified for maintaining confidentiality.

conflict of interest   Any personal, financial, and/or professional interest that might create a divergence with the ability to fairly and objectively carry out the responsibilities to an employer when one is in a position of influence.

consequential damages   Those damages or losses that arise from or in consequence of an action.

consideration   The exchange of value upon which a contract is based or something of value that is offered as an inducement by one party to another to enter into a contract.

consignment inventory   Inventory that is held in the possession of the customer without payment for future use but which is still owned by the supplier.

consignment   A procedure in which one business (the consignee) accepts goods from another business (the consignor) for sale on a commission basis.

consignee   A person or company (named in the bill of lading) to whom goods are shipped.

consortium   A legal grouping of organizations to fulfill a shared objective or undertake a common project that is intended to result in greater benefit to the participants than each would obtain individually.

constraint-based planning   A form of production planning based on the assumption that the production process is limited by certain bottlenecks (constraints). Possible bottlenecks that can have a significant influence on production include resources with low capacity (such as equipment) and materials that are available in limited quantities.

construction contract   An agreement between a general contractor and buyer that sets forth terms and conditions for the construction, repair, renovation, or restoration of a building or civil engineering work.

Consumer Price Index (CPI)   A measure of the change in the cost of living as determined by a market basket of goods and services, commonly used as a measure of inflation. It is published by the U.S. Department of Labor (DOL) on a monthly basis.

Consumer Product Safety Act (1972)   An act that established the Consumer Product Safety Commission with jurisdiction to reduce the risk of injuries and deaths from consumer products by developing voluntary standards with industry, issuing and enforcing mandatory standards and banning consumer products if no feasible standard adequately protects the public.

contingency planning   The process of developing a strategic plan that identifies alternative actions to be used to ensure a successful outcome if specified risk events occur.

contingency theory   The management theory of leadership that asserts the association between leadership orientation and group effectiveness is contingent upon how favorable the situation is for exerting influence.

continuous improvement   A quality philosophy that assumes the ongoing improvement of processes, products, programs, and services through incremental (progressive small steps) and breakthrough (giant step) actions.

Continuous Quality Improvement (CQI)   A philosophy and attitude for analyzing capabilities and processes and repeatedly improving them to achieve customer satisfaction.

contract   A legally enforceable agreement entered into by two or more parties to perform or not perform certain actions.

contraction   A government monetary policy of raising interest rates charged by the central bank in order to reduce spending.

Control Chart   A graphical tool showing upper and lower control limits that determine whether the statistical distribution of data values generated by a process is stable over time.

Convention on Contracts for the International Sale of Goods (CISG)   An international agreement that establishes uniform legal rules governing the formation of international sales contracts and the rights and obligations of the buyer and seller.

copyright   A grant of ownership for various forms of expressions such as works of art, literature, software programs, or audio/visual material with the exclusive right to sell, publish, or license.

corrective action   Change(s) made to bring expected future performance of a process into line with the requirements or plan.

corrective action process   The methods used to document, analyze, and correct deviations from standards or specifications.

corrective action request (CAR)   A report issued to activate a corrective action, usually initiated by a process failure or by findings during internal or external quality auditing.

correlation analysis   Analysis of the degree to which changes in one variable are associated with changes in another, measuring the strength of the relationship between the two variables.

Cost and Freight (CFR)   A pricing term indicating that the cost of the goods and freight charges are included in the quoted price. The buyer arranges for and pays insurance.

cost analysis   The process of determining the actual cost of a product or service by analyzing, evaluating, and examining data to determine the reasonableness and appropriateness of the costs.

cost avoidance   A purchasing action to ensure certain material or supplier increases are not incurred by the purchasing firm. It involves avoiding a future cost increase by delaying or reducing the impact of a proposed price increase.

cost center   An accounting term that refers to a department or function in the organization that incurs expenses. A cost center can be a program cost center, a project, or an organizational unit such as a department.

cost code   An accounting and budgeting category assigned to allocate cost to specific departments, projects, or functions.

cost containment   The process or strategy used to limit or control costs when companies implement new programs or modify existing programs.

cost of goods sold (COGS)   Accounting term used for the total cost of purchased direct materials and the labor for manufacturing finished products (if applicable).

cost reduction   Process to reduce the overall cost of a product.

cost reimbursable contracts   Contracts that provide for payment of allowable incurred costs, to the extent agreed upon in the contracts.

Cost, Insurance, and Freight (CIF)   A pricing term indicating that the cost of the goods, insurance, and freight is included in the quoted price.

cost-only contract   Used primarily by nonprofit organizations; covers reimbursement only for actual costs, without including a fee. This contract typically supplements one organization's capabilities and enables full utilization of the other's resources that might otherwise remain idle.

cost-plus-award-fee   A contract where all allowable costs are paid by the buyer, and an incentive is provided to the supplier by enabling the buyer to make a financial award in addition to the cost and negotiated fee for excellent performance.

cost-plus-fixed-fee contract   A contract where the buyer reimburses the seller for the seller's allowable costs plus a fixed fee negotiated in advance.

cost-plus-incentive-fee   A contract where the buyer reimburses the seller for the seller's allowable costs and the seller earns a formula-based adjustment that reflects the relationship of total allowable cost to total target cost.

cost-plus-percentage-of-cost   A now outlawed contract that provided reimbursement of allowable cost of services performed plus an agreed-upon percentage of the estimated cost as profit.

cost-ratio analysis   A method for comparatively evaluating a supplier's offers that weighs one supplier's bid in comparison to others by transforming the value of its offer to some equivalent percentage based upon its demonstrated performance or added value.

costs   The cash value of the resources used to produce or purchase a product or service.

cost-sharing contract   A contract that provides payment for only a share of allowable costs. Cost-sharing contracts are often awarded to motivate development of new technologies.

counseling   A behavioral control technique to help resolve performance problems.

counteroffer   The rejection of an offer to buy or sell and a second offer altering one or several terms and/or conditions of the offer as originally written. The counteroffer terminates the original offer. This process continues until both seller and buyer agree to all terms and conditions.

countertrade   The sale of goods or services paid for in whole or in part by the transfer of goods or services.

Cp   The measure of process capability equal to the difference between the upper specification limit and the lower specification limit divided by six sigma.

Cpk   A process capability index used to measure a process's ability to create product within specification limits. Cpk represents the difference between the actual process average and the closest specification limit over the standard deviation, times three. When the Cpk is less than one, the process is referred to as incapable. When the Cpk is greater than or equal to one, the process is considered capable of producing a product within specification limits. In a Six Sigma process, the Cpk equals 2.0.

Critical Incidents Review   A process where a review of a specific or key performance factor is made that separates effective from ineffective performance.

Critical Path Method (CPM)   A project management planning and control technique based on a series of activities and tasks with no built-in slack time. Any task that takes longer than expected will lengthen the time of the project.

cross functional team   Team consisting of individuals with different functional expertise working toward a common goal.

cure   In law, another term for remedy, referring to the legal or judicial means by which a right or privilege is enforced or the violation of a right or privilege is prevented, redressed, or compensated.

current ratio   A measure of an organization's liquidity or its ability to pay its short-term debts. Calculated by dividing current assets by current liabilities.

Customer Relationship Management (CRM)   The process used by an organization to manage interactions with its customers. It includes all business processes in sales, marketing, and service that reach the customer.

customization   The modification of a product or service to meet a customer's specific requirements.

cycle counting   A perpetual series of regularly scheduled inventory counts that "cycles" through all key items of inventory.

cycle time   The elapsed time to move a unit of work from the beginning to the end of a physical process.

D

damages   Financial compensation that a claimant seeks or a court awards for injuries sustained or property damaged by another.

data   A collection of facts and/or information represented in a readable language (such as numbers, characters, images, or other methods of recording) from which conclusions may be drawn.

data warehousing   The collection of information from multiple, disparate databases into one database, against which programs can be run to gather organization-wide business intelligence.

database management systems (DBMS)   A set of computer programs for organizing and storing information in a database. Typically, a DBMS contains routines for data input, verification, storage, retrieval, and combination.

decentralized purchasing   The allocation of purchasing responsibility away from a centralized Purchasing Department to locally dispersed departments.

Decision Support Systems (DSS)   Computerized information system that supports decision-making activities

decision tree   A decision-making, graphical tool used to analyze and represent alternate decisions and the possible outcomes.

de-escalation   A clause in a contract allowing for the reduction of prices as a result of specific conditions.

Define, Measure, Analyze, Improve, and Control (DMAIC)   A process for continued improvement and an integral part of a Six Sigma quality initiative. It is a systematic, scientific, and fact-based closed-loop process to eliminate unproductive steps, often focusing on new measurements and technology for improvement.

definite quantity contract   A contract that provides for a specific quantity of products or services within stated limits for a fixed period.

deflation   A decline in the general price level of goods and services that results in increased purchasing power of money. The opposite of inflation.

Delivered at Frontier (DAF)   A term of sale indicating that the exporter's obligation is fulfilled when the goods are delivered to a specified point at the frontier cleared for export.

Delivered Duty Paid (DDP)   A term of sale indicating the exporter's obligation is fulfilled when the goods have been made available at a specified point in the importer's country. The exporter is also responsible for payment of duties, taxes, and other customs clearance charges.

Delivered Duty Unpaid (DDU)   A term of sale where the seller fulfills its obligation to deliver when the goods have been made available at the named place in the country of importation. The seller has to bear the costs and risks involved in bringing the goods thereto (excluding duties, taxes, and other official charges payable upon importation), as well as the costs and risks of carrying out customs formalities. The buyer has to pay any additional costs and bear any risks caused by failure to clear the goods in time.

Delivered Ex Quay (DEQ)   Indicates that the exporter is responsible for making the goods available to the importer on the wharf at the port of discharge, cleared for import. This term cannot be used for airfreight shipments.

Delivered Ex Ship (DES)   A term of sale where the seller makes the goods available to the buyer on board the ship at the place named in the sales contract. The seller bears the full cost and risk involved in bringing the goods there. The cost of unloading the goods and any customs duties must be paid by the buyer.

Delphi method   A group decision-making technique in which individuals respond to questionnaires until a final composite list is obtained that represents the opinions of the group. This is not a group discussion technique since the group members do not typically or necessarily meet to talk about their responses to the questionnaires.

demand   The order for a specific item in a specific quantity or, more broadly, the overall quantities of goods or services consumers are willing and able to purchase at any given price over a given time.

demand management   Management of the functions related to forecasting customer demand, order entry, order promising, inventory optimization, and replenishment requirements, often through the use of decision support systems.

demand-based   A system of replenishment based on actual or forecasted customer demand.

Deming Prize   An annual prize meant to promote the continued development of quality control in Japan. It was originally established in 1950 to commemorate Dr. Edward Deming's contribution and friendship to Japan, and awards are still given each year.

demurrage   A charge to the receiver when freight cars, containers, or trucks are held for loading, unloading, or shipping instructions beyond the allowable time.

Departmentalization Principle   Maintains that similar activities should be grouped according to similarities in process, product lines, location, or purpose.

dependent demand   The demand for components and parts based upon incoming customer orders.

depreciate   Taking an accounting charge to current operations that distributes the cost of a tangible capital asset, less estimated residual value, over the projected useful life of the asset in a systematic and logical manner.

detrimental reliance   The legal principle that a buyer relied on what was told to the buyer to the buyer's disadvantage.

digital certificate   An electronic "credit card" that establishes credentials when doing business or other transactions on the World Wide Web.

digital signature   A method for proving that the holder of a private key is the originator of a message.

Digital Signature Standard (DSS)   A cryptographic signature algorithm that is part of many standards.

digital system   A system in which information is transmitted in a series of pulses using a binary code.

direct costs   Clearly identifiable costs that are directly attributable to specific products or services provided for sale. Some examples are labor hours or materials consumed in the production of an output.

direct labor   Labor costs directly attributed to the production of specific products or services for sale that include wages and associated fringe benefits.

direct material   Material incorporated into the product being sold.

directive counseling   Counseling that provides recommendations in a direct manner.

disadvantaged suppliers   A business concern which is at least 51 percent owned by one or more socially and economically disadvantaged individuals or, in the case of any publicly owned business, at least 51 percent of the stock is owned by such individuals and whose management and daily business operations are controlled by one or more of such individuals.

discipline   A form of corrective action and behavioral control taken when an employee is unwilling or unable to correct performance issues.

discrimination   The unfair or unequal treatment of an individual or class of individuals because of their age, sex, race, religion, or physical disability.

disintermediation   Removing the middleman or distributor in a sales transaction.

disqualified suppliers   Suppliers prohibited from doing business with the organization.

distributed system   A noncentralized network consisting of numerous computers that can communicate with one another and that appear to users as parts of a single, large, accessible "storehouse" of shared hardware, software, and data.

distribution   The process of delivering goods and services to the customer.

Distribution Resources Planning (DRP)   Software used to plan inventory requirements in a multiple plant/warehouse environment. DRP may be used for both distribution and manufacturing.

diversity suppliers   Minority-owned, women-owned, and service-disabled veteran–owned suppliers.

document control   A system whereby control is maintained over the initiation, reproduction, transmission, receipt, and destruction of documents.

due diligence The careful discovery, investigation, and complete analysis of the risks and value of a product or service that is to be purchased (or the organization from which it is to be acquired) in order to assist a buyer in making decisions about the purchase.

dumped Product offered for sale at prices below cost as a result of a governmental subsidy or in order to undermine the competition as a means of gaining market share.

Dutch auction An auction in which an item is initially offered at a high price that is progressively lowered until a bid is made and the item sold.

E

Early Supplier Involvement (ESI) A process of involving a supplier before or during the design phase of a project.

economic order quantity (EOQ) A calculation that determines the most cost effective quantity to order (purchased items) or produce (manufactured items) and finds the point at which the combination of order cost and carrying cost is the least. The standard formula is EOQ = Square Root [2 * (Annual Usage) * (Order Cost) / (Annual Carrying Cost/unit)].

electronic catalog A computerized system that presents goods or services for sale and enables users to buy goods or services electronically.

electronic commerce (EC) Electronic techniques for accomplishing business transactions, including electronic mail or messaging, World Wide Web technology, electronic bulletin boards, purchase cards, electronic funds transfer, and electronic data interchange.

Electronic Data Interchange (EDI) A set of computer interchange standards for business documents such as invoices, bills, and purchase orders to enable business transactions using computer systems.

electronic funds transfer (EFT) Any transfer of funds, other than a transaction originated by cash, check, or similar paper instrument, that is initiated through an electronic terminal, telephone, computer, or magnetic tape, for the purpose of ordering, instructing, or authorizing a financial institution to debit or credit an account.

electronic procurement (e-procurement) The business-to-business (B2B) automated purchase and sale of supplies and services over the Internet.

electronic purchase orders (EPOs) Purchase orders transmitted to the supplier electronically directly from a computer system.

e-mail (electronic mail) A method and tool used to send digital messages, usually text, electronically from one computer to another.

encryption A method of making data unreadable to everyone except the receiver.

encryption key A group of characters that initiate the encryption process. Each partner of a trading partner pair must have possession of the same key.

end-of-life   Products reaching the end of their marketing cycle due to declining demand or obsolescence.

end user   The ultimate consumer of a product or service.

End-User License Agreement (EULA)   The terms and conditions governing the use of software or other intellectual property.

Engineering Change Order (ECO)   A form or notice that signifies a change is required in documents, processes, work instructions, or specifications. Also referred to as ECN (Engineering Change Notice).

Enterprise Resource Planning (ERP)   An integrated, modular software system used to manage the important parts of an organization's operations, including product planning, parts purchasing, maintaining inventories, interacting with suppliers, providing customer service, and tracking orders.

Environmental Protection Agency (EPA)   An independent federal agency with primary responsibility for protection and enforcement of the environmental laws covering the pollution of air quality, water quality, and wetlands, in addition to protection against hazardous wastes and other environmental issues.

Equal Employment Opportunity (EEO)   Legislation that all employment-related actions are based on objective, nondiscriminatory criteria; firing, compensation, promotion, recruitment, and training in state and federal laws and regulations prohibit employment discrimination on the basis of race, color, religion, national origin, citizenship, sex, age, disability, Vietnam-era veteran status, or special disabled veteran status.

Equal Employment Opportunity Commission (EEOC)   A federal agency responsible for overseeing and enforcing nondiscrimination in hiring, firing, compensation, promotion, recruitment, training, and other terms and conditions of employment regardless of race, color, sex, age, religion, national origin, or disability.

Equal Pay Act (EPA)   Enacted in 1970, this act provides rights to the same contractual pay and benefits for individuals of each sex in the same employment, where the man and the woman are doing work rated as equivalent under an analytical job evaluation study.

escalation   A clause, generally found in long-term supply contracts, which provides for periodic price adjustment based on variations in any or all cost factors. "Escalating prices" are the opposite of "firm" prices, which are not subject to change over the life of a contract.

Ethical Code of Conduct   A management tool for establishing and articulating the corporate values, responsibilities, obligations, and ethical ambitions of an organization and the way it functions. It provides guidance to employees on how to handle situations that pose a dilemma between alternative right courses.

evaluated receipts settlement (ERS)   A process designed to eliminate or minimize the supplier invoice as a costly and unnecessary document. Payments are initiated by receipt of goods as they are logged on the buying organization's computer system.

evergreen contract   A contract with no expiration date.

ex works (EXW)   A term used in the sale of goods to denote that the price includes only the cost of the product at the warehouse/factory gates before any transportation costs are included.

Exception Management Principle   Suggests that routine duties are handled by subordinates and that the manager responds only to issues outside the normal course of events.

executive review   An annual meeting where executives from the buying and selling organizations come together to exchange business plans and technology road maps.

executive summary   A synopsis or abbreviated report of an action, project, situation, or contract.

expansion   A phase of the business cycle that extends from a trough to the next peak.

expediting   The process of increasing the priority level of a production or purchase order because of a past due condition or a change in the requirement date that necessitates compressing the normal lead time.

exponential smoothing   A statistical adjustment technique commonly used to forecast time series data or to smooth the values or predict a series.

express warranties   Spoken or written promises made by the seller of a product about what will be done if the product proves to be defective in manufacture or performance.

external audit   A review of financial statements and accounting records by an accountant not belonging to the firm to check that the system is effective, documented, and adhered to by all staff.

extranet   That part of a company's own intranet that is shared with a subset of external users.

F

fair and reasonable   A price that is fair to both parties, considering the agreed-upon conditions, promised quality, and timeliness of contract performance. "Fair and reasonable" price is subject to statutory and regulatory limitations.

fair market value   The price at which property changes hands between a willing buyer and a willing seller, neither being under compulsion to buy or sell and both having reasonable knowledge of the relevant facts.

Federal Acquisitions Regulations (FAR)   The body of regulations, uniform policies, and procedures that is the primary source of authority governing the federal government's procurement process.

Federal Reserve System   The central bank of the United States. Its primary duties include conducting the nation's monetary policy by influencing the money and credit conditions in the economy, supervising and regulating banking institutions, and maintaining the stability of the nation's financial system.

fiduciary   A legal relationship of trust and confidence to another, having a duty to act primarily for the other's benefit. A fiduciary has rights and powers that would normally belong to another person and must exercise a high standard of care in protecting or promoting the interests of the beneficiary.

field   Discipline or a branch of knowledge surrounding an area of interest.

file   A set of related records (either written or electronic) kept together.

File Transfer Protocol (FTP)   An Internet protocol that allows users to quickly transfer text and binary files to and from a distant or local PC, list directories, delete and rename files on the foreign host, and perform wildcard transfers between hosts.

finance lease   A lease in which the service provided by the lessor to the lessee is limited to financing equipment. All other responsibilities related to the possession of equipment, such as maintenance, insurance, and taxes, are borne by the lessee. A financial lease is usually noncancelable and is fully paid out and amortized over its term.

Financial Accounting Standards Board (FASB)   Nongovernmental authority for establishing accounting standards in the United States. FASB Statement 13 establishes standards for lessees' and lessors' accounting and reporting for leases.

finished goods (FG)   An item that is complete and in a salable form.

finished goods inventory (FGI)   Products completely manufactured, packaged, stored, and ready for distribution.

firewall   A combined hardware and software buffer that protects and filters the incoming data of a private network from users from other networks.

firm-fixed-price contract   Provides for a price that is not subject to any adjustment on the basis of the contractor's cost experience in performing the contract. This contract type places upon the contractor maximum risk and full responsibility for all costs and resulting profit or loss and provides maximum incentive for the contractor to control costs and perform effectively. It imposes a minimum administrative burden upon the contracting parties.

First In, First Out (FIFO)   An accounting term that describes the method of rotating inventory to use the oldest product first.

fitness for a particular purpose   An implied warranty of use that promises a product or good is fit for its ordinary purpose by a merchant who knows that a buyer intends to use a product or good for a particular purpose and has reason to know that the buyer is relying on the merchant's knowledge or expertise and that the product or good is suitable for the buyer's special use or particular purpose.

fixed costs   Operating expenses that remain constant, regardless of output.

fixed order quantity   An order of fixed size, placed whenever stock falls to a certain level. The size of reorder will depend on the rate of consumption and the lead time (the time taken from ordering supplies to supplies arriving and being prepared for use).

fixed-price contract   See *firm-fixed price contract*.

fixed-price-with-economic-price-adjustment contract   Provides for upward and downward revision of the stated contract price based on economic occurrences, including adjustments based on increases or decreases of established prices for materials used in manufacturing, in actual labor costs, or on cost indexes of labor or material.

fixed-price-with-incentive contract   A fixed-price contract that provides for adjusting profit and establishing the final contract price by application of a formula based on the relationship of total final negotiated cost to total target cost. The final price is subject to a price ceiling, negotiated at the outset.

fixed-price-with-price-redetermination contract   Provides a firm fixed price for an initial period of contract deliveries or performance and prospective redetermination, at a stated time or times during performance, of the price for subsequent periods of performance.

fixed-price, level-of-effort contract   Requires the contractor to provide a specified level of effort, over a stated period of time, on work that can be stated only in general terms.

Flat Organization   Describes a decentralized approach to management organization that reduces the management hierarchy and encourages high employee involvement in decisions. In this organizational structure, managers tend to have a more personal relationship with their employees.

flexible budget   Based on a set of revenue and expense projections at various volume levels, the cost allowances for each expense item are allowed to vary as income or production varies.

flowchart   A visualization technique representing the steps or activities in a process. Rectangles represent a step in the process. Diamonds represent decision points. Lines with arrowheads give the flow and direction of the process.

focus group   A carefully planned discussion lead by a trained moderator that is used to gain a deeper understanding of respondents' attitudes and opinions about a topic of concern. A focus group brings together from six to nine users to discuss issues and concerns about the features of a user interface.

force majeure   A standard clause in a supply contract that permits either party not to fulfill the contractual commitments due to events beyond their control by an overpowering force. These events may range from natural disasters such as earthquakes, floods, and war to strikes or export delays in producing countries.

forecast-based   A policy or process based on an estimation of future demand.

forecasting   The process of estimating future demand, coming events, or conditions.

forward auction   Selling companies post items they want to sell and allow buying companies to compete for the best prices acceptable by the selling companies for those items. Winning bidders (buyers) are obligated to buy items in forward auctions. A typical forward auction is the English auction, which is a single or multiple-item, open, ascending-price auction. The initiator specifies the opening bid and bid increment and optionally a reserve price. Each bidder submits a successively higher bid. At the end of the auction, bidders with the highest bids win. Each winning bidder pays a price equal to the highest bid made.

forward buying   Buying in advance of actual demand or forecasted needs. This process is generally used to ensure supply at a fixed price when prices are trending upward or market conditions indicate there may be potential shortages in supply.

free on board (FOB)   Term of sale where the invoice cost to the purchaser includes the cost of delivery, at an agreed point, beyond which all transportation and delivery costs and risks must be borne by the purchaser.

free trade   Trade between nations that is conducted on free market principles without tariffs, import quotas, or other restrictive regulations. In 1993, Canada, the United States, and Mexico entered into a trilateral free trade agreement, the North American Free Trade Agreement (NAFTA).

full payout lease   A lease in which the lessor recovers, through the lease payments, all costs incurred in the lease plus an acceptable rate of return, without any reliance upon the leased equipment's future residual value.

functional specifications   A specification that defines the task to be accomplished rather than the method by which it is to be performed.

functionality analysis   A procedure for analyzing behavior problems between the occurrence of problem behavior, antecedent, and consequence events through direct observation and the systematic manipulation of environmental events.

futures options   The right to buy or sell contracts for commodities, currencies, stock indexes, and other instruments at some time in the future.

G

Gantt chart   A graphical representation of the stages or activities in a project work plan over time, indicating the status of progress in relation to an established timeline. Progress is typically shown as a horizontal bar plotted on a calendar.

gap analysis   A fact finding process of comparing the difference between projected outcomes and desired outcomes.

General and Administrative Expenses (G&A)   A management, financial, and other expense for general management and administration of the business unit as a whole.

goal   A result to be achieved by an organization to address its critical issues and drive its actions.

Government Accounting Office (GAO)   An independent federal agency that acts as the investigative arm of Congress, making the executive branch accountable to Congress and the government accountable to citizens of the United States.

graphic rating scale   A scale on which individuals indicate their ratings of an attribute by placing a check at the appropriate point on a line that runs from one extreme of the attribute to the other.

gratuities   A voluntary payment or award (as for meritorious service) given without claim or obligation.

Gross Domestic Product (GDP)   A measure of total consumer spending, business investment, and government spending and investment, plus the value of exports, minus the value of imports, of the total market value of all final goods and services produced in the United States during any quarter or year.

Gross National Product (GNP)   The monetary value of all goods and services produced in a nation's economy. Unlike gross domestic product, it includes goods and services produced abroad.

Group Rank Ordering System   Requires the reviewing manager to place employees into a particular classification such as the top 25 percent or the bottom 25 percent. This forces a ranking according to group levels.

H

halo effect   A rating error that occurs when the evaluator tends to base overall judgments or evaluations on selected pieces of information rather than on all available relevant information. The halo effect can be reduced by rating and comparing all performance ratings on a single factor before going on to another factor.

harassment   Unsolicited words or conduct, such as unwanted sexual attention, bullying, intimidation, or abuse of power that tends to annoy, alarm, or abuse another person.

hard costs   Money spent that can be saved as additional profit.

Hawthorne Effect   The impact of the researcher on the research subjects or setting, notably in changing their behavior. The increase in worker productivity was observed when a worker was singled out and made to feel important.

hits   A measure of the number of times a website has been visited or requests for files have been made to a web server. Alternatively, the number of responses provided by a computer search.

hold harmless   In a contract, a promise by one party not to hold the other party responsible if it carries out the contract in a way that causes damage.

human relations theories   Theories governing the management and development of employees.

hypertext markup language (HTML)   The programming language of the Internet used to create and design web pages. HTML creates the page layout, formats text, and inserts graphics.

I

imperfect competition   A condition where the actions of at least one buyer or seller have an effect on the market price. Forms of imperfect competition include monopoly and oligopoly markets.

Implicit Price Deflator (IPD)   A series of price indices used to deflate the components of National Accounts to real terms relative to the index base. The IPD for expenditure on GDP and the IPD for private final consumption expenditure are widely used as general measures of inflation for an economy.

implied warranty   A guarantee of the condition of a thing or the truth of a statement that is created as a result of the actions of a party but is not written down.

incidental damages   An award in a lawsuit for breach of contract in compensation for commercially reasonable expenses incurred as a result of the other party's breach, such as costs of inspecting and returning goods that do not conform to contract specifications.

indefinite delivery contracts   A contract awarded to facilitate the delivery of specified supply and service orders at some date in the future.

indemnification   A process of protecting the buyer against any losses that have occurred or will occur.

independent demand   Demand generated from forecasts, customer orders, or service requirements.

indirect costs   Costs that are not directly charged to a product or project but which are associated with general operations such as utilities, building operations, legal services, or purchasing.

indirect material   Material used in the production process but not attributed to the production of specific salable units.

Individual Rank Ordering System   Requires the reviewing manager to list employees from highest to lowest during evaluations.

inflation   An increase in the amount of money or credit available in relation to the amount of goods or services available, which causes an increase in the general price level of goods and services. Over time, inflation reduces the purchasing power of a unit of currency, making it worth less.

information overload   Introducing too much information into the activity, making it difficult or impossible to find a satisfactory resolution.

information technology (IT)   Equipment or interconnected systems or subsystems of equipment, personnel, and processes that are used in the automatic acquisition, storage, manipulation, management, movement, control, display, switching, interchange, transmission, or reception of data or information.

infringement   Unauthorized use of intellectual property or violation, as of a law, regulation, or agreement; a breach.

injunction   A writ (order) issued by a court ordering someone to do something or prohibiting some act after a court hearing

in-kind exchange   A product or service that is traded with a second party for another product or service.

input devices   Hardware that is used to enter information into a computer. For example, a keyboard, mouse, or bar-code scanner.

insourcing   Sourcing for a product within the company.

Institute for Supply Management (ISM)   A not-for-profit association that provides opportunities for the promotion of the supply management profession and the expansion of professional skills and knowledge. It is considered the largest supply management association in the world as well as one of the most respected. ISM's mission is to lead the supply management profession through its standards of excellence, research, promotional activities, and education.

Institute of Electrical and Electronic Engineers (IEEE)   A professional society of engineering and electronics professionals serving the international community that focuses on electrical, electronics, computer engineering, and science–related matters, conducting research and helping to set standards for electrical and computer engineering.

intellectual property (IP)   The general term for intangible property rights that are a result of intellectual effort. Patents, trademarks, business methods, designs, and copyrights are the main forms of intellectual property rights.

interactive counseling   A combination of both nondirective and directive techniques.

interest rates   The price charged as a fee for lending or borrowing money.

intermediaries   Third party resellers or brokers of products and services.

internal audit   An examination of a company's records, policies, and procedures conducted by the company's own employees, who check for completeness, accuracy, and deviations from standard procedures.

International Commercial Terms (INCOTERMS)   Codification of terms managed by the International Chamber of Commerce that is used in foreign trade contracts to define which parties incur the various costs of shipment and at what specific point the costs are incurred.

International Organization for Standardization (ISO)   A federation of national standards organizations that develops and publishes international standards.

Internet   A worldwide system of computer networks in which any one computer can get information from or talk to any other connected computer using the TCP/IP protocols.

Internet Protocol (IP)   The standard that allows a variety of computer hosts to connect to each other through the Internet.

interoperability   The ability of one system to operate alongside, communicate with, and exchange information with another dissimilar system.

interviewing   Part of the employment selection process designed to assess past behaviors and accomplishments.

intranet   A private computer network used inside a company or organization.

inventory   Goods and materials held in stock for use in manufacturing or sale.

inventory management   Systems and processes that manage the replenishment and status reporting of stock items.

ISO 14000   A group of environmental management standards developed by the International Organization for Standardization (ISO).

ISO 9000:2000   A group of standards established by the International Organization for Standardization (ISO) in the 1980s as a basis for judging the adequacy of the quality control systems of companies.

J

joint venture   The agreement of cooperation or joint ownership between two or more individuals or enterprises in a specific business enterprise, rather than in a continuing relationship as in a partnership.

just-in-time (JIT)   A philosophy and methodology for optimizing manufacturing processes by eliminating all waste including wasted steps, wasted material, and excess inventory, with inventory arriving or being produced just in time for the shipment or next process.

K

Kaizen   A Japanese term that means continuous improvement, taken from the words *Kai* meaning "continuous" and *Zen* meaning "improvement."

Kanban   A Japanese term for maintaining an orderly and efficient flow of materials throughout the entire manufacturing process by signaling the need for inventory and controlling inventory levels through a system of cards sent from the using location to the supplying location.

Key Performance Indicators (KPI)   Measurements that are used in progress reports to reflect the critical success factors of the operation.

Kyoto Agreement   A United Nations–sponsored agreement to prevent global warming signed by 38 developed countries. At a summit held in 1997, those signing the treaty agreed to reduce their emission of greenhouse gases by the year 2012. Also known as the *Kyoto Protocol*.

Kyoto Protocol   See *Kyoto Agreement*.

L

lagging (trailing) indicators Economic indicators that follow behind rather than precede the country's overall pace of economic activity.

landed cost The cost of a product after transportation and customs costs are paid.

landed price The price of a product (as quoted by a supplier) that includes transportation and customs duties.

Last In, First Out (LIFO) An inventory management and valuation method that describes the method for using the most recently acquired inventory first.

latent defects Hidden defects that are likely to surface at a later time. The supplier must disclose to a purchaser any serious latent defects of which it has knowledge.

Law of Agency Legal relationship of an individual (called the agent) who acts on behalf of another person, company, or government, which is known as the principal and is authorized to make commitments on its behalf.

law of diminishing marginal utility The principle that as additional units of a product are consumed during a given time period, the added satisfaction decreases.

lead time The amount of time, defined by the supplier, that is required to meet a customer's request or demand.

leadership The ability to set goals and directions for the future and to communicate those goals to others and motivate them in such a way that they voluntarily and harmoniously work together to accomplish those goals.

leading indicators Market indicators that signal a change in the state of the economy for the coming months. Some of the leading indicators include the average manufacturing work week, initial claims for unemployment insurance, orders for consumer goods and material, the percentage of companies reporting slower deliveries, changes in manufacturers' unfilled orders for durable goods, plant and equipment orders, new building permits, the index of consumer expectations, change in material prices, prices of stocks, and change in money supply.

learning curves A graphical curve reflecting the rate of improvement in performing a new task as learners practice and use their newly acquired skills.

lease A short-term (usually five to ten years) written agreement between a lessor and a lessee that stipulates the payment and conditions under which the lessee may possess the property or equipment for a specified period of time.

lessee The party that is granted the right to use equipment or property under the terms of a lease and is obligated to pay the rentals to the lessor during the lease term.

lessor The party to a lease agreement who has legal or tax title to the equipment, grants the lessee the right to use the equipment for the lease term, and is entitled to the revenues from the rentals.

Letter of Credit (LC)   A document that consists of specific instructions by a buyer of goods and is issued by a bank to the seller who is authorized to draw a specified sum of money under certain conditions, e.g., the receipt by the bank of certain documents within a given time. It may be revocable or irrevocable.

Letter of Intent (LOI)   A letter from a potential buyer to a seller indicating the seriousness of the potential buyer's interest and agreeing to hold in strict confidence any data provided by the seller to assist the buyer in evaluating the property or equipment being sold. It is usually required by the owner of an agency from a prospective buyer before sharing proprietary information.

leveraged lease   In this type of lease, the lessor provides an equity portion (usually 20 to 40 percent) of the equipment cost, and lenders provide the balance on a nonrecourse debt basis. The lessor receives the tax benefits of ownership.

liability   Any legally enforceable obligation that is due either currently or at some time in the future. It could be a debt or a promise to do something.

license   The legal right to use intellectual property granted by the owner.

licensing agreement   A contract granting the legal right to use a patent or trademark in exchange for consideration. See also *license*.

limited competition   A condition where competition in a particular industry is limited to only a few suppliers within a geographical area, commonly due to the existence of franchises or large initial investments required to enter the business, and the buyer finds it financially impractical to extend procurement beyond that limited area

linear regression analysis   An algorithm for drawing a straight line through a series of events that are plotted on an x and y axis. Once the formula for the line is calculated, it is possible to determine the value of either variable, given the value of the other. As a result, linear regression using time as one variable can be used to calculate a value at some future time.

Line-Staff Principle   Distinguishes production (or operational) functions from support functions.

liquidated damages   The contractually agreed-upon amount required to satisfy a loss resulting from breach of contract.

local area network (LAN)   A group of computers and other devices in a relatively limited area (such as a single building) that are connected by a communications link that enables any linked device to interact with any other device on the network.

logistics   The management of processes in transferring goods through manufacture, storage, and transportation to business customers and end consumers.

lot for lot (L4L or LFL)   An inventory replenishment system where an order is placed for exactly what is needed for a given period. With respect to the quantity, exactly enough is always ordered to avoid a stock outage while ordering as little as possible. With respect to timing, the order is always placed in time to ensure that no outages occur.

Lower Control Limit (LCL)   The measurement point below the center line in a process control chart or report that indicates an out-of-bounds condition or warning signal.

lower level (item)   A component or material (child) used in the production of an upper-level item (parent).

M

M1   Measure of the U.S. money stock that consists of currency held by the public, travelers checks, demand deposits, and other checkable deposits, including NOW (negotiable order of withdrawal) and ATS (automatic transfer service) account balances and share draft account balances at credit unions.

M2   Measure of the U.S. money stock that consists of M1, certain overnight repurchase agreements, certain overnight Eurodollars, savings deposits (including money market deposit accounts), time deposits in amounts of less than $100,000, and balances in money market mutual funds (other than those restricted to institutional investors).

macro economics   The study of economics in terms of whole systems with reference to general levels of output and income and to the interrelations among sectors of the economy.

mainframe   A very large and expensive computer capable of supporting hundreds or even thousands of users simultaneously.

Maintenance, Repair, and Operations (MRO)   Purchased inventory used to maintain equipment and facilities, as well as administrative supplies such as office supplies.

make or buy   A decision process to determine if a particular process should be performed within the organization or purchased from a supplier.

Malcolm Baldridge National Quality Award (MBNQA)   The American Society for Quality (ASQ) administers the President's Malcolm Baldridge National Quality Award under a contract with National Institute of Standards and Technology. The award is given for best practices in Total Quality Management.

management   The people who administer a company or project, create policies, and provide the support necessary to implement the organization's objectives. Also, the process of controlling activities within an organization.

management by exception   A management system in which exceptions to the baseline or plan are identified on a regular basis and acted upon rather than reviewing every detail in every monitoring cycle. It assumes work is done according to orchestrated systems and standards.

Management by Objective (MBO)   Method of goal setting in which performance objectives are agreed upon by subordinates and managers. In the process, periodic reviews of progress toward objectives take place and rewards are allocated on the basis of this progress.

management control   An internal control performed by one or more managers. See also *management*.

management styles   The pattern of supervision methods employed by a manager to control employees and activities.

Manufacturing Resource Planning (MRPII)   A system used for the effective planning of all resources of a manufacturing company, linking various operations such as manufacturing planning and shop floor control with finance and sales.

margin   Gross profit; net sales minus the cost of goods and services sold.

market analysis   Research of the supply-and-demand conditions in a specific area to discover future trends.

market conditions   The characteristics of market forces in a particular industry, including supply-and-demand conditions, the number of competing products, the level of competitiveness, and the growth rate.

markup   The difference between cost and selling price. It can be expressed as a percentage of the selling price.

Master Production Schedule (MPS)   The detailed, optimized manufacturing plan for which all variable demands upon the manufacturing facilities (such as available labor, equipment, and supplies) have been considered. The MPS is a statement of what the company expects to build and purchase listed by items, specific quantities, and dates required.

Master Purchase Agreement   An agreement or contract governing the terms and conditions of the sale and purchase of specific products from a supplier.

Master Services Agreement   An agreement or contract governing the terms and conditions of the sale and purchase of specific services from a supplier.

Master Supply Agreement   An agreement or contract governing the terms and conditions of the sale and purchase of specific products and services from a supplier.

material   The tangible goods that are used in the production and delivery of products and services.

Material Requirements Planning (MRP)   Methodology for defining the raw material requirements for a specific product, component, or subassembly ordered by a customer or required by a business process.

Material Requisition (MR)   A form completed by the user to request materials and services ordered from suppliers through the Purchasing Department. These forms are also traditionally used to document approval authority by recording the signatures of those authorizing the purchase. See also *purchase requisition*.

material   A tangible substance; goods or products. Also used in legal and accounting terminology to signify importance.

material standardization   The process of using the least number of parts and materials across the various products produced in a manufacturing operation.

materials management   The combined process of managing the receiving, warehousing, inventory planning and control, internal material distribution, and shipping function in a manufacturing organization.

maverick purchases   Purchases made by internal users outside the existing contracted supply base or preferred supplier list.

mean time between failure (MTBF)   A measure of reliability as an estimate of the average time a product can be expected to fully perform its function without breaking down.

measures of dispersion   Measurements that record differences in data sets. Some examples include range, standard deviation, and variance.

mediation   A process that attempts to settle a contractual dispute through active participation of a neutral third party outside of the court system.

Memorandum of Understanding (MOU)   A preliminary contract jointly prepared and signed by buyer and seller defining the terms under which the parties will cooperate to move forward with the operations of a business relationship prior to the development of a contract that contains a statement of work (SOW).

mentoring   An educational process where a trusted and experienced professional serves as a role model, trusted counselor, or teacher who provides opportunities for professional development, growth, and support to less experienced individuals in career planning or employment settings. Individuals receive information, encouragement, and advice as they plan their careers.

merchantability   The state of being fit for market; ready to be bought or sold.

metrics   Various measures and parameters used to indicate the status or progress toward a goal or standard of quality.

minicomputer   A small digital computer, normally able to process and store less data than a mainframe but more than a microcomputer or PC while doing so less rapidly than a mainframe but more rapidly than a microcomputer.

Minority Business Enterprises (MBE)   A supplier which is at least 51 percent owned by one or more citizens of the U.S. who are determined to be socially or economically disadvantaged.

mirror image rule   The legal principle that an acceptance must exactly match the original offer to be considered an enforceable contract rather than a counteroffer.

mission statement   A general statement of the role or purpose by which an organization intends to serve its stakeholders; it describes what the organization does (current capabilities), who it serves (stakeholders), and what makes the organization unique (justification for existence). Mission statements always exist at the top level of an organization but may also be set for different organizational levels or components.

money supply   Total stock of money in an economy, consisting primarily of currency in circulation and deposits in savings and checking accounts.

multiperson comparison   Compares one employee's job performance with that of others in the same function or at the same level of compensation.

mutual agreement   An agreement between two parties on a particular issue.

N

National Bureau of Standards (NBS)   Former name of the National Institute of Standards and Technology (NIST).

national income   The sum of the incomes that all individuals in an economy earned in the forms of wages, interest, rents, and profits. It excludes government transfer payments and is calculated before any deductions are taken for income taxes.

National Institute of Standards and Technology (NIST)   A nonregulatory federal agency within the U.S. Commerce Department's Technology Administration. Its mission is to develop and promote measurement, standards, and technology to enhance productivity, facilitate trade, and improve the quality of life.

negotiated savings   When the buyer and seller reach a mutually satisfactory agreement concerning a reduction of cost on a product or service.

negotiation   The act of discussing an issue between a buyer and a seller with the objective of reaching a mutually satisfactory agreement.

net lease   A lease arrangement under which the lessee is responsible for all property taxes, maintenance expenses, insurance, and other costs associated with keeping the asset in good working condition.

net national product (NNP)   The total market value of all final goods and services produced by citizens of an economy during a given period of time, after adjusting for the depreciation of capital.

net operating margin   Net operating income divided by revenues, expressed as a percentage.

Net Present Value (NPV)   An approach used in capital budgeting where the present value of cash inflow is subtracted from the present value of cash outflows. NPV compares the value of a dollar today versus the value of that same dollar in the future after taking inflation and return into account.

network operating system (NOS)   System software that controls the network and enables computers to communicate with each other by taking messages from the application programming interface, changing it into a packet by affixing proper addressing, and sending it to the network communications driver, the interface card driver, and the interface hardware.

network   A group of computers and associated peripherals connected by a communications channel capable of sharing files and other resources between several users. A network can range from a peer-to-peer network connecting a small number of users in an office or department to a local area network (LAN) connecting many users over permanently installed cables and dial-up lines or to a wide area network (WAN) connecting users on several different networks spread over a wide geographic area.

new product introduction (NPI)   The complete business process of introducing new products to market. It spans the entire product life cycle from initial identification of market/technology opportunity, conception, design, and development through production, market launch, support, enhancement, and retirement.

nonconforming   Term used to describe products, materials or services that do not meet customer specifications or accepted standards. Also used to describe bids or contract offers and counteroffers that do not meet stated requirements.

nondirective counseling   A technique used in counseling employees that summarizes what has been said. Using the nondirective approach you might say, "You feel stressed because you have not had enough team support in conducting the project."

Non-disclosure Agreement (NDA)   A legal agreement by which the parties involved agree to keep the information exchanged confidential. See also *Confidentiality Agreement*.

not-to-exceed (NTE)   A cost or schedule estimating term that defines the highest realistic estimate.

O

objectives   The anticipated and quantified outcomes or benefits that are the expected results of implementing a strategy. They are described in measurable terms and indicate a specific period of time during which these results will be achieved.

obligations   Represent commitments of orders placed, contracts awarded, services received, and similar transactions during a given period, regardless of when the funds were appropriated and when the future payment of money is required.

Occupational Safety and Health Association (OSHA)   The branch of the U.S. government that sets and enforces occupational health and safety regulations.

offer   The terms of a contract proposed by one party to another.

off-the-shelf   A ready-to-use hardware or software product that is packaged and ready for sale, as opposed to one that is proprietary or has been customized.

on-the-job training (OJT)   Training conducted at the job site, usually on a one-on-one basis, while either performing or simulating the job or task to be learned.

open bidding   A bidding process that is open to all qualified suppliers.

open competition   A bid or proposal process that is open to all suppliers who are qualified to bid.

open orders   Purchase orders that have not yet been fulfilled.

open stores   Materials stored in open locations that are accessible directly by production staff. Record keeping is typically loose, relying primarily on physical cycle counting to reconcile on-hand inventory levels.

open-to-buy budgets   Primarily used in retail operations to control inventory restocking, funds are allocated to each budgeting period and released based on a planned investment schedule.

operating budgets   Detailed financial plan for each cost center during the budget period that reflects day-to-day operating activities involving both revenues and expenses.

operating lease   A type of lease in which the contract period is shorter than the life of the equipment, and the lessor pays all maintenance and servicing costs. It is considered a short-term, cancelable lease that is expensed rather than capitalized.

operating system   A computer program that lets multiple, simultaneously executing computer programs coexist effectively on one physical computer.

operational control   The authority delegated to a manager to perform those functions of command over subordinate forces involving the composition of labor, the assignment of tasks, the designation of objectives, and the authoritative direction necessary to accomplish the project. Operational control includes directive authority for training.

options   A contract for a specified product and amount to be delivered at some future date. Frequently used in financial markets, it is a type of contract that gives the buyer the rights to complete a transaction within a given time period.

order point   A specified inventory level used to trigger a reorder when the total of current on-hand inventory and open scheduled receipts falls below that level. The order point is set to cover demand expected until the order is received and often includes a buffer based on past variability in the demand or the lead time.

Original Equipment Manufacturer (OEM)   The original company that actually creates the product or writes the software that customers ultimately buy.

output device   An item of hardware to which the computer writes data, such as a monitor or printer, often converting the data into a human readable form.

outsourcing   The transference of functions formerly administered and performed in-house to a supplier in order to cut costs.

overhead   The ongoing administrative expenses of a business, such as rent, taxes, utilities, and insurance.

overhead costs   Those costs generally connected with the operation of the organization as a whole and that cannot be directly connected with any specific operational activity.

P

packing slip   The paperwork that accompanies a shipment, pallet, or smaller unit and describes its contents and quantities. It should normally reference the customer order number involved.

paired comparison   A method where the reviewing manager compares each employee with every other employee in the group and rates each as either superior or weaker of the pair. After all comparisons are made, each employee is assigned a summary or ranking based on the number of superior scores received.

parol evidence   Oral or verbal evidence rather than written evidence given in court. The parol evidence rule limits the admissibility of parol evidence that directly contradicts the clear meaning of terms of a written contract.

parts per million (PPM)   A quality measure of the number of defective items observed or projected out of a population of one million.

patent   The exclusive right to the benefits of an invention or improvement granted by the U.S. Patent Office.

payment terms   Terms under which a buyer will pay a seller for purchases. Payment terms may range from cash-in-advance to an open account with extended payment terms such as payment 120 days from date of purchase. A common payment term is 2/10, N/30, meaning that 2 percent may be deducted from the face amount of the invoice if paid within 10 days and the invoice must be paid in full in 30 days.

perfect competition   An ideal market structure characterized by a large number of qualified firms, identical products sold by all firms, freedom of entry into and exit out of the industry, and perfect knowledge of prices and technology. Perfect competition efficiently allocates resources.

performance appraisal   A periodic, formal assessment of evaluating an employee's or team's effectiveness on the job over a given period of time and assessing potential for future development.

periodic   Actions that are taken at designated intervals, usually referring to physical inventory counts or ordering cycles.

periodic order quantity   Requires that the quantity ordered should be enough to cover requirements for a fixed number of periods.

perpetual   A continually up-to-date process, as in *perpetual inventory*, below.

perpetual inventory   A book inventory kept in continuous agreement with stock on hand by means of a detailed recording of issues and receipts.

personal computer (PC)   A computer specifically designed for use by one person at a time, equipped with its own CPU, memory, operating system, keyboard and display, and hard/floppy disks, as well as other peripherals when needed. Originally associated with a product produced by IBM.

personal digital assistant (PDA)   A handheld device that allows for electronic calendars, cell phones, e-mail, and address books to be combined.

personal income   The total income received by the members of the domestic sector, which may or may not be earned from productive activities during a given period of time, usually one year. After adjusting for income taxes, personal income forms the basis for consumption expenditures on gross domestic product.

platform   Refers to an operating system, such as Windows and the Mac OS, that can be used to run other software programs. A computer program built to run on one platform will generally not run on another unless it is rewritten for that other platform.

policy   A set of guidelines for a plan or course of action adopted by an organization.

portal   A website that functions as a central point of entry, combining multiple functions such as search engines, forums, catalogs, news articles, and shopping services.

posted offer to buy   Government contracting requirements are often posted in a public bidding document or online. This ensures that the general public has open access to the process.

post-operational control   A system used to measure how activities were actually conducted and providing input to management to help determine areas for process improvement.

preferred supplier   Suppliers who have proven capabilities that make them especially valuable to the buying organization. Often they are suppliers who provide exceptional service or favorable pricing.

pre-operational control   Management controls that can be categorized according to the timing of their occurrence.

presentations   The act of providing a formal proposal or report, generally accompanied by printed handouts or PowerPoint slides.

price index   An average price comparing relative prices or changes in group prices over a base time period (usually one year). Such an index is a handy indicator of overall price trends.

priority system   Type of system where activities are established and ordered to address specific needs.

procedures   Formalized operating steps developed within the organization to ensure that standard methods are employed across the enterprise to accomplish goals and objectives.

process capability (Cpk)   The ability to create product within specification limits. Cpk is a measurement of this ability.

procurement   The activity and process of selecting, ordering and acquiring goods, equipment and services for an organization.

procure-to-pay   Activities, transactions, and ERP system settings within the buying through settlement business cycle.

Producer Price Index (PPI)   An index of the prices domestic producers receive from selling their output, which is published monthly by the Bureau of Labor Statistics for all commodities.

product analysis   Examines products or services in terms of the functionality they provide, evaluating each element as a separate cost factor so that a comparative analysis of features can be made.

product liability   Financial responsibility of manufacturers, distributors, and sellers for products sold to the public to deliver the products free of any defects that can harm an individual.

product mix   The number of individual products produced or sold by an organization. The mix is developed through the industry and manufacturing environment and management strategies that position the company.

production   The act of creating value or the process of manufacturing a product.

professional development   The ongoing process of improving a person's personal skill sets, knowledge, and abilities in order to improve job performance and further one's career.

Profit and Loss Statement (P&L)   Summary of the revenues, costs, and expenses of an organization during an accounting period. Together with the balance sheet as of the end of the accounting period, it constitutes a company's financial statement.

project budget   Tracked expenditures by a specific project so that profit (or loss) can be attributed to a particular contract.

promoting   Advancing an individual to a higher professional level.

proprietary information   Any information that provides an entity with some kind of business advantage and is not generally known to the public. This includes but is not limited to inventions; operational information; strategic information about the entity's current and future business plans; supplier's pricing and specifications; research; records such as financial, customer, or personnel records; or information designated as confidential or proprietary.

public key encryption   A code that is known by the public so that they can encrypt or decrypt messages on the Internet.

Public Key Infrastructure (PKI)   The mechanisms used both to allow a recipient of a signed message to trust the signature and to allow a sender to find the encryption key for a recipient.

publicly held   A company that issues stock to the general public and therefore gives the public the right to own a portion of that company.

purchase order (PO)   A contract used to convey requirements and authorization from the buyer to the supplier. It will contain a standard set of terms and conditions, description of the goods or services and quantity ordered, and price paid, and it will state how and when the goods or services should be shipped or completed. The purchase order is also used to process and track receipts and supplier invoices or payments associated with the purchase.

Purchase Price Variance (PPV)   The difference created by the actual price paid to a vendor for material as compared to the standard cost.

purchase requisition (PR)   A form completed by the user to request materials and services ordered from suppliers through the purchasing department. They are also used to document approval authority by recording the signatures of those authorizing the purchase.

purchasing card (P-card)   Designed as a credit card to help companies maintain control of purchases while reducing the administrative cost associated with authorizing, tracking, paying, and reconciling those purchases. Can be used by employees outside of Procurement up to a certain spending limit.

Purchasing Manager's Index (PMI)   A composite index based on the seasonally adjusted diffusion indexes for five of the indicators (new orders represent 30 percent, production represents 25 percent, employment represents 20 percent, supplier deliveries represent 15 percent, and inventories represent 10 percent) by the varying weights.

Q

qualifiable suppliers   Suppliers that can potentially achieve qualification status.

qualified suppliers   Suppliers that meet the established standards and requirements for quality, delivery, and price.

quality assurance (QA)   A formal methodology designed to assess and specify acceptable material and process parameters and measure actual performance in meeting defined quality standards for the product/service involved. Quality assurance includes formal review of care, problem identification, corrective actions to remedy any deficiencies, and evaluation of actions taken.

quality control (QC)   System of control meant to guarantee, by periodic inspections, that a certain level of quality is being maintained during the production of the product in question. Quality control usually requires feeding back information about measured defects to further improvement of the process.

Quality Functional Deployment (QFD)   Applied in the early stages of the design phase so that the customer's requirements are incorporated into the final product, it is used to translate customer requirements to engineering specifications. It is a link between customers, design engineers, and manufacturing.

quantitative analysis   An assessment of specific measurable values such as information derived form the organization's balance sheet and income statements to make investment decisions. It also includes measurements of performance used to help identify areas for improvement.

quid pro quo   Latin term meaning "something for something." Typically, an exchange of concessions in a business negotiation.

R

Radio Frequency Identification (RFID)   Wireless electronic devices attached to an object that electronically transmits data to an RFID receiver such as is normally found in bar-code information. RFID has advantages over bar codes, such as the ability to hold more data and the ability to change the stored data as processing occurs. It also does not require line-of-sight to transfer of data and is very effective in harsh environments where bar-code labels won't work.

rate of exchange   The price of one nation's currency in relation to that of another nation's currency, usually determined in a foreign exchange market where foreign currency is traded.

rationalize   A standardization process based on the logic of overall needs. Supplier rationalization, for example, is a consolidation of suppliers to the minimal number required for effective competition based upon a set of selection criteria.

raw material (RM)   The basic materials a manufacturer converts into a finished product.

receiver   A form used to document the receipt of goods and notify users of their receipt. Receiving documents are typically submitted with the shipment (as a packing slip and/or bill of lading) and should include information directly from the original purchase order.

reciprocity   Mutual exchange of privileges between states, nations, organizations, or individuals.

record   Collection of related data arranged in fields and treated as a unit. The data for each item in an electronic database constitutes a record.

reengineering   The fundamental rethinking and radical redesign of business processes to bring about dramatic improvements in an organization's operations.

regression analysis   A statistical technique used to measure and estimate trends and predict the value of a dependent variable; for example, a regression analysis could be used to predict which website characteristics are most influential in a person's likelihood of returning to the site.

Rehabilitation Act   Federal law entitling individuals with disabilities to vocational rehabilitation and independent living services. This law also prohibits discrimination on the basis of disability by various entities including the federal government, recipients of federal financial assistance, and federal contractors.

reports   Written statements that furnish organized information and summarize the status or a particular aspect of a project or activity.

Request for Information (RFI)   A formal document sent by a buyer to a potential supplier asking for specific information about its organization, products, and capabilities.

Request for Proposal (RFP)   A formal request to a potential supplier by a buying organization outlining the available details for a particular requirement and requesting a proposal satisfying those requirements.

Request for Quotation (RFQ)   A formal document including detailed specifications sent by a customer to a supplier requesting a price quotation and other specific details such as lead time.

requirement   A set of measurable user needs and wants incorporated into a project or application.

requirements contract   A contract in which an organization agrees to purchase all of its requirements of a particular category of goods or services from one supplier in exchange for some form of additional consideration.

requisition   A paper or electronic document that requests the procurement of materials or services and is normally initiated by the using department. It usually includes requested delivery dates and quantities but may leave the determination of pricing and vendor sourcing to a purchasing agent. MRP generations often treat accepted requisitions as a scheduled receipt in the same manner as a purchase order.

requisitioner   The individual or staff member originating a purchase requisition.

restricted bidding   A bidding process open only to a specific group of suppliers due to the requirements of a regulatory process (e.g., minority or small business set-asides) or to ensure that sensitive information does not get into the wrong hands.

Return Authorization (RA)   A method used to document the required return of materials to the supplier. Typically, a supplier will issue an RA number that is recorded internally as the supplier's authorization to ship back the product. This is also known as "Return Materials Authorization (RMA)."

Return on Investment (ROI)   A calculation of how much money will be saved or earned over time as the result of an investment.

Return on Net Assets (RONA)   Operating income before interest paid and taxation, expressed as a percentage of average net assets. Often used to gauge the efficiency of an organization's management.

Return on Total Assets (ROTA)   A measure of the profitability of a firm's assets. Calculated by dividing the sum of net income and interest expense by average total assets.

Reverse Auction (RA)   A buyer-initiated auction in which a buyer posts its product or service needs and invites real-time bids from multiple sellers with prices moving downward as vendors compete against each other. The price decreases as sellers compete for the buyer's business, with the lowest bid considered the winner.

reverse marketing   A proactive, market-oriented approach to procurement using aggressive recruiting and persuasion in order to develop a source to meet the organization's needs.

root cause   The root cause is the underlying cause of a problem and the original reason for nonconformance within a process. When the root cause is removed or corrected, the nonconformance will be eliminated.

root cause analysis   A process improvement and error or defect prevention method that examines the individual processes within a system, identifies the control or decision points, and determines what actually caused a failure, as opposed to what appears to have been the cause.

royalty   A payment made for the use of intellectual property, especially a patent, copyrighted work, franchise, or natural resource. The amount is usually a percentage of revenues obtained through its use.

S

safety stock   The inventory that is held above normal needs as a buffer against delays in receipt of supply or changes in customer demand, allowing for lead time and usage.

Sarbanes-Oxley Act of 2002 (SOX)   Legislation including provisions addressing audits, financial reporting and disclosure, conflicts of interest, and corporate governance at public companies. The act also establishes new supervisory mechanisms, including the new Public Company Accounting Oversight Board, for accountants and accounting firms that conduct external audits of public companies.

Scalar Principle   A hierarchical system of work distribution, where authority and accountability move directly from the highest levels in the organization to the lowest level of competency.

scientific management   The study of workers to find the most efficient way of doing things and then teach people those techniques. This methodology was originated by Frederick Taylor.

scope of work   A detailed description of the project or task to be accomplished, including measurable objectives useful for determining successful completion, such as the goals, objectives, activities, and timelines.

scorecard   An evaluation process that specifies the criteria customers will use to rate a business's performance in satisfying its requirements.

sealed bid   A bid submitted in a sealed envelope to prevent dissemination of its contents before the deadline for the submission of all bids; usually required by policy, law, or rule on major procurements to enhance fair competition.

search engine   A tool that enables users to locate information on the World Wide Web. Search engines use keywords entered by users to find websites that contain the information sought.

seasonal cycles   Regularly repetitive fluctuations of demand or supply, most commonly linked to the time of year.

Securities and Exchange Commission (SEC)   An independent, nonpartisan, quasi-judicial regulatory agency that is responsible for administering the federal securities laws. These laws protect investors in securities markets and ensure that investors have access to all material information concerning publicly traded securities. Additionally, the SEC regulates firms that trade securities, people who provide investment advice, and investment companies.

semi-variable costs   Costs that have both fixed and variable elements.

Service Level Agreement (SLA)   The agreed-upon level of service that will be provided by the supplier to the customer upon purchase of product or service; it could include channels supported, hours of the day, days of the week, response times, and on-site support.

Sherman Act   The first antitrust law passed in the United States (in 1890) which outlawed monopoly or any attempts to monopolize a market.

single source   Condition created by the buying organization where only one supplier provides the product or service.

Six Sigma   A quality movement and improvement program that grew from TQM. As a methodology, it focuses on controlling processes to +/– three standard deviations from a centerline, which is the equivalent of 3.4 defects per million opportunities (where an opportunity is characterized as a chance of not meeting the required specification).

Small Business Administration (SBA)   An independent agency of the United States government that protects the interests of small businesses and ensures that they receive a fair share of government contracts.

Society of Automotive Engineers (SAE)   A professional organization that shares information and exchanges ideas for advancing the engineering of mobility systems.

soft costs   Savings of costs that do not actually result in the elimination of cost, such as reduced head count or lower rent.

soft dollars   The savings amount reported as soft costs.

software application   A computer program that provides tools to do work for one particular function, such as a word processor or a database.

sole source   The only supplier capable of providing a particular product or service.

sourcing   The process of identifying, conducting negotiations with, and forming supply agreements with vendors of goods and services.

Span of Control Principle   A principle that describes the number of subordinates that report to a specific manager.

specific duties   Duties imposed as a flat rate for some specified measure of goods, for example $6.00 per ton.

specification   A clear and accurate description of the essential technical requirements for items (hardware and software), materials, and processes that includes verification criteria for determining whether the requirements are met.

Specification Change Order (SCO)   Changes to specifications or additional requirements that apply to goods and services previously ordered but not delivered that are monitored and documented through a formal control process; also known as an Engineering Change Order (ECO).

split order   A large order that is broken into smaller segments to be executed one at a time to avoid affecting the market price.

spot buying   Strategy where minimum amounts are purchased as needed, often on a daily basis.

spot price   The price at which a physical commodity for immediate delivery is selling at a given time and place.

spyware   Technology that assists in gathering, tracking, and reporting information about a person or organization without their knowledge. On the Internet, spyware is programming that is put in someone's computer to secretly gather information about the user and relay it to advertisers or other interested parties.

stakeholder   A person or group that can affect or is affected by an action and has a vested interest in the successful outcome of an action. Stakeholders influence programs, products, and services.

standard cost   The specified cost used as the basis for measurement against the actual price paid. Standard costs for manufactured items include labor, material, and overhead, as well as acquisition, freight, duty fees, and other categories for purchased items.

standard deviation   The spread of the distribution of measurements.

Standard Operating Procedures (SOPs)   A detailed written set of instructions specifying the normal steps and procedures for performing a specific activity.

standardization   The methods used to develop uniformity and reduce or eliminate custom, one-time, and seldom-used components and processes that introduce variability, potential added costs, and quality problems. Standardization techniques include rationalizing product line offerings and performing cost studies to determine the true costs associated with designing, documenting, and performing a custom or variable process.

standards   Statements of model criteria and expectations for meeting a specified level of performance. Standards for specific products commonly include content and performance criteria.

statement of work (SOW)   A document specifying the work requirements and expected outcomes for a project or program. It is used in conjunction with specifications and standards as a basis for a contract. The SOW is used to determine whether the contractor meets stated performance requirements.

Statistical Process Control (SPC)   A quality control methodology that focuses on continuous monitoring and plotting on charts of quality levels during the production process itself rather than post-production inspection of the items produced. The intent is to produce no defective items. By recording quality results on a chart at frequent regular intervals, trends toward defective production can be spotted.

status checks   The process of obtaining updated information from a supplier regarding shipment dates and quantities.

Statute of Frauds   The legal statute dictating what types of contracts must be in writing to be enforceable.

statutory law   Law enacted by the legislative branch of government (Congress), as distinguished from case law or common law.

storage media   The physical device onto which data is recorded such as magnetic tape, optical discs, floppy disks, or hard disk drives.

stores   A system based within the warehouse operation that enables supplies to be purchased in large quantities for organization-wide usage and issued to a specific section as needed. The supplies are charged to the using department when distributed.

strategic plan   A document used by an organization to enable it to respond in a focused, effective, and innovative way to the challenges of its environment and constituents. The strategic plan states goals, objectives, and action steps developed through a process that identifies strengths, weaknesses, and critical needs of the organization, all within the context of the institutional mission.

structured interview   An employment interview process structured to assess the candidate's past behaviors and accomplishments.

subassemblies   A unit assembled separately but designed to integrate with other units in a manufactured product.

subcontracting   The formation of a contract and the delegation of work between a primary supplier and secondary sources.

subject matter expert (SME)   A person who has had extensive training or experience in a particular area and performs tasks that require a high degree of problem solving, data analysis, and synthesis; a professional or specialist in a specific area.

supplier certification   Determines that the supplier's internal system for measurement and control of quality is sufficient to ensure it will meet the minimum quality level required without performing further incoming inspections.

supplier development   The processes used in the formation of supplier alliances for competitive advantage, identification of potential new sources for key goods and services, supplier consolidation, and increased use of small, minority, women-owned, or disadvantaged businesses.

Supplier Managed Inventory (SMI)   A method of optimizing supply chain performance in which the supplier is responsible for maintaining the buyers inventory levels. This is also known as "Vendor Managed Inventory (VMI)."

Supplier Master Record   Database file that maintains information about the particular supplier such as address, key contact personnel, and payment terms.

supplier performance   Measures of supplier support such as quality improvement and performance relative to goals, on-time delivery, responsiveness to service requests, flexibility to accommodate late scheduling, favorable return policy, and overall reliability.

Supplier Quality Engineering (SQE)   A group or section within the organization that is responsible for ensuring suppliers' compliance with regulatory agencies, government regulations, engineering specifications, customer requirements, and company policies/procedures. In addition, it provides support to supplier quality performance improvement activities.

Supplier Relationship Management (SRM)   A comprehensive approach to managing an organization's interactions with the suppliers of the goods and services it uses. The goal of SRM is to streamline and make more effective the processes between an organization and its suppliers, just as customer relationship management (CRM) is intended to streamline and make more effective the processes between an enterprise and its customers.

supplier scorecard   An evaluative report summarizing supplier performance in specific areas (such as cost, quality, and service) during a specified time and compared with prior performance, benchmarks, or goals.

supply chain   The linked set of organizations, activities, and flow of resources and processes that begins with the sourcing of raw material and extends through the delivery of end items to the final customer. It includes suppliers, manufacturing facilities, logistics providers, internal distribution centers, distributors, wholesalers, and all other entities that lead up to final customer acceptance.

supply management   As defined by the Institute for Supply Management: "The identification, acquisition, access, positioning, and management of resources an organization needs or potentially needs in the attainment of its strategic objectives."

supply positioning analysis   Methodology for categorizing the key areas of spending by cost and associated risk, dividing them into categories and formulating a strategy for managing each of them.

suspension   A period of time where normal business is canceled between two parties due to prior progressive problems with their relationship.

SWOT analysis   The process of identifying *strengths* and *weaknesses*, which are internal to the organization or project, and *opportunities* and *threats*, which come from outside the organization, and formulating strategic and business plans.

system theory   The transdisciplinary study of the abstract organization of phenomena, independent of their substance, type, or spatial or temporal scale of existence. It investigates both the principles common to all complex entities and the (usually mathematical) models that can be used to describe them.

systems software   A general term for software that supervises, sequences, and coordinates programs. Systems software may include programs such as operating systems, assemblers, interpreters, compilers, software debugging programs, text editors, utilities, and peripheral drivers.

systems theory of management   Views the organization as an interrelated, interdependent group of elements that functions as a single entity, developing synergy from these interdependent elements to create a greater whole than the theoretical sum of its parts.

T

take or pay   A type of contract that specifies the amount being purchased during a given time frame but not the specific delivery dates. However, the buying organization cannot cancel it and must pay for it at the end of the contractual period even if it is not used.

tariff   A duty or tax levied upon goods transported from one nation to another. Tariffs raise the prices of imported goods, thus making them less competitive within the market of the importing country.

technical competition   Created when only a limited number of suppliers are available for a particular product due to patents or limited production capability.

technical specifications   The physical characteristics of the material or product being purchased such as dimensions, grade of materials, physical properties, color, finish, and any other data that defines an acceptable product.

technology road map   Planning process driven by the projected technology needs of tomorrow's markets. It helps companies identify, select, and develop technological options and suppliers to satisfy future service, product, or operational needs.

termination   A cancellation of business or a contract between two parties due to completion or prior progressive issues. Also refers to the discharge of an employee.

Terms and Conditions   The contractual specifications that spell out the rights and privileges of both the buyer and the seller and what actions each may or must take.

Theory X   A management methodology that assumes that people inherently dislike work, that they must be coerced or controlled to do work to achieve objectives, and that they prefer to be directed. This theory supports a strong, closed management style.

Theory Y   A management methodology that assumes people view work as being as natural as play and rest, that they will exercise self-direction and self-control toward achieving objectives they are committed to, and that they learn to accept and seek responsibility. This theory supports an open management style, which encourages creativity in personnel.

third party logistics (3PL)   Businesses that provide one or many of a variety of logistics-related services, such as public warehousing, contract warehousing, transportation management, distribution management, and freight consolidation. A 3PL provider may take over all receiving, storage, value added, shipping, and transportation responsibilities for a client and conduct them in the 3PL's warehouse using the 3PL's equipment and employees, or it may manage one or all of these functions in the client's facility using the client's equipment, or any combination of the above.

three-way-match   An accounts payable function that matches a receiving document, purchase order, and invoice prior to paying a supplier.

time and materials (T&M) contracts   A contract that defines the relationship whereby the client pays a separately negotiated or agreed-to fee for labor and the expenses that the supplier encounters. It specifies a price for different elements of the work such as cost per hour of labor, overhead, and profit. Such a contract may not have a maximum price or may state a price "not to exceed" a specified amount.

time-in-motion   The actual clock time it takes an employee to perform a specific task or activity.

time series analysis   A visualization forecasting technique that uses an organization's historical data to discover a pattern or patterns in particular operations over time.

tolerance   The upper and lower limits of some dimension or parameter relating to a component part, material, or assembly that an actual item must comply with in order for it to be acceptable in procurement or manufacturing. Pursuing a "tight" tolerance usually results in higher costs than costs encountered to achieve "loose" tolerance.

tolerance stack-up   Used to measure the cumulative variations of each of the items in an assembly that goes into a final product.

total cost of ownership (TCO)   The cumulative consideration of all the costs that might be associated with a product or service over its lifespan in the organization.

total operating income   A calculation of sales less direct costs.

Total Quality Control (TQC)   A comprehensive set of principles that focuses organization-wide attention on the aspects of design, production, and logistics and that leads to quality conformance and customer acceptance. It maintains a cross-functional view of the processes involved.

Total Quality Management (TQM)   A business improvement methodology designed to constantly motivate, support, and improve the quality of products, services, and marketing processes. A practitioner of TQM will continuously analyze the flow of work, seeking ways to make the process more consistent, less variable, less wasteful, and more serviceable than it was before. Statistical process control is an integral part of this practice.

trade deficit   A condition where a nation's imports are greater than its exports.

traffic   The amount of activity over a system during a given period of time.

training methods   Types of processes used to train employees, such as on-the-job training, job rotation, instructor-led classroom training, and computer-based training.

transformational bidding   Weighs one supplier's bid in comparison to others by transforming the value of their offer to some equivalent percentage based upon their demonstrated performance or added value. Comparatively evaluating suppliers' offers can be implemented through the use of a weighted bid analysis or cost-ratio analysis.

Transmission Control Protocol/Internet Protocol (TCP/IP)   The method by which data on the Internet is divided into packets of bytes. Information is divided into packets of information. Each packet is delimited with header information that includes the destination address to where the packet is to be routed when it is transmitted over the Internet and how it is to be reassembled with the other packets containing the coherent data on the other end.

Traveling Requisition   A form containing standard information, such as descriptions and part numbers, that is passed from department to department in order to request repetitive purchases or the release of production materials under a blanket order from the supplier.

trend analysis   The process of analyzing data to identify underlying longer-term trends, e.g., failure patterns that are not due to seasonality or random noise. Analyzing trends is useful in detecting patterns that could lead to future quality problems and in forecasting future demand.

tunneling protocol   Networking technology that supports multiprotocol virtual private networks (VPN), enabling remote users to access corporate networks securely across operating systems and other point-to-point protocol (PPP)–enabled systems.

turnover   The ratio of annual sales to total inventory that determines the theoretical average number of times an item is used during the year. Low turnover is a sign of inefficiency, since inventory usually has a rate of return of zero.

turns   See *turnover.*

U

Uniform Commercial Code (UCC)   A set of business-related laws dealing with the sale of goods, their transportation and delivery, financing, storage, and payments and various other commercial transactions. These model laws have been adopted, with minor modifications, by most states to provide some consistency among states' commercial laws.

uniform resource locator (URL)   Also known as an Internet address or web address. The standardized address that tells a web browser how to locate a file or other resource on the Web; for example, http://www.netscape.com. URLs can be typed into the browser's address bar to access web pages. URLs are also used in the links on web pages that you can click to go to other web pages.

Uniform Trade Secrets Act (UTSA)   Model legislation drafted by the National Conference of Commissioners on Uniform State Laws designed to prevent misappropriation of an organization's trade secrets. Forty-two states have enacted various statutes modeled after the USTA.

unilateral contract   A contract in which only one party makes an enforceable promise. An insurance policy is an example of a unilateral contract.

unilateral mistake   A mistake of a material fact involving the contract that is made by just one of the parties.

unit of measure (U/M)   The standard quantity of measurement for an item as it is purchased and tracked in the inventory system. The most common unit of measure is "each" (EA), which means that each individual item is considered one unit.

United Nations Commission on International Trade Law (UNCITRAL) The core legal body of the United Nations system in the field of international trade law.

upper control limit (UCL) The measurement point above the centerline in a process control chart or report that indicates an out-of-bounds condition or a warning signal.

using department The end using group that requests a purchase requisition and assists in the development of a statement of work (SOW) or specification.

V

value added network (VAN) A private network provider (sometimes called a turnkey communications line) that is hired by a company to facilitate electronic data interchange (EDI) or provide other network services.

value added reseller (VAR) A company independent of a manufacturer that takes a product and adds a customer-perceived value to it and repackages it and sells it to customers on its own.

value analysis An approach to cost reduction in which components are studied carefully to determine if they can be redesigned, standardized, or made by less costly methods of production. The process attempts to define cost, quality, and customer acceptance parameters in determining the value and possible redesign or reengineering of a given function.

variable cost An operating expense that varies directly with the volume of production including direct material, direct labor, and variable overhead costs.

Vendor Managed Inventory (VMI) See *Supplier Managed Inventory.*

virtual private network (VPN) A private data network that makes use of the public telecommunication infrastructure, maintaining privacy through the use of a tunneling protocol and security procedures.

virus A program or piece of code that is installed on your computer without your knowledge to cause some unexpected and usually undesirable event, such as lost or damaged files. Most viruses can also replicate themselves and spread to other computers.

Volume Purchasing Agreement (VPA) An agreement or addendum to a contract that sets the pricing for specific goods or services over a designated period of time. VPAs are usually based on some agreed volume during a specific time period.

W

Warehouse Management System (WMS) Computer software designed specifically for managing the movement and storage of materials throughout the warehouse.

warranty   A signed statement or representation that promises or guarantees the condition or continued usefulness of a product or service or guarantees the truth of the facts set out in a statement.

Waste Electrical and Electronic Equipment (WEEE) Directive   A European Union directive that encourages and sets criteria for the collection, treatment, recycling, and recovery of electrical and electronic waste.

web browsers   Software that gives a user access to the World Wide Web. Web browsers provide a graphical interface that lets users click buttons, icons, and menu options to view and navigate web pages.

web-based sourcing   Internet-based tools that automate and speed up many of the more tedious procurement processes such as RFIs and RFPs and that have enabled organizations to improve their supplier selection and reduce prices through standardization methods that would otherwise be cost prohibitive.

weighted average   An average of a data segment (usually an element of evaluation) multiplied by some assigned numerical value that expresses its importance to the overall rating.

weighted bid analysis   Weighs one supplier's bid in comparison to others by transforming the value of their offer to some equivalent percentage based upon their demonstrated performance or added value.

wide area network (WAN)   A network communications system that connects computers and other devices across a large geographical area.

win-win   The condition where each party in a negotiation feels it has achieved its objectives.

work in process (WIP)   Inventory that is being processed in a manufacturing operation but has not yet reached its final stage. It is also an inventory account that represents the value of materials, labor, and overhead that has been issued to manufacturing but has not yet produced a salable item.

work standardization   The process that specifies each step of a job so that it can be performed uniformly over time by various individuals.

workstations   Personal computers with powerful calculating and graphics capabilities that can be connected to a local area network (LAN) or used in a stand-alone mode.

World Wide Web (WWW)   A collection of electronic documents, or "pages," that can be viewed on computers using a web browser. While many users think of the World Wide Web and the Internet as the same thing, the Web is actually only part of the Internet.

worm   A malicious, self-replicating computer program that reproduces itself over a network.

written reprimand   A formal letter to an employee that outlines previous efforts to solve a current problem and required actions to be taken by the individual to correct the problem.

wrongful termination   The illegal discharge of an employee from employment.

X

X12   An American National Standards Institute (ANSI) standard that defines EDI processes for many American industries.

XML (Extensible Markup Language)   A superset of HTML (hypertext markup language) that is the common language of the web. XML defines both elements for data and elements for data about data, or metadata, to explain what kind of information is being transmitted.

Z

zero-based budget   A budget that starts fresh at the beginning of a period from a zero base. As a result, each item must be justified separately, usually in terms of the organization's current goals.

Index

Note to the Reader: Throughout this index **boldfaced** page numbers indicate primary discussions of a topic. *Italicized* page numbers indicate illustrations.

E

F

Project Management Skills for all Levels

TELL US WHAT YOU THINK!

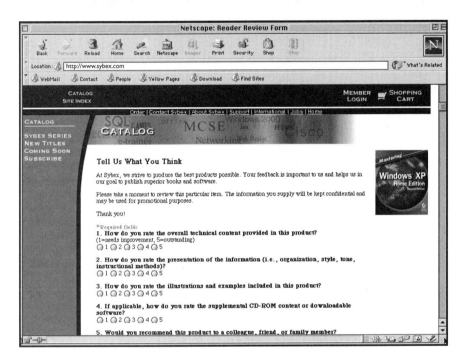

Your feedback is critical to our efforts to provide you with the best books and software on the market. Tell us what you think about the products you've purchased. It's simple:

1. Go to the Sybex website.
2. Find your book by typing the ISBN or title into the Search field.
3. Click on the book title when it appears.
4. Click **Submit a Review.**
5. Fill out the questionnaire and comments.
6. Click **Submit.**

With your feedback, we can continue to publish the highest quality computer books and software products that today's busy IT professionals deserve.

www.sybex.com

SYBEX Inc. • 1151 Marina Village Parkway, Alameda, CA 94501 • 510-523-8233

Harbor Light Press
and
The Story of the Fresnel Lens

© Courtesy of U.S. Coast Guard

Invented in 1822 by Frenchman Augustin Fresnel (pronounced Fray-nell), the multiprismed lens depicted on the Harbor Light Press logo was hailed by sailors for making coastlines around the world more navigable. A dramatic technological improvement over the reflector lenses previously used in lighthouses, the Fresnel lens was capable of capturing 83% of the light from the flame produced by an oil lantern and projecting a beam up to eighteen miles into the distance.

Fresnel lenses are divided into seven "orders"—technically, one through six, with the oddball Third and one-half order included to keep things interesting. First order lenses, at over seven feet tall, were used in the tallest seacoast lighthouses, while lower order lenses could be found in smaller lighthouses on lakes, harbors, and breakwaters.

Although new electric beacons now light the world's coastlines and waterways, the elegant Fresnel lens remains a striking symbol of guidance provided by modern technology coupled with classic craftsmanship.

HARBOR
LIGHT
PRESS